R x

Biography today : 1992
annual cumulation :

Biography Today

Profiles of People of Interest to Young Readers

1992
Annual
Cumulation

Laurie Lanzen Harris
Editor

1992 is first volume
they published lal
12-10-97

Omnigraphics, Inc.

Penobscot Building
Detroit, Michigan 48226

Laurie Lanzen Harris, *Editor*
Cherie D. Abbey and Margaret W. Young, *Contributing Editors*
Barry Puckett, *Research Associate*

Omnigraphics, Inc.

Frank R. Abate, *Vice President, Dictionaries*
Eric F. Berger, *Vice President, Production*
Laurie Lanzen Harris, *Vice President, Editorial Director*
Peter E. Ruffner, *Vice President, Administration*
James A. Sellgren, *Vice President, Operations and Finance*

* * *

Frederick G. Ruffner, Jr., *Publisher*

ISBN 1-55888-139-5

Printed in the United States

Letter from the publisher—

The enthusiastic response to this new magazine for young readers has not only delighted us, but has validated our belief in the need for such a publication. We have been encouraged from the start by teachers and librarians, and now we are further motivated by appreciative reviews. *Booklist* finds our journal useful for elementary and middle schools, and for public library children's collections; a Texas school district is using the publication to tempt reluctant readers; the Library Power Project has selected *Biography Today* as a recommended title; and students themselves give hearty endorsement, which we accept as a high compliment.

The concept of *Biography Today* is unique in that the subjects profiled here are not necessarily people of great or lasting stature. Many are, of course, noted writers or public figures who have made important contributions to the world we live in, but a goodly number of entries are biographies of modern sports heroes and entertainment personalities. These we have included in direct response to the interests of the young. They want to read about the athletes and actors and musicians whose names are familiar to them, and whose fame and talents are the current rage.

The one element we have kept in mind in launching this publication is that youthful readers have youthful interests. We have tried to give each biography a light and very personal touch without sacrificing the content. Certain terms and concepts that might have no meaning to this new generation are explained, often in detail, since we cannot assume that readers so young have the background knowledge that we take for granted. Even the trim size and the typeface were evaluated for their appeal to young readers.

Biographical dictionaries and encyclopedias abound—good reference works that our children will turn to and depend upon throughout their adult years. But we feel that *Biography Today* answers their existing needs with an appealing, story-telling approach. If a class assignment can also be a "good read," then we have met that challenge.

Frederick G. Ruffner, Jr.

Contents

6

Preface

Biography Today is a new publication designed and written for the young reader—aged 9 and above—and covers individuals that librarians tell us young people want to know about most: entertainers, athletes, writers, illustrators, cartoonists, and political leaders.

The Plan of the Work

The publication was especially created to appeal to young readers in a format they can enjoy reading and readily understand. It is available as a quarterly magazine and as a hardbound annual. Each quarterly issue contains approximately 15-20 sketches arranged alphabetically; this annual cumulation contains 78 entries. Each entry provides at least one picture of the individual profiled, and bold-faced rubrics lead the reader to information on birth, youth, early memories, education, first jobs, marriage and family, career highlights, memorable experiences, hobbies, and honors and awards. Each of the entries ends with a list of easily accessible sources designed to lead the student to further reading on the individual and a current address. A few of the famous people profiled here prepared autobiographical sketches for *Biography Today*. Obituary entries are also included, written to provide a perspective on the individual's entire career. Autobiographies and obituaries are clearly marked in both the table of contents and at the beginning of the entry.

Biographies are prepared by Omni editors after extensive research, utilizing the most current materials available. Those sources that are generally available to students appear in the list of further reading at the end of the sketch.

This annual cumulation contains updated entries for those people whose careers have changed significantly since we covered them. These entries include those of the presidential candidates Bill Clinton, George Bush, and Ross Perot, as well as athletes Magic Johnson, Larry Bird and Wayne Gretzky.

Indexes

To provide easy access to entries, each quarterly issue of *Biography Today* contains a Name Index, General Index covering occupations, organizations, and ethnic and minority origins, Places of Birth Index, and a Birthday Index. These indexes cumulate with each succeeding issue. This annual cumulation contains the cumulative indexes, with references to both the quarterly issue and to the annual cumulation.

Our Advisors

This new magazine was reviewed by an Advisory Board comprised of librarians, children's literature specialists, and reading instructors so that we could make sure that the concept of this publication—to provide a readable and accessible biographical magazine for young readers—was on target. They evaluated the title as it developed, and their suggestions have proved invaluable. Any errors, however, are ours alone. We'd like to list the Advisory Board members, and to thank them for their efforts.

Sandra Arden	Troy Public Library Troy, MI
Gail Beaver	Ann Arbor Huron High School Library and the University of Michigan School of Information and Library Studies Ann Arbor, MI
Marilyn Bethel	Pompano Beach Branch Library Pompano Beach, FL
Eileen Butterfield	Waterford Public Library Waterford, CT
Linda Carpino	Detroit Public Library Detroit, MI
Helen Gregory	Grosse Pointe Public Library Grosse Pointe, MI
William Jay Jacobs	Westport, CT
Jane Klasing	School Board of Broward County Fort Lauderdale, FL
Marlene Lee	Broward County Public Library System Fort Lauderdale, FL
Judy Liskov	Waterford Public Library Waterford, CT
Sylvia Mavrogenes	Miami-Dade Public Library System Miami, FL
Carole J. McCollough	Wayne State University School of Library Science Detroit, MI
Deborah Rutter	Russell Library Middletown, CT
Barbara Sawyer	Groton Public Library and Information Center Groton, CT
Renee Schwartz	School Board of Broward County Fort Lauderdale, FL

12

Lee Sprince	Broward West Regional Library
	Fort Lauderdale, FL
Susan Stewart	Birney Middle School Reading Laboratory
	Southfield, MI
Ethel Stoloff	Birney Middle School Library
	Southfield, MI

Our Advisory Board stressed to us that we should not shy away from controversial or unconventional people in our profiles, and we have tried to follow their advice. The Advisory Board also mentioned that the sketches might be useful in reluctant reader and adult literacy programs, and we would value any comments librarians might have about the suitability of our magazine for those purposes.

Your Comments Are Welcome

Our goal is to be accurate and up-to-date, to give young readers information they can learn from and enjoy. Now we want to know what you think. Take a look at this volume of *Biography Today*, on approval. Write or call me with your comments. We want to provide an excellent source of biographical information for young people. Let us know how you think we're doing.

And here's a special incentive: review our list of people to appear in upcoming issues. Use the bind-in card to list other people you want to see in *Biography Today*. If we include someone you suggest, your library wins a free issue, with our thanks. Please see the bind-in card for details.

And take a look at the next two pages, where we've listed those libraries and individuals who received free copies of Volume 1, Issues 1-4, for their suggestions.

Laurie Harris
Editor, *Biography Today*

THANK YOU!

Our thanks to the following individuals and libraries who received a free copy of *Biography Today* for suggesting people who appear in Volume I:

Aliez I.S.D.
Aliez, TX
Shirley Rosson

Alberto Bender
Marshall, TX

Brainerd Branch Library
Chicago, IL
Mary L. Jones

City Cerritos Public Library
Cerritos, CA
U. Sigurdson

Eastover Elementary School
Charlotte, NC

Fletcher Hills Library
El Cajon, CA

Friendship High School Library
Wolfforth, TX
Terry Parish

Jefferson Middle School
Grand Prairie, TX
Lynn Witherspoon, Librarian

Klein Forest High School Library
Houston, TX
Mary Jo Cooper

Lake Jackson Intermediate School
Lake Jackson, TX
Sandra Lea

Mears Junior High School
Anchorage, AK

North Miami Beach Library
North Miami Beach, FL
Sylvia Freireich

Paris High School Library
Houston, TX
Glenna Ford

Paschal High School Library
Fort Worth, TX
Cheryll Falcone

Pflugerville Middle School Library
Pflugerville, TX
Donna Hector

Suffren Free Library, Suffren, NY
Sue Arnold

Wells Academy High School
Chicago, IL
Q.E. Jackson

Weslaco High School Library
Weslaco, TX
Debbie Benedict

Westlane Middle School Library
Indianapolis, IN
Clara Shelton

Paula Abdul 1962-
American Singer, Dancer, Choreographer
Recording Artist Whose Work Includes
Forever Your Girl and *Spellbound*

BIRTH

Paula Abdul was born June 19, 1962, in California. She has one older sister, Wendy. Her father, Harry Abdul, of Syrian-Brazilian heritage, was at one point a cattle rancher and later owned a sand and gravel business; her mother, Lorraine Abdul, a former concert pianist and assistant to the famed movie director Billy Wilder, is French-Canadian. Writers often make note of this mixed heritage to explain Paula Abdul's exotic good looks.

YOUTH

Abdul grew up in Van Nuys, California, in the San Fernando Valley, the origin of the term "Valley Girls." Her parents were divorced when she was seven, and she lived thereafter with her mother and sister. Abdul started taking dance classes at about that time, eventually studying ballet, jazz, modern, and tap.

EARLY MEMORIES

Abdul became interested in dance from watching old musicals. Even as a child she fantasized about becoming a performer: "I think it all started when I was about six, and I first saw Gene Kelly dance in *Singing in the Rain*. That was it. I was well and truly hooked." Starting in elementary school, her teachers would ask her to help stage the school performances. "I was into choreography before I knew what it was," Abdul has said. "This is all I've ever wanted to do since I was a little girl growing up and watching Fred Astaire and Gene Kelly musicals."

EDUCATION

Abdul attended Van Nuys High School. She was an active student—head of the cheerleading squad, senior class president, and a member of the debate and science teams. Yet she also maintained a 3.85 grade point average (out of a possible 4.0).

After high school Abdul enrolled at California State University at Northridge. She planned to major in sports broadcasting, but also took courses in music, dance, and acting. According to Abdul, "I always knew that I wanted to be in show business, but I wanted something to fall back on. So I thought I'd go into sports broadcasting." Abdul soon got her chance at show business, and she dropped out of college after six months.

FIRST JOBS

Abdul's big break came while she was still a student at Cal State. She decided to audition for a spot on the Los Angeles Lakers' cheerleading squad, which performs during breaks in the basketball action. But she wasn't very optimistic about her chances: at only 5'2", she knew that she didn't fit the typical image of a tall, leggy dancer. "See, growing up, my dreams of being a professional dancer seemed shot to hell because of my height. So I get down to the tryout, and there were hundreds of tall, beautiful girls there, and I say to myself, 'I'm not going to do this.' It was like that big moment at the end of *Flashdance*, when Jennifer Beals struts her stuff." Yet despite Abdul's lack of confidence, in a very quick sixty-second tryout she thoroughly impressed the judges and earned a spot as a Laker Girl. A few months later, when the cheerleaders' choreographer left the team, she took over the job.

The cheerleaders' innovative dance steps soon brought Abdul a lot of attention. Members of the Jackson family, who were big fans of the Lakers, admired the new routines and asked to meet the choreographer. The Jacksons hired Abdul to choreograph the stage dancing for their 1984 concert tour and the video for their song "Torture"; this first video earned Abdul a "Best Video of the Year" nomination from the American Video Awards. In addition, her work with the Lakers' cheerleaders was seen by a record company executive, who asked her to work with Janet Jackson.

CAREER HIGHLIGHTS

The pairing of Abdul and Janet Jackson proved to be an inspired match. Jackson's own training as a dancer coupled with her funky dance music perfectly suited Abdul's style, which Jackson described as a "great mix of street and jazz moves." Abdul choreographed videos for four Jackson songs—"Control," "What Have You Done for Me Lately?" "When I Think of You," and "Nasty," which won the 1987 Best Choreography Award from MTV. These videos established Abdul's reputation. Her exuberant style combines technical training with street moves, which are quick-cut dance steps reminiscent of her cheerleading days (what she calls "real snap and flash").

Abdul went on to choreograph for a wide range of performers, including, to name just a few, ZZ Top, the Pointer Sisters, Duran Duran, Kool & the Gang, Dolly Parton, and the cast of "The Tracey Ullman Show," for which she won an Emmy. Yet she aspired to become a performer in her own right: not only to create routines for others, but to move to the front of the camera as a singer and dancer. She has often discussed her desire to be not just a dancer, but an all-round entertainer: "I grew up just adoring all those old MGM musicals," she has said. "Back then, you had to do it all. To be a superstar, you had to sing and dance and entertain and not just stick to one thing."

In 1988 Abdul made her move into music with a pop album, *Forever Your Girl*. Although it initially bombed, it has sold over twelve million copies since its debut and has produced four hit singles. Sales were almost certainly helped by the frequent play on MTV of several videos from the album, including "Straight Up" and "Opposites Attract." In the latter, Abdul dances with the animated, street-wise M.C. Scat Cat, showing her debt to Gene Kelly's duet with an animated mouse in the movie *Anchors Aweigh*. After the success of her first album, a host of new opportunites opened up for Abdul, including choreographing the Oscar Awards telecasts, working on several movies, and appearing in television commercials for such products as Coca-Cola, Reebok shoes, and L.A. Gear. In spring 1991, she released a new album, *Spellbound*, that has sold over two million copies to date and has spawned two hit singles, "Rush Rush" and "Promise of a New Day." Her latest tour, "Under My Spell," has been praised as a tightly scripted visual extravaganza, full of superb lighting effects, snazzy costumes, and intense, fast-paced choreography.

Abdul's move to pop singer was greeted with skepticism. Some reviewers have criticized her mediocre singing voice, limited vocal range, selection of material, and the overly processed, technological sound of much of her music. Yet even her detractors point to her willingness to work hard, her desire to learn, and her sincerely nice personality in an often ugly business. And no matter what her critics might say, her phenomenal record sales attest to the devotion of millions of fans.

MARRIAGE AND FAMILY

Although Abdul is unmarried, she is frequently linked in the gossip columns with a host of Hollywood personalities; she routinely denies these rumors. She lives alone in a recently purchased mansion in the Hollywood Hills.

MAJOR INFLUENCES

Abdul has mentioned several entertainers who have had a great influence on her work, including Debbie Allen, Fred Astaire, Sammy Davis, Jr., Bob Fosse, Gregory Hines, and Gene Kelly.

RECORDINGS

Forever Your Girl, 1988
Spellbound, 1991

HONORS AND AWARDS

Choreographer of the Year Award (National Academy of American Video
   Arts and Sciences): 1987
MTV Music Video Award: 1987, for choreography in "Nasty"; 1989, for
   best female video, best choreography, best dance video "Straight Up"
Emmy Award: 1989, for outstanding achievement in choreography
   "The Tracey Ullman Show"; 1990, for American Music Awards Show
Grammy Award: 1990, for best music video "Opposites Attract"
American Music Award: 1990, for dance music favorite artist and pop/rock
   favorite duo or group
People's Choice Award: 1990 and 1991, for best female musical performer

FURTHER READING

PERIODICALS

Current Biography, Sept. 1991
Ebony, May 1990, p.118
New York Times, May 12, 1991, II, p.30
People, Mar. 23, 1987, p.101; Mar. 12, 1990, p.64
Sassy, Sept. 1989, p.48
Time, May 28, 1990, p.87
Us, June 27, 1991, p.19

ADDRESS

10000 Santa Monica Blvd.
Suite 400
Los Angeles, CA 90067

* *UPDATE* *

Paula Abdul married actor Emilio Estevez on April 29, 1992.

Andre Agassi 1970-
American Professional Tennis Player
Winner of 1992 Wimbledon Tournament

BIRTH

Andre Agassi (AH-gus-see) was born April 29, 1970, in Las Vegas, Nevada, to Emmanuel (Mike) and Elizabeth (Betty) Agassi. He is the youngest in a family of four that also includes a brother, Philip, and two sisters, Rita and Tamee.

YOUTH

Andre was groomed from infancy to be a court star. His father, although Armenian by heritage, was born in Iran and boxed for that country in the 1948 and 1952 Olympics. He moved to the

United States in the mid-1950s and married. Mike Agassi had been so intrigued by the game of tennis since his own youth that he decided to settle his family in Las Vegas, where the climate would be suitable for year-round play. He then taught the game to all of his children, with the goal of eventually producing a champion. By the time Andre was born, Mike had fine-tuned an early training plan that would develop both interest and skill, and in his young son he saw the prospect of stardom.

When Andre was a baby, his father strung a moving tennis ball above his crib for "eye coordination." By the time the child could sit in a high chair, Mike Agassi was tossing water-filled balloons toward the paddle he had strapped to his son's little hand. At two, Andre was serving on a full court—on his fourth birthday, he was a crowd-pleaser as he practiced with tennis great Jimmy Connors during a Las Vegas resort exhibition. The young prodigy further developed his game on the family's backyard court, pounding away at balls fired from as many as eight machines set at different angles.

There was little doubt about Agassi's remarkable skills, but tennis—and more tennis—was the focal point of his young life. Part way through the eighth grade, and still only thirteen years old, Andre was sent to the famous Nick Bollettieri Tennis Academy in Bradenton, Florida, for intensive coaching. His play there with other teenage hopefuls was often less than sensational. The pressures of being away from home and family and of trying to live up to his father's expectations began to show in his personality. He became resentful at losing, arrogant at winning, and verbally abusive toward the other players. Some time later, after confronting his problems, much of this offensive attitude was channeled into the showmanship, gaudy wearing apparel, and funky hairstyles for which he has become famous.

EDUCATION

Agassi attended traditional school in Las Vegas before transferring to the Bollettieri Academy, where private tutors work a shortened academic program around the long hours of tennis instruction. He was not known as much of a student during those years, but eventually he earned a high-school diploma through correspondence courses. His formal education has been spotty at best, yet a childhood friend, Perry Rogers, who himself went on to university study, insists that the young tennis phenomenon has a quick and eager mind.

CAREER HIGHLIGHTS

Andre Agassi turned pro on May 1, 1986, two days after his sixteenth birthday. His performance at Bradenton may have been erratic, but with this move away from the juniors, a natural ability and competitive spirit seemed to shift into high gear. He quickly made his presence known in early tournaments that year, astounding established players with his aggressive, hard-hitting style. A discouraging slump followed, but by the end of 1987, the brash young man with the racquet had regained confidence and surged ahead in the rankings from number 91 to number 25. He captured his first career title on the year's final stop at the SuL [South] American Open in Itaparica, Brazil, by defeating (in succession) Brad Gilbert, Martin Jaite, and Luiz Mattar.

Staggering success was just around the corner, and so was unbelievable celebrity. In 1988, the sassy, teenage marvel racked up six titles in seven finals and reached the semifinals of both the U.S. and French Open tournaments. He also made his debut that same year on the U.S. roster of the Davis Cup international competition, compiling a 3-0 record. Breaking hearts along the way with his often-noted "come-hither grin" and "exotic Middle Eastern surf-rat looks," Agassi's demeanor was described at about that time in *Sports Illustrated* like this: "Being Just Andre means blowing kisses to the crowd, belting balls into the stands and handing out haberdashery—even a pair of his with-it signature denim shorts—to the courtside maidens."

There were critics, too. Tennis traditionalists were irritated by his bizarre mode of dress, and he was accused of faking injuries, skipping out on exhibitions, and "tanking" sets (purposely losing to conserve energy for the next set). In general, his hotdog antics endeared him to some while offending others.

Agassi forged ahead, grabbing the spotlight by winning matches from such top players as Jimmy Connors, Boris Becker, and Stefan Edberg. He reached number-three ranking in the world, his best up to the present time. Then, with 1989, came a series of struggles, and Agassi often reacted immaturely to his losses. "I guess you could basically say that I got too big for my britches," he finally admitted. Criticism rose when he turned his back on

England's famed Wimbledon tournament. His explanation smacked of arrogance when he and his brother/manager Philip implied that Wimbledon was just another contest. Others speculated that Andre's real reason was a fear of embarrassing himself playing on grass, which is not his best surface—and further, a reluctance to forgo his trademark attire for the tournament's required tennis whites.

The sudden slide in early 1989 was reversed when Agassi won the Italian Open, then reached the semifinals at the U.S. Open by beating Jimmy Connors for his first ever five-set victory. Other wins and losses have followed in what has been described as a roller-coaster career. Agassi was runner-up in 1990 in two Grand Slam events, the U.S. and the French Open, and made it to the finals again at the French in 1991. He returned to Wimbledon that season after a three-year absence, but reached only the quarter-finals. Inconsistent play marked most of his year except for some solid wins in Davis Cup play.

Frustrated in his continuing failure to win a major tournament, Agassi decided, as 1992 began, to rededicate himself physically and mentally. The strategy paid off on a simmering Sunday afternoon in July—victory at last. He entered Wimbledon as a long shot No. 12 seed and battled his way to center court past two former champions, John McEnroe and Boris Becker. In a stirring five-set triumph over Croatia's Goran Ivanisevic, Agassi won the first major title of his life. "He didn't just wave away the memory of haunting failures in previous championship finals," wrote a *Detroit Free Press* columnist the next day. "What he did—with style and talent and, yes, grit—was lend substance to transparency."

A stunned Agassi sank to his knees and collapsed in tears. "I was Wimbledon champion, Grand Slam winner," he said after regaining his composure. "It is quite an irony. I really have had my chances to fulfill a lot of my dreams, and I have not come through in the past. To do it here is more than I could ever ask for."

Andre Agassi at last has lived up to the expectations of his defenders—and lived down the doubts of his detractors.

MAJOR INFLUENCES

According to Agassi, it is religion that has had the greatest influence on him. Tennis observers notice the transformation from a rebellious, often vulgar, show-off whose antics raised criticism wherever he played, to a more thoughtful (although still colorful) competitor.

By his late teens, Agassi began to realize how troubled and unhappy he was, and how out of control. He said later that he "was facing a lot of questions" in his life and felt that "there had to be more important things than tennis, money, and fame." With the encouragement of Fritz Glauss, the traveling minister of the pro tour who had earned his trust, he joined other players in Bible study. What has emerged is a somewhat restrained, and certainly more gracious, young man. Few doubt his sincerity in saying that renewing his childhood faith in Christianity offered him peace of mind and "the understanding that it's no big deal if you get beat."

MARRIAGE AND FAMILY

Agassi, now twenty-two, is unmarried, but frequently is seen in the company of Wendy Stewart, who is said to be his steady girlfriend. When he is not on tour or staying in Bradenton, he goes home to his parents in Las Vegas. The Agassis form a close family, and all the siblings either are, or have been, involved in tennis. Rita, the eldest, a former pro, is married to the legendary Richard (Pancho) Gonzales, who rose to court fame in the 1950s and was eight times world professional tennis champion. Philip, who is Andre's manager and traveling companion, once played on the satellite tour, and Tamee played collegiate tennis in Tyler, Texas.

FURTHER READING

PERIODICALS

Current Biography Yearbook 1989
New York Times, July 6, 1992, p.C3.
Sports Illustrated, Mar. 13, 1989, p.66; June 17, 1991, p.34; Sept. 30, 1991, p.12
Tennis, Sept. 1992, p.186
World Tennis, Mar. 1991, p.22

ADDRESS

International Marketing Group
One Erie View Plaza
Suite 1300
Cleveland, OH 44114

Kirstie Alley 1955-
American Actress
Co-Star of "Cheers" TV Series

BIRTH
Kirstie Alley was born January 25, 1955, in Wichita, Kansas, to a well-to-do lumber company owner, Robert Alley, and his wife, Mickie. She has an older sister, Collette, and a younger brother, Craig, both of whom still live in Wichita.

YOUTH
Growing up in a typical midwestern family of the 1950s, Kirstie Alley was the feisty, daring middle child who strained against the limits of convention. She stood up for herself and her offbeat notions from a tender age and always was willing to do the unusual to get attention. Her lifelong best friend, Sarah Campbell, told *People* a couple of years ago that the "closest Kirstie came to

27

an interest in acting [in those days] was when she read the movie magazines in my mom's beauty shop. Maybe she was too embarrassed to admit it." More than likely, she was dreaming, even then, of being a star.

By the time she had reached her teens, Alley was into a free-wheeling lifestyle that unnerved her parents, whose other children showed no such sign of willfulness. "I guess I was wild, but not promiscuous wild," she says now, recalling those disturbing times. "I was an artsy, troubled, searching, obnoxious kid, the one they [her parents] worried about. I was insecure about everything and uncomfortable with myself." Alley hated her unique name (a Scottish variation of Christina), her husky voice, and having to conform to normal expectations, so she rebelled by sneaking out in "geeky" clothes and running around town in fast cars and on motor-cycles, either with or looking for boys.

Shortly before her mother was killed in an auto accident in 1982, Alley wrote home apologizing for what she called all the "rotten things" she had ever done, and for being such a difficult child to raise. "The day she died," Alley reveals with sorrow, "I got her answer in the mail. She had written back saying that during all our conflicts, she had always been trying to protect me because she loved me. The biggest regret in my life is that my mother never got to see me be successful....She would have loved my success. My mother always gave to me. How I wish I could have given something back to her."

EARLY MEMORIES

A touch of outrageous behavior has always been part of Alley's emotional makeup. "When I was a child, I said stupid things which turned out to be shocking," she recalls. "I would think of something that would really pique your interest, not that it was necessarily sane....something like 'Have you ever been in a fire?'...One day my dad decided I'd become too bizarre and offered me a silver dollar if I would not talk for an hour. I made it for two minutes."

EDUCATION

Alley graduated from Wichita High School Southeast where, she says, she never fit the image of the wholesome, midwestern cheerleader-type (she did, however, make the cheerleading squad). With her defiant attitude, her rangy, unkempt looks, and her offbeat attire, she was not accepted by the "in" crowd. Alley went on to Kansas State University to study literature and art, but stayed less than two years. Although she transferred to the University of Kansas, she remained restless and soon dropped out of school altogether.

FIRST JOBS

Returning to Wichita, and inspired by a Doris Day role in the light romantic comedy *Pillow Talk,* Alley started working for a design firm as a free-lance interior decorator. "I was a good decorator," she says of that first career, "but I snorted up all my profits." Still bored and basically unchallenged, she got hooked on cocaine, most weeks spending as much as $400 on her habit. "Finally," she admits, "it caught up with me and I realized what a jerk I was." The day of reckoning came when her sister dropped in for an unexpected visit with her children, and Kirstie was in such a fog that she could not even relate to her family.

Twenty-six years old and ready for a new start, Alley quit cocaine "cold turkey," quit her job, too, and moved to Los Angeles. There she entered the Church of Scientology's Narconon, a drug rehabilitation program, and sought out an acting career. Today, she is one of the many celebrities (Tom Cruise, John Travolta, jazz pianist Chick Corea, Mimi Rogers, Anne Archer, and Olympic gymnast Charles Lakes are a few of the others) who continue to defend the controversial Scientology "self-help" cult, and who credit it with giving new direction to their lives. Scientology, however, is rejected by many critics and was described in a lengthy special report last year by *Time* as a "hugely profitable global racket that survives by intimidating members and critics in a Mafia-like manner."

CHOOSING A CAREER

Giving herself a year to break into show business, Alley made the usual rounds of agents and studios with unusual grit and perseverance. She pounded the pavements and beat on doors "in a town," says *Good Housekeeping*, "where almost everybody was beautiful and at least a few dozen were talented." Finally, she was called to read for a part in *Star Trek II: The Wrath of Khan*, but that was the week that her parents were in a tragic car accident that took her mother's life and left her father near death. Her dad survived, and Alley returned to the studio to win the role of Lieutenant Saavik, Mr. Spock's pointy-eared protegé.

CAREER HIGHLIGHTS

After *Star Trek*, Alley had a starring run in "Masquerade," a short-lived television series, then moved on to parts in *Runaway*, a film with Tom Selleck, and the miniseries "North and South," in which she and husband Parker Stevenson appeared as brother and sister. The actress's further credits included a number of less-than-memorable parts as she moved back and forth from movies to television.

Then, in 1987, came "Cheers," the enormously successful TV comedy set against the backdrop of a fictional Boston bar that has showcased her considerable talents as a comedienne. She replaced the Emmy-winning Shelley Long, who had left the series to pursue a career in films. Alley's character was cast with a different angle, and her own wacky disposition has been instrumental in shaping her pivotal role in the hit series, now in its eleventh, and final, season. She plays the uptight, overachieving Rebecca Howe with vulnerability and comedic talent, and she has been a major force in helping the sitcom climb to first place in the ratings.

Alley's career runs on a fast track as she "crams six lifetimes into one," her husband tells a *People* interviewer. Her role in *Look Who's Talking*, a surprise comedy hit of 1989, was followed by a well-received sequel, *Look Who's Talking Too*. Other films have brought mixed reviews, but the actress's confidence is unshaken in the belief that one day her big break in movies will come. She says that "there's this untapped territory which is actually exciting to me. It keeps a future there for me." Kirstie Alley—still daring to go out on a limb.

MARRIAGE AND FAMILY

Kirstie Alley has been married since December 22, 1983, to Parker Stevenson, the Princeton-graduate actor of *Hardy Boys* and "Baywatch" fame. As yet, they have no children, but their San Fernando valley estate shelters a menagerie of dogs, cats, parrots, exotic fish, monkeys, rabbits, and geese (close to fifty in all), attesting to the actress's love of animals, her passionate advocacy of animal rights, and her long-standing interest in ecology.

The estate, which encompasses lush acreage and a huge swimming pool, once belonged to old-time vaudeville and film entertainer Al Jolson and later to the actor Don Ameche. Alley, however, has put her own creative decorator touches on the mansion. In addition to the California property, she and Stevenson own a ranch in Oregon and a colonial-revival home at Isleboro, a tiny island village on the coast of Maine.

HOBBIES AND OTHER INTERESTS

Narconon, which helped Alley overcome her addiction to cocaine, remains one of her most important interests; she serves as an international spokesperson for that rehabilitation program. She also devotes much of her time to issues involving animal rights and the environment, and has been instrumental in producing *Cry Out*, a primer for junior environmentalists. She is a member of the Earth Communications Office.

HONORS AND AWARDS

Emmy Award: 1991, for Outstanding Lead Actress in a Comedy Series
Golden Globe Award: 1991, for Best Actress in a Musical/Comedy Series
People's Choice Award: 1991, for Best Female Television Performer

FURTHER READING

Cosmopolitan, Dec. 1990, p.84
Good Housekeeping, Mar. 1990, p.132
Ladies Home Journal, Oct. 1991, p.48
People, Oct. 30, 1987, p.122; Oct. 29, 1990, p.82
Redbook, Oct. 1987, p.10
Time, May 6, 1991, p.50
TV Guide, Nov. 14, 1987, p.8
Us, Feb. 1992, p.41
USA Today, June 25, 1990, p.18; Oct. 25, 1990, p.1D

ADDRESS

1033 Gayley
Suite 208
Los Angeles, CA 90024

Terry Anderson 1947-
American Journalist
Longest-Held American Hostage in Lebanon

BIRTH

Terry Anderson was born October 27, 1947, in Lorain, Ohio, to Glenn Richard and Lily Anderson. He was the fourth in a family of six children that included Glenn Richard, Jr., Peggy, Bruce, and twins Jack and Judy.

YOUTH

The man whose frightful ordeal as a hostage in Lebanon brought his name and face to the attention of the world grew up in circumstances that could not have prepared him for the experience

31

that was to come. His early years were spent in the western New York State town of Albion, near Batavia and about 30 miles west of Rochester. The Andersons' family life was characterized by tight finances and little structure. According to Peggy (Anderson) Say, the sister who fought for six-and-a-half years to keep Terry's memory alive, the household was one of constant friction. In *Forgotten,* her 1991 book about the relentless crusade to free her brother, she writes that Terry, as a kid, "managed to carve a place for himself that nobody much noticed...as if he wanted to stay removed from the chaos around him. Our house heard a lot of screaming and every time there was a conflict you could bet Terry would be out in the car with a book."

By all accounts, Anderson was well-behaved and able to function normally in the midst of what his sister describes as a malfunctioning family. He did well in school and became an Eagle Scout. As he grew to young adulthood, he and his father became very close. "As far as Terry was concerned," Peggy remembers, "Dad could do no wrong. To Dad, Terry was the star of the family." In later years, Glenn Anderson would visit his son in Japan, and again in Beirut.

EDUCATION

Terry Anderson was a high school honor student, but upon graduation in 1965, turned down college scholarship offers to enlist in the Marine Corps. He served six years in all, including two tours of duty in Vietnam as a combat correspondent and a posting to Japan for part of that time. Anderson returned to the United States to resume his education, and subsequently graduated from Iowa State University.

FIRST JOBS

While studying for his college degree, Anderson worked as a radio and television newsman in Des Moines, Iowa. He was hired by the Associated Press (AP) in 1974, and assigned to the agency's Detroit bureau, but soon left for a job at the Ypsilanti (Michigan) Press. He rejoined the AP in Louisville, Kentucky, in 1975.

CAREER HIGHLIGHTS

Reporting the news from his subsequent posts in Tokyo, in New York City where he worked on the foreign desk, and in Johannesburg, South Africa, Terry Anderson was making a name for himself in journalism. Nevertheless, this "rollicking, restless man" *(Newsweek)* was looking for a bigger challenge, and jumped at the chance to go to Lebanon on a temporary AP assignment in 1982, after the Israeli invasion. A person who "likes to be where the action is," he found himself in the thick of it, and soon became news editor in the Beirut office. He was named the bureau's chief Middle East correspondent within a year.

A powerful writer and forceful editor, he plunged into the world of war reporting and the dangers that surround it. He loved his work and shared the daily risks of the war-torn region with his associates. Where there was action, there too was Terry Anderson. None of this, however, could have foretold the next chapter in his life. He was to say, years later, "you summon up the energy from somewhere, even when you think you haven't got it, and you get through the day. And you do it day after day after day."

Anderson was returning home from a tennis game with AP photographer Don Mell on the morning of March 16, 1985, when he was ambushed by armed Shi'ite Muslim gunmen on a street in West Beirut. His abductors were members of the extremist Islamic Jihad (the name means Holy War), a faction of the pro-Iranian Hizballah, or "Party of God." Blindfolded and shackled, he began a 2,455-day test of endurance. He was held in as many as fifteen to twenty different locations during his nearly seven years in captivity—an imprisonment longer than that of any of the other Americans taken. He eventually became a sort of team leader, endlessly hounding his cellmates to talk and to debate, in an effort to keep everyone alert and sane. He boldly challenged his captors for better conditions, and finally won their grudging respect. In a story of his survival through beatings, filthy conditions, and "near despair," *Newsweek* told, after his release, how his "strong will and quick mind sustained him."

Anderson never gave in. He continued his role as a reporter during times of solitary confinement, passing messages and whatever bits of information he could learn from the guards in a simplified sign language he had taught to his fellow hostages. He begged for books and more books, studied and memorized long passages from the Bible and, in 1990, was provided with a shortwave radio by his captors. He fought boredom in every way that he could devise. After the hostages were allowed to be together, Anderson organized "cutthroat games of Hearts" which they played with scraps of paper he had fashioned into a deck. He obsessively "cleaned" and mended; and, from Thomas Sutherland, a dean at the American University of Beirut and the man with whom he spent most of his captivity, he learned French. He also wrote a collection of 32 poems. Anderson had rediscovered his lapsed Catholic faith shortly before he was kidnapped, and later would speak often of the strength that faith had given him in his darkest moments.

For some of the years of imprisonment, there were two clergymen in the group—Rev. Benjamin Weir and Father Lawrence Martin Jenco—and services were allowed (although mocked) in what the hostages called their "Church of the Locked Door." The captives, men of interesting and varied backgrounds, also used their long, empty hours keeping journals and working out math equations or talking about their careers. There were "imaginary tours" of foreign lands, recitations and readings, and every possible conversational and mental activity that would keep their spirits alive. Through all this, they endured acts of unspeakable cruelty (three Americans died in captivity—nine hostages in all).

At home, Peggy Say continued her quest to free her brother and *all* the hostages. "A simple housewife is what I am," she told the media. "I don't pretend to be anything else." But Say put aside a modest, uncomplicated life to talk to the White House, the State Department, the pope, Yasser Arafat and, always, to the press. It was as much her persevering fight to keep the hostage story alive, as it was any other single effort, that resulted in the final releases negotiated by the United Nations' representative, Giandomenico Picco, who traveled around the dangerous Middle East for six months bargaining with the captors.

Anderson was finally released in December 1991, and he returned to the enthusiastic welcome of an entire nation. While he was held hostage, the Iran-*contra* scandal unfolded, the Berlin Wall came down, the U.S. engaged in a war in the Persian Gulf, and the Soviet Union collapsed. On a more personal level, Anderson's father and elder brother died of cancer. Still, when the subject of bitterness was raised during a talk with newspaper publishers and editors in New York five months after his release, he said, "I have no room for it, I have no time for it. My hating them is not going to hurt them an ounce; it's only going to hurt me." As for being courageous, he added, "People are capable of doing an awful lot when they have no choice and I had no choice....Courage is when you have choices."

Since his release, Anderson has made no announcement of long-term career plans. He has accepted a fellowship from the Freedom Forum Media Studies Center at Columbia University for one year, which he will spend writing a book.

MARRIAGE AND FAMILY

At the time of his release from captivity, Anderson's personal affairs were in a tangle. He was still married to Mihoko (Mickey), his wife of twenty-three years, who had left Beirut in 1984 with their daughter, Gabrielle, to return to her parents' home in Iwakuni, Japan. A divorce had been under way since before his kidnapping, but there was also another family situation waiting to be resolved: a second daughter, Sulome, had been born to Anderson's fiancée, Madeleine Bassil, less than three months after he was abducted. When legal matters are straightened out, Anderson plans to marry Bassil and make his home with her and their child. Gabrielle, now sixteen, remains in Japan with her mother. Anderson spent Christmas of 1991 in Japan with his elder daughter.

Little Sulome's face became familiar to television viewers during the latter years of Anderson's imprisonment as she spoke shyly to him on videotape and danced ballet steps for the daddy she had never known. Although

Sulome was born in the United States, where her Christian-Lebanese mother had come to stay briefly with Anderson's relatives, most of her young life has been spent in Nicosia, Cyprus. Mother and daughter lived there near friends and family for nearly six years, waiting for the day that Anderson would be released.

After their reunion, and with the first flurry of public appearances behind them, the family of three vacationed quietly for four months on the Caribbean island of Antigua.

MEMORABLE EXPERIENCES

Anderson nearly gave in to despair on one particular day during his years in captivity. "The worst day I had was Christmas of 1986," he revealed at a news conference. He was in solitary, but had eye contact with Thomas Sutherland and others. There was no way to communicate except through the sign alphabet, so they passed messages back and forth that way. "One thing we could do was 'talk' to each other. Then I took off my glasses and dropped them and broke them. My eyes are very bad. Couldn't see. End of silent cell-to-cell dialogue. End of story. *That* was a bad day." Other hostages told of how, in his frustration, he beat his head against the wall of his cell until blood ran down his face. His glasses were later repaired, but were still in patched-up condition when he first appeared on television after his release.

In an interview on "Dateline NBC" on May 5, 1992, Anderson told that there were other moments, too, especially in the early days after his kidnapping, when he almost abandoned hope. "Sometimes I wanted to die," he admitted, "but I *couldn't* give in." He denied ever being a hero, though, emphasizing that "you can do anything you have to—human beings are infinitely strong."

HOBBIES AND OTHER INTERESTS

Books have been an important part of Terry Anderson's life since his schooldays in western New York. His sister Peggy tells of the hundreds of volumes he had "tucked away in a trunk" at his apartment in Beirut. Music is another of his passions—and cooking, too. He is known among his friends for the "three-alarm chili" he prepared for parties, and for his special touch with Irish coffee, which his sister calls "a concoction of renown."

Anderson also is a physically active man who played tennis regularly before that March day in 1985 when he was snatched off the street in Beirut. Even during his long imprisonment, he exercised whenever possible in his confined space—this, no doubt, contributed to his surprisingly good health upon release.

HONORS AND AWARDS

National Hostage Awareness Day: October 27, 1989, Terry Anderson's forty-second birthday; designated as a special honor for the man who had become a symbol of the Americans still held (at that time) against their will in Lebanon

President's Award (Overseas Press Club): 1992, for lifetime achievement in foreign reporting

Free Spirit Award (Freedom Forum): 1992, for contributions to free press, free speech, free spirit (including a cash award of $245,500 given to Anderson, equaling $100 for every day he spent in captivity)

FURTHER READING

BOOKS

Say, Peggy, and Peter Knobler. *Forgotten: A Sister's Struggle To Save Terry Anderson, America's Longest-Held Hostage,* 1991

PERIODICALS

Maclean's, Apr. 30, 1990, p.40
New York Times, Dec. 11, 1991, p.A6
Newsweek, Dec. 16, 1991, p.34
Time, Dec. 16, 1991, p.16
Washington Post, Dec. 13, 1991, p.C1

ADDRESS

Associated Press
Human Resources Dept.
50 Rockefeller Center
New York, NY 10020

Roseanne Arnold   1952-
American Comedian
Co-Creator and Star of ABC's "Roseanne"

BIRTH

Roseanne (Barr) Arnold was born November 3, 1952, in Salt Lake City, Utah. Her parents, Jerry and Helen Barr, sold religious items door-to-door. Roseanne has a brother, Ben, and two sisters, Geraldine and Stephanie.

YOUTH

Growing up Jewish in mostly Mormon Salt Lake City made Roseanne feel like an outsider almost from the beginning. At Christmastime, she usually was asked by her teacher to sing a popular Hanukkah song about the dreidel, a toy associated with that Jewish holiday. "So I would sing the dreidel song, and then explain why I didn't believe in Jesus," she recalls. "I was the designated heathen."

In her autobiography, *Roseanne: My Life as a Woman*, Arnold remembers feeling that her family was different and eccentric. She writes about an uncle who was convinced that the Coca-Cola Company was trying to make him confess to the Lindbergh kidnapping (a notorious case of 1932, in which the baby son of famed aviator Charles A. Lindbergh was kidnapped from his crib and murdered). She also relates that her maternal grand-mother would repeatedly phone the local radio talk show to argue with anti-Semitic callers. Still, Roseanne managed to set herself apart. "Life was not easy for Roseanne," her mother commented to *People* in an inter-view several years ago. "It wasn't easy for me, either, because I'd never met anyone like her."

When she was three, Roseanne hit her head in a bad fall, and her facial muscles were paralyzed. The rabbi's prayers did not help, and her mother called a Mormon faith healer in desperation. The paralysis went away. Mrs. Barr, taking that as a sign from God, began to include Mormonism in the family's spiritual life. "My life was a total dichotomy," Arnold says in speaking of their involvement in contradictory religions. "My mother sent me to study the Talmud (a collection of commentaries on biblical texts) at the Jewish school at the same time she sent me to church to appreciate Jesus."

A medical textbook that Roseanne picked up when she was fifteen or sixteen years old provided another answer. Upon discovering that her paralysis as a toddler was, in fact, Bell's palsy, a condition that usually disappears after only days, she became angrily disillusioned about her Mormon "miracle." She reacted by breaking several Mormon taboos: drinking alcohol, smoking cigarettes and marijuana, and trying, but failing, to instigate a sexual encounter with her Mormon boyfriend. In her defiant state, she wandered down a busy highway until she was run over by a passing motorist. She suffered a concussion, as well as injuries to both legs. Roseanne, seriously injured in the accident and emotionally confused as well, was persuaded by counselors to check into the Utah State Hospital, a mental facility, to recuperate. She entered in August 1969, and stayed there for eight months. "I learned everything I need to know there. It made me everything I am," she says. "It's an incredible thing to have a group of insane people be your family for a year."

EARLY MEMORIES

According to Arnold, some of her childhood memories were repressed until very recently. In 1991, Arnold accused her parents of physically and sexually abusing her as a child. She claimed that she and her sisters were regularly beaten and molested in the Barr home. "What's so horrible is that the people you love most in the world hurt you," she says. "When I came forward with my story, I had to let go of the fantasy that I had a family. It's like they drove off a cliff."

Jerry and Helen Barr admit that they beat their children, sometimes severely. But they hotly deny the accusations of sexual abuse. "It wasn't sexual," Jerry told *TV Guide.* "It wasn't abuse. It was *parenting."* Stephanie and Geraldine also deny having been sexually abused. This disagreement among family members, which has been widely covered in the press, has contributed to Roseanne's reputation for generating controversy.

EDUCATION

Arnold never completed high school. Although she had been a good student when she was young, she had trouble concentrating and remembering after the accident. She returned briefly to school after she left the mental hospital, and then quit to go to work.

FIRST JOBS

After dropping out of high school, Roseanne left Utah for good. She traveled for awhile and then settled in 1971 in Colorado, where she lived in an artists' commune and worked as a dishwasher. In 1973 she married Bill Pentland, the only person in their Denver community with a bathtub, she would joke. In fact, she has often said that it was love at first sight. After their marriage, they moved to a six-foot wide trailer outside Denver and had three children over the next five years. Arnold's friends from Denver have said that her life during that period greatly resembles the Connor household on "Roseanne." At first she stayed at home with her children for several years, and then she took part-time jobs, as a window dresser and later as a cocktail waitress, to help support her family. It was the latter job that revealed her talent as a comedian. When her male customers made offensive remarks, she was always able to defuse the situation and make them laugh with her cutting responses. They convinced her to try out at a local comedy club.

CHOOSING A CAREER

In 1981, Roseanne began to do stand-up routines at a Denver comedy club, where she offered comic rebuttal to what she saw as the male comedians' sexism. She also joined a collective at a women's bookstore and began to explore feminist ideas. When the club owner told her that her feminist views were offensive, she began to perform at coffeehouses, to mostly lesbian audiences. "Thirty-five lesbians would show up," she told the *Advocate* early last year, "and then we'd put it in the paper that the show was sold out! And that would get me future bookings because I'd say, 'Hey, I've got a following.' Those women really gave me my start."

Having extended her performances to punk clubs and motorcycle bars, Roseanne still struggled with reworking her material to appeal to a wider audience. She softened her rough-edged message, drew on her own domestic experiences, and took the funny new act on the road in 1984, while her husband stayed home with the children. When discovered by Mitzi Shore, owner of Los Angeles' prestigious Comedy Store, Roseanne decided to move to that city and make comedy her vocation.

CAREER HIGHLIGHTS

After a two-week gig at the Comedy Store in 1985, Roseanne was signed to the television special "Funny." She continued touring clubs and striking familiar chords in audiences with a style and subject matter that few had dared to present. Overweight, often crude, and adamantly working-class, she punctured the popular view that feminism applied only to white, upper-class, professional women. She skewered men, children, and the family in general, while lampooning her own slovenliness. Commenting on her husband asking if there were any Cheetos left in the house, she wisecracked, "Like he couldn't go over and lift up the sofa cushions himself."

Her fame blossomed quickly. Three appearances on the "Tonight" show led to a performance backing Rodney Dangerfield on an HBO special, and

then to a special of her own on that network in 1987. The latter show won her an Ace Award for best female in a comedy and led to the creation of her hit situation comedy, "Roseanne."

"Roseanne" depicts the often-chaotic life of the Connors, a working-class family with three children. The show focuses on their real-life problems—lost jobs, failed businesses, financial hardship, health problems, teen sexuality and depression. The series also features the talented John Goodman as Roseanne's husband Dan. According to *L.A. Style,* "it all revolves around Roseanne Connor: obnoxious, sarcastic, whining, lazy, imperfect in almost every way—in all, a very funny characterization by Roseanne Arnold, based, one assumes, on herself."

Arnold insisted on creating a character based on her real-life experiences as a working-class mother. "I'm not gonna play a damn person who's making $500,000 a year and call that real American life," she said at the time. "I see myself as sort of like Ralph Kramden [of the famous "Honeymooners" sitcom]....I'm proud to be a working-class person." Roseanne also wanted to portray gender struggles within the home without resorting to the stereotypes that she believes are rampant in TV comedy.

Roseanne has managed the difficult feat of appealing to a broad audience while keeping the intellectual honesty necessary to make what some see as powerful political points. Barbara Ehrenreich, writing in the *New Republic,* praises the show's realism, citing Arnold's "bleak and radical vision....Yeah, she's crude, but so are the realities of pain and exploitation she seeks to remind us of. If middle-class feminism can't claim Roseanne, maybe it's gotten a little too dainty for its own good."

"Roseanne" was an instant hit when it premiered on ABC in 1988. While some viewers were repelled by a character they saw as crude, most audiences sided with critics like Cathleen Schine, writing for *Vogue.* Schine noted that Roseanne brought "a strangely comfortable dignity" to the proceedings and called her "the voice of reason." In making "Roseanne" the country's number-one show, viewers clearly identified with both the sarcasm and vulnerability Arnold brought to her character.

In spite of high audience ratings and critical approval for "Roseanne," strong differences of opinion started to disrupt the production. The star fought with then-co-creator Matt Williams for control of the scripts, complaining that the network was insisting on making the characters unsympathetic. "I want a portrait of working folks with a little warmth and dignity," she commented, "not buffoons. Bad grammar doesn't mean you're an idiot." She eventually gained control of the show, but remained upset about all the negative publicity. Roseanne believes that other stars are not singled out when they replace staff members, and that she has received such hostile criticism because the television industry doesn't tolerate powerful women.

Arnold once again provoked a raging controversy when she performed the national anthem at a San Diego baseball game in 1990. She sang off-key and, in an attempt to parody athletes, she spat and grabbed her crotch. What she saw as satire, the fans, and the tabloids, saw as a desecration. Roseanne has apologized for any offense she might have caused, but her reputation for controversy continues unabated.

"There is something in Roseanne's psyche that cannot tolerate silence," her former publicist Jim Dobson told *TV Guide.* "When it gets calm, she needs to go public with controversy." Arnold herself has a more relaxed take: "It's rock and roll. It's living life on the edge. I don't want to be normal. I couldn't ever be even if I wanted to be....I hope never to be boring."

With her show in its fifth year and currently among the top two programs, and with unchallenged creative control, Roseanne Arnold stands as the most powerful woman in television. Like the working-class people she still claims as her source and inspiration, she has taken her shots and fired back in what Ehrenreich calls a "rags-to-revolution tale."

MAJOR INFLUENCES

Roseanne's father, a self-described funnyman who never went on stage, introduced his daughter to the stand-up acts that she now credits as her influences. She admired the recordings of Mort Sahl and Lenny Bruce, as well as the appearances of tamer comics on television. "I can feel Jack Benny in me, Totie Fields, Henny Youngman," she says.

MARRIAGE AND FAMILY

Roseanne married her first husband, Bill Pentland, in Denver in 1973. They had three children—Jessica, now seventeen; Jennifer, sixteen; and Jake, fourteen. The two were divorced in 1990. She then married Tom Arnold, a comedian she had met seven years earlier in Minneapolis. Tom Arnold has worked as a writer and story editor on her show, and Roseanne credits Tom with helping her to be more assertive.

While she has often been sarcastic in her stage and screen persona about family duties ("I figure by the time my husband comes home at night, if those kids are still alive, I've done my job"), she is in fact fiercely loyal and protective toward her children. She has stood by her daughters through emotional and drug problems, and says she'd put them up against anyone's children.

Roseanne also has a daughter, Brandy, born twenty-one-years ago out of wedlock and adopted by another family. They have recently been reunited. The Arnolds say that they are planning to have a child of their own.

HOBBIES AND OTHER INTERESTS

Roseanne and Tom Arnold, who stay in Hollywood only when necessary, are building a large neo-Victorian home on 1,600 acres in Tom's hometown of Ottumwa, Iowa. They enjoy establishing a home life and working together. True to their roots, they plan to have a bowling alley built in the mansion.

HONORS AND AWARDS

Ace Awards: 1987, for Best Female in a Comedy and Best HBO Special
American Comedy Awards: 1988, for Funniest Female Performer in a Television Special for "On Location: The Roseanne Bar Show"; 1989, for Funniest Female Performer in a Television Series (Lead)
People's Choice Award: 1989, for Favorite New Television Series and for Female Performer in a New Program; 1990, for Female Performer in Television and for All-Around Favorite—Female Entertainer

WRITINGS

Roseanne: My Life as a Woman, 1989

FURTHER READING

BOOKS

Barr, Roseanne. *Roseanne: My Life as a Woman,* 1989

PERIODICALS

Current Biography Yearbook, 1989
Ladies Home Journal, Sept. 1989, p.137
New Republic, Apr. 2, 1990, p.28
People, Apr. 28, 1986, p.105; Oct 7, 1991, p.84
Redbook, Jan. 1991, p.26
TV Guide, Feb. 23, 1991; Jan. 4, 1992, p.6
Vogue, Nov. 1988, p.246

ADDRESS

c/o Wapello County Productions
500 S. Sepulveda #400
Los Angeles, CA 90049

OBITUARY

Isaac Asimov   1920-1992
American Writer and Scientist
Author of Nearly 500 Books of Science Fiction
and Nonfiction for Young Readers and Adults

BIRTH

Isaac Asimov was born on January 2, 1920, in Petrovichi, Russia, to Judah and Anna Rachel (Berman) Asimov. Judah Asimov worked in the family grain business, earning a comfortable income. But there was a great deal of uncertainty and upheaval in the new Soviet Union at that time, shortly after the Bolshevik Revolution (1917) and World War I (1914-18). The family decided to join Anna Asimov's half-brother in America. They emigrated to the United States in 1923, when Asimov was three years old, and he became a naturalized American citizen five years later. Asimov was the oldest child in the family, with a sister, Marcia, and a brother, Stanley.

YOUTH

The Asimov family settled in a poor neighborhood in Brooklyn, New York, along with many other immigrants. There Judah Asimov held a series of jobs before buying, in 1926, the first of several neighborhood stores that sold candy, tobacco, and newspapers and magazines. The elder Asimov liked being his own boss, even though it meant working very long hours, from 6:00 A.M. to 1:00 A.M., seven days a week. Isaac was in second grade at the time, and he and the whole family began helping out in the store. While the business didn't make them rich, the Asimov family did get through the Great Depression without suffering much hardship.

The Asimov family valued education. Judah and Anna encouraged their children to work hard and to read good books. Their son Isaac was a very bright child. He taught himself to read at the age of five and always excelled at school—so much so that he skipped several grades. But he also had trouble fitting in. About the only time he was able to get along with his classmates was when he was telling stories. He frequently got in trouble with his teachers, and he was so boastful about being smart that the other students picked on him. Years later, he said, "Even when, as the result of skipping, I ended up the youngest pupil in the class by better than two years, I was still the smartest and knew it and made sure *they* knew it." This robust self-esteem, evident here in Asimov's own words from his two-volume autobiography *In Memory Yet Green* and *In Joy Still Felt*, is frequently mentioned by his biographers as a key personality trait throughout his life.

EARLY MEMORIES

Working in the family store every day, Isaac Asimov soon became fascinated with the glossy magazines that filled the racks. His father, though, refused to let him waste his time on what he considered junk—until young Isaac hit on a plan. By pretending that the new magazine *Science Wonder Stories* was really about science, young Isaac soon won his father's permission to indulge his love of science fiction. As he later recalled, "I started reading science fiction at the age of nine. My father wouldn't let me read anything else. He thought that science fiction dealt with science. That was his mistake. Later on, of course, I read other books, but nothing interested me as much as science fiction. It stretched my mind."

Those early stories got him started on his career. At age eleven he began writing his first novel, which he set aside after eight chapters. Beginning in 1934, several of his letters were published in one of his favorite science fiction magazines, *Astounding Stories*. Encouraged by this success, Asimov soon began writing stories and working with John W. Campbell, an influential author and editor of science fiction. Campbell once described the young Asimov as "lean and hungry and very enthusiastic. He couldn't write, but he could tell a story. You can teach a guy how to write, but not how to tell a story."

EDUCATION

After graduating from Boys High School in Brooklyn at the age of fifteen, Asimov entered Columbia University. He received his bachelor's degree there in 1939 and his master's degree in chemistry in 1941. During World War II, Asimov took a break from his education to assist in the war effort. He went to work as a chemist at the Naval Air Experimental Station in Philadelphia and then served in the Army in 1945-46. After his discharge as a corporal, he returned to Columbia University and earned his Ph.D. in chemistry in 1948. He finished up his work at Columbia by doing postdoctoral research on nucleic acids.

CHOOSING A CAREER

In 1949, Asimov accepted a teaching position at Boston University School of Medicine, ready to begin his career as a research scientist. At the same time, he was starting to have some success as a writer. He had already sold a few pieces—his first short story, "Marooned Off Vesta," appeared in the October 1938 issue of *Amazing Stories*, and "Nightfall," the most popular story of his career, appeared in 1941. Since its publication, "Nightfall" has repeatedly been voted the best science fiction short story of all time by both science fiction writers and readers.

Asimov continued to write while teaching at Boston University. *Pebble in the Sky*, his first science fiction novel, was published in 1950; *I, Robot*, his famous collection of stories, appeared that same year; and he and two colleagues wrote a medical textbook, his first nonfiction work, two years later. He also completed the original "Foundation" trilogy at about this time. In 1958, Asimov quit teaching to write full-time. As he later recalled, "I had thought of myself as a research chemist (or, later, biochemist) for a dozen years. To be sure, I was a writer also, but that was my avocation, not my profession. Writing was a spare-time activity, a sideline, something to make a little extra cash with and to gain a little extra importance with. I was beginning to think of myself as a writer and that was crucial."

CAREER HIGHLIGHTS

Before his death in New York on April 6, 1992, of heart and kidney failure, Asimov had completed almost 500 books, 350 short stories, and some 2000 articles. Asimov loved to write. His daily routine was to wake by 6:00 A.M., sit down to write by 7:30 A.M., and continue to work most days until 10:00 P.M. He worked very quickly, typing 90 words per minute, with very little rewriting. In addition, he preferred to work without assistance, handling his own typing, phone calls, letter writing, research, proofreading, and indexing. An amazingly prolific author with wide-ranging interests, Asimov wrote a tremendous amount on many different topics. In addition to science fiction, he wrote nonfiction science books, for both youthful readers and adults, on such subjects as biology, chemistry, astronomy, physics, and mathematics. He also published books on the Bible, Shakespeare, the origin of words, ancient and modern history, and dirty limericks. In most of these works, particularly those on scientific topics, Asimov was widely acclaimed for his ability to interpret complicated technical issues for the general reader. He explained difficult concepts with a straightforward, clear, humorous, and easy-to-understand style. His appeal was perhaps best summarized by the astronomer Carl Sagan, who called Asimov "the greatest explainer of the age."

Asimov's science fiction stories and novels remain his best-known and best-loved works—and the Robot and "Foundation" series are widely considered the best of the best. The Robot series began with a group of short stories first collected in *I, Robot* (1950). In one of them, "Runaround" (1942), Asimov created the "Three Laws of Robotics," which define and describe the relationship between robots and humans:

1. A robot must not injure a human being or, through inaction, allow a human being to come to harm.
2. A robot must obey the orders given it by human beings except where those orders would conflict with the First Law.
3. A robot must protect its own existence, except where such protection would conflict with the First or Second Law.

Asimov's depiction of robots as machines that would help but never harm humans was profoundly influential in the field. It helped many people to overcome their fears about new technology. His view eventually became so popular that it was generally accepted by readers and other writers as an accurate description of what robots would become. To this day many modern scientists, particularly those working in the field of artificial intelligence, credit Asimov with inspiring them to become scientists by encouraging them to dream about what could be.

The "Foundation" series began as several stories and novellas that were then grouped into three novels: *Foundation* (1951), *Foundation and Empire* (1952), and *Second Foundation* (1953). The "Foundation" trilogy, considered one of the most influential works in science fiction, won a Hugo Award in 1966 as the "Best Novel Series of All Time." The work is often described as a "future history" patterned after the renowned *Decline and Fall of the Roman Empire* by nineteenth-century historian Edward Gibbon. The "Foundation" trilogy describes the dissolution and subsequent rebuilding of a galactic empire of the future consisting of perhaps 25 million inhabited worlds. Asimov repeatedly returned to the themes of the "Foundation" and Robot stories, writing new works that eventually linked the two series. This combined series now totals fifteen books, including a final title, *Forward the Foundation*, to be published in late 1992. With the mature dialogue and themes of these works, Asimov is often credited with helping to elevate the genre of science fiction from pulp-magazine status to a more intellectual level. While some critics fault Asimov's literary technique, particularly his writing style and creation of characters, his broad and imaginative vision of a future society continues to entrance readers.

"What characterized all his writing," according to University of Michigan professor of English Eric Rabkin, "was the ability to find the tantalizing details that led his readers to go on and do further thinking. For example, in one of his essays, he wondered whether the Renaissance was created by the invention of eyeglasses, because it suddenly tripled the number of available scholars in the world. It's one of those absolutely impossible things to prove, but tantalizing. Asimov walked with one foot in the land of fiction and one foot in the land of fact."

MARRIAGE AND FAMILY

Asimov met Gertrude Blugerman on Valentine's Day, 1942, and they were married just a few months later, on July 26, 1942. They had two children: David, born in 1951, and Robyn Joan, born in 1955. Asimov and his first wife were divorced in 1973, and he married Janet Jeppson, a retired psychiatrist, on November 30, 1973.

SELECTED WRITINGS

THE "FOUNDATION" AND ROBOT BOOKS

Fifteen of Asimov's novels, the "Foundation" and Robot books, comprise a series about the future of humanity. According to Asimov, he did not write them in the order in which they were intended to be read. The following list presents the titles in chronological order, according to the historical narrative:

1. *The Complete Robot*, 1982 (includes stories from the original collection *I, Robot*, 1950)
2. *The Caves of Steel*, 1954
3. *The Naked Sun*, 1957
4. *The Robots of Dawn*, 1983
5. *Robots and Empire*, 1985
6. *The Currents of Space*, 1952
7. *The Stars, Like Dust*, 1951
8. *Pebble in the Sky*, 1950
9. *Prelude to Foundation*, 1988

10. *Forward the Foundation* [to be published in 1992]
11. *Foundation,* 1951
12. *Foundation and Empire,* 1952
13. *Second Foundation,* 1953
14. *Foundation's Edge,* 1982
15. *Foundation and Earth,* 1986

OTHER SCIENCE FICTION

Fantastic Voyage, 1966
Nightfall and Other Stories, 1969
The Gods Themselves, 1972
The Bicentennial Man and Other Stories, 1976

SCIENCE FICTION FOR YOUNG READERS

David Starr, Space Ranger, 1952
Lucky Starr and the Pirates of the Asteroids, 1953
Lucky Starr and the Oceans of Venus, 1954
Lucky Starr and the Big Sun of Mercury, 1956
Lucky Starr and the Moons of Jupiter, 1957
Lucky Starr and the Rings of Saturn, 1958
Norby, the Mixed-Up Robot, 1983
Norby's Other Secret, 1984
Norby and the Invaders, 1985
Norby and the Lost Princess, 1985
The Norby Chronicles, 1986
Norby and the Queen's Necklace, 1986
Norby Finds a Villain, 1987
Norby: Robot for Hire, 1987
Norby through Time and Space, 1988
Norby and Yobo's Great Adventure, 1989
Norby Down to Earth, 1989
Norby and the Oldest Dragon, 1990
Norby and the Court Jester, 1991

All the David and Lucky Starr books were written under the pseudonym Paul French; all the Norby the Robot books were written with Janet Asimov.

SCIENCE FOR YOUNG READERS

The Moon, 1966
Stars, 1968
ABC's of Space, 1969
Great Ideas of Science, 1969
ABC's of the Ocean, 1970
ABC's of the Earth, 1971
ABC's of Ecology, 1972
Comets and Meteors, 1972
"How Did We Find Out About" Series, 35 vols., 1972-1992

OTHER

In Memory Yet Green: The Autobiography of Isaac Asimov, 1920-1954, 1979
In Joy Still Felt: The Autobiography of Isaac Asimov, 1954-1978, 1980

Asimov was also the editor of many anthologies; a contributor of short stories and editorials to magazines and anthologies; a contributor of articles to science magazines; and the author and editor of a vast collection of other books of mystery, history, etymology, and other nonfiction.

HONORS AND AWARDS

Hugo Award (Science Fiction Achievement Award, given by the World Science Fiction Convention): 1963, Special Award for Distinguished Contribution to the Field of Science Fiction; 1966, *The Foundation Trilogy,* for Best Novel Series of All Time; 1973, *The Gods Themselves,* for Best Novel; 1977, "The Bicentennial Man," for Best Novelette; 1983, *Foundation's Edge,* for Best Novel

James T. Grady Award (American Chemical Society): 1965

American Association for the Advancement of Science—Westinghouse Science Writing Award: 1967

Nebula Award (given by the Science Fiction Writers of America): 1973, *The Gods Themselves,* for Best Novel; 1977, "The Bicentennial Man," for Best Novelet; 1987, as "Grand Master"

Washington Post/(Children's Book Guild Nonfiction Award): 1985

FURTHER READING

BOOKS

Asimov, Isaac. *In Memory Yet Green: The Autobiography of Isaac Asimov, 1920-1954,* 1979

Asimov, Isaac. *In Joy Still Felt: The Autobiography of Isaac Asimov, 1954-1978,* 1980

Contemporary Authors New Revision Series, Vol. 19

Encyclopedia Britannica

Erlanger, Ellen. *Isaac Asimov: Scientist and Storyteller,* 1986 (juvenile)

Who's Who in America, 1990-91

World Book Encyclopedia

PERIODICALS

Current Biography, 1953, 1968
Los Angeles Times, Apr. 7, 1992, p.A1
New York Times, Apr. 7, 1992, p.B7
Time, Dec. 19, 1988, p.80
Washington Post, Apr. 7. 1992, p.B6

James Baker   1930-
American Politician, Former White House
Chief of Staff, Secretary of State, and
Secretary of the Treasury

BIRTH

James Addison Baker III was born on April 28, 1930, in Houston,
Texas. His father, James Addison Baker, Jr., worked in the family
law firm, while his mother, Bonner Means Baker, was a
homemaker. James Baker has one younger sister, Bonner Baker,
named after their mother.

YOUTH

Biographical profiles of James Baker give little sense of what he
was like as a boy, what he liked to play or study at school.

Instead, they focus on his family heritage. Baker, known to friends and family as Jimmy, is a member of one of Houston's oldest, best-known, and wealthiest families. He is one in a long line of first sons named James Baker. In 1872 his great-grandfather, a state judge, added his name to the law firm Gray & Botts, formed some six years earlier; it soon became Baker & Botts. His grandfather, known as Captain Baker, was a powerful attorney and financier, known for his great influence on city affairs. He often receives credit for building the family concern into what is now considered the most notable firm in Houston and one of the 20 or so largest in the country. Captain Baker used to advise young attorneys to "Work hard, study hard, and keep out of politics." Yet according to one of his partners, "Captain Baker ran the firm, and he ran the city." Even his grandson Jimmy has said that "Grandfather was a behind-the-scenes player." Of all his family, it is Captain Baker that James Baker is said to resemble most.

His father, a strict disciplinarian, was known as "the Warden" by James Baker's friends. Each morning "the Warden" expected young Jimmy to get out of bed immediately; if not, he would pour a pitcher of ice cold water over his head, soaking him and the bed. "Gets you up real fast," Baker now admits. Yet he was very close to his father, who encouraged his skill as an outdoorsman and athlete. They started hunting together when young Jimmy was only six or seven, and began playing tennis together a few years later.

EDUCATION

James Baker started out at the Kinkaid School and then, like his father, went to the Hill School, near Philadelphia, Pennsylvania. At that exclusive Eastern private prep school, Baker was a good student as well as captain of the tennis team.

After graduating from the Hill School, Baker attended Princeton University in Princeton, New Jersey. He was co-captain of the freshman tennis team, but switched over to rugby, he has said, because the rugby team took a trip to Bermuda. He majored in history and classics and received his bachelor's degree from Princeton in 1952. Baker served as a lieutenant in the Marine Corps from 1952 to 1954, becoming an expert marksman.

After military service, Baker returned to Texas and enrolled in law school at the University of Texas at Austin. To please his father, he joined a fraternity there, even though he was seven years older than the other pledges, the only graduate student, and by then a married man. During Hell Week, the ritual hazing period, Baker had to wear a dead fish on a string all week. "I did that for my father," he has said. "He wanted me to do it because he had done it. He believed it was the smart thing to do. If you're going to practice law in Texas, you go to the law school in Austin and make all the contacts you can. They'll pay off later." Baker received his law degree from the University of Texas in 1957.

MARRIAGE AND FAMILY

Baker met his first wife while a sophomore at Princeton. During that rugby trip to Bermuda, he met Mary Stuart McHenry, then a student at Finch College in Ohio. According to Baker, he never really dated anyone else after he met Mary Stuart. They were married in Dayton, Ohio, her hometown, in November 1953, and had four sons: James, John, Stewart, and Douglas. She died in 1970, after a sixteen-month battle with breast cancer.

EARLY CAREER

After completing law school in 1957, Baker began his career in Houston. The family firm had enacted a rule against nepotism (showing favoritism for family members), and he was unable to work there. Instead he went to work for Andrews, Kurth, Campbell, & Jones, another prestigious corporate law firm in Houston. With his mastery of technical issues, organizational skill, attention to detail, hard work, and unaffected manner, he was very successful there. He was made managing partner within a decade.

It was during this time that he first met George Bush. The two became friends on the tennis court, where they often paired up in doubles tournaments at the Houston Country Club. Also, Baker's wife, Mary Stuart, was an active Republican who worked on Bush's congressional campaigns. Baker considered himself a Democrat, but was more likely to go hunt than go vote on election day, as others recall. Still, the Baker and Bush families soon became close friends, and George and Barbara Bush stood by Baker when Mary Stuart became ill, spending hours at her bedside.

Baker's whole direction in life changed, though, after her death in 1970. Bush had recently announced his candidacy for the U.S. Senate, and he asked Baker to direct the campaign in Harris County, which includes Houston and the area around it. According to Baker, "Within a month after Mary Stuart died, he asked me to run his Houston campaign. I think he did it to give me something to do, to get me involved." With that move, they forged a partnership that has endured to this day. Bush lost that election, but he did win a majority in Harris County. Baker was hooked: "I went back to practicing law, but it didn't hold the same fascination." He switched political parties then, becoming, in his own words, "absolutely, totally, pure Republican." In 1972, he worked on the reelection campaign of Republican President Richard Nixon, and soon after was appointed state Republican finance chairman. In addition, Baker continued to work at the law firm of Andrews, Kurth until 1975.

REMARRIAGE AND FAMILY LIFE

The early 1970s was a period of transition for Baker in both his career and family life. Raising four young sons alone was difficult. "It was the only time when I have felt at a loss as to the future," Baker has said. "I did maintain my work habits, and I couldn't satisfy the emotional needs of the boys. I couldn't be both mother and father to them. We had a succession of housekeepers—not a happy experience. This was 1970, and a tough time to be raising kids." Two of the children, it has been widely reported, eventually developed serious drug problems that required treatment in a hospital.

In 1973 Baker married Susan Garrett Winston, who had been one of his wife's closest friends. She had three children from her first marriage— Elizabeth, James, and Will Winston—and together they all moved into the Baker home. It was chaotic at first, according to Baker: "We recognized it wasn't going to be easy to put seven kids from two families together, and boy, it wasn't, that first year." As she recalls, "There were times when we wondered if the roof would stay on the house for all the emotion and conflict. But we've survived—very well." Both agree that their family life came together with the birth of their child, Mary Bonner Baker, in 1977. A devout Christian, Susan Baker has, since their move to the capital, started a prayer group for Washington wives. With Tipper Gore, the wife of Democratic Vice President-elect Al Gore, she also cofounded the Parents Music Resource Center, an anti-pornography group that fought for labeling rock records.

LATER CAREER

Baker has been active in politics since 1975. At that time, he was offered a position as Under Secretary of Commerce in the Republican administration of Gerald Ford, who had become president after Richard Nixon resigned in 1974 following the Watergate scandal. In 1976, when Ford was campaigning against Ronald Reagan and others for the Republican nomination for president, he asked Baker to join his campaign team as a delegate counter. In the weeks leading up to the nominating convention, Baker kept track of exactly how many delegates had pledged their support to Ford. His success in persuading delegates to support the president so impressed Ford that he hired Baker to manage his campaign against Democratic challenger Jimmy Carter. At that time, Ford was running some 30 points behind Carter; President Ford lost the election by only one percent of the vote, and Baker received much of the credit for Ford's come-from-behind effort. With that campaign, Baker began to develop his reputation as a skilled and astute political strategist.

Following Ford's defeat, Baker briefly returned to practicing law in Houston. In 1978 he made his only attempt at elective office, running for Texas attorney general. He lost. Baker then signed on as manager for George Bush's 1980 campaign for the Republican nomination for president. Although Bush was considered an underdog, he made a very respectable showing in the early primaries. Yet later in the season, it was clear that Ronald Reagan would win enough delegates to secure the nomination.

Baker urged Bush to withdraw from the race before the primary in Reagan's home state of California, but Bush refused. Baker took matters into his own hands and announced to the press that Bush was withdrawing from the race. As Baker later explained, "What I'll admit to, but George never will, is that the Veep thing [the vice presidency] was always the fallback. It was always on my mind. That's why, at every opportunity, I had him cool his rhetoric about Reagan." Baker's plan worked, and Reagan selected Bush as his running mate.

THE REAGAN YEARS

Following the Republican nominating convention in August 1980, Reagan asked Baker to serve as senior adviser during the fall campaign. They worked closely together in preparing for the debates against President Carter. Reagan's masterful performance in those debates was both a deciding factor in his success as well as a great credit to Baker's coaching abilities. Ten days after winning the election, President Reagan offered Baker the job of White House chief of staff. The move surprised many. Reagan is known to be very loyal, and it was expected that the post would be filled by one of his circle of close friends and advisers from his days in California government.

As chief of staff, Baker worked closely with long-time Reagan aides Edwin Meese III and Michael Deaver. Baker was responsible for directing all the day-to-day activities of the White House, including the press office, Congressional relations, speech writers, personnel matters, and relations with elected officials throughout the U.S. He also controlled access to the president. It is a position of great power, and Baker is widely credited with employing that power masterfully, particularly in his relations with members of the press and the U.S. Congress. It was in this position, in particular, that Baker developed his reputation for efficiency, competence, ambition, discipline, hard work, caution, and political pragmatism: he is not considered a visionary, but rather an expert at implementing the vision of others. During his tenure as chief of staff from 1981 through 1985, Baker is widely credited with securing passage of Reagan's controversial tax reform bill and budget cuts.

After Ronald Reagan's 1984 landslide reelection, Baker left his White House post in January 1985 to become Secretary of the Treasury. He served in that Cabinet-level post for three-and-a-half years. Commentators agree that his major achievements during that era include the 1986 tax-reform act, the U.S.-Canada trade agreement, and an international forum on economic policy, which brought about the devaluation of the dollar. Some critics, though, fault Baker for ignoring the savings and loan crisis, which developed during his tenure as Treasury secretary.

THE BUSH YEARS

In August 1988, Baker left his Cabinet post to become the director of Bush's 1988 presidential campaign against Democratic challenger Governor Michael S. Dukakis. It has been widely reported that Baker was reluctant to leave the Treasury department: he wants to be seen as a statesman, not a politician. Despite his reluctance, he took the job for his old friend. For Bush, it paid off. Baker joined the campaign when Dukakis was leading by seventeen points, and Baker has received much of the credit for Bush's come-from-behind win. The day after the 1988 election, President-elect Bush appointed Baker Secretary of State. Because of the importance of that position and his long friendship with Bush, Baker was widely considered the most powerful figure in the administration.

Baker served as Secretary of State from January 1989 until August 1992. It is a demanding job—he logged some 251,000 miles of travel to 40 countries in 1991. It is, perhaps, premature to judge Baker's accomplishments as a statesman. Still, political commentators applaud his work on arms-control agreements and his handling of the Mideast peace talks between Israel and the Arab states. Their views are more mixed, however, on the administration's responses to political changes in Germany, the U.S.S.R, and other Eastern-bloc nations; some fault the policies as too cautious, while others applaud this restraint. The state department's role leading up to and during the war against Iraq, though, receives widespread criticism, focusing on the administration's support for Iraq in the long war with Iran, its failure to predict Iraq's invasion of Kuwait, and its inability to avoid war.

In August 1992, Bush appointed Baker chief of staff and again asked him to lead his presidential campaign against Democratic challenger Governor Bill Clinton. As in 1988, there was widespread conjecture that Baker was unwilling to leave his post. Despite the political skill and organization that he brought to the race, Clinton won the election. Baker's political appointment will come to an end when the Bush administration leaves Washington in January 1993. When asked what he planned to do after the election, Baker has said that he will go to his ranch in Wyoming.

Over the years, there has been much speculation in the press about Baker's own political ambitions. Many believe that he will one day run for president, possibly in 1996. Others discount this idea. While praising his skill at behind-the-scenes maneuvering, they point to his lack of a grand vision and his disdain for campaigning and fundraising. With a Democratic administration in power, his immediate prospects are uncertain, yet few doubt that Baker will continue to play a major role in American politics.

HOBBIES AND OTHER INTERESTS

Although he has had little free time in recent years, Baker still enjoys hunting, fishing, and camping out, particularly on his 1300-acre ranch in Wyoming. His spread is completely undeveloped—no buildings, no electricity, no running water—just an old tent that he throws out when it starts to rot. "I call it the Rock Pile Ranch," Baker says, "and that's about all that's on it. Nothing else but some water wells and turkey feeders. Coming here is the closest I get to therapy. I'm not really into material things, but land, well, they're not making any more of it."

HONORS AND AWARDS

Woodrow Wilson Award (Princeton University): 1983

Jefferson Award for Distinguished Service (American Institute for Public Service): 1985

Award for Distinguished Public Service (John F. Kennedy School of Government, Harvard University): 1986

Finance Minister of the Year *(Euromoney* magazine): 1986

George F. Kennan Award (American Committee on U.S./Soviet Relations): 1990

Hans J. Morganthau Award (National Committee on American Foreign Policy): 1990

Presidential Medal of Freedom: 1991

FURTHER READING

PERIODICALS

Current Biography Yearbook 1982
New York Times, Aug. 14, 1992, pp.A1, A24
New York Times Magazine, May 6, 1990, p.34
New Yorker, May 7, 1990, p.50
People, Aug. 31, 1981, p.62
Texas Monthly, May 1982, p.148
Time, Feb. 13, 1989, p.26
Vanity Fair, Oct. 1992, p.214
Washington Post Magazine, Jan. 29, 1989, p.17

ADDRESS

The White House
1600 Pennsylvania Ave.
Washington, D.C. 20500

Charles Barkley 1963-
American Professional Basketball Player
Recently Traded from the Philadelphia 76ers
to the Phoenix Suns

BIRTH

Charles Wade Barkley was born February 20, 1963, to Frank and
Charcey Mae (Gaither) Barkley in Leeds, Alabama, a small town
about fifteen miles northeast of Birmingham. He is the only child
of that union. He has two half-brothers—Darryl Barkley, three
years younger; and John Glenn, seven years younger, born to his
mother in a later marriage.

YOUTH

Barkley, now a man of massive, overpowering size, was a severely
anemic infant who required blood transfusions for the first six

months of his life. After his parents separated when he was only thirteen months old, Charles and his mother (now Charcey Mae Glenn) moved in with his grandmother, Johnnie Mae Edwards, and her second husband, Adolphus Edwards. The family was poor, but Barkley recalls no deprivation. He remembers how both mother and grandmother "made sure I had everything I needed, even though they had to go without paying bills." He looks back on his life in the projects (government housing) as a clean and relatively safe place, in those years, to be born and raised. Charcey Mae worked as a maid in the white neighborhoods of Leeds to help support her little boy, and Johnnie Mae was a beautician.

There was a missing link in family life, however, since Frank Barkley had run off to California, and the child had no contact with his father until they met again when Charles was nine years old. In his 1992 auto-biography, *Outrageous!*, written with Roy S. Johnson, he talks about the bitterness he felt then and still has not completely resolved, although father and son have developed some closeness in recent years. "I had no real idea of who he was, what type of person he was, nothing. . . . I hated the fact that he left my mother alone to fend for herself. . . . I came to think of him only as an evil man," he says, "because only an evil man would leave his wife and son." Adolphus Edwards, whom Charles called "Little Daddy," filled the void as best he could by being a positive male influence. He was good to Charcey Mae and all of her children, even after he and the grandmother were divorced, but Charles "was his heart."

Because his mother and grandmother were quite strict and did not allow him and his brothers to roam the streets, young Charles became focused on one recreation: basketball. "It was the only fun Mama'd let me have," he remembers. He worked hard at it, usually by himself when the other kids had left the playground. He would even practice jumping—a skill that has had a tremendous impact on his game—by leaping back and forth across a three-and-a-half-foot fence for two or three hours at a time. He is certain now that it was the fence-jumping that gave his legs their incredible strength.

EARLY MEMORIES

Young Barkley was, by his own admission, headed in the wrong direction by the time he was in junior high school. Probably because of boredom—as he says, "when you're a poor kid in the projects, you'll do anything for excitement"—he and his friends started stealing small items or boxed cakes from the stores downtown. But one night they got rowdy as they ripped through the bakery boxes and started throwing cakes at one another. The police came and chased after them into the dark woods. Barkley, in his panic to get away, ran face first into a tree at full speed, and "when I hit the ground, I thought I was dead." The boys were not caught, but after that frightening experience, Barkley realized that he had to find something better to do with his time. He stuck to basketball.

EDUCATION

Barkley attended elementary and junior high school in Leeds and graduated from Leeds High School in 1981. He then spent three years at Auburn University (in his home state) on a basketball scholarship before declaring hardship and entering the 1984 draft of the National Basketball Association (NBA). While at Auburn, he majored in business management.

CHOOSING A CAREER

Even as a five-foot-ten, 220-pound high school junior, Barkley insisted at the time that he was going to make it in the NBA. His single-mindedness paid off, but he now admits to having harbored doubts. "I had no hope," he says. "Most people who brag are insecure, and I was insecure because I wasn't that good." Then, a one-year growth spurt of six inches allowed him to become a quick forward rather than a slow guard, won him a scholarship to Auburn, and set him on a course to stardom.

CAREER HIGHLIGHTS

At Auburn, Barkley led the Southeastern Conference in rebounding for three straight years, despite carrying close to 300 pounds on his almost six-foot-five frame. His unusual body type and surprising combination of skills earned him the nickname "The Round Mound of Rebound." Additionally, the controversy that has dogged his career first came to light: Barkley began to be seen as an overly fierce loudmouth on the court, but as apathetic and lazy in practice. His attitude led to his being cut from the 1984 Olympic team by the famed disciplinarian and coach of Indiana University, Bobby Knight, for whom Charles had no sufferance. "I hate the S.O.B.," Charles said at the time, but recently he has somewhat grudgingly softened his feelings.

Although his weight and discipline problems caused many teams to be wary of Barkley, the powerful Philadelphia 76ers felt that he had enough talent to overcome his weaknesses, and they drafted him fifth overall. It took a little time for the newly dubbed "Sir Charles" to excel in the NBA. He played every game of his rookie season, though rarely as a starter. He made the starting lineup in the 1985-86 season, averaging twenty points and thirteen rebounds per game, a remarkable feat for a man of his height.

In his third year as a pro, Barkley became the shortest player ever to lead the league in rebounding, making up for his lack of height with quickness, intelligence, and determination. Barkley was named to the NBA All-Star team that year. After carrying his team to an Atlantic Division title in 1989-90, he finished second in MVP (Most Valuable Player) balloting.

As the Sixers have declined as a team, Barkley's star has risen—yet, the controversies have multiplied as well. He is clearly one of the game's dominant players, but has drawn criticism for his outspokenness and temper, blasting coach, management, teammates, and fans. He has had trouble with the law on more than one occasion, for fighting and flaunting league rules, and in general makes life as rough on himself as on others. With both mouth and fists, he has earned the adjectives "outrageous" and "fearsome." He made perhaps his most offensive remark of all in November 1990: "This is a game that if you lose, you go home and beat your wife and kids," he joked, following a win over the then-lowly New Jersey Nets.

Those who know Barkley, however, paint a different picture. Charles is a kind, decent man, they insist, adding that his emotional outbursts and competitiveness can give people the wrong impression. "Charles is the exact opposite of most modern athletes," says former Sixers public relations director Dave Coskey. "Most of these guys are jerks who want you to think they're nice guys. But Charles is a genuinely nice guy who wants you to think he's a jerk."

In June 1992, Barkley was traded to the Phoenix Suns. He says that he probably will continue to play for a while, although he once announced that he would quit at thirty (that would be February 1993), then "never get up before noon again." Regardless, his unusual combination of court skills—rebounding, shooting, jumping, and intimidating—make Charles Barkley, the league's shortest forward, into one of its best in decades.

MAJOR INFLUENCES

It is not easy to get a fix on Barkley's true impressions of people and their impact on his life except, of course, for what he feels about the women who brought him up. "I owe everything I have to my mother and grandmother," he writes in his autobiography. "They were...my support and my security. They were everything I needed." Moses Malone, a former Sixers teammate, is another person Barkley credits with being an inspiring

presence. "Moses filled a gap in my life that had burdened me since my father abandoned my family. He was always there for me. . . .The day he was traded to the Washington Bullets [was] one of the saddest days of my life."

Barkley cites Larry Bird, the Boston Celtics superstar, as the man from whom he learned the most about NBA play. Bird's ability to appear calm under extreme pressure has intimidated opposing players for years, and Barkley has developed a similar style. "Clutch play," he says, "is all mental."

MARRIAGE AND FAMILY

Charles Barkley married wife Maureen, a former legal-aid secretary, February 9, 1989. They lead a quiet life in suburban Philadelphia with their three-year-old daughter, Christiana. The Barkleys are aware that their inter-racial marriage prompts controversy, but say that they are determined not to let it spoil the happiness they share.

HOBBIES AND OTHER INTERESTS

Barkley likes to listen to pop music and relaxes by watching television. He enjoys poking fun at life, too—offering his own philosophy that "if you're not enjoying it, you might as well be dead."

This "most quotable" of sports stars is concerned with the plight of black athletes who, he says, remain the victims of discrimination. He is generous in helping others, but for all his outspokenness, he keeps his personal life private, and insists that his extensive contributions to charity go unpublished.

WRITINGS

Outrageous!: The Fine Life and Flagrant Good Times of Basketball's Irresistible Force, with Roy S. Johnson, 1992

HONORS AND AWARDS

Southeast Conference College Player of the Year: 1983-84
NBA All-Star Team (6 Times): 1987-92
NBA All-Star Game Most Valuable Player: 1991
U.S. Olympic Basketball Team: Summer 1992

FURTHER READING

BOOKS

Barkley, Charles, and Roy S. Johnson. *Outrageous!: The Fine Life and Flagrant Good Times of Basketball's Irresistible Force*, 1992

PERIODICALS

Current Biography Yearbook 1991
New York Times Magazine, Mar. 17, 1991, p.26
Sport, Feb. 1990, p.21
Sports Illustrated, Mar. 9, 1992, p.186

ADDRESS

Phoenix Suns
2910 N. Central Ave.
Phoenix, AZ 85012

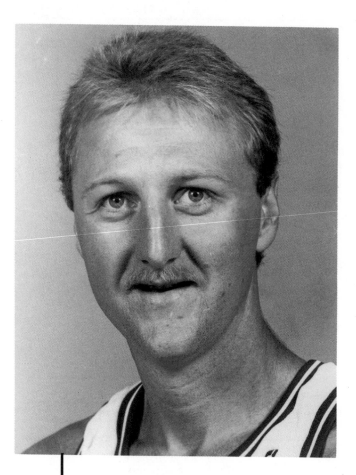

Larry Bird 1956-
American Former Professional Basketball Player
Member of the Boston Celtics Basketball Team

BIRTH

Larry Joe Bird was born December 7, 1956, in West Baden, Indiana, a village close to the once-famous mineral springs resort town of French Lick. He was the fourth of Joe and Georgia Bird's six children: Mike, Mark, and Linda were older, and Jeff and Eddie were several years younger.

YOUTH

Times were hard during Bird's early years. His father's various jobs provided only basic needs for the growing family, and there was seldom any money for extras. After the parents divorced in 1972, Georgia Bird supported her children as a restaurant cook and, later, with a better-paying job in a nursing home. The boys took turns living with their grandmother, Lizzie Kerns, because there was never enough room at home, but they continued to help their mother with chores around the house. All of the children, including Linda, were athletic, and they played ball whenever and wherever they could. "We played lots of baseball, soft-ball, rubber ball—we played ball all the time," Bird once told a reporter. But growing up in that part of the Midwest really means basketball above all other sports, and by the time the future star was in high school, this had become his game of choice. Indiana is nicknamed the Hoosier State (from *husher*, or *hoozer*, an old regional term for the pioneer men, meaning large and tough). It is a place where interest in basketball is so keen that high school and college competition creates a special kind of excitement known as "Hoosier Hysteria." Good players become heroes almost over-night, and Larry Bird more than fit that image. Mostly, he says, he was on the court to have fun, but he practiced every day and into the evening, in season and out, and it was that combination of work and play that developed his athletic talents, making him a high school all-star.

EARLY MEMORIES

Bird says now that he became a good team player because of his upbringing. His father taught the children to "stick up for one another, no matter what," and that prepared him to always "be there" for his team-mates. Larry Bird has written a book called *Drive: The Story of My Life,* and in it he tells about his father and the many good times the family shared with him. He writes with sadness of his father's tragic suicide on February 3, 1975, and remembers that "he was always trying to push us to be better. I missed him as soon as he was gone and I still miss him."

EDUCATION

Bird played guard during his sophomore and junior years at Springs Valley High School in French Lick, but it was not until his senior year, when he had grown to his full height of 6'9", that his skill and size came together to make him the team's star attraction. By this time, he was averaging 30.6 points and 20 rebounds a game. Although many college scouts tried to recruit him, he wasn't anxious to go far away from home, and so, in the fall of 1974, he enrolled at Indiana University in nearby Bloomington. Being a small-town boy, Bird felt out of place right away on such a big campus, and said later that it was not his idea of a school at all, but "more like a whole country." He left before official practice even began. He tried classes for two weeks at Northwood Institute in his hometown of West Baden, but was unhappy and dropped out to take a job with the local public works department.

It was not until the following year that he returned to college, this time at Indiana State University in Terre Haute. He could not play basketball for a year, under the transfer, or "redshirt," rules of the National Collegiate Athletic Association (NCAA). When he became eligible to join the lineup in the 1976-77 season, he led his teammates, the Sycamores, to a 25-3 record, their best in nearly 30 years. The following season, they reached the country's Top Ten. In Bird's senior year, they ranked first, remaining undefeated until the NCAA finals, when they suffered their only loss of the season to Magic Johnson's Michigan State team.

Bird had been a first-round draft pick by the Boston Celtics in 1978 when he was only a junior, but he chose to remain in school to earn his degree in physical education before turning pro.

FIRST JOBS

Delivering newspapers was one of the many jobs that Bird had when he was a schoolboy. He remembers being afraid to approach one particular house on his route because it was in such run-down condition that he thought that "ghosts lived there." Odd jobs around the neighborhood also came his way and, at one time, he was employed at his uncle's gas station. During the year after he dropped out of Indiana University, he did road clearing and snow removal for the town of French Lick, and occasionally worked "putting up hay" for a farmer.

MAJOR INFLUENCES

In interviews with Larry Bird, whenever he mentions his parents, he says how much their care and encouragement meant to him during his young years. But it is his Grandmother Kerns of whom he speaks so often and so fondly. He cherishes the time he spent with her, and wishes that she could have lived to know that he would dedicate his book to her. Other people made a difference in his life, too. Jim Jones, his first basketball coach, taught him the fundamentals of the game and helped him to gain confidence in himself. The Celtics' Red Auerbach was also a positive influence, and Bird is generous in his praise of all the people who stood behind him and urged him to be all that he could be.

CHOOSING A CAREER

By the time that Bird had begun to show his tremendous ability on the court, there was little doubt that he would make basketball his career. But he loved softball and baseball, too, and played both games before college and during summers between college semesters. His right index finger was badly injured in a softball game soon after he was drafted by the Boston Celtics, and there was some worry that his professional basketball career would be threatened. Bird, however, worked to strengthen the other fingers of that hand, and the injury, although still apparent, has never been a problem.

CAREER HIGHLIGHTS

In 1979, his very first year in professional basketball, Larry Bird fulfilled the hopes that the Celtics had placed in him by bringing the lagging team back to the heights their fans had come to expect. His career soared, and so did the standings of the Celtics, which has ranked among the top teams of the National Basketball Association (NBA) every year since he has been in the lineup. Playing forward, he excels at pinpoint passing to the open man, and is equally skillful at shooting and rebounding. Bird was the first player in NBA history to shoot 50% from the floor and 90% from the foul line. He scored his 20,000th career point in February of the 1990-91 season.

Larry Bird is considered one of the greatest players in the history of basketball. He is neither flashy nor particularly fast, but his determination and his great strength and court sense have contributed to his spectacular success. He is a true team player. He studies the patterns of the game and knows where every player is. He feels that perhaps one of his best assets is the ability "to make the right move at the right time."

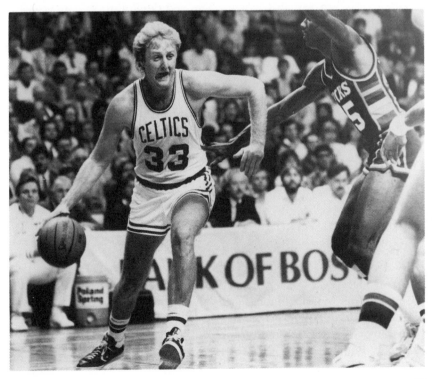

In recent years, injuries have slowed Bird's play to some extent, but his talent is still remarkable. If he can stay healthy, he hopes to give more good years to the Celtics.

MARRIAGE AND FAMILY

Bird's brief, early marriage to Janet Condra ended in divorce. Their fourteen-year-old daughter, Corrie, lives in Indiana with her mother. On October 1, 1989, Bird was married to Dinah Mattingly, whom he had known since his college days at Indiana State. They were friends for a long time before their romance began, and he says now that it was she who raised his spirits and helped him through the difficult time after his father's suicide and his own divorce.

HOBBIES AND OTHER INTERESTS

Larry Bird is a modest man with simple, homespun interests. He dresses casually, and likes to work around his own home and lawn whenever possible, although fans make it difficult for him to have this kind of privacy. He follows baseball, listens to country music, hunts and fishes, and plays active sports at every opportunity. He is involved in several charitable causes, one of them being an annual golf tournament to benefit the Terre Haute Boys' Club. He also helps to run the Larry Bird All-Star Classic Scholarship basketball game in Indianapolis, which raises money for educational scholarships for youngsters in Indiana; many of his endorsement companies support this special project.

Bird and his wife live in suburban Boston during the basketball season, but often spend time in Indiana. When his playing days are over, he probably will return to his home state, where he has business ventures—a hotel in Terre Haute and an automobile dealership in Martinsville.

WRITINGS

Drive: The Story of My Life (with Bob Ryan), 1989

HONORS AND AWARDS

NCAA All-American and Player of the Year: 1979
NBA Rookie of the Year: 1980
NBA All-Star Team (eleven times): 1980-90
All-Star Game Most Valuable Player: 1982
NBA Most Valuable Player: 1984, 1985, 1986
NBA Most Valuable Player in Championship Series: 1986
Player of the Year, *Sporting News:* 1986

FURTHER READING

BOOKS

Bird, Larry, and John Bischoff. *Bird on Basketball,* 1988
Bird, Larry, and Bob Ryan. *Drive: The Story of My Life,* 1989
Newman, Matthew. *Larry Bird,* 1986 (juvenile)
Rosenthal, Bert. *Larry Bird: Cool Man on the Court,* 1981 (juvenile)
Who's Who in America, 1990-91

PERIODICALS

Current Biography Yearbook 1982
Gentlemen's Quarterly, Feb. 1990, p.210
Sports Illustrated, Dec. 11, 1989, p.42

ADDRESS

Boston Celtics
North Station
Boston, MA 02144

* UPDATE *

After winning a Gold Medal in the 1992 Summer Olympics as part of the U.S. basketball team, Larry Bird retired from the game. He made his announcement in August 1992, citing continuing problems with his back.

Judy Blume 1938-
American Author of Juvenile and Adult Fiction
Writer of *Deenie, Forever, Superfudge, Tiger Eyes,*
and Other Books

BIRTH

Judy Blume (born Judy Sussman) was born on February 12, 1938,
to Rudolph and Esther Sussman.

YOUTH

Blume spent her youth in Elizabeth, New Jersey, with the exception of two years during which she lived in Miami Beach, Florida.

Her father, Rudolph, was a dentist with an outgoing personality; Judy was especially close to him. Her mother, Esther, was a homemaker who was quiet and shy and loved to read. Growing up, Judy had many interests: she liked movies, radio shows, and books, and began taking dance lessons at the age of three.

As a teenager, Blume recalls, she "had a lot of tensions and problems. . . .I was a good girl, had to do well, please everyone. That was my role in life." Despite her close relationship with her father, Blume didn't feel comfortable talking to him about the social and emotional difficulties of adolescence. As she once said, "My father delivered these little lectures to me, the last one when I was ten, on how babies are made. But questions about what I was feeling, and how my body could feel, I *never* asked my parents." In her family, she states, "we kept our feelings to ourselves." Later in life Blume became strongly interested in improving communication between young people and their parents. In 1981, she founded KIDS Fund, an organization that contributes about $40,000 each year to non-profit groups designed to help children talk with their parents.

EARLY MEMORIES

Blume has particularly fond memories of going to the public library. "I not only liked the pictures and the stories but the feel and the smell of the books themselves. My favorite book was *Madeline* by Ludwig Bemelmans. I loved that book! I loved it so much I hid it in my kitchen toy drawer so my mother wouldn't be able to return it to the library. . . . I thought the copy I had hidden was the only copy in the whole world. I knew it was wrong to hide the book but there was no way I was going to part with *Madeline*."

EDUCATION

Blume first attended public school in Elizabeth. When she was in the third grade, her brother became ill with a kidney infection. She moved with him and her mother to Miami Beach, where they hoped the warm climate would help David's health. Judy and David went to school there and later returned to New Jersey.

A very good student, Blume especially liked her English and journalism classes but did not enjoy science. She also participated in a variety of extra-curricular activities. She was co-feature editor of the school paper, sang in the chorus, and studied dance. After graduating with honors from Battin High School, Blume enrolled at Boston University, but she became ill with mononucleosis after only two weeks and had to leave school. The following year, she transferred to New York University, earning her bachelor's degree in early childhood education in 1960.

MARRIAGE AND FAMILY

After graduating, Blume did not go on to the teaching career for which she had prepared. Instead, she decided to begin a family with her husband, John Blume, whom she married after her junior year in college, on August 15, 1959. They had two children: Randy Lee, now an airline pilot, was born in 1961, and Lawrence Andrew, now a film maker, was born in 1963. Judy and John Blume divorced in 1975. In 1976 she married Thomas A. Kitchens; they were divorced in 1979. In 1987 she married George Cooper, with whom she has one stepdaughter, Amanda.

CHOOSING A CAREER

The decision to write children's stories was, in her words, "an accident. My kids were about three and five and I wanted to do something, but I didn't want to go back to classroom teaching, which is what I was qualified for. I read my kids a lot of books, and I guess I just decided—Well, I could do that too. So when I washed the dinner dishes at night I would do imitation Dr. Seuss rhyming books; and each night by the time I'd done the dishes I would have a whole book. I would send some of them in to publishers and they would be rejected. They were terrible. That's how I started."

Blume was not immediately successful as an author. It was two-and-a-half years before any of her books were accepted for publication. She decided to enroll in a graduate course at New York University on how to write for young people. She enjoyed the class so much that she took it twice. In the process she sold a couple of stories to magazines and completed a draft of *The One in the Middle Is the Green Kangaroo,* a story about a middle child who feels left out of the family. She also worked on *Iggie's House,* a story about a child who learns about tolerance from a friend. Blume treated this book as a home-work assignment, completing one chapter each week to turn in to her class.

Her first published book was *The One in the Middle is the Green Kangaroo.* When it appeared in 1969, she was "overjoyed, hysterical, unbelieving! I felt like such a celebrity."

CAREER HIGHLIGHTS

Blume's next work, *Are You There God? It's Me, Margaret,* published in 1970, established her reputation as the author of honest novels based on her own memories of childhood and adolescence. These works deal with real-life concerns and often taboo subjects.*Are You There God? It's Me, Margaret* combines humor with serious treatment of a girl's worries about religion, menstruation, physical development, and acceptance by her friends. Many adults attacked the novel because of its treatment of such controversial topics, but Blume's youthful readers wrote her thousands of letters saying that they loved the book and that it was just like their own lives.

Writing steadily since that time, Blume has published over 17 books that describe the experiences of young people and adolescents. Like *Are You There God? It's Me, Margaret* and *Iggie's House,* most focus on the same types of issues that her readers deal with in their own lives: struggle for acceptance by others *(Otherwise Known as Sheila the Great),* children's cruelty to each other *(Blubber),* sibling rivalry *(Tales of a Fourth Grade Nothing, Superfudge, Fudge-a-mania),* divorce *(It's Not the End of the World),* illness *(Deenie),* masturbation *(Deenie),* teenage sex *(Forever),* drugs and alcohol use *(Tiger Eyes),* and death *(Tiger Eyes).*

Blume's works have been criticized by some adults because of their vulgar language, mature themes, and straightforward treatment of sexuality. Unlike most earlier authors of youth fiction, Blume avoids providing simple solutions to her characters' problems, and her stories don't end by punishing characters who are sexually active. Some parents feel that this challenges their authority and their religious teachings. Many of her books, especially *Are You There God? It's Me, Margaret* and *Forever,* have been censored by schools and libraries.

Yet many other readers, both young and adult, appreciate Blume's realistic, often humorous and sympathetic treatment of important issues. They especially value her understanding of her readers' feelings. Her capacity for what she describes as "total recall" of experiences from her own youth is one of the reasons for her great popularity with her readers, who enjoy her descriptions of feelings and situations like their own. In a conversation about her own writings Blume has said, "I knew intuitively what kids wanted to know because I remembered what I wanted to know. I think I write about sexuality because it was uppermost in my mind when I was a kid: the need to know, and not knowing how to find out." In addition, her use of "first-person narration," or speaking in her works as "I," combined with her ability to write like a younger person, make her works realistic and believable—they have been described as sounding like diaries or journals.

FAVORITE BOOKS

As a child, according to Blume, "My favorite [book] was *Madeline*. When I was older I liked the Betsy-Tacy books by Maud Hart Lovelace, and the Oz Books, and Nancy Drew mysteries. But I didn't find real satisfaction in reading until I was older. Because there weren't any books with characters who felt the way I felt, who acted the way I did, with whom I could identify. I think I write the kinds of books I would have liked to read when young."

HOBBIES AND OTHER INTERESTS

Blume enjoys movies, theater, reading, dancing, needlepoint, and baseball, especially the New York Mets.

WRITINGS

FOR YOUNG READERS

The One in the Middle Is the Green Kangaroo, 1969
Are You There God? It's Me, Margaret, 1970
Iggie's House, 1970
Freckle Juice, 1971
Then Again, Maybe I Won't, 1971
It's Not the End of the World, 1972
Otherwise Known as Sheila the Great, 1972
Tales of a Fourth Grade Nothing, 1972
Deenie, 1973
Blubber, 1974
Forever, 1975
Starring Sally J. Freedman as Herself, 1977
Superfudge, 1980
Tiger Eyes, 1981
The Pain and the Great One, 1984
Letters to Judy: What Your Kids Wish They Could Tell You, 1986
Just as Long as We're Together, 1987
Fudge-a-mania, 1990

FOR ADULTS

Wifey, 1978
Smart Women, 1984

HONORS AND AWARDS

Outstanding Book of the Year *(New York Times)*: 1970, for *Are You There God? It's Me, Margaret*; 1974, for *Blubber*

Children's Choice Award (International Reading Association and Children's Book Council): 1981, for *Superfudge*; 1985, for *The Pain and the Great One*

A Best Book for Young Adults *(School Library Journal)*: 1981, for *Tiger Eyes*

Literary Lions (New York Public Library): 1987, for *Letters to Judy*

Blume has also received numerous awards from state and local organizations throughout the United States

FURTHER READING

BOOKS

Contemporary Authors New Revision Series, Vol. 13
Lee, Betsy. *Judy Blume's Story,* 1981
Something about the Author, Vol. 31
Weidt, Maryann N. *Presenting Judy Blume,* 1990

PERIODICALS

Christian Science Monitor, May 14, 1979, p.B10
Current Biography 1980
Newsweek, Oct. 9, 1978, p.99
New York Times Magazine, Dec. 3, 1978, p.80
People, Oct. 16, 1978, p.47; Mar. 19, 1984, p.38
Teen, Oct. 1982, p.30
Time, Aug. 23, 1982, p.65

ADDRESS

Bradbury Press
866 Third Ave.
New York, NY 10022

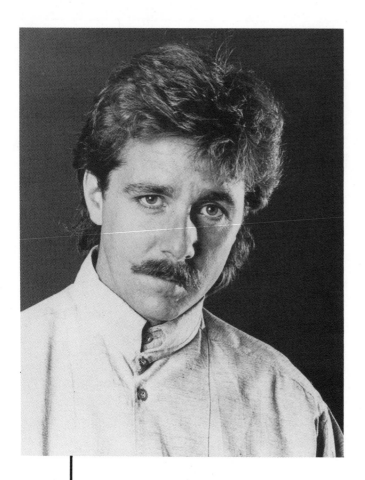

Berke Breathed   1957-
American Cartoonist
Creator of the Comic Strips "Bloom County"
and "Outland"

BIRTH

Berke Breathed (Guy Berkeley Breathed; rhymes with method)
was born on June 21, 1957, in Encino, California. His father, John,
was an oil equipment executive, while his mother, Jane, was a
homemaker.

YOUTH

The family moved from southern California to Houston, Texas,
in 1971, following the oil boom. According to Breathed, his youth
was unremarkable. He was a bit of a loner with a rather unusual

hobby: he collected snakes. "During most of the years that boys were going through puberty and finding girls, I was finding reptiles." But he also had a keen sense of humor that was appreciated by his teachers, although he recently said, "I was never the class clown. The only way I could apply my wit was on paper."

EDUCATION

Breathed attended the University of Texas at Austin, where he received a B.A. in photojournalism in 1979. While there he worked on the school newspaper, the *Daily Texan*, as a columnist, writer, and photographer. As a junior he started a comic strip, "Academia Waltz," the precursor to "Bloom County."

CAREER HIGHLIGHTS

After graduating from college, Breathed sent two anthologies of his works to the major syndicates that distribute comic strips to newspapers throughout the country. He was routinely rejected, but his luck soon changed. He was working at *UTmost*, a university student magazine, when Al Leeds, the sales manager for the Washington Post Writers Group, called the office of the *Daily Texan*. Leeds planned to commission a new cartoon and hired Breathed to create it.

"Bloom County," a new series based loosely on Breathed's earlier "Academia Waltz," was syndicated by the Washington Post Writers Group beginning in December 1980. Initially, there was very limited interest in the strip. It started out in only 27 newspapers, but nine years later it appeared in almost 1000 papers with an estimated readership of 40 million. Breathed ended "Bloom County" on August 6, 1989, explaining that "A good comic strip is no more eternal than a ripe melon. The ugly truth is that in most cases, comics age less gracefully than their creators. 'Bloom County' is retiring before the stretch marks show."

"Bloom County" was known for its frequently silly tone, satirical approach, sense of absurdity, commentary on current issues, and odd assortment of characters, featuring Opus the penguin. The strip often angered political conservatives and religious fundamentalists, and it even sparked controversy among cartoonists. In 1987, the strip won the prestigious Pulitzer Prize for Editorial Cartooning. This angered other cartoonists, who felt that Breathed's work was not serious political commentary. Breathed responded that "Bloom County" was not specifically a political cartoon. He did not intend the strip to present one particular viewpoint or to focus consistently on political events; instead, it covered a wide range of current social issues as well as people in the news. As he once explained, "I really am a schizophrenic cartoonist. . . .There's a side of me that reads the *New Republic* and wants to spill out on paper all the anger I might have on a particular issue. But I can also really lose myself in a fantasy like the work of Walt Disney or *Winnie the Pooh*. So I have those two sides tugging me in opposite directions. I may read the morning paper and get riled up, but by four in the afternoon, I'm wishing I was living in the Hundred Acre Wood with Pooh. 'Bloom County' should be seen as a hybrid: It'll never satisfy purists on either side."

After "Bloom County," Breathed created a new strip, "Outland," that debuted on September 3, 1989. Appearing only on Sundays, "Outland" features a recurring cast of characters, including Opus, Ronald Ann, and Bill the Cat from "Bloom County." Like Breathed's previous strip, "Outland" uses satire to comment on personalities and social issues.

Breathed once tried to explain what he set out to accomplish in drawing these comic strips. While describing his reaction to reading "Peanuts" by Charles Schulz, Breathed said: "I was bowled over by the depth of Schulz's simplicity. It wasn't until I really studied those old strips, with their underlying themes and symbolic approach to dealing with life's problems, that I began to realize the inner dynamics of a comic strip are not immediately apparent. It's not just a matter of getting a political point across or squeezing out a giggle from somebody. It's about creating your own universe, which is a real challenge. Few cartoonists succeed in doing it, but it's become my goal."

MAJOR INFLUENCES

Several sources have influenced his comic strips, according to Breathed. He has mentioned the imagery in the works of such children's writers as Dr. Seuss and Norman Juster, author of *The Phantom Toolbooth*. In response to a question about cartoons, Breathed once stated, " 'Doonesbury' is the only one that had an active influence on me, especially in my college years. I hadn't read strips before 'Doonesbury.' Others had an influence on me later: 'Pogo' in its drawings, and 'Peanuts' in more subtle things such as characterization and pacing."

The influence of Garry Trudeau, creator of "Doonesbury," has been part of the controversy surrounding Breathed's work. Many reviewers considered "Bloom County" derivative of "Doonesbury," citing similarities in format, pacing, and characterization. Even Breathed has acknowledged the influence, saying "I've never been a comics fan. 'Doonesbury' was the first strip I ever paid attention to and followed regularly—which may explain the obvious roots of 'Bloom County.' " Yet in recent years many reviewers have said that despite surface similarities, Breathed's work is truly original.

MARRIAGE AND FAMILY

Breathed met his future wife, Jody Boyman, while competing in the New

Mexico State Fair Celebrity Goat Milk-off in 1985. Boyman, a photographer, was covering the event; Breathed was milking goats. He came in last. They were married on May 10, 1986.

HOBBIES AND OTHER INTERESTS

Breathed's hobbies include traveling, boating, motorcycling, water skiing, and rock climbing. He also used to enjoy piloting ultralight airplanes, but he quit after an accident in which he broke his back. In addition, Breathed is involved in the animal rights movement.

WRITINGS

Bloom County: ''Loose Tails,'' 1983
Toons for Our Times: A Bloom County Book, 1984
Penguin Dreams: And Stranger Things, 1985
Bloom County Babylon: Five Years of Basic Naughtiness, 1986
Billy and the Boingers Bootleg, 1987
Tales Too Ticklish to Tell, 1988
The Night of the Mary Kay Commandos: Featuring Smell-O-Toons, 1989
Classic of Western Literature, 1990
Happy Trails, 1990

HONORS AND AWARDS

Harry A. Schweikert, Jr. Disability Awareness Award (Paralyzed Veterans of America): 1982, for "Bloom County"
Pulitzer Prize: 1987, in editorial cartooning, for "Bloom County"
Fund for Animals Genesis Award: 1990, for "outstanding cartoonist focusing on animal welfare issues"

FURTHER READING

BOOKS

Contemporary Authors, Vol. 110
Contemporary Authors New Revision Series, Vol. 27

PERIODICALS

Los Angeles Times, Nov. 26, 1987, V, p.1
People, Aug. 6, 1984, p.93
Time, Dec. 25, 1989, p.10

ADDRESS

Washington Post Writers Group
1150 15th St. NW
Washington, DC 20071

SIGH.

Garth Brooks 1962-
American Singer and Guitarist
Country and Western Star

BIRTH

Troyal Garth Brooks was born on February 7, 1962, in Tulsa, Oklahoma. His father, Troyal Raymond Brooks, was a former Marine and an oil company draftsman. Garth describes him like this: "If I could wrap my dad up in two words, it would be thundering tenderness. He's a man with the shortest temper I ever saw, and at the same time he's got the biggest heart. . . . I learned from him that you gotta be thankful for what you got and treat people like you want to be treated. My dad drilled that into my head all my life. . .we're a lot alike in that way." Garth's mother, Colleen Carroll Brooks, was a country singer during the 1950s who

80

performed on TV with Red Foley's "Ozark Mountain Jubilee." Recording for Capitol, later her son's label, she released four singles in 1955-57. According to Garth, "We kids felt that she had cut her career short because of us, and we wanted to carry on the tradition for her." His mother, though, disputes this point. Today, people often say that Garth inherited his personality from his father and his desire to perform from his mother.

YOUTH

Brooks grew up in a small town near Oklahoma City named Yukon, which he calls "an average city in the middle of average Oklahoma in the middle of average America." He was the youngest in a houseful of kids. His parents' union was the second marriage for both. They had four children from their first marriages—Jim, Jerry, Mike, and Betsy—and added two more, Kelly and Garth.

The Brooks home was always filled with music. Garth's parents enjoyed listening to a style of country music known as honky-tonk, and they often played the music of George Jones and Hank Williams, Sr., as well as Merle Haggard and Marty Robbins. "We had music around the house 24 hours a day, it seemed," Brooks remembers. All the children learned to play guitar and sing, too.

EDUCATION

At Yukon High School, Brooks played occasionally in a band, but he devoted most of his time to sports. In football, he played quarterback (on a team that lost its first five games); in baseball, he was a decent pitcher and outfielder; and in track and field, he tried running, pole vaulting, the discus, and the shot put. He even played basketball for a while. A good student, Brooks was popular and well liked. His teachers, counselors, and fellow students have described him as personable, friendly, and down-to-earth, "genuinely a nice guy." Brooks graduated from Yukon High School in 1980.

Brooks often speaks of an experience he had shortly before starting college. Although he had listened to country music as a child, more recently he had become a fan of the singer-songwriters James Taylor and Dan Fogelberg, as well as many 1970s rock bands, including Kansas, Journey, and Boston. One day, though, he heard country singer George Strait. His sound was, for Brooks, completely new: "I heard Strait do "Unwound" on my car radio, and that's the exact moment it all changed," Brooks has said. "I became a George wannabe and imitator for the next seven years."

Brooks attended Oklahoma State University in Stillwater. He financed his education with grants, help from his parents, and odd jobs, selling shoes, delivering pizza, and working in a nightclub. He also received a partial track scholarship, competing in the javelin. Brooks is a large man—6'1",

81

225 pounds—and he was able to throw the javelin 200 feet and bench-press over 300 pounds. Athletics dominated his college years until he was a senior, when he failed to earn a place at the Big Eight conference finals in track and field. But he also played music at local bars and played duets with Ty Englund, then a roommate and now a guitarist with his band. Brooks graduated in 1984 with his bachelor's degree in advertising.

MARRIAGE AND FAMILY

During one college job, he worked as a bouncer at Tangleweeds, the local club. One night a brawl broke out in the women's rest room, and he was sent in to break it up. There he met his future wife, Sandy Mahr, a fellow student at Oklahoma State and rodeo champion. Trapped in the bathroom by a jealous former girlfriend of a man she had dated, Mahr threw a punch—just to scare her, she says—and promptly got her fist stuck in the wall. According to Brooks, all she said then was "I missed." He recently recalled that first meeting: "I threw her out of the club. That's how we met, and I couldn't take my eyes off her. I asked her to go home with me that first night, and she told me to drop dead." But he persisted, and they eventually began to date. They married in May 1986, and their first child, Taylor Mayne Pearl Brooks, was born on July 8, 1992. They currently live on a 20-acre spread in Nashville.

FIRST JOBS

After graduating from Oklahoma State, Brooks decided to seek his fame and fortune in Nashville, Tennessee, the home of the Grand Ole Opry and the center of the recording industry for country music. He lasted less than 24 hours before he decided to return to Oklahoma, first to his parents' home and then to Stillwater. "I thought the world was waiting for me," Brooks has said, "but there's nothing colder than reality." In Stillwater, he joined a band called Santa Fe. For the next year and a half they toured throughout the Southwest, playing mostly at bars and fraternity parties in college towns. In 1986, the group decided to move to Nashville and try to land a recording contract.

Although Santa Fe broke up within a few months, Garth and Sandy decided to remain in Nashville. They were broke at first, but gradually their luck began to change. They both found jobs working in a boot store, where Garth met several musicians who joined his new band, Stillwater. In 1987 and 1988, he started making contacts in the record industry, meeting songwriters, recording commercials, and finding a management team. His managers circulated his demo tapes and he even auditioned at Capitol Records, but he was repeatedly turned down. Finally, he attended an amateur night showcase at a Nashville club and, at the last minute, won a spot on the program when one act didn't show. His intense live performance so impressed a Capitol executive in the audience that he offered Brooks a recording contract on the spot.

CAREER HIGHLIGHTS

Brooks's rise to stardom has been meteoric. Just four years ago, he was a complete unknown working a day job selling boots and trying to make a name for himself in Nashville; today, he is the hottest singer in the country. With the release of *Garth Brooks*, his first album (1989), he catapulted from being just one more honky-tonk singer to becoming a headlining star. Four songs from the album hit No. 1 on the country charts, including "If Tomorrow Never Comes," his signature song. His next album, *No Fences* (1990), shipped gold, meaning that the album generated advance sales of over 500,000 before its release. One of the songs provoked a great deal of controversy—and ultimately a great deal of publicity as well. "The Thunder Rolls" portrays the theme of domestic violence. Its video, with Brooks playing the role of the abusive husband, was banned on two country music video networks, yet still won a major award from the Country Music Association. Brooks has said that he wrote the song to focus attention on the problem of domestic violence. Following the release of *No Fences*, he was named "Entertainer of the Year" by the Country Music Association, the industry's most prestigious award and one that he received again in 1992. His next album, *Ropin' the Wind*, started at the No. 1 spot on two *Billboard* magazine lists, country and pop. The album made country music history by becoming the first country record ever

to debut at No. 1 on the pop charts. Brooks repeated that feat with his most recent offering, *The Chase* (1992), which had advance sales of almost four million. Currently, all five of Brooks's albums, including his selection of Christmas songs, *Beyond the Season* (1992), rank in the top 15 spots on the *Billboard* country chart. To date, Brooks has sold over 27 million records in less than four years —a phenomenal achievement, and testimony to the depth of his appeal to both country and pop audiences.

Yet cataloging Brooks's album releases and sales figures doesn't begin to explain his appeal. Industry insiders marvel at his ability to attract mainstream pop listeners while not sacrificing his traditional country audience. His success, according to many, derives from three areas: his own personal charm, traditional country sound, and flamboyant stage shows. First, his personality contributes greatly to his popularity. Onstage and off, Brooks is consistently described as modest, polite, self-effacing, and grateful to fans, band members, and others. Second, his music is often described as mainstream country, including poignant lyrics, romantic and sad ballads, and rowdy honky-tonk music, all using such standard country instruments as acoustic guitars, pedal steel, and fiddles. His concerts, though, are very different from those by traditional country stars. Intensity, energy, and charisma are the words most often used to describe his stage persona. According to many, his concerts have the energy, excitement, and theatrical antics usually associated with rock and roll shows—Brooks has been known to smash guitars, pour water on band members, climb rope ladders, and flirt with the audience.

FAME AND FAMILY LIFE

Yet success has taken a toll on his personal life. Both Garth and Sandy have spoken publicly about their marital difficulties. Garth has admitted to a period of infidelity when he went on tour in 1989, after his first album was released and he became an overnight success. He now regrets his poor judgment in those first months of becoming a superstar, and he has long since recommitted himself to his marriage.

His career is currently in a state of transition. During the past year, Sandy's difficult pregnancy—she was hospitalized with a threatened miscarriage—and the birth of their daughter have inspired Brooks to reconsider his demanding schedule of songwriting, recording, touring, and promoting his records. As he says, "Kids deserve a lot of attention, so I think I'll be around for her." At first he suggested that he might retire; recently he has said that he wants to take a long break, for about eight months or so, beginning in December 1992. Explaining his change in attitude, Brooks recently said, "For the last few years, business always came before family. But the future will be extremely different. If that upsets people, I'm sorry. But with a kid coming, your life has to be slower. Years are the one thing you can't buy back."

MAJOR INFLUENCES

Brooks paid homage to his two greatest musical influences when he accepted the Entertainer of the Year award at the 1991 Country Music Association awards: "I know this embarrasses these two guys every time I say this, but I don't think an entertainer is anybody without his heroes. I love my Georges, George Strait and George Jones. Thank you, guys."

MEMORABLE EXPERIENCES

One of the biggest events in his career came when Brooks was inducted into the Grand Ole Opry in October 1990, becoming its youngest member.

Brooks has said that he considers his acceptance into this select group to be his greatest professional achievement. As he later described it, "That was it, man. They gave me an award you can't get anywhere else. They gave me membership in a family, a family that includes people like Mr. [Roy] Acuff and Ms. [Minnie] Pearl. [My wife] Sandy and Ms. Pearl have become friends, and they can go off and have a great time, but I can't relax. It's funny, but it's an 'I'm not worthy' kind of thing.

"When someone asks to take a picture of me with Mr. Acuff, I'll go up there and smile, but inside I'll be thinking, 'I can't believe I'm doing this.'"

HOBBIES AND OTHER INTERESTS

Brooks enjoys lifting weights, playing golf and baseball, and watching John Wayne movies on his VCR.

RECORDINGS

Garth Brooks, 1989
No Fences, 1990
Ropin' the Wind, 1991
Beyond the Season, 1992
The Chase, 1992

HOME VIDEO RELEASES

Garth Brooks, 1991
This Is Garth Brooks, 1992

HONORS AND AWARDS

Academy of Country Music Awards: 1991 (6 awards), Entertainer of the Year, Male Vocalist of the Year, Album of the Year for *No Fences*, Single Record of the Year for "Friends in Low Places", Song of the Year for "The Dance," and Video of the Year for "The Dance"; 1992 (3 awards), Special Achievement Award, Entertainer of the Year, and Male Vocalist of the Year

Country Music Association Awards: 1990 (2 awards), Horizon Award for best new artist and Video of the Year for "The Dance"; 1991 (4 awards), Entertainer of the Year, Album of the Year for *No Fences*, Single of the Year for "Friends in Low Places," and Video of the Year for "The Thunder Rolls"; 1992 (2 awards), Entertainer of the Year and Album of the Year for *Ropin' the Wind*

American Music Awards: 1991, Best Country Song of the Year for "If Tomorrow Never Comes"; 1992 (3 awards), Best Country Male Vocalist of the Year, Best Country Album of the Year for *No Fences*, and Best Country Song of the Year for "The Thunder Rolls"

Billboard Music Awards: 1991 (4 awards), Top Country Artist, Top Pop Album Artist, Top Country Album Artist, and Top Country Singles Artist

Grammy Award: 1992, Best Male Vocal Performance, Country, for *Ropin' the Wind*

People's Choice Awards: 1992 (2 awards), Best Male Country Performer and Best Male Musical Performer

FURTHER READING

BOOKS

McCall, Michael. *Garth Brooks,* 1991

PERIODICALS

Country Music, Jan. 2, 1991, p.30; Jan. 2, 1992, p.4
Current Biography, Mar. 1992
Entertainment Weekly, Sep. 20, 1991, p.20
Life, July 1992, p.55
People, Sept. 3, 1990, p.91; Oct. 7, 1991, p.40
Saturday Evening Post, July/Aug. 1992, p.38
Time, Mar. 30, 1992, pp.62, 67
Us, Oct. 1991, p.71
USA Weekend, Feb. 7-9, 1992, p.4

ADDRESS

Doyle-Lewis Management
1109 17th Ave. South
Nashville, TN 37212

Barbara Bush 1925-
American Public Figure
Former First Lady of the United States

BIRTH

Barbara Pierce Bush was born June 8, 1925, in New York City to Marvin and Pauline (Robinson) Pierce of Rye, New York. She was the third child in a family of four, which included an older sister and brother, Martha and James, and a younger brother, Scott.

YOUTH

The young girl who would grow up to be First Lady of the United States lived a privileged childhood in the prosperous suburb of Rye. She was reared in a household that provided the material things of life, but one that also mirrored qualities of refinement and consideration. The children were trained "to look after other people's feelings."

Marvin Pierce, who counted among his early relatives America's fourteenth president, Franklin Pierce, was an executive of McCall Corporation, the publishing company that produced *McCall's* and *Redbook* magazines, and a series of widely used pattern catalogues. Mrs. Pierce, the daughter of an Ohio Supreme Court justice, was involved in community affairs, collected antiques, and was an enthusiastic gardener. According to her now-famous daughter, Pauline Pierce was "not perfect, but the world was more beautiful because my mother was there. She taught us all a lot of good lessons."

EARLY MEMORIES

Barbara Bush remembers her schoolgirl days as being typical for a child reared in an upscale suburban setting. The family did not want for anything. She talks of tennis and swimming lessons, tree houses, bicycling, and dancing lessons, as well as quieter pursuits, such as paper dolls and games of imagination. Dogs were always her special love. Books were, too, and in those early years she developed her lifelong passion for reading. Often quoted is a comment she made in an interview given a few years ago for the *New York Times Book Review:* "I think of my dad sitting in his chair by the fireplace and my mother on the couch reading, and after we children could read, everyone was curled up with something." This eagerness for the printed word would one day lead the First Lady to focus her energies on promoting literacy in America.

EDUCATION

Bush attended public school for six years, transferred to the private Rye Country Day School for four more grades, and then, as was common in her social circle, was sent away to an exclusive boarding school to complete her secondary education. It was while she was home for the Christmas holidays that she met her future husband, George Bush, at a country club dance. Apparently it was love at first sight for both teenagers. They exchanged frequent letters after returning to their respective schools—she to Ashley Hall in Charleston, South Carolina, and he to Phillips Academy in Andover, Massachusetts. They arranged visits together and with one another's families during school breaks and summer vacation.

World War II had just started, and George Bush enlisted in the Navy immediately after his graduation. Barbara Pierce went back to Ashley Hall as a senior. The next year she attended Smith College in Northampton, Massachusetts, but there she paid little attention to her studies. A quote from a recent biography tells why: "The truth is, I just wasn't very interested. I was just interested in George." She dropped out of college at the beginning of her sophomore year to plan a December wedding, unaware that her fiancé's Navy plane had been shot down in the Pacific. George Bush was rescued at sea and returned home for a wedding delayed by only a few weeks.

FIRST JOBS

Although she has given much of her time to volunteer activities, the only employment paychecks made out to Barbara Bush over the years have come from the Yale Co-op, where she worked after her husband enrolled at that university, and from a 1942 summer job in a small factory in Port Chester, New York.

MAJOR INFLUENCES

Marvin Pierce, who died in 1969, is remembered lovingly by his daughter as *the* truly important figure in her childhood. He was the closest to her of her parents—an understanding man with a delightful sense of humor and a deep affection for his family. She recalls that he always took her side and was, in fact, her hero.

The strong influence in her adult years has been George Bush. She says of her marriage, "it was the biggest turning point in my life."

MARRIAGE AND FAMILY

Barbara Pierce and George Herbert Walker Bush have been married since January 6, 1945. They have five children: George Jr.; John Ellis (Jeb); Neil Mallon; Marvin Pierce (named for his maternal grandfather); and Dorothy (Doro) Walker Bush LeBlond (named for the president's mother). The second child born into the family died of leukemia shortly before her fourth birthday in 1953; she was Pauline Robinson, called Robin, and named in memory of Barbara Bush's mother, who had been killed in an automobile accident two months before the child's birth.

The Bushes have twelve grandchildren.

CAREER HIGHLIGHTS

The President's wife has devoted much of her life to volunteer work, but her special focus has been the promotion of literacy. During the years her children were growing up, son Neil suffered from dyslexia (a reading disability). In working with him to overcome the problem, her interest became a cause. She is honorary chairperson of the Barbara Bush Foundation for Family Literacy; a sponsor of the Laubach Literacy Volunteers; and honorary chairperson of equally active groups such as the National Advisory Council of Literacy Volunteers of America, the National Committee on Literacy and Education of the United Way, and the Reading is Fundamental Advisory Council.

Mrs. Bush also serves in an honorary capacity on the boards of the National Association of Partners in Education, the Business Council for Effective Literacy, and the Washington Parent Group Fund. Her volunteerism extends further afield—to the Leukemia Society of America, the Washington Home, the Sloan-Kettering Cancer Center, the Children's Oncology Services of Metropolitan Washington, and the Girl Scouts of America.

HOBBIES AND OTHER INTERESTS

Barbara Bush is a reader, a swimmer and golfer, and an unpretentious woman who enjoys time in her garden at the family home in Kennebunkport, Maine. All of America is familiar with her love of dogs through her books and through the headlines made by her English springer spaniel, Millie, whose puppies were born in the White House.

The President's wife puts her family first—this, she says, is her major interest. The Bush children have affectionately dubbed their mother the "Silver Fox," (for her grandmotherly white hair which she refuses to color). By all accounts, she is warm, loyal, and straightforward, and always able to poke fun at herself. She is known to be opinionated, too, but even on those occasions when her well-publicized wit shows a sharp edge, she is quickly apologetic—and easily forgiven.

WRITINGS

C. Fred's Story: A Dog's Life, 1984
Millie's Book: As Dictated to Barbara Bush, 1990

HONORS AND AWARDS

Outstanding Mother of the Year Award: 1984
Distinguished Leadership Award (United Negro College Fund): 1986
Woman of the Year Award (USO): 1986
Distinguished American Woman Award (College of Mount St. Joseph):
   1987

FURTHER READING

BOOKS

Behrens, June. *Barbara Bush: First Lady of Literacy,* 1990 (juvenile)
Blue, Rose, and Corinne J. Naden. *Barbara Bush: First Lady,* 1991 (juvenile)
Heiss, Arlene. *Barbara Bush,* 1991 (juvenile)
Radcliffe, Donnie. *Simply Barbara Bush,* 1989
Who's Who in America 1990-91

PERIODICALS

Current Biography Yearbook 1989
People, Spring 1990, p.31
Time, Jan. 23, 1989, p.22

ADDRESS

The White House
1600 Pennsylvania Avenue
Washington, DC 20500

* *UPDATE* *

George Bush lost his bid for reelection to the presidency, and the Bushes
now plan to settle in Houston, Texas, and will possibly build a home there.

George Bush   1924-
American Political Leader
Former President of the United States

BIRTH

George Herbert Walker Bush was born June 12, 1924, in Milton, Massachusetts, to Prescott Sheldon and Dorothy (Walker) Bush. He was the second in a family of five children, which included Prescott, Jr., Nancy, Jonathan, and William T.

YOUTH

Before young George was a year old, the Bushes moved to a large house in Greenwich, Connecticut, about an hour away from New York City. It was in that wealthy suburban setting that he grew up, living in comfort and surrounded by his closely knit family and an army of friends "who were always swarming around the house." His sister Nancy, now Mrs. Alexander Ellis, tells of those happy days, and of how George and Prescott, Jr., were "thick as thieves. They were a twosome. They shared the same room and [the same] friends." She adds that she and her four brothers did a lot of things as a group, too, and that their parents reared them strictly but fairly, and with old-fashioned values. The youngsters were expected to do small jobs around the house for extra spending money. They were taught to be honest, modest, and generous—George learned the latter lesson so well that he was called "Have Half" for his willingness to share with others. The Bush children also were encouraged to take part in sports, and there were frequent family games and family trips, as well. The president says of his parents today that they were "our biggest boosters."

Prescott Bush, Sr., who died in 1972, was an investment banker in New York during his children's growing years and later served as United States senator from Connecticut. Mrs. Bush, now in her ninety-first year, is the daughter of a wealthy St. Louis businessman, George Herbert Walker, who owned a summer retreat overlooking the Atlantic Ocean at Kennebunkport, Maine. Here, every summer at Walker's Point, the Bush children enjoyed "the best of all possible adventures." They swam, played tennis, hiked, went deep-sea fishing, and ran free. Grandfather Walker was "Pop" to his own children, so it was natural that his devoted young namesake would be called "Poppy," a nickname that stuck for many years.

EARLY MEMORIES

One particular childhood episode stands out in George Bush's mind. He and his brother Prescott had been taught by their grandfather to handle *Tomboy,* the Walker sailboat but, on their first time out alone, a sudden storm blew up and tossed them around. They were frightened, yet they managed to return to dock and to their worried family. The President tells now, in talking about the incident, that "Grandfather said he knew we could do it. That gave me confidence that's lasted all my life."

EDUCATION

Bush attended the private Greenwich Country Day School before entering Phillips Andover Academy in Massachusetts for high school. At Andover, an exclusive eastern preparatory school, he earned good grades and was an exceptionally popular student. He was president of his senior class, played varsity basketball, and captained both the baseball and soccer teams. He still is spoken of by those who knew him in prep school as an "all-time soccer great."

World War II had started during George Bush's senior year at Andover, and after graduation, he chose to delay his college education to join the

93

U.S. Naval Reserve. He enlisted as a seaman second class on his birthday, June 12, 1942, and was sent to Chapel Hill, North Carolina, for flight training. Receiving his wings and commission while still eighteen years old, he became the Navy's youngest pilot. On September 2, 1944, Bush's plane was hit by antiaircraft fire over the Bonin island of Chichi Jima, 600 miles south of Japan. Although the plane was on fire and severely damaged, he completed his strafing run on the Japanese installation before heading out to sea. He bailed out and was rescued by the submarine *USS Finback* but, tragically, his two crew members were killed. Bush was decorated for courageous service in the Pacific Theater.

When the war ended, Bush entered Yale University, where he studied for a degree in economics and served as captain of the varsity baseball team. He was graduated Phi Beta Kappa (for scholastic achievement) in 1948.

MARRIAGE AND FAMILY

On January 6, 1945, George Bush married Barbara Pierce of Rye, New York. They have five children: George Herbert Walker, Jr.; John Ellis (Jeb); Neil Mallon; Marvin Pierce; and Dorothy (Doro) Walker Bush LeBlond. Their second child, Robin (named Pauline Robinson) died of leukemia in 1953, shortly before her fourth birthday. The Bushes have twelve grandchildren.

President and Mrs. Bush are residents of Houston, Texas. They are members of St. Martin's Episcopal Church, where the President is a former vestryman. When in Washington, they attend services at St. John's Episcopal Church. The President serves on the vestry of St. Ann's Episcopal Church in Kennebunkport.

MAJOR INFLUENCES

Fitzhugh Green, author of *George Bush: An Intimate Portrait*, asked Barbara Bush some years ago about what lasting impressions Prescott and Dorothy Bush had made on the son who would become President of the United States. "His father had enormous influence on him," she answered, "and his mother had ten times more." She told that the children were in awe of their father, an imposing man, full of energy and business, but "their mother had the most influence, and not in a bossy way. As a young woman she was a great athlete, even-tempered, fair, loving. . . . She brought those kids up under the most extraordinary values."

The President himself has often said that it was from his mother that he learned to get along with people. Others note, too, that it is from her that he inherits his competitive edge.

CHOOSING A CAREER

Bush had all the right business connections and could have had a job with a large corporation, or on Wall Street with his father. He chose instead to move with his wife and small son to Texas after college, where he worked for Dresser Industries as an oil field supply salesman. Dresser was headed by Neil Mallon, a family friend for whom the Bushes later named their third son.

By 1951, after working in California and again in Texas, Bush started a small royalty firm with John Overby. Two years later, Bush-Overby Oil Development Company merged with an independent oil exploration company run by two brothers from Oklahoma, William and Hugh Liedtke. The four young men called their new endeavor Zapata Petroleum Corporation, borrowing the catchy name from a heroic Mexican rebel leader, Emiliano Zapata. Then, in 1954, at the age of thirty, George Bush became co-founder and president of a third firm, Zapata Off-Shore, which pioneered in experimental off-shore drilling. He and his family were living in Houston by this time, and Bush was becoming interested in politics.

CAREER HIGHLIGHTS

After an unsuccessful bid in 1964 as Republican candidate for the U.S. Senate, Bush returned briefly to his oil business. In 1966, he resigned from Zapata Off-Shore to run for Congress. This time, he was elected to the House of Representatives from Texas' Seventh District. He was reelected to the House two years later but, in 1970, lost a second campaign for the Senate.

The next year, Bush was appointed U.S. Ambassador to the United Nations, a post he held until 1973, when he became chairman of the Republican National Committee. In the autumn of 1974, George and Barbara Bush went to Beijing, for his assignment as chief of the U.S. Liaison Office, at an important time in the developing relationship between the U.S. and the People's Republic of China.

Bush returned from the Far East in early 1976 to take up duties as director of the CIA (Central Intelligence Agency). When Jimmy Carter, a Democrat, took office as president the following January, Bush returned to Texas and private life but, by May 1979, he was back into politics, making a bid for the White House. Ronald Reagan won the party's nomination, however, and asked Bush to be his running mate. Their ticket won, and the two were sworn into office in January 1981. In the 1984 election, they won a second term.

After eight years as vice president, Bush was nominated for the presidency at the 1988 Republican National Convention. He made a controversial choice in selecting an ultraconservative young Indiana senator, J. Danforth Quayle, as his running mate, and even people in his own party questioned Bush's judgment. Nevertheless, George Bush carried forty states to win the election and, on January 20, 1989, was sworn in as the forty-first president of the United States.

As President, Bush's popularity initially soared, due perhaps in large part to the success of Desert Shield and Desert Storm, the military campaign to force Saddam Hussein's forces to leave Kuwait. His popularity has waned in recent times with worsening economic conditions and growing domestic troubles. Bush is currently preparing to run for reelection as President.

MEMORABLE EXPERIENCES

On a personal level, Bush's rescue at sea during World War II must be forever forged in his memory. He speaks of bailing out of his burning plane and of the battle raging above him as he bobbed in the water. One of his squadron buddies was able to help him by signalling the location of his floating raft, and other pilots helped by strafing and turning away enemy boats. It was a U.S. Navy submarine, the *Finback*, that finally surfaced to rescue him. Years later, in telling of the ordeal, Bush said, "I'll always be grateful to the *Finback* crew. They saved my life."

HOBBIES AND OTHER INTERESTS

Sports have always been important to Bush. He loves the sea, whether he is sailing, motorboating, or fishing. He is a good tennis player and an avid golfer—and likes the game of horseshoes so much that he had a pit dug on the White House grounds soon after he took up residence.

Bush spends much of his leisure time with his wife and family. He often says that his proudest accomplishment is that his children "still come home."

WRITINGS

Looking Forward: The George Bush Story, 1987

HONORS AND AWARDS

Air Medal
Distinguished Flying Cross
Gold Star (two)
Time Magazine "Man of the Year": 1990

FURTHER READING

BOOKS

Encyclopedia Britannica, 1991
Green, Fitzhugh. *George Bush: An Intimate Portrait,* 1989
Kent, Zachary. *Encyclopedia of Presidents,* 1989 (juvenile)
Sufrin, Mark. *George Bush: The Story of the Forty-first President of the United States,* 1989 (juvenile)
World Book Encyclopedia, 1991

PERIODICALS

Current Biography Yearbook 1983
People, Aug. 22, 1988, p.34
Time, Aug. 22, 1988, p.22; Jan. 7, 1991, p.32

ADDRESS

The White House
1600 Pennsylvania Avenue
Washington, DC 20500

* *UPDATE* *

George Bush lost to Bill Clinton in his race for reelection to the presidency, garnering 38% of the vote to Clinton's 43% and Ross Perot's 19%. After January 1993, the Bushes plan to move to Houston, Texas, and build a home there.

Fidel Castro   1927-
Cuban Revolutionary and Political Leader
President of Cuba and First Secretary of the
Cuban Communist Party

BIRTH

Fidel Alejandro Castro Ruz was born August 13, 1927, at his parents'
farm near Mayari, in Oriente Province, Cuba, the third of seven
children. His father, Angel Castro Argiz, was a Spaniard by birth
and a former army sergeant. His mother, Lina Ruz González, was
a domestic. Castro has two older siblings, Anjela and Ramón, and
four younger—Juanita, Raúl, Emma, and Augustina. He also has
two half-siblings, Lidia and Pedro Emilio, from his father's first
marriage.

As a boy, Fidel Castro worked in his prosperous father's sugarcane fields. His thirst for education led his parents to belatedly marry, in order that they might send him to Catholic school. While they had not originally planned to send their children to school at all, Fidel displayed his iron will early by threatening to burn down the family home unless they relented. This first revolutionary act was successful.

EDUCATION

Castro entered the LaSalle School in Santiago de Cuba, run by French Marianist brothers, at the age of six or seven. His birth year was changed to 1926 so that he would appear old enough to begin third grade, and he was baptized at this time. Two years later, he was enrolled at Colegio Dolores, a Jesuit institution also in Santiago. After his graduation, he enrolled at the Colegio Bolén, a Jesuit preparatory school in Havana and the most prestigious secondary institution in Cuba. There he not only excelled in history and Spanish, but also was voted the school's outstanding athlete in 1944. The Jesuits instilled in Castro a passion for discipline, order, and hard work—but he disliked their authoritarianism and rejected their belief in God. In 1945, he entered the University of Havana to study law, and was graduated in 1950. It was here that his political career began.

CAREER HIGHLIGHTS

When Fidel Castro entered law school, Cuba was in political turmoil, and that unrest expressed itself on campus through violent student demonstrations. Fidel's intellectual gifts, courage, and oratorical skill secured for him the leadership of the University Students Federation. He aligned himself in 1947 with the Partido del Pueblo Cubano (Party of the Cuban People) and thrust himself into national politics. He interrupted his studies that year to take part in an abortive coup against Dominican dictator Rafael Trujillo and, in 1948, traveled to Colombia to participate in the Bogotaza —another violent uprising. Despite his liberal orientation at this time, Fidel's lifelong commitment to internationalism was already evident.

In 1950, Castro set up a law practice in Havana with two partners, often representing poor and working-class clients for no fee. He ran for the Cuban Congress in 1952, but his bid was frustrated when Fulgencio Batista seized power in a military coup, canceling the election results. When the courts refused to declare the coup unconstitutional, Fidel turned to revolutionary struggle. He organized a small band of rebels and attacked the Moncada military barracks on the night of July 26, 1953. He was captured after the unsuccessful assault, but was spared execution when a university colleague intervened.

Castro gave his first important speech in defending himself at his secret trial. It was printed and circulated underground as *History Will Absolve Me,* increasing support for the rebel movement. In 1955, Fidel and his brother Raúl were released after serving two years of their fifteen-year sentences, and they and their supporters left for Mexico, forming there the "26th of July Movement" (named after the date of the Moncada defeat). In December 1956, they sailed for their homeland with 82 Cubans and the Argentine revolutionary Ernesto "Che" Guevara, aboard the yacht *Granma.* Only thirty survived an assault by Batista's troops. The survivors, including the Castros and Guevara, fled to the Sierra Maestra mountains. From there they launched the Cuban revolution.

THE CUBAN REVOLUTION

Aided by alliances with populist groups in the cities, deteriorating social conditions, the rampant corruption of Batista's dictatorship, and the bravery of their commanders, the rebels soon controlled much of eastern Cuba. Fidel ordered land redistribution in liberated areas, thus building further on his immense popularity. The rebels began a multifront offensive in mid-1958 that resulted in Batista's flight to exile on New Year's Day, 1959. Fidel Castro triumphantly marched into Havana, seizing the power he has held for more than 33 years.

Shortly after the revolution, tribunals were convened in an effort to execute former Batista officials. This caused the first uneasiness among Americans, who had previously been supportive of what they saw as a liberal-democratic revolution. When, in 1960, the Cuban government began to seize American-owned businesses as part of its economic program, the United States retaliated by sharply cutting its quota of sugar imports from Cuba. Rhetoric on both sides became more hostile, and historians still debate which country holds ultimate responsibility for Cuba's drift into Soviet influence. On January 3, 1961, the United States broke off diplomatic relations.

THE BAY OF PIGS AND CUBAN MISSILE CRISIS

Just over three months later, 1300 Cuban exiles staged an invasion of Cuba with American support. Cuban defense forces routed them, and the disastrous raid became infamously known as the "Bay of Pigs Invasion," named after the bay on the south coast of Cuba where the exiles landed. By the end of 1961, Castro had publicly proclaimed his faith in communism, tightened his ties with the Soviet Union, and set up a one-party state. Raúl Castro, now officially second-in-command, made several trips to the Eastern Bloc (the communist states of eastern Europe), making arrangements that brought the world to the brink of nuclear war. Soviet ballistic missiles were placed in Cuba, causing President John F. Kennedy to threaten a nuclear strike. The tense days in 1962, known as the Cuban Missile Crisis, ended when Soviet Premier Nikita Kruschev agreed to remove the menacing weapons.

Since 1963, Castro has consolidated his power and ruled Cuba with an iron hand. Admirers point to his stunning achievements—literacy, below fifty percent before the revolution, is now at a level comparable to that of the United States and Canada. Health care is guaranteed to all Cubans, as is employment and housing. More importantly, perhaps, to a politician, Fidel (as he is called by his countrymen) continues to enjoy the support of a vast majority of Cubans. Critics are no less vocal in their denunciations of human rights abuses; these include suppression of political dissidents and of homosexuals. They also accuse Cuba of attempting to export communist revolution to such places as Angola and Ethiopia, as well as to the rest of Latin America. However, few serious historians see Cuba as being on a par with the hemisphere's worst human rights abusers—Guatemala, Paraguay and, until recently, El Salvador.

The fall of the U.S.S.R. has placed the Cuban economy in a serious bind. Subsidized exports from Eastern Europe and the Soviet Union have been curtailed, leaving Cuba much more vulnerable to the continuing United States embargo. Castro has responded with a multitiered program: extreme austerity measures, further tightening of political controls, and encouragement of joint-venture projects with other Western countries. All of these tactics come at a cost. Ordinary Cubans are reportedly whispering, for the first time, that Fidel has outlived his usefulness. Also, there continues to be strong anti-Castro feeling among the growing Hispanic community in Florida. Cuba seems now to be, more than ever, one of the last bastions of a dying communist system.

Fidel Castro's appeal is a mystery to many North Americans—but to few who have met him. One of the world's most powerful orators, he can mesmerize a crowd for hours at a time. He is known as an engaging one-on-one conversationalist as well, though revolutionary rage is never far from the surface. Whether such a combination of charisma, ardor, and political repression is enough to hold power is an open question. "I would not work near Fidel," said José Luis Llovio, Cuba's former assistant culture minister, in an interview earlier this year with the *Montreal Gazette*. "He is like the sun. From a distance he warms. Up close he burns."

MARRIAGE AND FAMILY

While Castro has attempted to keep his private life secret, some details have become public knowledge, and rumors abound. He married Mirta Díaz-Balart, daughter of a prominent Cuban family, in 1948, and much of their tempestuous life together is detailed in Georgie Anne Geyer's 1991 biography, *Guerilla Prince*. The couple had one son, Fidel (Fidelito), born in 1949. Fidelito, who uses his mother's family name, graduated from Tomorrasov University in Moscow in 1972 with a degree in nuclear physics, and now heads Cuba's Atomic Energy Commission. He and his Russian wife have two children. Fidel and Mirta divorced in 1954, but still are in contact and reportedly continue to share strong feelings for each other.

Castro has a daughter, Alina, by a woman named Naty Revuelta. He has been linked to a number of other women, too, and when his longtime personal assistant, Celia Sánchez, died in 1980, Fidel was said to have been withdrawn for months. Rumors are that he has fathered as many as five other children out of wedlock.

HOBBIES AND OTHER INTERESTS
Castro leads a fairly simple life, devoting most of his energies to politics. He enjoys cooking and fishing. Once a major-league prospect as a pitcher, he remains an avid baseball fan. As part of an anti-smoking campaign, he has given up the cigars that were, for years, an important part of his image.

WRITINGS
History Will Absolve Me, 1958
Revolutionary Struggle, 1947-58, 1972
Fidel Castro Speeches: Volume I, 1981; Volume II, 1983; Volume III, 1985
Fidel Castro: Nothing Can Stop the Course of History, 1986
Fidel and Religion, 1987

HONORS AND AWARDS
Lenin Peace Prize: 1961
Order of Lenin: 1972
Somali Order, first class: 1977
Order of Jamaica: 1977
Dimitrov Prize (Bulgaria): 1980
Gold Star (Vietnam): 1982

FURTHER READING
BOOKS
Bourne, Peter G. *Fidel: A Biography of Fidel Castro,* 1986
Contemporary Authors, Vol. 129
Geyer, Georgie Anne. *Guerilla Prince,* 1991
Szulc, Tad. *Fidel: A Critical Portrait,* 1986

PERIODICALS
Esquire, Mar. 1992, p.102
Mother Jones, July/Aug. 1989, p.20
National Geographic, Aug. 1991, p.90
New Yorker, Apr. 27, 1992, p.52
Reader's Digest, June 1991, p.129
Scholastic Update, Feb. 9, 1990, p.18
U. S. News & World Report, June 24, 1991, p.38

ADDRESS
Office of the President
Palacio del Gobierno
Havana, Cuba

Bill Clinton   1946-
American Political Leader
President of the United States

BIRTH

Bill Clinton was born William Jefferson Blythe IV on August 19,
1946, in Hope, Arkansas, to Virginia (Cassidy) Blythe. His mother
was recently widowed; his father had been killed in an automobile
accident just three months before Bill's birth. In order to support
her son, Virginia Blythe left Arkansas for school in New Orleans
to become a nurse-anesthetist. Young Bill lived with his grandparents in Hope during his first four years. His grandfather ran
a small grocery store that provided the family with a modest
income, and both grandparents provided Bill with lots of love.

103

YOUTH

Young Bill's life changed when his mother married Roger Clinton. Virginia had returned to Hope after graduating from nursing school, where she met Roger, the local Buick dealer. After their marriage, when Bill was seven, the family moved to Hot Springs, Arkansas, where Roger Clinton went to work in his brother's Buick dealership. A resort town, Hot Springs at that time attracted visitors for the gambling, nightclubs, racetrack, and the medicinal quality of the mineral springs. When Bill was about ten, his half-brother and only sibling, Roger Jr., was born. Their mother, who has been called smart, strong willed, quick witted, and a free spirit, was devoted to her sons. As Hillary Clinton once explained, "The important thing about Bill Clinton's upbringing is that he was always surrounded by love. He had a mother who, despite all the heartbreak and tragedy in her life, got up every day optimistic and positive and determined to try to make the best of it—and to love her children."

Clinton's home life was deeply troubled. Roger Clinton was an alcoholic. Although good natured when sober, he was violent when drunk—so violent that once, during an argument with Bill's mother, he fired a gun in the house. Young Bill watched in despair for years, until he finally grew old enough—and big enough—to step in. As a teenager, he broke down the door to his parents' bedroom during a fight and threatened his step-father. Motioning to his mother and brother, Clinton warned, "You will never hit either of them again. If you want them, you'll have to go through me." During this difficult time Bill, at the age of fifteen, formally changed his name from Blythe to Clinton, in what he later called "an expression of family solidarity." Family troubles escalated, though, and his mother divorced Roger Clinton in May 1962, although they remarried three months later. Clinton kept his difficult home life a secret, and none of his friends, or the adults at his school or church, knew about these problems. In fact, it was only during the last few months of his campaign for the Democratic nomination, after repeated questioning by reporters, that Clinton began to discuss these issues publicly.

Despite such hardship, Clinton excelled in school, displaying early his strong intellect and driving ambition. According to Joe Klein, writing in *New York* magazine, "There are many possible ways to respond to an alcoholic parent. Bill Clinton's was to become the perfect child." He was a leader in many school activities, playing saxophone in the band, setting up concerts, participating in Boy Scouts, and volunteering with community organizations. He was so responsible, in fact, that his principal began to limit his activities, concerned that others were taking advantage of him. By high school, he was already involved in politics. As one friend recalled, "Bill was the kind of person who would come up to everyone new in high school and say: 'Hi. How are you? My name's Bill Clinton, and I'm running for something,' whatever it was. We always thought, well, someday Bill will be President."

EDUCATION

Clinton worked his way through college at Georgetown University in Washington, D.C., earning his bachelor's degree with a major in international studies in 1968. His experiences were largely shaped by two major social struggles, the movement for civil rights and the protest against American involvement in Vietnam. During his last two years at Georgetown he worked for the Senate Foreign Relations Committee and for one of his heroes, Arkansas senator J. William Fulbright, the committee chairman and an influential early critic of the Vietnam war. According to Clinton, "Those were the two years that they had all the big hearings on the Vietnam War and our policy in Southeast Asia and its relationship to China and the Soviet Union. It was an utterly fascinating time to be there." It was also during his final year at Georgetown that his stepfather, Roger Clinton, lay dying of cancer in a hospital in North Carolina. Bill Clinton made the long drive each weekend to see him, making peace with the past.

After finishing his undergraduate degree, Clinton spent two years studying at Oxford University as a Rhodes Scholar, a prestigious scholarship awarded to outstanding students from the U.S. and the British commonwealth. He completed his formal education by attending Yale University Law School, where he also met his future wife, Hillary Rodham. He earned his law degree in 1973. While still a student in Yale's very challenging program, Clinton also helped run the Texas campaign of George McGovern's unsuccessful bid for the presidency in 1972—Clinton's first involvement in a presidential campaign. Although he spent much of one year in Texas, he still managed to ace his exams.

FIRST JOBS

After a brief stint as a staff attorney for the House Judiciary Committee, Clinton returned to Arkansas. From 1973 to 1976, he worked as an attorney in private practice and as a professor at the University of Arkansas School of Law. In 1974, Clinton officially began his political career, running for a seat in the U.S. House of Representatives. In his first bid for election, he almost beat the four-term incumbent, losing by only four percentage points. In 1976, he headed Jimmy Carter's successful presidential campaign in Arkansas and also ran for office himself, becoming attorney general for a two-year term.

CAREER HIGHLIGHTS

GOVERNOR OF ARKANSAS

In 1978, Clinton was elected to his first term as governor of Arkansas. At 32, he was the youngest governor in the nation. He and his young aides attacked state government with enthusiasm, reforming existing programs and developing a wide range of new projects. Two years later, though, he was defeated in his bid for reelection, becoming the youngest ex-governor in the nation's history. Political observers chalked it up to immaturity, claiming that many Arkansas voters objected to his arrogance, zeal for reform, reliance on outside experts, and support for tax increases. In their view, he simply tried to do too much too soon. Many also objected to Hillary Rodham's use of her own name, which she later gave up to take her husband's name.

A year later, Clinton began his comeback campaign by appearing on television, apologizing to the voters, promising to listen to their concerns, and asking for another chance. "The people sent me a message," he later admitted, "and I learned my lesson." He was reelected governor in 1982, a position he has held ever since. Commentators generally describe the post-defeat Clinton as a changed man, one interested in moderation and compromise. While some see this as a virtue, others have labeled Clinton "Slick Willie" for his shifting opinions, carefully developed not to offend anyone. Few commentators agree on his record as governor. Most applaud his reforms of the education and welfare systems, but his environmental and tax policies are widely criticized.

There was one decision, though, for which Clinton is widely respected. In 1983, during his second term, his brother, Roger, was filmed by the state police selling crack cocaine to a police informant. Clinton authorized the sting operation that resulted in Roger's arrest and eventual imprisonment, and then followed up by undergoing counseling with the entire family. For this, Clinton is often credited with much personal courage.

RUNNING FOR PRESIDENT

On October 3, 1991, Clinton entered the race for president, declaring himself a candidate for the Democratic nomination. That day he presented many of the themes that he has returned to throughout the campaign. He defined his mission as "preserving the American Dream, restoring the hopes of the forgotten middle class, and reclaiming the future for our children." Calling for government that puts people first, he speaks of justice, compassion, and inclusion, emphasizing the need for all people to work together. Clinton has generally downplayed foreign policy issues and focused on domestic concerns instead. He is considered a moderate who proposes a more limited role for government than traditional Democrats. His administration, he contends, would develop programs to improve education, provide college scholarships, redefine welfare, create new jobs, provide tax breaks for the middle class, and devise other economic measures to fight the recession. But he would also expect something back from those who receive government help, some form of repayment of time, money, or services. With opportunities, according to Clinton, should come additional responsibilities. This is the "new covenant" between government and individuals that forms the cornerstone of his public policy.

During the 1992 presidential primaries, Clinton faced a field of five rivals for the Democratic nomination: Jerry Brown, Tom Harkin, Bob Kerrey, Paul Tsongas, and Douglas Wilder. After winning the majority of delegates in the primaries, Clinton selected Albert Gore as his running mate and secured his party's nomination at the Democratic convention in July 1992. At that time also, independent candidate H. Ross Perot, citing a "revitalized" Democratic party, announced that he was suspending his campaign, leaving a two-man race between Clinton and the Republican candidate, President George Bush.

Clinton's campaign has been dogged by controversy and potentially disastrous revelations. A great deal of press attention was devoted to rumors and allegations of his extramarital affairs. With wife Hillary at his side, Clinton publicly proclaimed on "60 Minutes" that their marriage had been troubled, but that they were committed to staying together and working out their problems. Clinton's draft record was also called into question. His 1969 letter to an Army R.O.T.C. colonel, which seems to contradict his earlier comments about his draft deferment during the Vietnam War, has painted him as a draft dodger for some voters. His stated desire in the letter "to maintain my political viability within the system"

despite his opposition to the war and his deferment strikes some people as overly calculating. Doubts were also raised by his evasiveness when reporters asked him whether he had ever smoked marijuana.

These and other issues have led to many questions about Clinton's credibility, his character, and, ultimately, his electability. Some commentators have argued that Clinton's character and personality directly result from his experiences as a child. Many observers, including Clinton himself, have described his early, almost obsessive achievements as one of several typical patterns for children of alcoholic parents. His secrecy about the past and frequent desire to avoid conflict by building consensus also fit into this pattern. Others, though, focus less on his background, describing him as a slick politician with no firmly rooted beliefs who will do anything for a vote. The key question, though—what the voters think— will be decided in November.

MARRIAGE AND FAMILY

Clinton met his future wife, Hillary Rodham, while both were students at Yale University School of Law. Like Clinton, Rodham was also an excellent student. She grew up outside Chicago and earned her bachelor's degree at Wellesley College before attending Yale, where she and Clinton began dating. Yet she intended to remain on the East Coast, while Clinton always planned to return to Arkansas. After Yale, they briefly separated, and she went to work in Massachusetts at the Children's Defense Fund. When that position ended after one year, she decided to try small-town life. As she later said, "I had no choice but to follow my heart there. Following your heart is never wrong."

In 1974, Rodham moved to Arkansas and accepted a teaching position at the University of Arkansas School of Law. She and Clinton were married in 1975, and they have one daughter, Chelsea, born in 1980. Hillary Clinton has worked as an attorney since her marriage and has been twice named by the prestigious *National Law Journal* to their annual list of the "100 Most Influential Lawyers in America." She has, of late, received a great deal of press attention because of the rumors of Clinton's infidelity and because of her presumed influence if he is elected president.

MAJOR INFLUENCES

In his acceptance speech before the Democratic convention in July 1992, Clinton explained a bit about his background and identified the people who have had the greatest influence on him.

"My mother taught me. She taught me about family and hard work and sacrifice. She held steady through tragedy after tragedy. And she held our family, my brother and I, together through tough times. As a child, I watched her go off to work each day at a time when it wasn't always easy to be a working mother. As an adult, I've watched her fight off breast cancer. And again she has taught me a lesson in courage. And always, always she taught me to fight. . . .You want to know where I get my fighting spirit? It all started with my mother. . . .

"When I think about opportunity for all Americans, I think about my grandfather. He ran a country store in our little town of Hope. . . .My grandfather just had a grade-school education. But in that country store he taught me more about equality in the eyes of the Lord than all my professors at Georgetown; more about the intrinsic worth of every individual than all the philosophers at Oxford; and he taught me more about the need for equal justice than all the jurists at Yale Law School. If you want to know where I come by the passionate commitment I have to bringing people together without regard to race, it all started with my grandfather.

"I learned a lot from another person too. A person who for more than 20 years has worked hard to help our children. . .all while building a distinguished legal career and being a wonderful loving mother. That person is my wife. Hillary taught me. She taught me that all children can learn, and that each of us has a duty to help them do it. So if you want to know why I care so much about our children and our future, it all started with Hillary."

MEMORABLE EXPERIENCES

One of the defining experiences of Clinton's life occurred when he was only seventeen. In 1963, he was selected as a delegate to the American Legion Boys' Nation convention in Washington, D.C. There he met and shook the hand of President John F. Kennedy, who remains one of Clinton's heroes. That meeting strengthened his resolve to enter politics. As his mother later recalled, "I'd never seen him get so excited about something. When he came back from Washington, holding this picture of himself with Jack Kennedy, and the expression on his face. . .I knew right then that politics was the answer for him."

HOBBIES AND OTHER INTERESTS

Clinton is an avid reader and golfer. He also enjoys playing the saxophone, as he recently demonstrated on the "Arsenio Hall Show."

HONORS AND AWARDS

Ten Outstanding Young Americans (U.S. Jaycees): 1979

MEMBERSHIPS

National Association of Attorneys General
National Governors' Association (chairman 1986-87)

Education Commission of the States (chairman 1986-87)
Lower Mississippi Delta Development Commission (chairman 1989-90)
Democratic Leadership Council (chairman 1990-91)

FURTHER READING

BOOKS

Allen, Charles F., and Jonathan Portis. *The Comeback Kid: The Life of Bill Clinton,* 1992
Moore, Jim, with Rick Ihde. *Clinton: Young Man in a Hurry,* 1992
Who's Who in American Politics, 1991-92

PERIODICALS

Current Biography Yearbook 1988
Fortune, May 4, 1992, p.85
Newsweek, Mar. 30, 1992, p.37; July 20, 1992, pp.23, 28, 32, 40
New York, Jan. 20, 1992, p.28
New York Times, July 16, 1992, p.A1
New York Times Biographical Service, Oct. 1991, p.1036; Mar. 1992, p.274
Rolling Stone, Sept. 17, 1992, pp.40, 42, 47, 55
Time, Jan. 27, 1992, p.14; Mar. 23, 1992, pp.14, 16, 24; Apr. 13, 1992, pp.22, 24; Apr. 20, 1992, p.38; June 8, 1992, p.62
U.S. News & World Report, Oct. 14, 1991, p.40; Mar. 30, 1992, p.28
Washington Post Magazine, July 12, 1992, p.12

OTHER

"A Vision for America: A New Covenant," Transcript from a speech given before the Democratic National Convention, July 16, 1992

ADDRESS

National Campaign Headquarters
P.O. Box 615
Little Rock, AR 72203

* UPDATE *

Clinton won the race for the presidency, capturing 43% of the popular vote to George Bush's 38% and Ross Perot's 19%. His sweep of the electoral college was more dramatic, where he garnered 370 electoral votes to Bush's 168. He will be sworn in as president in January 1993, and he is already actively directing his transition team, getting ready for his new position.

Bill Cosby   1937-
American Comedian and Entertainer
Co-Producer and Star of "The Cosby Show"

BIRTH

Bill Cosby (William Henry Cosby, Jr.) was born on July 12, 1937, to Anna and William Cosby. Bill was the oldest of four brothers: James, Russell, and Robert.

YOUTH

Cosby grew up in a poor, black neighborhood in Germantown, a suburb of Philadelphia, Pennsylvania, during World War II. When he was young his father had a job as a welder, and the family lived comfortably. Over time, though, his father lost his job, started to drink, and spent more and more time away from home. The family began to have money troubles. In addition, James died of rheumatic fever when Bill was eight. Soon after, their father left to join the United States Navy and was rarely home from that time onward. Bill's mother, Anna Cosby, went to work as a maid, usually working twelve hours each day, leaving him in charge of his brothers.

EARLY MEMORIES

Cosby has often spoken warmly of his mother's influence on his early years. "She is the most unselfish being I've ever known," he has said. "Many's the time I saw her come home from work exhausted and hungry—and give her supper to one of my brothers who was still hungry after he'd eaten his own. I promised her that some day she wouldn't have to work, and that's a promise I've kept." But there was a lighter side, too— she was also his first audience. She listened to his funny stories, laughed at his jokes, and encouraged him to learn.

EDUCATION

As a youth, Cosby attended Wister Elementary School, Fitz-Simons Junior High, and Central High School. He was not a good student. He was more interested in clowning around than studying or listening in class. As he later said, "I found I could make people laugh, and I enjoyed doing it....Telling funny stories became, for me, a way of making friends." He fondly recalls one early teacher, Mary Forchic Nagle, who encouraged this need to perform by casting him in several school plays. Although she wrote on his sixth-grade report card, "He would rather be a clown than a student and feels it his mission to amuse his class mates in and out of school," she also added, "He should grow up to do great things." While Cosby did poorly in his classes, he always excelled in sports. He was a star athlete on the football, baseball, and track teams. In high school, though, he spent so much time on sports and clowning around, and so little time on his schoolwork, that he had to repeat the tenth grade. Soon he dropped out of high school. After several jobs and a stint in the Navy, where he earned his high-school diploma, he enrolled at Temple University in Philadelphia in 1961 to become a gym teacher. He received a four-year athletic scholarship and played on the basketball, football, and track teams while also maintaining good grades in his courses. Yet he dropped out of school again, during his third year, this time to work as a comedian. Years later, Cosby returned to his studies. He was awarded an honorary bachelor's degree from Temple and later completed a master's and doctorate in education at the University of Massachusetts.

FIRST JOBS

Cosby began to work very early in life. At age nine he started shining shoes to help out the family. At eleven he spent the summer stocking shelves in a grocery store. He worked from 6:00 a.m. to 6:00 p.m., plus extra hours on weekends, for $8 per week. After dropping out of high school he worked in a shoe repair shop and a car muffler plant before joining the Navy in 1956 in search of a better job. Cosby continued to play sports and joke around while in the Navy, but he also became more serious about his studies and his job as a physical therapist for sick and injured soldiers at Philadelphia Naval Hospital.

CHOOSING A CAREER

Cosby's first job as an entertainer came while he was a student at Temple. During the summer after his second year, he got a job as a bartender to earn extra money for school. While working at The Underground in Philadelphia, he soon realized that he could make more money in tips if he was friendly. His funny stories and jokes were a success with the customers, and the owner offered him a job as a comedian in a room called The Cellar, with a ceiling so low that Cosby couldn't even stand up on stage! He soon began to receive bigger and better job offers, and he dropped out of Temple to become a full-time entertainer midway through his third year.

MARRIAGE AND FAMILY

In 1963, while performing in Washington, D.C., after leaving Temple, he began to date Camille Hanks, then a student at the University of Maryland. According to Cosby, he knew he wanted to marry her after their first date. They were soon engaged, but she broke it off at the request of her parents, who were worried about his uncertain future as an entertainer. Despite her parents' wishes Hanks and Cosby got back together again, and they were married on January 25, 1964. They have five children: Erika, Erinn, Ennis, Ensa, and Evin.

CAREER HIGHLIGHTS

In the almost thirty years since Cosby began performing professionally, he has recorded over twenty albums (including both comedy and jazz), performed in more than ten movies, written three best-selling books (including two that were among the top twelve nonfiction bestsellers of the 1980s), and starred in a variety of television shows. In his first series, "I Spy," Cosby teamed up with Robert Culp to play a pair of spies disguised as tennis bums. An instant success, the series broke television racial barriers by depicting a black man as brilliant and equal in every way to his white partner.

His long-running hit series "The Cosby Show" debuted in 1984. This show depicts day-to-day life in a comfortably middle-class New York family that resembles Bill's own. The Huxtable family consists of the father, Heathcliff, a doctor; the mother, Claire, a lawyer; and their five children. This show, like many of Bill's other projects, focuses on the similarities rather than the differences among people. Stories often emphasize the value of family ties, education, hard work, and self-respect, and consistently avoid violence and sexual or racial overtones. With gentleness and humor, the series depicts many of the poignant, bittersweet, silly, infuriating, and downright funny things that can happen in an ordinary loving family. "The Cosby Show," the highest-rated series of the 1980s, will come to an end at the close of the 1991-92 television season.

In late 1991, Cosby announced a new program to be shown beginning in fall, 1992. The new series, "You Bet Your Life," a revival of a classic Groucho Marx show, will be a comedy game show. In a departure for Cosby, though, the show will not be seen on any of the major networks. Instead, it will be sold in syndication to individual stations around the country. According to television insiders, this approach should increase Cosby's earnings.

In addition, Cosby has also been hired by many companies in recent years to star in television commercials for their products. All of these activities have combined to make Cosby one of the richest entertainers in the world.

FAVORITE BOOKS

According to Cosby, the famous American writer Mark Twain had a great influence on his early ideas of humor. "As a boy," Cosby once said, "my mother used to read Mark Twain to me....I was impressed with his fantastic sense of humor."

HOBBIES AND OTHER INTERESTS

In addition to his lifelong interest in sports and comedy, Cosby is an avid fan of jazz, especially the music of such great artists as Louis Armstrong, Charlie Parker, Charles Mingus, and Miles Davis. Their influence can be seen in his comedy routines, where Cosby has tried to imitate their ability to improvise, to take a theme and continually find new ways to treat it. Cosby has also been involved in several television projects that combine his interests in children and education, including an educational cartoon series called "Fat Albert and the Cosby Kids" and appearances on "The Electric Company," "Sesame Street," and "Captain Kangaroo's Wake Up." "All I do," Cosby once said, "has to do with some form of education, some form of giving a message to people." He has also been active in charity work, contributing both money and time to many causes. He has been especially generous in his donations to predominately African-American colleges and universities, including a 1987 donation to Spelman College of $20 million.

WRITINGS

The Wit and Wisdom of Fat Albert, 1973
Bill Cosby's Personal Guide to Tennis Power: or, Don't Lower the Lob, Raise the Net, 1975
You Are Somebody Special (contributor), 1978
Fatherhood, 1986
Time Flies, 1987
Changes: Becoming the Best You Can Be (contributor), 1988
Love and Marriage, 1989
Childhood, 1991

SELECTED RECORDINGS

Bill Cosby Is a Very Funny Fellow, Right! 1963
I Started Out as a Child, 1964
Why Is There Air? 1965
Wonderfulness, 1966
Revenge, 1967
To Russell, My Brother, Whom I Slept With, 1968
Bill Cosby, 1969
Bill Cosby Talks to Kids about Drugs, 1971
The Electric Company, 1971
Fat Albert, 1973
Bill Cosby Is Not Himself These Days, 1976
My Father Confused Me, 1977
Bill's Best Friend, 1978
Bill Cosby...Himself, 1982
Reunion, 1982
Those of You With or Without Children, You'll Understand, 1986
OH, Baby, 1991

HONORS AND AWARDS

Grammy Award: 1964, for *I Started Out as a Child;* 1965, for *Why Is There Air?;* 1966, for *Wonderfulness;* 1967, for *Revenge;* 1968, for *To Russell, My Brother, Whom I Slept With;* 1969, for *Bill Cosby;* 1986, for *Those of You With or Without Children, You'll Understand,* all as best comedy recording; 1971, for *Bill Cosby Talks to Kids About Drugs;* 1972, for *The Electric Company,* both as best children's recording
Emmy Award: 1966-68, for lead actor in "I Spy"; 1985, for "The Cosby Show" as outstanding comedy series
Seal of Excellence (Children's Theatre Association): 1973
Gold Award (International Film and Television Festival): 1981, for "Picture Pages" as outstanding children's program
Elmer Award *(Harvard Lampoon):* 1983, for lifetime achievement in comedy

Spingarn Medal (NAACP): 1985, "for recognition of his status as one of America's greatest humorists, social philosophers, and communicators of the human condition"

Golden Globe Award: 1985-86, for best actor in "The Cosby Show"

People's Choice Award: 1985, for male performer in new program "The Cosby Show" and for new comedy program "The Cosby Show"; 1986-91, for male performer; 1986-91, for favorite male entertainer; 1988-89, for "The Cosby Show" as favorite TV program

FURTHER READING

BOOKS

Adams, Barbara Johnston. *The Picture Life of Bill Cosby,* 1986 (juvenile)
Contemporary Authors New Revision Series, Vol. 27
Green, Carl R., and William R. Sanford. *Bill Cosby,* 1986 (juvenile)
Haskins, Jim. *Bill Cosby: America's Most Famous Father,* 1988 (juvenile)
Kettelkamp, Larry. *Bill Cosby: Family Funny Man,* 1987 (juvenile)
Woods, Harold, and Geraldine Woods. *Bill Cosby: Making America Laugh and Learn,* 1983 (juvenile)
World Book Encyclopedia, 1991

PERIODICALS

Current Biography Yearbook 1986
Ebony, May 1989, p.25
Life, June 1985, p.34
Newsweek, Sept. 2, 1985, p.50
Time, Sept. 28, 1987, p.62

ADDRESS

The Brokaw Company
9255 Sunset Blvd.
Suite 706
Los Angeles, CA 90069

Diana, Princess of Wales 1961-
English Member of the Royal Family
Wife of Prince Charles, Heir to
the British Throne

BIRTH

Diana, Princess of Wales, was born July 1, 1961, to Edward John
and Frances Burke (Roche) Spencer, then the Viscount and
Viscountess Althorp. Her birthplace was Park House in Norfolk,
England, on the edge of the royal estate at Sandringham, and it
was here that she spent the early years of her childhood. She has
two sisters, older by six and three years, respectively: Lady Sarah
McCorquodale and Lady Jane Fellowes (wife of Sir Robert
Fellowes, Queen Elizabeth's private secretary). Diana's brother,
three years her junior, is Charles, the ninth Earl Spencer, who

117

inherited the title upon his father's death March 29, 1992. Another brother, John, born eighteen months before the princess, lived for only a few hours.

Diana is descended from a long line of English nobility, linked by blood to kings and dukes, and by service to both court and state. The home where she was born was a royal grant to her maternal grandfather, Maurice Roche, the fourth Baron Fermoy, who later became a member of Parliament; the baron's Scottish wife, Ruth, Lady Fermoy, remains a close friend and member of the official household of Queen Mother Elizabeth. The Spencers, Diana's paternal ancestors, have served England's sovereigns for generations—her own father was equerry (officer by appointment) to both the present queen and her late father, George VI. The ancestral Spencer home, where the princess lived after her father inherited the earldom, is Althorp House in Northamtonshire, one of England's grandest estates.

YOUTH

As a child of privilege, the Honourable Diana Spencer was raised in an aristocratic country lifestyle that biographer Ingrid Seward describes in *Diana: An Intimate Portrait*, as "very much in the 'Upstairs, Downstairs' tradition, almost Edwardian in its order and routine." She was taken to parties with the royal princes, went on summer trips to the seaside, romped with her siblings and her animals, and made frequent visits to her grandparents at Althorp.

Diana's sisters were in boarding school by the time she and her little brother were ready for the classroom at Park House. Life should have been carefree and uncomplicated, but their world came to a shattering halt with the messy divorce of their parents. Lady Althorp had left her husband for an affair with wealthy wallpaper heir Peter Shand Kydd; she was branded an adultress and denied custody of her children. Diana and brother Charles, in particular, were bewildered and shaken by the turn of events, and the princess recalls how her parents were "busy sorting themselves out. I remember my mother crying, daddy never spoke to us about it. We could never ask questions. Too many nannies. The whole thing was very unstable."

In the England of the 1960s, scandalous divorce among members of the nobility was very much an embarrassment, and the young Spencers were deeply scarred by their parents' breakup. They alone among their schoolmates had lives that had been so publicly exposed and they felt, say their friends, "set apart." Family times as they knew them had ended, and they were shuffled around among grandparents and nannies, and between parents who had difficulty hiding their bitterness toward one another. It is thought by those who know the princess best that the impact of those traumatic years has influenced her strongly in the devotion and unstinting attention she gives to her own children.

Diana's mother, the Honourable Frances Shand Kydd, remarried in 1969 and moved to the Sussex coast. She currently lives on the Isle of Seil in Argyllshire, Scotland, and is separated from her second husband. In 1975, Diana's father was elevated to the peerage upon the death of his own father and, as Lord (Earl) Spencer, moved to the opulent manor at Althorp. His young son became the new viscount, and his daughters' titles were raised from "Honourable" to "Lady." The earl was soon married again—this time to Raine, the countess of Dartmouth and daughter of romance novelist Barbara Cartland. There was an uneasy relationship between the Spencer children and their new stepmother, reportedly stemming from jealousy, but most of it coming from what they considered her overbearing attitude and her mishandling of the family home and priceless treasures. However, since the death of their father in the spring of 1992, they have reclaimed their ancestral property and Charles has inherited the peerage.

EDUCATION

Diana's earliest education was at home with a governess before she attended primary day classes at nearby Silfield School. Then, at the age of nine, she was enrolled at Riddlesworth Hall, a Norfolk boarding school forty miles from Park House. It was the first time that the sensitive little girl had been away from her family, and the early weeks found her sad and lonely, particularly after the trauma of her parents' divorce. Biographer Seward explains that the "British boarding school is a strange institution . . . .Yet by its very routine and insistence on rules and order it can give a sense of security. Diana, like many other children from broken homes, found a stability there she might otherwise have missed." At Riddlesworth, Diana was only a passable student, but she is still remembered for her athletic abilities, her love of animals, and her exceptional kindness and helpfulness.

The princess's next boarding school venture was at West Heath, in a woodland park outside Sevenoaks in Kent where, by tradition, she followed in the footsteps of her sisters; her mother also had been educated here, as had Prince Charles's great-grandmother, the dowager Queen Mary. Again, success eluded Diana in the classroom, but she excelled at swimming and netball (a girls' game somewhat like basketball) and enjoyed community work. With children and with old people, her gentleness and concern were already evident. She also loved ballet, although at five feet, ten-and-a-half inches, she was too tall to consider dancing professionally.

Diana left West Heath at sixteen, after twice failing her "O" level exams, to attend the Institut Alpin Videmanette, an exclusive Swiss finishing school near Gstaad. Her stay among the more sophisticated European students was brief and miserable, and she returned to England, ending her formal education.

FIRST JOBS

Without qualification for even the most basic of professions, Diana went to work as a babysitter and sometime-housemaid for the upper-class friends of her family. For a short time, she lived in her mother's London quarters and, although her wealthy parents eventually bought her a flat in London's fashionable South Kensington neighborhood, the industrious young woman continued to work for pocket money. Doing occasional ironing or clean-up, say her former flatmates, was never beneath her.

At the time she became romantically involved with Prince Charles, Diana was a teachers' assistant at the Young England Nursery School in Pimlico (southwest London) and a babysitter for the son of an American oil executive two days a week. All was not drudgery, though, for she had several boyfriends (none serious) and was part of a young social set that lived and partied around Sloane Square and was teasingly identified in the press as the "Sloane Rangers."

PREPARING FOR MARRIAGE

Lady Diana and Prince Charles had known one another as neighbors at Sandringham, and Charles had once dated her elder sister, Sarah, but their own romance did not begin until 1980, when Lady Diana was 19. When the courtship became public knowledge in the autumn of that year, the media went into a frenzy about the bachelor prince and the beautiful young noblewoman. "Charles's quest for a wife," says Andrew Morton, a royal biographer, "had developed into a national pastime." Diana was hounded relentlessly by reporters and photographers, but managed to handle the attention with appealing humor and grace. It was during those months, before the formal engagement announcement was made in February 1981, that "Shy Di" became the darling of the press.

Diana had a brief vacation in Australia with her mother and stepfather before moving into Buckingham Palace to prepare for marriage. Barely out of girlhood, she had started down a path strewn with public expectations and had embarked on a royal career for which, many say, she was ill-prepared.

MARRIAGE AND FAMILY

The marriage of Lady Diana Frances Spencer to Charles Philip Arthur George, the Prince of Wales, took place July 29, 1981, at London's St. Paul's Cathedral, the beautiful edifice designed three centuries earlier by Sir Christopher Wren, one of England's greatest architects. The spectacular ceremony was attended by 2500 guests and watched on television by more than seven hundred million viewers around the world. Diana, who rode with her father in a glass coach from Clarence House, the home of the Queen Mother, arrived at St. Paul's to the thunderous applause of British subjects numbering in the hundreds of thousands. Even greater numbers of cheering onlookers had lined the Strand along the two-mile route to the church, waiting for a glimpse of the young noblewoman who would one day be their queen.

The marriage service was performed by Dr. Robert Runcie, Archbishop of Canterbury, and, in a break with royal tradition, prayers were offered by Catholic and other non-Anglican clergymen. Three orchestras, three choirs, and well-known operatic soprano Kiri Ti Kanawa provided majestic music for the lavish ceremony that came to be known as the "wedding of the century." Diana was attended by five young bridesmaids and two pageboys; Prince Charles had as his supporters his two brothers, Prince Andrew (now the Duke of York) and Prince Edward. All the bells of London pealed as the newlyweds rode from St. Paul's in an open landau (horse-drawn carriage) to Buckingham Palace for a private reception and a widely photographed public balcony appearance.

Two sons have been born to the royal couple: William Arthur Philip Louis on June 21, 1982, and Henry Charles Albert David (called Prince Harry) on September 15, 1984. The children are second and third in line to the throne, after their father.

The prince and princess have two major residences—their extensive London quarters at Kensington Palace, and Highgrove, their estate in the Gloucestershire countryside. In addition, there are Tamarisk, a tiny house on the Scilly Isles off southwestern England, and Craigowan on the Balmoral estate in central Scotland. The latter is royal property and is used only occasionally.

ROYAL CAREER

Press interest and public enthusiasm quickly made an idol of the new Princess of Wales. Immediately after her marriage, she plunged into her royal career with a grace and freshness rarely exhibited by the solemn Windsors. "Wherever she went," wrote *Current Biography* at that time, "whether attending exhibitions at the Victoria and Albert Museum...switching on the Christmas lights on Regent Street, or being present at the opening of Parliament, she was Great Britain's brightest star." Her public appearances at home and abroad were attended by hordes of reporters and photographers, and the willowy, elegantly dressed princess became a style-setter as well as a new national symbol.

Diana produced two sons within three years—"an heir and a spare," quipped the press—endearing her even further to the already-enchanted Britons. Her devotion to her children is legendary and, as they have grown, she is more often pictured with them than in the glamorous images of her early marriage. Surprisingly, for all her popularity, she had come under frequent criticism for her excessive and elaborate wardrobe and also for her obsession with dieting. In recent years, it has been rumored that she suffered from the eating disorders anorexia and bulimia during this period in her life.

When the twenty-year-old Diana first married the heir to the British throne, royal watchers looked upon their new life as a fairy tale. Here were a beautiful and fascinating princess and a dashing prince whose love affair would enhance the monarchy and reaffirm the traditions of the House of Windsor. "The pageantry and...delirium of the wedding celebration," said *Time* in those heady days, "are the distillation not only of national spirit but of a shared dramatic soul." Sadly, eleven years later, the public dream has ended and the royal marriage is spoken of as merely a working arrangement.

Rumors of a royal rift surfaced early and have escalated to such levels that there is now wide speculation that the couple may enter into a formal separation—or even a divorce. Several new tell-all books and dozens of tabloids have raised the whispers to screaming headlines. Prince Charles, it is said, is disenchanted with his wife and resentful of her enormous popularity. She, in turn, is reportedly bored with his middle-aged friends and interests (he is twelve years her senior), hurt by his indifference and frequent absences, and humiliated and betrayed by his continued relationship with an old (and married) girlfriend, Camilla Parker Bowles.

Friends on both sides point fingers of blame for the disharmony. Diana, a beloved and dazzling figure to the rest of the world, is said by Charles's contemporaries to be spoiled (her old nannies confirm that she was a willful child), given to tantrums and moods, and an intellectual lightweight. Charles is accused of coldness, inflexibility, and eccentricity, although he is also known as a man who can be both charming and witty. Andrew Morton, in his much-publicized new book *Diana: Her True Story*, writes that "this much-discussed union which began with such high hopes has now reached an impasse of mutual recrimination and chilling indifference."

This year alone, Queen Elizabeth has faced in stony silence the breakup of two other royal marriages, those of Princess Anne and Mark Phillips, and of "Fergie and Andy," the popular Duke and Duchess of York.

HOBBIES AND OTHER INTERESTS

The Princess of Wales enjoys dancing, swimming, and skiing, but does not share the rest of the royal family's conspicuous interest in horses. She fell from her mount as a child, and the memory of her injury has kept her wary of riding. It is said that Diana reads only light fiction or fashion journals, but the growing maturity and the new self-confidence she has shown in recent speaking appearances belie that unsubstantiated report. She is said to have a genuine devotion, beyond the call of her royal patronage, to issues involving children and the aging and has become an outspoken advocate for AIDS research.

FURTHER READING

BOOKS

Campbell, Lady Colin. *Diana in Private: The Princess Nobody Knows*, 1992
Davies, Nicholas. *Diana: A Princess and Her Troubled Marriage*, 1992
Giff, Patricia R. *Diana: Twentieth-Century Princess*, 1991 (juvenile)
King, Norman. *Two Royal Women: The Public and Private Lives of Fergie and Di*, 1991
Morton, Andrew. *Diana: Her True Story*, 1992
Seward, Ingrid. *Diana: An Intimate Portrait*, 1992

PERIODICALS

Current Biography Yearbook 1983
Esquire, June 1992, p.110
Life, Aug. 1992, p.26
Maclean's, Aug. 5, 1991, p.46; June 15, 1992, p.28
Newsweek, Aug. 3, 1981, p.35; Oct. 28, 1985, p.56; June 22, 1992, p.69
New York, Aug. 3, 1981, p.30
People, Nov. 11, 1985, p. 56
Time, Aug. 3, 1981, p.20

ADDRESS

Office of the Princess of Wales
St. James's Palace
London, England SW1 A1BS

* UPDATE *

On December 9, 1992, Buckingham Palace announced that Prince Charles and Princess Diana had agreed to separate. They do not plan to divorce, and both will continue their royal and constitutional duties. They plan to raise their children jointly. The announcement indicated that the succession to the throne remains unchanged and left open the possibility that Diana will someday reign as Queen, but the speculation is that the separation has dealt a decisive blow to the monarchy.

Shannen Doherty   1971-
American Actress
Plays Brenda Walsh on "Beverly Hills, 90210"

BIRTH

Shannen Doherty was born April 12, 1971, in Memphis, Tennessee, to Tom and Rosa Doherty. She has one brother, Sean, who is about four years older.

YOUTH

When Doherty was six, the family moved to Palos Verdes, California, a suburb of Los Angeles, so her father could expand the family trucking business. Ever since that time, acting has dominated her life. As she tells it, "When I was eight and a half, a friend invited me to watch her audition for a children's theater production of *Snow White* that was being held at a church. Acting wasn't anything I'd thought about up until that point, and when the director invited me to audition, at first I shied away. But after some prodding, I finally did. Boy, was I surprised when I landed one of the lead parts!" Encouraged by the recognition she received, Doherty wanted to become a professional actor. Yet her parents refused, worrying about the effects of the life style of a child actor. By her response, Doherty showed the self-confidence, determination, and perseverance for which she is known today. During the next two years, she kept up with her school work, her chores at home, and her roles with the children's theater, eventually convincing her parents to allow her to see an agent. Within a week, she had her first job: a voice-over part in the animated movie, *The Secret of Nimh.*

FIRST JOBS

After several commercials and a small part in the film *Night Shift,* Doherty landed her first role on television, on a two-part segment of "Father Murphy." The show's creator, Michael Landon, was so impressed with her skill and maturity that he soon cast her as Jenny Wilder in his new series, "Little House: A New Beginning." Doherty continued to act from that time onward, appearing in commercials, documentaries, and in guest-starring roles in "Airwolf," "The Voyagers," "The Outlaws," "Magnum, P.I.," "Highway to Heaven," "21 Jump Street," and "Life Goes On." She also appeared in a small role in the film *Girls Just Want to Have Fun* and in the made-for-television movies "The Other Lover" and "Robert Kennedy and His Times."

EDUCATION

Shannen's education was divided between regular schools and on-set tutors: television and movie studios are legally required to provide three hours of tutoring to young actors each day. She started out her freshman year in a parochial high school, but felt different from her classmates. She found it difficult to combine school hours with the many absences required by her acting jobs, and she felt left out of the cliques that developed. She later attended Lycee Francais, a private school whose headmistress was more tolerant of an actor's schedule. Although she has spoken of attending college, she has delayed those plans to continue her acting career.

CAREER HIGHLIGHTS

Doherty's next big break came in 1986, when she appeared in the television series "Our House" as Kris Witherspoon, a mature, responsible, perky, and hard-working teen. The series was on the air for three seasons. While working on "Our House," Doherty began to develop a reputation for her assertive manner and outspoken views. She felt strongly about the show's responsibility to present her character as a positive role model, and she often clashed with the directors and writers about any behavior or language that she considered inappropriate to any of the show's characters. Following "Our House," Doherty played the part of Heather Duke in the movie *Heathers*, a black comedy about high school life that also starred Winona Ryder and Christian Slater. *Heathers* has since become something of a cult favorite. Doherty didn't work much for about a year following that role, rejecting many parts that portrayed teens negatively. "I don't like playing airheads. Anything that's demeaning to women, I don't want to do. If I'm going to play a teenager, I'm going to play someone with brains, intelligence—a thinking young person."

In 1990, auditions began at the Fox Broadcasting Network for their new high-school series. Originally called "Class of Beverly Hills," the show would be produced by Aaron Spelling, the creator of such hits as "Charlie's Angels," "The Mod Squad," "The Love Boat," and "Dynasty." The Fox creative team auditioned many young actresses without finding anyone right for the role of Brenda Walsh—until Spelling's daughter Tori (who plays Donna Martin on the show) suggested Doherty based on her performance in *Heathers*. She got the job.

"Beverly Hills, 90210" is a weekly, one-hour dramatic series that depicts

the lives of a group of friends at fictional West Beverly High School. The group includes twins Brenda and Brandon Walsh, who have recently moved from Minnesota to southern California with their parents, Cindy and Jim, following his job transfer. With their devoted family ties and solid Midwestern values, the Walsh family represents the moral center of the show. Many of the stories have depicted Brenda and Brandon's internal struggles between their fascination with the more glamorous lifestyle of Beverly Hills and their respect for their parents' values. With time, however, Brenda and Brandon—as well as their friends—have come to appreciate the love, attention, and guidance that the Walsh family has to offer. Within this framework, the show has been able to explore many issues of concern to teens, including drug and alcohol use, date rape, sexuality, peer pressure, divorce, homosexuality, and teenage pregnancy. Many of these problems have concerned her relationship with her boyfriend on the show, Dylan McKay, played by Luke Perry. While the show received lukewarm ratings and scant press coverage with its October 1990 debut, it has since become a must-watch show for many young viewers. Observers agree that it is the show's honesty, forthrightness, and respect for teens that have won it such a devoted audience.

Doherty's character, Brenda, has evolved since the show began, from an often insecure and flighty young girl to a more confident and serious young woman determined to express her feelings—more and more like Doherty herself! Asked whether she identifies with Brenda, Doherty said, "In the beginning we had nothing common. [Brenda] was very insecure, would have done anything to be part of the clique. But she's maturing now, starting to realize some things...like she doesn't need a boyfriend for her life to be perfect, that she needs to stand on her own and find out who she is. That's an important lesson for any girl at any age." For Doherty, such lessons are vital. She feels a real sense of responsibility that her character and the show itself should provide positive role models, and she most enjoys the episodes that deal with serious issues. And the audience responds, sending Doherty and the other actors bags of letters describing their problems and asking for advice.

MAJOR INFLUENCES

Doherty has often spoken of her great respect and admiration for Michael Landon. "Working with Michael Landon," she has said, "was one of the most important stepping stones in my career. I credit him for guiding me in the right direction when I was very young."

MARRIAGE AND FAMILY

Throughout her career, Doherty's family has been crucial to her success. Despite their initial reluctance, her parents soon became supportive of her work. When Shannen was young, her mother, Rosa Doherty, accompanied her to the set each day to ensure that she wasn't overworked. Coming from such a close-knit family, Doherty found it especially difficult when her father, Tom Doherty, had a debilitating stroke when she was twelve. After a long and difficult recovery, he now works as an investment banker.

Doherty zealously guards her privacy. She currently lives alone in the Malibu Beach area, outside Los Angeles. She recently became engaged to her boyfriend Chris Foufas, a businessman from Chicago, with whom she has had a long-distance, commuter relationship. At press time, no information about wedding plans had been released.

HOBBIES AND OTHER INTERESTS

Doherty enjoys playing with her dogs, rooting for the L.A. Kings hockey team, horseback riding, painting, and all types of exercise, especially skiing and tennis.

FURTHER READING

BOOKS

Cohen, Daniel. *"Beverly Hills, 90210": Meet the Stars of Today's Hottest TV Series,* 1991
Mills, Bart, and Nancy Mills. *"Beverly Hills, 90210" Exposed!,* 1991
Reisfeld, Randi. *The Stars of "Beverly Hills, 90210": Their Lives and Loves,* 1991

PERIODICALS

People, Sept. 9, 1991, p.80
Rolling Stone, Aug. 8, 1991, p.81; Feb. 20, 1992, p.22
Seventeen, Dec. 1991, p.72
Teen, Jan. 1988, p.64; Dec. 1991, p.60
TV Guide, Feb. 13, 1988, p.32; Aug. 24, 1991, p.8

ADDRESS

Fox Broadcasting Company
P.O. Box 5600
Beverly Hills, CA 90209

Elizabeth Dole 1936-
American Red Cross President
Former U.S. Secretary of Transportation and Secretary of Labor

BIRTH

Elizabeth Hanford Dole was born July 29, 1936, in Salisbury, North Carolina, to John Van and Mary (Cathey) Hanford. She has one brother, John, thirteen years her senior. "Liddy," the widely recognized nickname that has followed her into adulthood, is her own baby pronunciation of her formal given name—Mary Elizabeth Alexander Hanford.

YOUTH

The little Southern girl who would grow up to acquire political stature shared by few women of her generation was drawn to public service from an early age. "As a child, as she would do so often as an adult," relates a *Washington Monthly* story, "Liddy Hanford campaigned. She was [barely more than] a toddler when she won a competition to be mascot of the high school graduating class of her brother. . .and in the third grade she was president of a class club."

Liddy's father, John Van Hanford, owned a successful floral business. She was raised in a prosperous family that gave her all the advantages of gracious living—piano, ballet, and riding lessons; summer camp; rail journeys across the country and into Canada; and a weekend house. Yet friends say that although she was doted upon, she was not a spoiled child. "Driven" is the adjective used most often in describing her, then and now. She was an excellent student, anxious to please, and laughingly admits that "as ringleader of neighborhood children, I was a precocious organizer." She tells of banding together her schoolmates during the days of World War II to collect wastepaper and tinfoil for recycling, although she and her friends had little understanding of war itself. Dole's need and willingness to be involved have echoed throughout her life.

As Liddy progressed through the grades in school, she became an avid reader and an essay writer; at one point she won a gold key and a certificate from a Chicago radio program called "Quiz Kids" for an essay she wrote about her teacher. Later she won a literary contest sponsored by the United Daughters of the Confederacy.

EARLY MEMORIES

One particular incident from Dole's childhood remains a touching memory to this day. Her brother was away in the Pacific during World War II, serving on the USS *Saratoga*, but eight-year-old Liddy had been, as young children are, insensitive to her parents' anxieties. Her mother, Dole recalls, "had worn a path" to the mailbox, hoping for news of Johnny's safety, and "her trial was made painfully vivid for me on [his] twenty-first birthday. That day, florist trucks that had been repainted to read 'J. Van Hanford and Son' appeared on the streets of Salisbury. When Mother first saw one, she pulled her car over to the side of the road and wept. Dad, without telling anyone, had used the occasion to make the family business a partnership. Mother just wanted to make sure her son lived to see it."

Other memories crowd in when Dole speaks of her childhood. She tells of the corrective glasses that she had needed since the age of three, and of how she complained to her mother during her grade-school years that, because of those glasses, "I'm always the last one when they choose sides" for games and sports. She remembers, too, or at least remembers being told, of her critical illness after her appendix burst when she was seven years old. There were no antibiotics then for the resulting bout of peritonitis (dangerous inflammation of the abdominal lining), and she nearly died.

EDUCATION

After graduating from Boyden High School in her hometown, Dole enrolled at Duke University in Durham, North Carolina, "for the simple reason," she says, "that my brother had gone there." The bright and ambitious young woman excelled in her studies and graduated in 1958 with honors in political science and a coveted key from Phi Beta Kappa (a prestigious scholastic society). But academics were not her only interest at college—her love of public service steered her into politics on campus, where she became president of the Women's Student Government and was elected student leader of the year. Dole also led an active social life, joining Delta Delta Delta sorority and dancing at the cotillions and "coming-out" balls that were so much a part of Southern custom both before and after the Second World War. Pretty and popular, she was chosen May Queen the year she graduated.

A brief course in English history and government at England's Oxford University was followed by graduate studies at Harvard University, where Dole earned a combined master's degree in education and government in 1960. She then attended Harvard Law School, from which she received her law degree in 1965. She began to practice law in Washington, D.C., several months later.

FIRST JOBS

Dole's first venture into the working world was in the autumn of 1958, a few months after her graduation from Duke. She moved north to Cambridge, Massachusetts, to take a job in the library of Harvard Law School. She made the most of her time in a part of the country so different from her own, and tells in her 1988 book, *The Doles: Unlimited Partners*, that ". . .all of New England became a classroom without walls. For a girl from Salisbury, there was something almost magical in the salt air of Marblehead and the icy perfume of a winter's morning in Vermont. I took to the ski slopes like a duck to water."

Dole taught history to eleventh-graders in suburban Boston the following year as part of her master's degree program at Harvard. She then worked on Capitol Hill during the summer of 1960, in the office of B. Everett Jordan, Democratic senator from North Carolina. Still later, while on summer breaks from law school, Dole held internships at the United Nations headquarters in New York.

CHOOSING A CAREER

From the day that she enrolled in the political science program at Duke University, there was never any question in Dole's mind about her life's work. She knew then—and maybe years before—that Washington would be her eventual destination, and everything she studied or was involved in prepared her for that goal.

CAREER HIGHLIGHTS

Elizabeth Dole started government work in 1966, during the Lyndon Johnson administration, as a staff assistant at HEW (the Department of Health, Education, and Welfare that is now the Department of Health and Human Services); there, she organized the first national conference on education for the deaf. As a community service, she also represented impoverished defendants in the District of Columbia courts. From 1968 to 1971, during the administration of Richard Nixon, she served on the President's Commission for Consumer Interests, first as associate director of legislative affairs, then as executive director.

Dole had been reared in an atmosphere of Democratic politics, but by the time Virginia Knauer tapped her to be deputy director in the White House Office of Consumer Affairs, a job she held from 1971 to 1973, she had registered as an independent. She met her future husband, Robert Dole, the Republican senator from Kansas, at about this time (Knauer introduced them), but they did not marry until 1975, when she was 39 years old. "I never felt any pressure. . . I was enjoying very much being single and going to graduate school and traveling," she explains. "But it happened with the person who was absolutely right for me, and I think I'm right for him. It's incredible to me that it meshed together so beautifully, so that two careers could go forward together without any adjustments." The Doles are often spoken of as a power couple, or even a "golden" couple.

Elizabeth Dole took a leave of absence from the Federal Trade Commission (FTC) in 1976 to campaign for her husband when he was the vice presidential candidate for the Republican Party, running with Gerald Ford. She resigned her post to help him in 1979 in the presidential primaries, and then campaigned for Ronald Reagan when her husband dropped out of the race. A *Vogue* profile of Liddy Dole, published a few years afterward, quoted an explanation of why she had become such a fervent Republican. "She once told me," said Jeffrey Edelstein, who knew her from her FTC days, "she felt the Republican Party had great challenges ahead of it, and it had to broaden its base. It had to be more sensitive to the concerns of women and minorities. She felt that the challenge would be exciting to work for."

Dole went to work for the Reagan administration, directing the transition team's human services' group in 1980. During the next two years, she headed the White House Office of Public Liaison, but never seemed to be in a position to press on the issues for which she had claimed the greatest empathy. Women's groups were disappointed. Eventually, "the White House began to realize that it had a serious problem with the gender gap," says *Vogue,* and in 1983, Dole was appointed to the Cabinet as secretary of transportation. In 1987, she again put her own career aside to help her husband in his second bid for the Republican presidential nomination.

Elizabeth Dole, known for her negotiating skills, was made secretary of labor in the new administration of George Bush in 1988—adding still another plum to her impressive resume. Her popularity remained high in most quarters; however, there was criticism throughout her tenure at both Transportation and Labor, says a 1991 *People* article, that "she produced more impressive-sounding press releases than results."

Dole has now moved on. In October 1990, she was named president of the American Red Cross, and quickly announced ambitious plans to streamline and revitalize the 110-year-old institution. She took no salary her first year (the job pays $200,000) because, she explained at the time, "I decided that the best way I can let volunteers know their importance is to be one of them—to earn the patches on my sleeve."

There is always speculation that Liddy Dole will appear on a Republican national ticket, but so far she remains committed to the Red Cross. She is often heard to say that she is not interested in running for public office, but she also says she has learned to "never say never."

MAJOR INFLUENCES

When Liddy Dole speaks of the forces that have motivated her, both personally and in public service, she always credits the influence of her family. She admits that, even now, she keeps her brother John "on a pedestal"—and together they agree that their mother has provided the support and shrewd advice that has directed them into productive lives. Mary Cathey Hanford, says Dole, "was not only there for me to lean on, but she worked to make leaning unnecessary." In addition to the enormous influence of her own mother, she also identifies with her maternal grandmother, Cora Alexander Cathey, who was "more than a role model....She lived her life for others."

MARRIAGE AND FAMILY

Elizabeth Hanford was married December 6, 1975, to Robert Joseph Dole, the senior senator from Kansas who now serves as minority leader of the United States Senate. Their wedding ceremony, which they say had to be "scheduled around the congressional calendar," took place in Bethlehem Chapel of the noted Washington Cathedral (more properly named the Cathedral of St. Peter and St. Paul.)

There are no children from this union, but Senator Dole has an adult daughter, Robin, from a previous marriage. Elizabeth and Robert Dole live in an apartment at the Watergate, the Washington complex that became famous in 1972, during the Nixon administration, as the site of the burglary of Democratic Party national headquarters.

Charismatic and extremely witty herself, Liddy Dole is credited for softening the "nasty edge" *[Newsweek]* of her husband's notoriously caustic humor. They are an interesting and devoted pair who say that they have learned not to take themselves too seriously.

HOBBIES AND OTHER INTERESTS

Committee meetings, traveling, and insanely long hours were leaving little time for Dole in her private life, so she has been trying to add balance. "I reached a point several years ago where I reassessed my priorities and decided that my life should not be built around my career, that there were other things that were important to me," she says. She takes time now to be more responsive to family, friends, and church work. She and her husband regularly attend Foundry Methodist Church in Washington, have brunch with friends, and make every effort to keep their overloaded work calendars from infringing on their Sundays together.

Liddy Dole likes to ski (both on water and snow) when time permits, and is said to be a fanatic about using the treadmill and exercycle she keeps at home.

WRITINGS

The Doles: Unlimited Partners (with Bob Dole and Richard Norton Smith), 1988

HONORS AND AWARDS

Arthur S. Fleming Award for Outstanding Government Service: 1972
One of America's Two Hundred Young Leaders *(Time)*: 1974
Esquire Woman of the Year: 1988
Humanitarian Award (National Committee Against Drunk Driving): 1988
Distinguished Alumni Award (Duke University): 1988
One of World's Ten Most Admired Women (Gallup Poll): 1988

FURTHER READING

BOOKS

Dole, Bob, and Elizabeth Dole (with Richard Norton Smith). *The Doles: Unlimited Partners*, 1988
Mulford, Carolyn. *Elizabeth Dole, Public Servant*, 1992 (juvenile)

PERIODICALS

Cosmopolitan, Jan. 1986, p.166
Insight, Oct. 28, 1991, p.20
McCall's, Apr. 1988, p.131
People, June 24, 1991, p.87
Saturday Evening Post, May/June 1990, p.44
Time, Mar. 21, 1988, p.22
Washington Monthly, Sept. 1987, p.29

ADDRESS

American Red Cross
17th and D Streets, N.W.
Washington, DC 20006

David Duke 1950-
American Politician
Former Grand Wizard of the Louisiana Ku Klux
Klan and Former Presidential Candidate

BIRTH

David Ernest Duke was born July 1, 1950, in Tulsa, Oklahoma, to David Hedger and Maxine Crick Duke. He was the second of their two children; his sister Dottie (now Dorothy Wilkerson) is five years older.

YOUTH

Duke's early life was unsettled. His father, a petroleum engineer for Shell Oil Company, moved the family throughout the Midwest, the South, and to the Netherlands for a brief period, before finally settling in New Orleans. By this time, Maxine Duke had become an alcoholic, which made her young son embarrassed and angry. He would not bring friends to the house, and reportedly once threatened to set his mother on fire unless she stopped drinking. Maxine Duke became so terrified of David that she often spent nights at her housekeeper's home.

In spite of this home life, Duke idolized his extremely strict father, although they later would be separated for David's teenage years while David, Sr., worked in Southeast Asia for the U.S. Agency for International Development. The senior Duke insisted on his children reading for three straight hours every day and writing a book report on what they had read—winter and summer. Dottie Duke Wilkerson told, in a 1992 television interview, that she rebelled, but David "just shone. He loved to read and it was just what he wanted to do." Duke now paints his childhood as idyllic, but researchers and biographers insist that it was troubled and possibly scarring.

EARLY MEMORIES

According to Duke, his life was changed at the age of fourteen when his teacher at an all-white Christian academy gave him an assignment to write an essay opposing racial integration. The book he read, *Race and Reason—A Yankee View,* by Carlton Putnam, argues that blacks are genetically less intelligent than whites and that integration would fail. "I couldn't put it down," he says.

EDUCATION

Duke attended early grade school in the Netherlands, then in both the city of New Orleans and suburban Metairie, where his family had moved to an all-white neighborhood. He also studied at the Clifton L. Ganus Christian School in New Orleans which was, at that time, all white. When his father went to Asia to work, Duke was enrolled at a military academy in Georgia, but returned to New Orleans and graduated from the John F. Kennedy High School. It was at Kennedy that he read and re-read Adolf Hitler's *Mein Kampf* and otherwise exhibited signs of having added anti-Semitism to his already formed racist beliefs. A former neighbor recalls that a Nazi flag hung on the wall of Duke's room.

In 1968, he enrolled at Louisiana State University (LSU). An average student, he formulated his racist views into a system of beliefs from which he has not strayed. He became known as a radical rightist through his bitter and abusive lecturing against blacks and Jews at LSU's open-air commons, known as "Free Speech Alley." Undeterred by jeering crowds, he declared himself a National Socialist in a 1969 speech. "You can call me a Nazi if you want to," he said then.

Duke majored in history and, although he interrupted his education to participate in activities of the National Socialist White People's Party, he graduated in 1974.

One incident from his college years is often mentioned today. Duke picketed an appearance at Tulane University by radical attorney William Kunstler—wearing a swastika armband and carrying a sign reading "Kunstler Is A Communist Jew." While Duke now dismisses the episode as a "college prank," he says that he learned then not to address audiences except in the tone they expected. Critics point to this as evidence that the former Klansman's conversion to more moderate politics is merely a false power grab and that Duke is as much a Nazi as ever.

MAJOR INFLUENCES

During his adolescence, when his father was so long away from home, Duke fell under the influence of James Lindsay, a local real estate developer. Lindsay, using the pseudonyms Jack Lawrence and Ed White, spread racist politics, admired Hitler, and was active in an organization called the Ku Klux Klan. The modern Klan, or KKK, was formed in Georgia in 1915 as a secret fraternal society whose aims were to maintain white supremacy, fundamentalism in religion, and militant patriotism. The original Klan, which dates from post-Civil War days, was a terrorist group that inflicted whippings and lynchings on blacks (and some sympathetic whites) who were moving into positions of equality and power. Klan members rode the countryside in strange disguises of hoods and flowing white sheets, posing as spirits of the Confederate dead. The Klan was banned by many states after the Second World War, but still functions in limited form.

During his teen years, Duke began devouring obscure literature that supported the cause of white supremacy and questioned the reality of the Nazi Holocaust against Jews, Poles, Russians, Gypsies, Communists, and gays. Duke still claims admiration for Nathan Bedford Forrest, who oversaw the establishment of the original Klan in 1865. He contrasts the founders of the society against the current "guys with green teeth" who have made the KKK synonymous with racial terror. Historians of the Reconstruction Era dispute that there ever existed a peaceful Klan dedicated to protecting the "Flower of Southern Womanhood."

FIRST JOBS

David Duke's only job before entering politics full-time was teaching in the Asian republic of Laos for six weeks during the Vietnam War, a position he reportedly obtained through the influence of his father. He has since claimed that he served heroically in the Vietnam conflict, but this civilian job was, in fact, his only contact with the war theater.

CHOOSING A CAREER

A year after completing college, Duke became Klan Grand Wizard of Louisiana, head of the state organization. He announced that he would lead the group to power through the ballot box and by admitting Catholics and women for the first time.

CAREER HIGHLIGHTS

Early in his career, Duke worked to increase the respectability of the former "secret empire" of the Klan, portraying it as a pro-white, rather than anti-black, organization. Yet at about the same time, he wrote a manual called *African Atto* (1973) under the pseudonym Mohammed X. Portraying himself as a black man teaching street fighting techniques, he was, in fact, collecting names of subscribers to compile a list of radical blacks for the Klan. In his political work, he began speaking about issues that appealed to the conservative middle class—issues such as busing, affirmative action, and illegal immigration. This political savvy allowed him to run twice as an independent, and as an open member of the Klan, for the Louisiana State Senate in the late 1970s, garnering a third of the vote each time.

Duke is accused of having Nazified the Klan during this same period, through his increased focus on anti-Semitism and his open admiration for Hitler, for whom he repeatedly had "birthday parties" well into the eighties. He also denied that the gas chambers in the concentration camps were used for mass executions, claiming that their primary purpose was the delousing of inmates. This view is widely denounced by scholars and historians, who offer documented proof that the Nazis exterminated millions of people. In addition, Duke was implicated (although never charged) in a planned coup against the government of Dominica, an island in the Caribbean, and later was videotaped selling secret Klan membership lists to a rival faction.

After resigning from the Klan in 1980 to form the National Association for the Advancement of White People, Duke fell out of the media spotlight. He concentrated on bringing the NAAWP into the modern era by casting it as a white civil rights movement and training its members in a leadership program based on the principals of "est," Werner Erhard's controversial personal development philosophy.

In the late 1980s, Duke returned to the public eye with a flurry. He ran for president in 1988, first as a Democrat and then with the extreme-right Populist Party. "If Jesse Jackson can speak for the Rainbow Coalition, why can't we of European descent have a Sunshine Coalition?" he asked. He received less than one percent of the vote, but people were again paying attention. When, running now as a Republican, Duke won a vacant seat in the Louisiana legislature, he was thrust again into the national spotlight.

In 1990, David Duke ran for the United States Senate against Bennett Johnston, the Democrat holding that office. Scorned by the Republican Party and largely dismissed by the press, he used his toned-down message to win forty-four percent of the vote. His ploys had set him up for his next, and closest, approach to major political power. The year 1991 brought Duke into full national prominence when he and former Governor Edwin Edwards both finished ahead of the incumbent Buddy Romer, leading the former Klansman and the scandal-ridden Democrat into a runoff for the post of governor of Louisiana. Duke was masterful in his national televised appearances, coming off as an unfairly scorned gentleman who only advocated what most of the white majority thought—that they had been unfairly discriminated against through job quotas and the welfare system. But he appeared to have reached his threshold. A majority of voters, even in conservative Louisiana, simply could not swallow Duke's purported transformation from an extremist to a more mainstream political figure. Edwards won with a comfortable margin.

Duke decided to run once again for the U.S. presidency, but his campaign was "rendered stillborn" in 1992 by the appearance of former presidential speech writer and newspaper columnist Patrick Buchanan. While he has also campaigned from an extreme right-wing, conservative platform, Buchanan has had no involvement in Klan or Nazi activities. Buchanan's views have led some to refer to him as "Duke without the baggage." Short of money and kept off the ballot in many states, David Duke officially withdrew from the race on April 22, 1992, stating "I know that my role in this presidential election is over." Duke has talked of taking a break from politics, but few doubt that he will be back. He hints that he may someday run for Congress.

MARRIAGE AND FAMILY

David Duke married Chloe Hardin of West Palm Beach, Florida, on September 9, 1972. Two daughters were born to them—Erika Lindsay (named after Duke's Klan mentor) in 1975; and Kristin Chloe in 1977. After several years of separation, the Dukes were legally divorced in 1986, and Chloe Hardin Duke is now married to Don Black, the former "Grand Dragon" of the Klan for the state of Alabama, and once a political confidant of her ex-husband.

HOBBIES AND OTHER INTERESTS

Duke enjoys his suburban home, reading (mostly political tracts), and films that many would expect him to denounce. In a recent candidate's survey, he chose the raw-edged and feminist *Thelma and Louise* as his current favorite.

WRITINGS

African Atto, 1973 [written under pseudonym Mohammed X]

FURTHER READING

BOOKS

Who's Who in American Politics 1991-92
Zatarain, Michael. *David Duke: Evolution of a Klansman*, 1990

PERIODICALS

American Spectator, Oct. 1990, p.16
Maclean's, Nov. 25, 1991, p.32
New York Times, Nov. 10, 1991, p.A1
People, Mar. 6, 1989, p.215
Times-Picayune (New Orleans), Nov. 3, 1991, p.A1
Vogue, Nov. 1991, p.280

ADDRESS

500 N. Arnoult
Metairie, LA 70001

Gloria Estefan 1958-
Hispanic-American Singer, Composer, and Dancer
Recording Artist Whose Hits Include
Cuts Both Ways and *Into the Light*

BIRTH

Gloria Estefan, the dynamic lead singer for the Miami Sound Machine, was born Gloria Maria Fajardo on September 1, 1958, in Havana, Cuba, to Jose Manuel and Gloria Fajardo. Her father was a motorcycle policeman whose job was to guard the wife of Fulgencio Batista, the former dictator of Cuba, who was ousted in the revolution of 1959 that brought Fidel Castro to power. The Fajardo family left Cuba and moved to Miami in the wake of Castro's victory. Gloria has one sister, Becky, who is five years younger.

YOUTH

In 1961, Jose Fajardo took part in the disastrous Bay of Pigs operation, a CIA-backed invasion of Cuba designed to overthrow Castro. He was captured and imprisoned for nearly two years in Cuba. Gloria and her mother lived in a small apartment behind Miami's Orange Bowl while her dad was in prison. With newspapers as bed sheets and supper cooked in tin cans, their life was one of deprivation and disappointment.

EARLY MEMORIES

Estefan recalls these early days with touching humor: "I remember a little birthday party I had when I was 5. I was real sad because my dad hadn't shown up. I knew where he was. But my mother kept telling me he was on the farm. So I would tell people, 'Don't tell my mom my dad's in prison. She thinks he's a farmer'."

When her father was released, he moved the family to Texas and joined the Army. He served in the Vietnam War, an experience that brought him home with a debilitating illness that affected his mind and body. It was finally diagnosed as multiple sclerosis. Gloria's mother contended that the slowly degenerating disease Jose Fajardo was suffering from was directly related to his exposure to Agent Orange. Agent Orange is a defoliant—a chemical weapon designed to destroy plant life—that was used in Vietnam and that has been linked to a number of illnesses suffered by Vietnam veterans. Gloria Fajardo fought the U.S. Government for a full pension and won, with the government acknowledging that her husband's condition was directly related to his service. With the proceeds, she sent Gloria to Our Lady of Lourdes, a Catholic high school.

EDUCATION

Gloria's years at Lourdes were shadowed by her father's illness. She was an A-student and a shy, withdrawn girl. She spent a great deal of her time caring for her father, while her mother, a former teacher, took courses that would allow her to teach in U.S. schools. Gloria helped out her mother by translating her papers from Spanish into English. "My mother leaned on me a lot and I thought I had to be strong for her. I was holding onto my emotions so much that I wouldn't cry. Instead I just sang." To escape from the sad atmosphere, Gloria would go to her room and sing and play the guitar. "Music was just my own thing, my personal thing that I loved. I would lock myself up in my room for two, three hours and sing to myself." When her father lost total control of his body, he was moved to a Veterans' Administration (V.A.) hospital, where Gloria would visit him every day to feed him dinner. He died in 1980.

After high school, Gloria studied psychology and communications at the University of Miami. She also worked for the Department of Immigration as a translator, and at that time, she planned a career in translation. She also taught guitar.

FIRST JOBS

It was Estefan's first job with a band called the Miami Latin Boys that determined her career. The head of the band was a fellow Cuban immigrant named Emilio Estefan, of mixed Cuban and Lebanese background, who came to the U.S. in 1967. He formed the Miami Latin Boys in 1974, while working as head of Hispanic marketing at Bacardi. Estefan knew he was breaking new ground with the addition of a female to the traditionally all-male Latin band, but the choice proved to be prophetic. The group, now renamed the Miami Sound Machine (MSM), was a hit. The original band, made up of Gloria, Emilio, Enrique "Kiki" Garcia, and Juan Marcos Avila, began recording in 1976, while Gloria was still in college. Their first record had one side in Spanish and one side in English. The Spanish song, "Rehacer," was #1 on Spanish radio stations in Miami for 16 weeks. The band toured Mexico, Central America, and South America, but were unknown outside of the Miami Hispanic community. "We would play for like 50,000 people in Lima and then we would come back to Miami and do a wedding," Estefan recalls.

MARRIAGE AND FAMILY

But there was more than a professional relationship going on between Gloria and Emilio. He often teased her that she could improve "95%," and her response was "so, you only like 5% of me?" They began to date and were married in 1978, the year she graduated summa cum laude from the University of Miami. A son, Nayib, was born in 1980.

CAREER HIGHLIGHTS

The year 1978 marked the release of the Miami Sound Machine's first album, and over the next several years, the band recorded four albums in Spanish. MSM's big break came in 1984 with the hit "Dr. Beat," from their first English-language album, *Eyes of Innocence*. The band had succeeded as a "crossover" group, appealing to an audience outside the Hispanic market. MSM's music is a combination of salsa, conga, and samba, with a driving beat that makes audiences want to get up and dance.

Their next big hit was "Conga," from the album *Primitive Love*, a recording that sold 2 million copies and made their name across the country. It also resulted in fans forming ever-longer conga lines wherever they performed. In Burlington, Iowa, 11,142 fans formed what's believed to be the world's longest conga line at an MSM concert. After the success of *Primitive Love*, a Miami-area street was renamed Miami Sound Machine Boulevard. Pepsi made a commercial using "Conga," and the music of MSM began to appear in such movies as *Top Gun* and *Three Men and a Baby*. *Primitive Love* also included a love ballad written by Gloria, "Words Get in the Way," which proved her ability as a songwriter and the band's ability to produce something besides dance tunes.

Gloria, who describes herself as a "shy and chubby" teenager, was gaining the reputation as a vibrant and attractive star. She began a rigorous weight control and exercise routine, training like a professional athlete to keep up with the demands of her performing schedule. The group began to make music videos, which continued to broaden their appeal.

In 1987 MSM released *Let It Loose,* which produced four Top 10 hits for the group, including "Anything for You," their first #1 hit. The album sold three million copies. In 1988, Emilio left the group as a performer to devote himself to writing and producing. The group now became known as "Gloria Estefan and the Miami Sound Machine," and their next album, *Cuts Both Ways,* featured Gloria, solo, on the cover. Gloria wrote seven of the 10 songs on the album, with two songs in Spanish. In recognition of her continuing success as a composer, Gloria was named BMI Songwriter of the Year in 1988.

In 1990, Gloria hosted the American Music Awards, and in March of that year, she was asked to visit the White House, where President George Bush talked with her about an anti-drug billboard campaign.

THE ACCIDENT

Shortly after her White House visit, Gloria and the MSM were traveling through a snowstorm in their customized tour bus on their way to Syracuse, New York, when they were involved in a horrible accident. They were struck from behind by a truck with such force that Gloria, who had been sleeping on a sofa in the bus, was thrown to the floor. "I remember lying on my back on the floor in excruciating pain," she recalls. "I had the strangest taste in my mouth, almost electrical, and I knew instantly I had broken my back." Her first thoughts were for Emilio and Nayib, but once she knew they were alright, the pain brought her back to her own condition, and to the fear uppermost in her mind: that she would be an invalid like her father.

After battling the snowstorm, a rescue squad reached the bus, and Gloria was strapped to a board and carried through a hole that used to be the windshield. When she reached the hospital in Scranton, Pennsylvania, the doctors confirmed her worst fears: she had broken a vertebra in her back and nearly severed her spinal cord. She was faced with two options: a body cast for six months, with little hope of recovery, or surgery, with the possibility of a return to 95-100% mobility, but also the risk of infection and permanent paralysis. She chose the surgery.

She was helicoptered to the Hospital for Joint Diseases in New York, where her surgeon, Dr. Michael Neuwirth, made a 14-inch incision in her back and inserted two 8-inch metal rods with hooks on either side of her broken vertebra. The operation was a total success, and Gloria Estefan began a painful road back to recovery.

Meanwhile, thousands of fans responded with love and concern for the star: "I received four thousand flower arrangements and more than forty-eight thousand cards," she said. "I distributed the flowers to other patients and the AIDS ward at the local V.A. hospital."

A rigorous physical therapy routine began, for six hours a day. "She was in pain so much of the time," remembers Emilio, "but she never complained. Not once." Her recovery has been rapid, but Gloria refused to perform until she was sure she was ready. "I wouldn't want to get back on that stage and be less than I was. I'm trying to even go beyond what I did before."

Her first post-accident appearance was on the American Music Awards in January 1991. She was dancing, singing, and ready to launch a new tour with a new album, aptly named *Into the Light*, and inspired by her recovery: "Coming out of the dark, I finally see the light now, It's shining on me. Coming out of the dark, I know the love that saved me."

MAJOR INFLUENCES

Estefan has named her husband, Emilio, as her personal hero. "We met when I was just out of high school. I was very, very shy and he was my first boyfriend. He always makes me think I can be better than I am."

ON BEING HISPANIC

Gloria Estefan continues to be an important role model for many Hispanics in the U.S. "Everywhere I go, it's not that people look at me as a Cuban, they look at me as an Hispanic. That's great. I do think it's necessary to be unified and help each other out."

RECORDINGS

Eyes of Innocence, 1984
Primitive Love, 1985
Let It Loose, 1987

Cuts Both Ways, 1989
Into the Light, 1991

HONORS AND AWARDS

Tokyo Music Festival: 1986, Grand Prize for "Conga"
American Music Award: 1988, Best Pop/Rock Group
BMI Songwriter of the Year: 1988
Lo Nuestro Latin Music Awards: 1990, Crossover Artist of the Year

FURTHER READING

BOOKS

Stefoff, Rebecca. *Gloria Estefan,* 1991
Who's Who among Hispanic Americans, 1991-92

PERIODICALS

Ladies Home Journal, Aug. 1990, p.100
Miami Herald, Oct. 18, 1987, pG1
Newsweek, Nov. 4, 1991, p.74
People, Oct. 27, 1986, p.77; Apr. 9, 1990, p.81; June 5, 1990, p.79
Rolling Stone, June 14, 1990, p.73
USA Today, July 10, 1989, p.D1

ADDRESS

Epic Records
P.O. Box 4450
New York, NY 10101

Mikhail Gorbachev   1931-
Russian Political Leader
Former President of the Soviet Union

BIRTH

Mikhail Sergeyevich Gorbachev (MEE-kile GAWR-buh-chawf) was born March 2, 1931, in Privolnoye, a village in the Russian Republic's Stavropol territory, to Sergei and Maria Panteleyevna (Gopkalo) Gorbachev. He has a younger brother, Aleksandr.

YOUTH

Descended from Ukrainian cossacks (free peasant-soldiers), Gorbachev, called "Misha" by his family, grew up in a collective farming community during the dictator Joseph Stalin's great purge of the 1930s. It was a time of brutal politics and total government control over production and distribution. Misha's paternal grandfather, Andrei, was one of the unfortunates whose name had appeared on Stalin's "list." He had been dragged away by secret police, for trumped-up reasons, and sentenced to nine years in the Gulag, which is the Soviet penal system.

Young Gorbachev grew up as a typical country boy of that time and place. He was ten years old when his father was called to army duty in World War II, after the Germans invaded the Soviet Union. The war years were extremely hard on the family. Gorbachev worked on the collective farm after school hours and during summer vacations. At one period, he had to drop out of school because there was no money for shoes. When his father learned of this, he wrote home from his army post instructing Misha's mother to sell whatever she could in order to buy shoes and send the boy to school. "He *must* study," he said.

Friends who remember Gorbachev as a youth say that he studied hard and was a boy of strong opinions—always ready for a lively argument. He often had "testy outbursts," but later learned to control his temper. Gail Sheehy, author of a Gorbachev biography, tells of how he took on manly responsibilities during his father's five years away from home. "Men twice his age would seek his views on war and domestic decisions," she writes, "and that must have helped develop in him the powerful self-assurance he shows today." No one recalls his ever having an interest in athletics, yet he kept fit as a result of long and tedious hours in the fields. Sergei Gorbachev returned to Privolnoye and his tractor station job at the war's end. The following year, Aleksandr, called "Sasha," was born, but the boys were so far apart in age, they never really shared the same experiences, nor did they become close. Aleksandr Gorbachev is now a mid-level official in the Ministry of Defense in Moscow.

EDUCATION

Gorbachev attended the village primary school, but had to walk ten miles every day to the town of Krasnogvardeiskoye for his secondary education. He rented a room away from home in the final year of school. About this time, he joined the youth organization Komsomol—his first step toward becoming a full member (in 1952) of the Communist Party. The young Gorbachev gained notice as a model student and worker, winning a coveted government award, the Order of the Red Banner of Labor. This honor made it possible for him to apply for entrance to the highly regarded Moscow State University. There, the ambitious young man from the country distinguished himself as a leader and a brilliant speaker and earned a law degree in 1955.

FIRST JOBS

After graduation Gorbachev returned to Stavropol, this time to the city itself, where he was assigned as Komsomol party organizer. His wife, Raisa, whom he had married while both were university students, took a teaching job. In 1963, Gorbachev became chief of the agricultural department for the Stavropol region and, to further his knowledge in that particular field, studied at night for five years to earn a diploma in agronomy (field crop production) from the Stavropol Agricultural Institute.

MAJOR INFLUENCES

Many people have made a difference in Gorbachev's life—some of them family members, some of them politicians with whom he associated during his rise in the government power structure. During Gorbachev's boyhood, he spent much of his time with his vigorous, outspoken mother and her parents. His paternal grandfather, Pantelei Yefimovich Gopkalo, was the chairman of the local collective farm and, as such, probably encouraged the boy's dedication to communism. Yet the independence of his other grandfather, who had refused to buckle under a repressive government, influenced him, too. It is felt that he learned early to stand up for his own beliefs, but to compromise when necessary. This may explain his complex character even today, and his understanding of the need for change.

Despite their importance, it is generally agreed that no single person has had more influence on him than has his wife. Bright and ambitious, she became his "good right hand," in a society that seldom recognized the contributions of women. From their earliest days together, she studied politics and economics, and became a sounding board for his theories and his plans to implement them. The research she did for her doctorate also helped to advance her husband's career.

MARRIAGE AND FAMILY

Mikhail Gorbachev has been married since 1954 to Raisa (rah-EE-sah) Maximovna Titorenko, a philosophy student whom he met at Moscow University. Born January 5, 1931, in Rubtsovsk, Siberia, she and her family later moved to the Rostov territory near Stavropol. The Gorbachevs have a daughter, Irina, a physician, who is married to a surgeon, Anatoli Viragovskaya. There are two granddaughters, Ksenia and Anastasia.

CAREER HIGHLIGHTS

Gorbachev's rise to power began in 1970 with his appointment as a deputy within the Supreme Soviet. Four years later, he became chairman of the Youth Commission and, in 1978, succeeded his patron, Fyodor Kulakov, as secretary of the Central Committee for Agriculture. Kulakov's death under suspicious circumstances was a blow to Gorbachev, but it turned out to be one of the forces that shaped his future.

In 1979, at the age of 48, Mikhail Gorbachev was made a nonvoting member of the Politburo (political bureau), the committee of party members in control of the government. The next year, he became the youngest member of that policy-making body. By now, in Moscow again, he and his wife had a more comfortable life; they were sent abroad on official business and were exposed to Western ideas and culture. During these years, Gorbachev began to build his reputation as a likable, charming politician. Soon he would "establish his style as a statesman—leadership through personal chemistry."

With the death of Leonid Brezhnev in 1982, Yuri Andropov became general secretary, and Gorbachev, whose career Andropov had furthered, was made second in command. Nevertheless, at Andropov's untimely death after only fifteen months in office, Gorbachev was considered too young to succeed him, and Konstantin Chernenko was chosen for the top post in the Soviet Union. The old and ailing Chernenko died a year later and, within hours, on March 11, 1985, Mikhail Gorbachev became general secretary. Sweeping reforms began, with *glasnost* (openness) and *perestroika* (restructuring), and the formation of a new Congress of People's Deputies. By 1989, Gorbachev was elected head of state, with the title Chairman of the Supreme Soviet.

New hope was born as Gorbachev started his nation on the road to reform and opened discussions that were aimed at world peace. He was awarded the Nobel Peace Prize in 1990, and it has been reported that he donated the cash prize (about $710,000) to a fund for the young victims of the 1986 nuclear accident at Chernobyl.

However, Gorbachev's leadership style, once considered decisive, proved ineffective against the inflation, unemployment, and civil disorder that overtook his country. Disapproval began to set in, although those at home were reluctant to speak out publicly. Even abroad, where he remained personally popular, there were serious concerns about domestic conditions in the Soviet Union and strong criticism of his handling of the Chernobyl disaster.

The people grew desperate about their overwhelming problems and, by mid-1990, his one-man rule began to slip away. Individual republics within the country called for independence. As the presidents of the republics worked with Gorbachev to create a new treaty calling for a looser union of states, hard-liners in the government responded. On August 18, 1991, Gorbachev and his family were held under house arrest at their summer home in the Crimea. The coup failed after four days when Soviet army troops refused to participate, and Gorbachev returned to Moscow. Boris Yeltsin, the popularly elected President of the Russian Republic of the Soviet Union, rose to national prominence during this time with his support of Gorbachev and his democratic and progressive ideas. Yeltsin, along with the leaders of the Soviet republics Ukraine and Byelorussia, announced the formation of the Commonwealth of Independent States and declared that the Soviet Union had ceased to exist. Shortly afterward, in the words of the *New York Times*, "Gorbachev, a president without a country, [announced] his resignation." As of this writing, the political future of Gorbachev and the Commonwealth of Independent States remains uncertain.

Author Gail Sheehy writes that the Soviet president, "whatever his ending, will surely take his place among giants. . . . Mikhail Gorbachev—the man who changed the world and lost his country."

HOBBIES AND OTHER INTERESTS

Gorbachev is said to enjoy classical music, poetry, and both the theater and the ballet. He reads world literature and history and, in his leisure hours, enjoys hiking.

WRITINGS

A Time for Peace, 1985
The Coming Century of Peace, 1986
Perestroika: New Thinking for Our Country and the World, 1987

HONORS AND AWARDS

Order of the Red Banner of Labor
Order of Lenin (three decorations)
Order of the October Revolution
Time Magazine "Man of the Year": 1987
Nobel Peace Prize: 1990

FURTHER READING

BOOKS

Butson, Thomas G. *Gorbachev: A Biography,* 1986
Medvedev, Zhores. *Gorbachev,* 1986

Oleksy, Walter. *Mikhail Gorbachev—A Leader for Soviet Change,* 1989 (juvenile)
Sheehy, Gail. *The Man Who Changed the World,* 1990
Time Magazine Editors. *Mikhail S. Gorbachev: An Intimate Biography,* 1988

PERIODICALS

Current Biography Yearbook 1985
New York Times, Dec. 9, 1991, p.A1; Dec. 26, 1991, Sec. A
Time, Jan. 4, 1988, p.18; Sept. 2, 1991, p.20

ADDRESS

Russian Embassy
1125 16th St.
Washington, DC 20036

Steffi Graf 1969-
German Professional Tennis Player
Ranked among the Top Players
in Women's Tennis

BIRTH

Stefanie Maria (Steffi) Graf was born June 14, 1969, in Mannheim, (West) Germany. Her parents are Peter and Heidi Graf, and she has a younger brother, Michael.

YOUTH

The little girl who was to become a world tennis champion was not yet four years old when she started begging to learn the game. Both of her parents were avid tennis players, and her father held first-place ranking at their club. Peter Graf cut down the handle of a small racket, strung up a makeshift net in the living room, and played small games of challenge with his earnest little daughter. Looking back now, the family realizes that Steffi had the makings of a champion even then. She swung so hard at the balls that she broke lights on the chandelier. Practice finally had to be moved to the game room downstairs, where ice cream and strawberries were offered as the reward for getting the ball over the net fifteen—and then twenty—times. Steffi Graf consumed a great deal of ice cream in those early days. Her father tells of giving tennis lessons to eight-year-olds who were not as good at the game as his child was at four. "She had more strength," he said in a magazine story a few years ago, "and always kept her eyes on the ball. Nothing distracted her. Even if the phone rang, she never looked away."

Moving from basement room to tennis court by the age of five, little Steffi progressed so quickly that she won her first junior tournament the next year in Munich. Her father soon sold his business interests in Mannheim and settled the family in the nearby town of Brühl, where he opened a tennis school and was able to spend more time helping his daughter develop her considerable talent.

EARLY MEMORIES

Graf's childhood years revolved around tennis, and there was no holding her back. She never tired of playing and although her father taught her technical skills and coached her carefully, the real drive came from within the girl herself. One story often repeated by her family tells of how she refused to go to a birthday party because it would interfere with her daily game of tennis. Only at her parents' insistence did she join the other children at the party.

EDUCATION

When she was only thirteen and in the eighth grade at Brühl's *Realschule,* Graf quit school to become a professional player. She traveled with a tutor for a couple of years, but did not complete the courses she would need to qualify for a diploma. She is an intelligent young woman and is known to read and appreciate Hemingway. Stephen King is also one of her favorites.

MAJOR INFLUENCES

No one has been more important to the young tennis star's success than her father. It was he who first recognized her extraordinary talent, who coached her and nurtured her skills, and who gave up his own interests to devote himself to her career. Pavel Slovil, former Davis Cup player for Czechoslovakia, is her hitting coach and practice partner, but Peter Graf plans her training regimen and manages her professional and business affairs. His attitude around tennis officials and the press often is arrogant and abrasive, and most people consider him to be a domineering parent. On one occasion, he was cited for illegal coaching from the stands (resulting in a penalty for his daughter), and for some time he was watched carefully so that he could not give secret signals during matches.

In spite of the overbearing image the father has carved for himself in the tennis world, he insists that it is she, not he, who is driven. "Normally I am very aggressive," he admits, "but I do not have to push Steffi. I am the one who tells her to slow down and relax. She is critical of herself." However, her steely will and her passion to win come directly from her father. A friend is quoted as saying, "The way Steffi is on the court, that is Peter everywhere else."

The family seems to have maintained a close and loving relationship in spite of a 1990 public scandal that implicated Peter Graf in a paternity suit and exposed his participation in a blackmail scheme to keep the accusation quiet. A blood test later cleared him of paternity charges, but tabloid reports of his extramarital affair took its toll on all the Grafs.

MARRIAGE AND FAMILY

Steffi Graf is unmarried and, at last report, there was no special romantic interest in her life. She and her parents live in adjoining houses in Boca Raton, Florida, part of every year, but their place in Germany remains their real home.

CAREER HIGHLIGHTS

Often described, even by competitors, as the best female tennis player ever, Graf was only fifteen when she reached the Wimbledon quarter-finals in 1984. That same year, she won the invitation tournament at the Los Angeles Olympic games. She continued her climb into the record books with numerous victories in 1986 and, in August 1987, the girl with the "devastating, cannonlike forehand and serve" reached the top women's ranking in the world. Until seventeen-year-old Monica Seles slipped ahead of her during a time of personal difficulties, Graf was the youngest person ever, male or female, to win the first spot.

In 1988, Steffi Graf won the "grand slam" of tennis, with victories in the Australian, French, All-England (Wimbledon), and United States championship tournaments. That year also brought her two Olympic medals—a gold for singles and a bronze for doubles. She continued her winning streak in 1989, capturing the championship in three of the four grand-slam events, and losing only in the finals of the French Open.

The Australian Open title was hers again in 1990, but sinus surgery and a painful thumb injury suffered in a skiing accident helped to keep Graf out of the winners' circle the rest of the year. Her family troubles added to her woes. However, there were other factors, too—namely, the rise of three other talented women's players: Monica Seles, Gabriela Sabatini, and tennis' newest sensation, fifteen-year-old Jennifer Capriati. Graf may have stumbled, but she continues to pursue her game of power and precision, and her goal to "play perfectly" has not been abandoned.

MEMORABLE EXPERIENCES

A young lifetime of championships and honors might make it difficult to say which moment is best remembered. Yet, Steffi Graf, in a *Tennis* magazine article last spring, tells of how she felt on August 17, 1987, when she defeated Chris Evert in the final of the Virginia Slims Tournament in Los Angeles to reach number-one ranking for the first time. "I'll never forget that feeling," she said. "I told my father, 'Now I should stop and start something different. This should be it.' But I never had that feeling again. Not even close."

HOBBIES AND OTHER INTERESTS

Popular music is a big part of Graf's private life. She checks out the rock-concert schedule in each of her tournament cities and goes to as many performances as she can fit in. Pavel Slovil says that since leaving the men's tour to coach her, "I have never heard so much music in my life." Graf is also a movie fan and has a real interest in motion pictures that were made before she was born. Photography and skiing are other special interests.

When Graf is at home in Brühl, she plays with Enzo and Max, her German shepherds, and Ben, the boxer.

HONORS AND AWARDS

German Sportswoman of the Year: 1986-88

Grand Slam of Tennis: 1988

Olympic Gold Medal (singles): 1988

Olympic Bronze Medal (doubles): 1988

Player of the Year (Women's International Tennis Association): 1988

Professional Sportswoman of the Year (International Women's Sports Association): 1988

FURTHER READING

BOOKS

Monroe, Judy. *Steffi Graf*, 1986 (juvenile)
Who's Who in Germany 1990
World Book Encyclopedia, 1991

PERIODICALS

Current Biography Yearbook 1989
People, June 9, 1986, p.49
Sports Illustrated, June 26, 1989, p.78; Sept. 26, 1990, p.42; Mar. 18, 1991, p.66
Tennis, Feb. 1990, p.46, 72

ADDRESS

Advantage International
Suite 450 East
1025 Thomas Jefferson St. NW
Washington, DC 20007

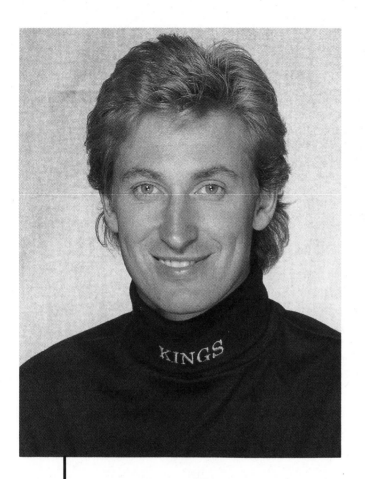

Wayne Gretzky   1961-
Canadian Professional Hockey Player
Member of the Los Angeles Kings Hockey Team

BIRTH

Wayne Gretzky was born January 28, 1961, in Brantford, Ontario, Canada, to Walter and Phyllis Gretzky. He is the eldest in a family of five children, which includes a sister, Kim, and brothers Keith, Glen, and Brent.

YOUTH

The man who is now a hockey superstar grew up in a small city of 75,000 that lies in southeastern Ontario. Brantford's other claims to fame are as an early home to Alexander Graham Bell, the inventor of the telephone, and as the headquarters for the Iroquois tribe of Six Nations. While young Gretzky showed talent in other sports, including baseball, his first love was always hockey. He learned to skate when he was two-and-a-half years old, and practiced constantly in his backyard, which his father flooded to turn into an ice rink each winter. Walter (Wally) Gretzky, himself a mediocre amateur player, became an extraordinary coach for his precocious little son. He taught Wayne his distinctive style of skating, which appears awkward but actually affords perfect balance: Gretzky leans forward, with his arms held away from his body. One piece of advice still stands out: "Skate to where the puck's going to be," his dad told him, "not to where it has been." Wayne Gretzky was to become hockey's best ever at anticipating the flow of the play.

At six, Gretzky began to play organized hockey, making the all-star team of a league for players up to the age of eleven. He next moved up to Ontario's Bantam League where he proved, at eight, to be one of the best in a league for fourteen-year-olds. When he was eleven, he scored 378 goals for the Brantford Nadrofsky Steelers. The most painful moment of his youth came when, at fourteen, he had become such a celebrity in his hometown that he was forced to move to Toronto for some sort of privacy. "It was just to try and escape all the unnecessary pressures specific parents lay on kids," he said later. "But the older in life I get, the more bitter I am. . . . I hate it now more than I did three years ago. . . . We just got to the point where it became uncomfortable being stared at."

EDUCATION

Gretzky attended public schools in Brantford, Toronto, and Canada's Sault Sainte Marie, completing his formal education in the latter city while playing there for the Junior A Greyhounds in 1977-78. He finished a few courses short of a high school diploma.

FIRST JOBS

When he was seventeen years old, Gretzky signed a contract with the Indiana Racers of the World Hockey Association (WHA). After playing only eight games, the financially troubled team sold his contract to Peter Pocklington, owner of the league's Edmonton Oilers, who were considered likely to be invited into the National Hockey League (NHL) when the WHA folded. "We feel that if we're going to be in the NHL," Pocklington said at the time, "we need a superstar. And Wayne is going to be one."

CHOOSING A CAREER

Gretzky embarked on his career in hockey earlier in life than virtually anyone in the sport's history. His father, a telephone technician, convinced him that the years of practice and sacrifice were a small price to pay for achieving stardom rather than spending his life in wage-labor. By the time the boy was six, few had any doubts about what his life's work would be.

CAREER HIGHLIGHTS

Wayne Gretzky burst upon professional hockey as a star. He was voted rookie of the year in the WHA's final season of 1978-79. The next year, he became the youngest NHL player ever to score fifty goals and 100 points (goals plus assists) in a season, and the youngest ever to be awarded the Hart Trophy as the league's most valuable player. He also received the Lady Byng Memorial Trophy for gentlemanly play. Gretzky led the league in assists with eighty-six to his credit.

His phenomenal success continues to the present day. The Hart Trophy went to Gretzky for a record eight consecutive years. He became the youngest player ever to score 300 goals, and the first ever to average more than two points per game in a season (1980-81). As a fine team player, he helped others to improve and led the Oilers to four consecutive Stanley Cups (NHL championships) between 1984 and 1988. He holds more than fifty NHL records, including career assists, career points, and single-season goals (92), assists (163), and total points (212).

While his numbers demonstrate his superiority, it is Gretzky's style of play that has astonished and fascinated observers. He is neither large nor especially fast, the two characteristics that usually predict success in the NHL. He does not engage in the roughhouse play that has been the league's black eye. What he can do is "see" the ice perhaps better than any player in history. "His greatness lies in the fact that he does things nobody else will," says former St. Louis Blues coach Red Berenson. "He has that second- and third-level depth perception of what is happening within the framework of the game....He has the ability to make poor players look great." Indeed, Gretzky often stands behind the opponents' goal, using it as a screen as he flips passes to his oncoming teammates. His ability to anticipate situations and positions has often led analysts to compare him to a chess master.

A crucial moment in Gretzky's career came in the summer of 1988, when he was traded (with his consent) to the Los Angeles Kings, then a struggling franchise. The deal sent shock waves throughout Canada, a proud nation that had revered Gretzky as one superstar who had not sought greener pastures south of the border. The costly deal, which Kings' owner Bruce McNall had expected to take years to show a profit, already has shown signs of running "in the black." The Kings now sell out almost every game and have turned from also-rans into one of the league's more competitive teams. Wayne Gretzky, known to hockey fans as "the Great One," is turning thirty-one, but shows few signs of slowing down.

His $31 million contract will expire at the end of the 1997-98 season, but most observers (including McNall) expect that he will continue playing beyond that point if he is still productive. His wife, Janet, supports that view. She said to a *Sports Illustrated* interviewer last year, "You know how a kid cries if his Little League game is rained out? That's Wayne. At 4:30 on game day, he starts to sweat a little bit, and he can't wait to go. There is never a time that he dreaded going to a hockey game." Gretzky says that his one remaining ambition is to win another Stanley Cup.

MAJOR INFLUENCES

Although his father was his first and most significant coach, Gretzky's boyhood idol was hall-of-famer Gordie Howe, who played twenty-six seasons between 1946 and 1980, and who holds the all-time goal scoring record (801) for the NHL. Gretzky has mixed feelings about breaking that record, the only significant one that he does not yet own. "I wish I could stop at 800," he said last season. Wishes aside, he probably will score goal number 802 by 1993.

On a personal note, Gretzky speaks of both his parents' lasting influence on his life. He pays touching tribute to his father in *Gretzky: An Autobiography,* the book he wrote last year with Rick Reilly of *Sports Illustrated,* saying, "You taught me to be fair, to do the right thing, to respect people and, most of all, to be a man. Not that it was tough to learn. All I had to do was watch."

Wally Gretzky underwent brain surgery in October 1991, and the worry about his father's illness has affected the son's play so far this season. In a recent *Detroit News* story, he is quoted as saying that he can't remember ever playing so poorly, but is making a special effort to put personal concerns out of his mind while he is on the ice. Father and son have remained unusually close throughout Gretzky's career.

MARRIAGE AND FAMILY

In a ceremony described at the time as "Canada's Royal Wedding," Gretzky married American actress Janet Jones in Edmonton, Ontario, on July 16, 1988. Hundreds of guests, security people, and newspaper and television reporters were in attendance, and ten thousand fans waited outside St. Jasper's Cathedral to get a glimpse of the wedding party. The Gretzkys now live in Beverly Glen, California, with their two children—Paulina Mary Jean, who is three years old, and Ty Robert, one-and-a-half.

MEMORABLE EXPERIENCES

Gretzky is thoughtful and courteous, but also famous for keeping his feelings and his personal life extremely private. Yet, one special memory he openly shares with his fans. In his autobiography, he speaks of holding the Stanley Cup for the first time and how, as a kid, he had watched all the great players "pick up that cup. . . .I must have rehearsed how I would do it ten thousand times. And when it came true on that May night in 1984, it was like an electric jolt up my spine."

No less a cherished memory for Gretzky is remembering Janet as she approached the altar on their wedding day. "It was one of the most stunning moments of my life," he writes in his book. "When I looked back and saw this beautiful woman, really radiant, really incredible. . . .But more than just how she looked, I realized that I was marrying someone I could spend this lifetime with, and about nine others past that."

HOBBIES AND OTHER INTERESTS

Wayne Gretzky owns fourteen thoroughbred horses with McNall. He had a remarkable run of luck in 1990 when the stable won two of world racing's most prestigious events, the Arlington Million and the Prix de l'Arc de Triomphe, within one month.

WRITINGS

Gretzky: An Autobiography (with Rick Reilly), 1990

HONORS AND AWARDS

World Hockey Association Rookie of the Year: 1979
NHL Lady Byng Memorial Trophy for Gentlemanly Play: 1980
NHL Hart Trophy for Most Valuable Player: 1980-87
NHL All-Star Team: 1980-90
NHL Art Ross Trophy: 1981-90
Sportsman of the Year, *Sports Illustrated:* 1982
NHL Lester B. Pearson Award: 1982-87
NHL Conn Smythe Award: 1985-86

FURTHER READING

BOOKS

Encyclopedia Brittanica, 1991
Gretzky, Wayne, and Rick Reilly. *Gretzky: An Autobiography,* 1990
Raber, Tom. *Wayne Gretzky: Hockey Great,* 1991
World Book Encyclopedia, 1991

PERIODICALS:

Current Biography Yearbook 1982
Sports Illustrated, Jan. 28, 1991, p.36
U.S. News & World Report, Nov. 5, 1990, p.18

ADDRESS

Los Angeles Kings
3900 West Manchester Blvd.
The Forum
Inglewood, CA 90306

* UPDATE *

Wayne Gretzky announced in September 1992 that he would be out of the game of hockey indefinitely because of a back injury. He is suffering from a severely herniated disk, and whether surgery or therapy will correct the condition and allow Gretzky to return to the game is not known.

Matt Groening   1954-
American Writer and Cartoonist
Creator and Co-Executive Producer of the
Television Series "The Simpsons" and Creator
of the Comic Strip "Life in Hell"

BIRTH

Matt Groening (Matthew Groening—rhymes with raining) was
born on February 15, 1954, in Portland, Oregon, to Homer Philip
and Margaret Ruth (Wiggum) Groening. He is the third of five
children. The family lived in a neighborhood located between the
new and the former Portland Zoo, where he and his friends often
played in the abandoned animal caves and pools.

YOUTH

Groening grew up in a household where creativity and individuality were encouraged. Much of that came from his father, whom Groening has called "the hippest dad in the neighborhood." As he once explained, "My dad is a cartoonist, film maker and writer who has lived by his wits. By example, he showed that you could do whatever you wanted to do in life—that a certificate didn't matter and that you could do creative stuff."

EARLY MEMORIES

Throughout his youth, Groening demonstrated a disdain for conforming and authority. While his parents were supportive, his teachers often were not: he was routinely sent to the principal's office. "I revolted against my school, my teachers and various administrators, because it was impossible to revolt against my perfect parents—who were very supportive; they thought the teachers were idiots, too. I got in trouble in school for drawing cartoons. Yeah, they used to get confiscated. In fact, one of the great thrills of my life is that I now get paid for doing what I used to get sent to the principal's office for. So, anyway, I spent many, many long hours in the principal's office staring at the ceiling and counting the little dots in the tiles. And at a very early age, I decided I had to somehow make this time that was being wasted pay off. And so I wrote about it. I kept a diary, and I eventually turned part of it into a series of comic strips, and then I wrote a book called *School Is Hell*. If I had known that I was really gonna do it—go off and be a cartoonist who got to write a book called *School Is Hell*—I would have been a much happier kid. In fact, to this day, I get a thrill when kids write to me and say they wore a SCHOOL IS HELL T-shirt to class and got kicked out. I say, "All right, I'm still annoying those teachers!"

EDUCATION

Groening attended Evergreen State College in Olympia, Washington, a progressive school that had no tests, grades, or required courses. The unstructured atmosphere suited Groening. While there he worked as a cartoonist on the student newspaper, where he became friends with fellow cartoonist Lynda Barry, known for her "Ernie Pook's Comeek" as well as several novels and plays. Groening received his bachelor's degree from Evergreen State in 1977.

CHOOSING A CAREER

Groening didn't set out to become a cartoonist. Instead, he moved south to Los Angeles in 1977 after graduating from Evergreen, hoping to become a writer. As he once explained, "My goal in life was to be a writer, and [Barry's] was to be a fine artist. We did cartooning as this other thing and neither of us expected it to be part of how we paid the rent." In Los Angeles he worked at a succession of odd jobs—ghostwriting the autobiography of an aging Hollywood director, landscaping a sewage treatment plant, and working at a record store. He was often unemployed, and he was miserable. Rather than write complaining letters to all his old friends about life in Los Angeles, Groening created a comic book. Called "Life in Hell," it featured a rabbit named Binky who was constantly angry at the world. Groening started out by sending copies of his comic books to his friends, and then began selling them for $2.00 each from the record store where he worked. In 1979 he began working for the new alternative weekly *Los Angeles Reader* as the circulation manager, a job that actually entailed delivering the magazine to its readers. He later began writing for the magazine and continued to work there until 1985. His comic "Life in Hell" appeared in the magazine for the first time in 1980. According to Groening, "I had no idea I was going to make cartooning a career. I was doing it merely to assuage my profound sense of self-pity at being stuck in this scummy little apartment in Hollywood."

MARRIAGE AND FAMILY

Groening met his future wife, Deborah Caplan, while they were both working on the *Los Angeles Reader,* he in the editorial department and she in advertising. They jointly quit in 1985 to set up the offices of Life in Hell, Inc., which distributes the comic strip to newspapers and markets related merchandise. Groening has often praised Caplan's business sense and credits her with much of his success. Groening and Caplan were married in 1986. They and their two children, Homer and Abraham, live in California.

CAREER HIGHLIGHTS

Groening's first creative success, "Life in Hell," features Binky, who evolved from being constantly angry to constantly victimized, his girlfriend Sheba, their illegitimate one-eared son Bongo, and two identical entrepreneurs, Akbar and Jeff, who always wear fezzes and Charlie Brown striped shirts. Unlike many conventional comic strips, "Life in Hell" usually deals with such important subjects as childhood, education, work, love, and sex. While the strip is often funny it is also disturbing, filled with disappointment, mockery, cruelty, and betrayal. The drawings appear quite simple— Groening chose rabbits for his characters because they were easy to draw—but the language is sharp and incisive. "I'm not so much interested in the visual aspect of it," Groening has said. "What's important to me are the ideas embodied in the cartoon. I'm much more interested in words." The strip currently appears in about 200 alternative newspapers and has been collected in several best-selling books, including *Work Is Hell, Love Is Hell, Childhood Is Hell, School Is Hell,* and others.

One fan of "Life in Hell" was James L. Brooks, who had helped create the hit television shows "Taxi" and "The Mary Tyler Moore Show" and the movies *Terms of Endearment* and *Broadcast News*. As producer of "The Tracey Ullman Show," Brooks asked Groening to create some short cartoons to show between comedy skits. The fifteen- to twenty-second spots were so successful that Groening was hired to create a new animated prime-time television show. Since its debut in January 1990, "The Simpsons" has become wildly popular. The show depicts a family of appealing but misfit characters: Homer, the father, dim-witted and ineffectual; Marge, the mother, best known for her towering blue beehive hairdo; Bart, the star of the show, who is always in trouble, especially at school; Lisa, the younger sister, the smart and soulful sax player; and Maggie, the baby, seen always with her pacifier.

"The Simpsons" owes its popularity to several factors. It depicts events and people from a kid's, rather than an adult's, point of view. Consistently irreverent and anti-authority, the show pokes fun at teachers, other educators, parents, and bosses. As Groening explains it, "[Bart] has latched onto a secret that kids respect. *The entire world of grown-ups is corrupt and stupid.*" Many adults have objected to the show because of such attitudes. Some schools initially banned Simpsons items, especially Bart T-shirts announcing UNDERACHIEVER AND PROUD OF IT! Groening responded with typical aplomb: "I have no comment, other than my

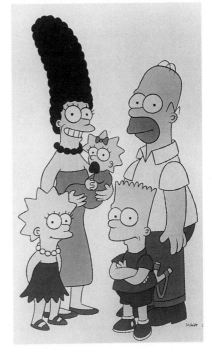

folks taught me to respect elementary-school principals, even the ones who have nothing better to do than tell kids what to wear. Is it possible that grade-school principals have lost their sense of humor?" More recently, Groening remarked: "I think in a world of *Friday the 13th* and Megadeth T-shirts, Bart Simpson fun wear is a little mild. Kids are smarter than a lot of adults give them credit for. I feel sorry for authority figures who are troubled by kids having fun."

MAJOR INFLUENCES

Groening acknowledges that his works have been influenced by several writers and comic artists: Dr. Seuss, Walt Kelly (creator of "Pogo"), Charles Schulz (creator of "Peanuts"),

Mad Magazine, and the underground comic artist R. Crumb.

WRITINGS

Love Is Hell, 1985
Work Is Hell, 1986
School Is Hell, 1987
Childhood Is Hell, 1988
Akbar and Jeff's Guide to Life, 1989
Big Book of Hell, 1990
Greetings from the Simpsons, 1990
Postcards That Ate My Brain, 1990
The Simpsons' Rainy Day Fun Book, 1990
The Simpsons' Xmas Book, 1991
With Love from Hell: A Postcard Book, 1991

HONORS AND AWARDS

Emmy Award: 1991, for best animated series "The Simpsons"

FURTHER READING

PERIODICALS

Current Biography Yearbook 1990
Mother Jones, Dec. 1989, p.28
Newsweek, Sept. 28, 1987, p.70; Apr. 23, 1990, p.58
People, Dec. 18, 1989, p.108
Rolling Stone, Sept. 22, 1988, p.81; June 28, 1990, p.41

ADDRESS

Fox Broadcasting Company
P.O. Box 900
Beverly Hills, CA 90213

OBITUARY

Alex Haley   1921-1992
American Writer and Lecturer
Author of *Roots*

BIRTH

Alexander Palmer Haley was born in Ithaca, New York, on August 11, 1921. His father, Simon Alexander Haley, was a student at Cornell University at the time of his birth, and his mother, Bertha George (Palmer) Haley, was a teacher. Haley had two younger brothers, George and Julius.

YOUTH

Haley spent his early years with his maternal grandparents, Will and Cynthia Palmer, in the town of Henning, Tennessee, while

169

his father finished his degree. Both of Haley's parents put a great emphasis on education: his mother was the first person in his family to go to college, and his father worked his way through undergraduate school in grinding poverty while studying agriculture. The sacrifices his parents made in the pursuit of education were a major influence on the young Haley. He often referred to an incident in his father's life that changed the course of the family's fortunes. While working as a porter on a railroad one summer, his father met a white man, R.S.M. Boyce, who was so impressed with Simon Haley and his aspirations that when the young man returned to school, he found that Boyce had paid his tuition in full. This allowed Simon to concentrate on his studies and to earn entrance to Cornell University, where he completed a graduate degree. He later became a professor at Alabama A & M University. Of Boyce's generosity, Haley said: "Instead of being raised on a sharecrop farm, we grew up in a home with educated parents, shelves full of books, and with pride in ourselves."

EARLY MEMORIES

While his father completed his degree at Cornell, Haley grew up in the atmosphere that would prove to be the greatest influence on his life and career. His grandmother and his great aunts loved to tell the young boy the stories of his ancestors, whom they were able to trace back to one they called "The African," a man named "Kintay," who had been brought to this country as a slave at the end of the eighteenth century. Haley remembered the power and the pleasure of this experience: "There, in the summer early evenings, my. . .grandmother and her sisters, my great aunts, used to sit in their rocking chairs on the front porch, dipping their Sett Garrett snuff and 'skeeting' its amber fluid in little shots at the lightning bugs all around the white-blooming honeysuckle vines. Night after night, they'd reminisce about our family members who had been slaves in somewhere called Alamance County, North Carolina, and then were freed by the Civil War and came in a wagon train led by grandma's grandpa."

EDUCATION

Despite his love of reading and history and his parent's expectations, Haley was never much of a student. He graduated from high school at 15 and went on to Elizabeth City Teachers College in North Carolina. Much to his father's dismay, he continued his rather lackadaisical ways and dropped out of college after two years.

FIRST JOBS

At his father's urging, Haley joined the Coast Guard in 1939, where he remained for 20 years. His first experience as a writer came from composing love letters for his fellow sailors, for which he charged $1.00 each. He began to submit articles to magazines, and after collecting a great pile of rejection slips, began to see his articles published. When he left the Coast Guard in 1959, he was at the level of chief journalist, a rank created for him.

CHOOSING A CAREER

After his discharge, Haley decided to try to make his living as a writer. The assignments were few and far between, and in another often-told piece of his personal history, Haley related how he found himself "down to 18 cents and two cans of sardines when a friend called with the offer of a job in the civil service. I turned him down." Then a writing job came his way that allowed him to continue in his chosen career, but Haley kept the sardine cans and framed them. They still hung on the wall of his home in Tennessee at the time of his death.

In 1962, Haley conducted a long discussion with jazz giant Miles Davis, which was published as the first *Playboy* interview, now a major feature in the magazine. This led to additional interview assignments for the magazine, in which Haley questioned such famous (and infamous) people as Martin Luther King, Jr., Johnny Carson, the American Nazi leader George Lincoln Rockwell, and Malcolm X.

CAREER HIGHLIGHTS

The interview with Malcolm X led to Haley's first major work, *The Autobiography of Malcolm X* (1965), which has sold six million copies to date. The book is currently in the news again because film director Spike Lee is preparing a movie on the life of Malcolm X, the powerful black political leader and spokesman for the Nation of Islam. The manuscript was completed just before Malcolm X's assassination in February 1965. Haley felt that the book "represents the best I could put down on paper of what Malcolm said about his own life from his own mouth. I'm glad the book exists because otherwise Malcolm would be a pile of apocryphal and self-serving stories."

But it was *Roots* (1976) that brought Haley fame and fortune and changed the way that African-Americans viewed themselves and their ancestry. In the mid-1960s, inspired by the stories his grandmother and great aunts had told him, Haley began a 12-year search into his past that began at the National Archives in Washington and led him around the world, to the village of Juffure, in Gambia, West Africa. He went to Gambia to find the *griot*, or oral historian, whom he hoped could give him more information on the history of his family, especially the background of "Kintay"—spelled "Kinte." In Haley's words, the *griots* were "almost living archives, men trained from boyhood to memorize, preserve, and recite—on ceremonial occasions—the centuries-old histories of villages, of clans, of families, of great kings, holy men and heroes." In the retelling of the Kinte family history, the *griot* came to the point at which Haley's personal history and his African heritage came together. The griot told how the eldest son of Omoro and Binta Kinte, Kunta, "went away from this village to chop wood—and he was never seen again."

Haley felt "as if I were carved out of rock. What that old man in back-country Africa had just uttered dovetailed with the very words my grandmother had always spoken during my boyhood on a porch in Tennessee, telling a story she had heard from her father, Tom, who had heard it from his father, George, who had heard it from his mother, Kizzy, who had been told by her father, the man who had called himself Kintay: that he had been out, not far from his village, chopping wood, intending to make himself a drum, when he had been set upon by four men and kidnapped into slavery."

The revelation in the village in Gambia was the culmination of 6,500 hours of research for Haley, during which he had consulted over 1,000 records in over 50 libraries. This quest he transformed into *Roots*. The work relates seven generations of Haley's family, from the birth of Kunta Kinte to the present generation. *Roots* was referred to by the author as "faction," a combination of fact and fiction in which historical events are given a fictional cast to heighten the narrative effect. It begins with the story of Kunta, brought to the United States in horrifying conditions aboard a slave ship bound for Annapolis, Maryland, where he is sold to a Virginia slave owner. He is renamed Toby, a name he refuses to accept. Caught trying to escape, Kunta is punished by having a part of his foot cut off. He proves to be the inspiration of the Kinte clan, and he raises his children to take pride in their African heritage, to treasure and preserve it. Kunta's legacy is passed on to later generations, spanning the nineteenth and the twentieth centuries, the Civil War and the movement of the family to Alabama and Tennessee, where Haley first heard the family story from his grandmother.

Roots proved to be a phenomenon in American publishing and television history. The book was published in 1976 and received both the Pulitzer Prize and a special National Book Award, since, according to the judges for that award, it did not fall into the realm of either fiction or history. The hardback edition has sold six million copies, and millions more have been sold in paperback editions. The work has been translated into 37 languages.

But it was the television adaptation of *Roots* that truly brought Haley to the attention of the American public. Broadcast in January 1977, the work was one of the first mini-series ever produced for television, in part because network executives did not believe there would be a broad audience for a show about blacks that spanned several weeks. How wrong they were! The eight episodes of *Roots* were seen by more than 130 million people, making it one of the top-rated television shows of all time. It won more than 145 awards, including 9 Emmys.

But *Roots* inspired controversy as well as praise. Two lawsuits were filed against Haley claiming copyright infringement—that Haley had used the words of another author without permission in his novel. One suit was dismissed, and one was settled out of court. The work was also the center of critical controversy as commentators debated whether the work, admittedly a blend of fact and fiction, was based on research or creativity. Overall, however, *Roots* is regarded as a tremendously important work that inspired people, both black and white, to learn about their past and to be proud of their heritage. People all over the world were motivated to do what Haley had done: to examine the genealogical records of births, marriages, and deaths to trace their ancestry.

Haley became a favorite on the lecture circuit: "One calendar year, I spent 226 nights in motels," he claimed. In his warm and conversational style he combined the influence of both his grandmother and the *griot*, relating to his audiences the inspiring story of his own search for "roots." Haley was certainly surprised by his success. "Do you know what it's like to go from the YMCA to the Waldorf? If I'd known I'd be this successful, I would have typed faster."

But the life of a lecturer did not leave much time for writing, and when the demands of his schedule proved to be too much, Haley would book passage on a freighter and spend months at sea, writing. "At sea," he said, "I will work from 10 at night until daybreak. Then comes that magic moment when you start to dream about what you are writing, and you know that you are really into it."

Two subsequent television series continued the story of the Kinte clan: *Roots: The Next Generation*, which aired in 1979 to great audience response, and *Roots: The Gift*, which appeared in December 1988.

Haley never again published a work with the impact of *Roots*. Only one book appeared before his death, *A Different Kind of Christmas*, which depicts the escape of a slave through the Underground Railroad. When Haley died in Seattle, Washington, on February 10, 1992, he was working on two books. One was a tribute to the people of Henning, Tennessee, where he had grown up and where his family home is now a state historic site. The other was an examination of his father's side of the family and of his white ancestors. Tentatively titled "Queenie," the work explores the life of his grandmother, Queen Haley, who was born on a plantation near Florence, Alabama. "Her father was the master and her mother a mulatto weaver," said Haley. "She was raised as the servant of her half-sisters.

She was what they called 'a child of the plantation'. " As Juan Williams reported in the *Washington Post,* Haley's idea "was that this next book would take America beyond *Roots* by breaking down what he called the artificial lines that too many conclude are walls." Haley, according to Williams, "clearly saw it as the final message to emerge from his lifetime of listening to stories and collecting secrets. America is poorer for having missed that message."

MARRIAGE AND FAMILY

Haley married three times. He and his first wife, Nannie Branch, were married in 1941 and had two children, Lydia Ann and William Alexander. They divorced in 1964. He married Juliette Collins in 1964, and the couple had one child, Cynthia Gertrude. The second marriage also ended in divorce, in 1972. Haley married Myra Lewis in 1974, a researcher who had been his assistant at the time of the publication of *Roots.* They were separated at the time of his death. He had four grandchildren. Haley is survived by his two brothers, George, who is a lawyer, and Julius, an architect.

WRITINGS

The Autobiography of Malcolm X, 1965 [with Malcolm X]
Roots: The Saga of an American Family, 1976
A Different Kind of Christmas, 1988

HONORS AND AWARDS

Emmy Awards (Nine): 1977, for "Roots"
National Book Award: 1977, for *Roots* [special citation]
Pulitzer Prize: 1977, for *Roots*
Springarn Medal (NAACP): 1977

FURTHER READING

PERIODICALS

DAR Magazine, Aug.-Sept. 1984, p.460
Essence, Feb. 1992, p.88
Los Angeles Times, Feb. 12, 1992, p.A1, p.F9
New York Times, Feb. 11, 1992, p.C19
People, Oct. 18, 1976, p.84; Dec. 12, 1988, p.126
Reader's Digest, Feb. 1991, p.55
Washington Post, Feb. 11, 1992, p.A1, E1; Feb. 16, 1992, p.C2

Hammer   1963-
American Rap Singer, Musician, Dancer
Recording Artist Whose Works Include *Please
Hammer Don't Hurt 'Em* and *Too Legit To Quit*

BIRTH

Hammer (formerly known as M.C. Hammer) was born Stanley Kirk
Burrell in East Oakland, California, on March 30, 1963. He was the
youngest of seven children. His father was the manager of a legal
gambling club, while his mother worked at a variety of jobs. They
were divorced when Hammer was five, and he was raised primarily
by his mother. "We were definitely poor," Hammer has said.
"Welfare. Government-aided apartment building. Three bedrooms
and six children living together at one time." East Oakland was "a
very tough area," according to Hammer: "Of the fifteen guys I hung
with on my block ten of them went to San Quentin."

YOUTH

As a child, Hammer enjoyed writing poetry, making up his own commercials, and singing and dancing. He was still very young when he began performing for his family. "I saw James Brown's appearance on TV when I was three or four years old and sort of emulated it. I did the whole routine of 'Please, Please, Please,' falling to the ground and crawling while my brother took a sheet and put it over my back as a cape."

Yet Hammer's first love was baseball. His brothers worked for the Oakland Athletics, and he often went to see them play. One day, when he was about eleven, he was in the parking lot of the Oakland Coliseum doing imitations of James Brown. The Athletics' owner, Charlie Finley, happened to see him. Finley was so impressed with his performance that he invited Hammer to join him in the owner's box. Hammer spent seven years with the Athletics, traveling with the team when he wasn't in school. He worked as a batboy and ran errands in the front office. At one point Finley named him Executive Vice-President and paid him $7.50 per game to provide play-by-play commentary on the telephone whenever Finley couldn't attend a game. Hammer received his nickname while with the Athletics, from a ballplayer who noticed his resemblance to the famed hitter "Hammerin' Hank" Aaron. For many years he used the name "M.C. Hammer," for Master of Ceremonies, although he recently dropped the initials M.C.

EDUCATION

In 1981, Hammer graduated from high school and left the Athletics. He decided to attend college, hoping to complete a communications degree and to prepare for a major league baseball career. He was unsuccessful at both. He tried out for the San Francisco Giants but was unable to make the team, and he dropped out of college. He soon returned to East Oakland.

FIRST JOBS

Back at home and out of work, Hammer had few prospects for a job. He briefly thought about becoming a neighborhood drug dealer. "Everyone who had any pocket change had it because they were dealing a little drugs. I was thinking about doing that, though I never touched the stuff. My father woke me up one day so disappointed I knew he wanted to cry. 'Son, I hear you're dealing drugs now.' I said, 'Daddy, I ain't dealing no drugs, you know I wouldn't do that.' But I sat up in bed and thought about how I had lived a clean life, a positive life, and suddenly there I was, considering being reduced to no more than the average drug dealer. I went to the nearest recruiting office, got all fifty questions on the test right, and joined the Navy." Hammer spent most of his time in the Navy in California, except for six months in Japan.

MARRIAGE AND FAMILY

Hammer and his wife, Stephanie, have one young daughter, Akeiba Monique. Hammer guards their privacy very carefully and allows little information about his family to be released to the public.

CHOOSING A CAREER

Hammer got his start in music in Oakland. After he left the Navy, he began checking out the local music scene. He also began seriously studying the Bible. His new-found interest in religion led him to become, in his own words, a "gospel rapper, the Holy Ghost Boy," in the local clubs. This marked the beginning of his rap career. He soon persuaded two ballplayers from the Athletics to invest $20,000 each, and he formed his own record company, Bustin' Records, in about 1987. He sold his first single, "Ring 'Em," out of the trunk of his car. It eventually reached number one in the Oakland/San Francisco area.

CAREER HIGHLIGHTS

Hammer began assembling a "posse," including dancers, backup singers, disc jockeys, and bodyguards. They worked out strenuously, practicing their routines twelve to fourteen hours per day. They soon recorded Hammer's first album, *Feel My Power*. After a talent scout from Capitol Records saw him perform at a local club, the record company signed him to a multi-album contract and gave him a $750,000 advance. They also re-released his first album in 1988, changing the title to *Let's Get It Started*, reworking one song, and adding four new songs. The new release sold over one-and-a-half million copies.

Hammer and his posse began touring throughout the United States, appearing in shows with other rap groups. After spending part of his advance from Capitol Records on $50,000 worth of equipment for the back of the tour bus, he used his time on the road to record his next album. *Please Hammer Don't Hurt 'Em*, released in 1989, went on to become the biggest-selling rap album of all time. It has sold over fifteen million copies and brought Hammer to national attention. He released a new album, *Too Legit to Quit*, in late 1991.

Hammer has toured extensively since the release of *Please Hammer Don't Hurt 'Em*, appearing in concert in 250 cities in the United States and throughout the world. His stage show is much more elaborate than most rap acts. The performances are fast-moving and intense, featuring over 30 singers, dancers, and musicians, tight choreography, flashy spandex costumes, and Hammer's trademark "genie" pants.

Despite his success, he has received criticism on several fronts. He was sued by the two baseball players who loaned him money to start his own record company; they claimed that he failed to repay them. There have been complaints from former members of his entourage who felt that the practice schedules were too demanding, the rules were too rigid, and the discipline was too strict. In addition, some critics say that his rhymes are simplistic and that he lifts too much material from other songs. Still, his nonsexist and nonviolent lyrics, his anti-drug and anti-gang message, his exuberant performances, and his fun and funky music have earned him millions of fans.

MAJOR INFLUENCES

Hammer has said that his music and performances have been influenced by his musical heroes, James Brown, George Clinton, The Jacksons, Earth, Wind & Fire, and Prince.

HOBBIES AND OTHER INTERESTS

The success of *Please Hammer Don't Hurt 'Em* has allowed Hammer to move into other areas. He has acted in an hour-long video and an upcoming movie and has been involved in the production of a new half-hour television cartoon, "Hammerman," which is loosely based on his life. He has also been hired to appear in television commercials for several different companies, including Pepsi-Cola and British Knights tennis shoes. In addition, Hammer will begin producing albums for artists in his entourage.

RECORDINGS

"Ring 'Em," 1987 [date uncertain]
Feel My Power, 1987; re-released as *Let's Get It Started,* 1988
Please Hammer Don't Hurt 'Em, 1989
Too Legit to Quit, 1991

HONORS AND AWARDS

MTV Video Music Award: 1990, for best rap video, best dance video "U Can't Touch This"
American Music Award: 1990, for *Let's Get It Started* as favorite album, rap favorite new artist; 1991, for *Please Hammer Don't Hurt 'Em* as favorite album, soul/rhythm and blues favorite album, soul/rhythm and blues favorite single "U Can't Touch This," rap favorite artist, soul/rhythm and blues favorite male vocalist
Grammy Award: 1990, for best rap solo, best video—long form *Please Hammer Don't Hurt 'Em,* best rhythm and blues song "U Can't Touch This"
Soul Train Music Award: 1990, Sammy Davis, Jr. Award for Oustanding Achievement in Music and Entertainment; 1991, for best rap album, best rhythm and blues/urban contemporary song "U Can't Touch This"
People's Choice Award: 1991, for favorite male musical performer

FURTHER READING

PERIODICALS

Current Biography, Apr. 1991
Ebony, Dec., 1990, p.40
Jet, Sept. 17, 1990, p.54; Feb. 18, 1991, p.59
Newsweek, Dec. 3, 1990, p.68
People, Aug. 6, 1990, p.59
Rolling Stone, July 12, 1990, p.29; Sept. 6, 1990, p.49
Time, Aug. 13, 1990, p.73

ADDRESS

Capitol Records
1750 North Vine
Hollywood, CA 90213

AUTOBIOGRAPHY

Martin Handford   1956-
English Author and Illustrator
Creator of *Where's Waldo?* Series

BIRTH

I was born in London on September 27, 1956, an only child. My earliest memories are probably the ones we all have of playing with my toys. My favorites were my Teddy Bear, of course, my own toy train set, and the very many plastic toy figures which I arranged into crowds and armies.

YOUTH

I grew up in Hampstead, a very pleasant part of north London.

My passions were watching TV (especially anything funny), going on walks around the area and noting all the different people, and visiting the local cinema to watch swashbuckling adventure films such as: *The Vikings, The Adventures of Robin Hood, El Cid, Zulu,* and my all time favorite—*The Alamo.* I would rush back home and spend hours drawing incidents from these films in great detail.

EDUCATION

My first recollection of school was a hutch which contained the school pets—guinea pigs. I loved caring for them and assumed the responsibility of being their friend! It was the start of my long-term commitment to animals.

History lessons were my favorite, especially in primary school. It was here that my passion for nineteenth century American History was ignited. However, secondary school was not as enjoyable, and I worked more and more on my special interests at home to supplement anything I felt I was missing at school. Art college came as a release, and I throughly enjoyed both the studies and the social life. I received a Bachelor of Arts degree in illustration from Maidstone College of Art.

FIRST JOBS

My first job was as an insurance clerk. I was a very gregarious teenager and this was the ideal occupation for me at the time. I was able to meet people and feel part of a company which respected the job I was doing. Although the insurance job is a far cry from the illustrations I am known for now, I feel it was a very happy time which enabled me to make decisions concerning my future with more confidence later on.

CHOOSING A CAREER

My choice of a career was a natural progression. I had always drawn in much the same way you see now. I had gained some very favorable notice over the years and so it was something I always hoped I could spend all of my time doing. I started drawing single pictures. The books were an obvious and very happy development giving me a huge audience for my work which I appreciate very much.

MEMORABLE EXPERIENCES

My favorite book as a child and one which I still think of daily (though sadly I can not now find a copy) was *The Golden History of the World* illustrated by Cornelius Witt. In 1990, I received a letter and a painting from Cornelius who had read of my esteem for his wonderful pictures. It was a wonderful moment—25 years after first seeing his work to be in touch with such an inspiring artist.

181

FAVORITE BOOKS

Apart from the above, I love all illustrated history books, especially those which pay great attention to military costumes and period detail. I look at as many comics as possible and particularly like the educational magazines of the sixties and early seventies.

HOBBIES AND OTHER INTERESTS

Obviously drawing remains my true passion. But I also love pop music, history, collecting toy soldiers, movies, books, comics, animals, and trivia of all kinds. Favorite groups: The Clash, The Bee Gees (it is still my dream to be in a band!). Favorite TV show: "Sergeant Bilko." Favorite animal: Labrador. Favorite time of day: night (when I work and watch TV and listen to tapes). Favorite holiday resort: home—I don't like to travel very much. My ambition is to produce lots more Waldo books and keep Waldo fans happy.

WRITINGS

Where's Waldo?, 1987
Find Waldo Now, 1988
The Great Waldo Search, 1989
Waldo: The Ultimate Fun Book, 1990
Where's Waldo? The Magnificent Poster Book, 1991

HONORS AND AWARDS

I have received various illustration awards over the years but I feel that the greatest honor I received is the vast quantity of fan mail from my fans around the world. It is the best part of what I do and I can't thank them enough.

FURTHER READING

PERIODICALS

Chicago Tribune, May 3, 1990, V,p.1
Newsweek, Aug. 13, 1990, p.50
New York Times, Jan. 18, 1990, p.C1
People, Nov. 11, 1991, p.89

ADDRESS

Where's Waldo?
8255 Beverly Blvd.
Los Angeles, CA 90048

Stephen W. Hawking   1942-
British Theoretical Physicist and Mathematician
One of the World's Foremost Cosmologists and
Author of *A Brief History of Time*

BIRTH

Stephen William Hawking was born in Oxford, England, on January 8, 1942, exactly three hundred years to the day after the death of Galileo. His parents, Frank and Isobel Hawking, had recently lived in London. But with the German bombing of London during World War II, they decided to move back to Oxford, where they had both attended school, when Isobel was pregnant with Stephen. His father was a doctor and medical researcher at Oxford's National Institute for Medical Research, eventually becoming the head of the Department of Parasitology.

He specialized in tropical illnesses and was frequently away on research trips to Africa. Stephen was the oldest child in the family, with two sisters, Mary and Philippa, and a brother, Edward.

YOUTH

After the war, the Hawking family lived in London for a few years before moving in 1950 to St. Albans, a small cathedral city north of London. An intellectual family, they valued education and good books highly. At the age of eleven, Hawking entered St. Albans School, a British public secondary school (what would be called a private school in the United States), which his parents hoped would prepare him for Oxford University. He was unhappy at school, unpopular with his classmates, and unskilled at athletics. He was also, at that time, an undistinguished student. Although he had a good intuitive grasp of scientific and mathematical concepts, he did little schoolwork and received only fair grades.

Then and now, the British educational system requires students to pick a field of specialization in their early teens. Hawking was most interested in mathematics, which worried his father, who hoped that he would go into medicine. "I reacted against my father to the extent that I did not go into medicine. I felt that biology and medicine were too descriptive, not exact enough. Had I known about molecular biology I might have felt differently. I wanted to specialize just in mathematics and physics, and my father was very unhappy about that, because he did not think there would be any jobs for mathematicians." The younger Hawking acquiesced and chose to concentrate on chemistry, physics, and a little math. Yet he rarely studied, and received poor grades. His parents were concerned, but needlessly: he scored near perfect marks on the physics part of the entrance examination and was accepted at Oxford University, one of the oldest and most prestigious universities in England.

EDUCATION

Hawking entered University College at Oxford in 1959. Initially he was bored and lonely, with little interest in his studies and no friends. Soon, though, he joined his college's rowing team as coxswain, the person who steers. He became very popular, known for his long hair, interest in classical music and science fiction, and keen wit. He has described the prevailing attitude among his fellow students as "very antiwork." According to Hawking, "At Oxford, you were supposed to be brilliant without effort or to accept your limitations and get a fourth-class degree. To work hard to get a better class of degree was regarded as the mark of a gray man, the worst epithet in the Oxford vocabulary." Hawking fit in perfectly with this attitude. Yet he was "completely different from his contemporaries," according to his physics tutor (or professor), Robert Berman. "Undergraduate physics was simply not a challenge for him. He could do any problem put before him without even trying." In 1962, Hawking received his B.A. with a first, or highest honors.

Hawking then went to Cambridge University to study cosmology, a branch of theoretical physics that investigates the origin and structure of the universe. At about the same time, though, he began to have trouble, on occasion, with tying his shoelaces and speaking, and even fell a few times for no apparent reason. After many tests, the problem was diagnosed in early 1963 as amyotrophic lateral sclerosis (ALS), or motor neuron disease; it is also known as Lou Gehrig's disease, after the New York Yankees' first baseman who died from it. A fatal illness, ALS gradually destroys the nerve cells in the spinal cord and brain that control muscular activity. Early symptoms include difficulty walking, trembling hands, and trouble with speech and swallowing. Over time, as nerve cells deteriorate, the muscles they control atrophy and cease to function. The disease is painless, though, and the brain functions normally throughout. Usually, the muscles that control breathing eventually fail, and death comes for most within just a few years.

When first diagnosed, Hawking didn't expect to live long. His immediate reaction was depression. He spent most of his time in his room, listening to classical music, primarily Richard Wagner, reading science fiction, "drinking a fair amount," and ignoring his studies. According to Hawking, "The doctors offered no cure or assurance that it would not get worse. At first, the disease seemed to progress fairly rapidly. There did not seem to be much point in working on my research because I didn't expect to live long enough to finish my Ph.D." After about two years, though, the progression of the disease stabilized. At about the same time, he became engaged to Jane Wilde, whom he had met in 1963. He has often credited his engagement with changing his life, saying that it motivated him to finish his degree so he could support his future wife. As he has said, "When you are faced with the possibility of an early death, it makes one realize that life is worth living and that there are lots of things you want to do." He returned, with enthusiasm, to his doctoral research, and received his Ph.D. from Cambridge University in 1966.

CHOOSING A CAREER

Hawking decided very early in life what kind of work he planned to do: "From the age of twelve, I had wanted to be a scientist. And cosmology seemed the most fundamental science." Considering the limitations imposed by ALS, the choice has proven to be a good one. In cosmology, Hawking can do all the work in his head; in addition, he isn't required to lecture, which his current speech disability would have ruled out.

CAREER HIGHLIGHTS

Hawking's serious intellectual and theoretical work began while doing his doctoral research at Cambridge. He became intrigued by the work of another physicist, Roger Penrose, on singularities and black holes. Physicists had been speculating for years about black holes. They believed that these theoretical objects could be created if a massive star were to collapse in on itself. Its intense gravity would cause it to shrink to a point of infinitely dense matter, which would prevent any light or other matter from escaping from the surrounding space. Penrose helped to show how a singularity, an infinitely small point of infinite density, could exist at the center of the black hole.

Collaborating with Penrose, Hawking took the idea one step further. He applied the idea of a singularity to the Big Bang theory, the belief by physicists that the universe was created by an explosion in the distant past—perhaps fifteen billion years ago—and continues to expand to this day. In his doctoral dissertation, Hawking took Penrose's conclusions about individual black holes and applied them to the universe as a whole. He also applied Penrose's ideas in reverse, going back through space and time to find a singularity at the creation of the universe. By hypothesizing that the universe had been created from a singularity, Hawking and Penrose's work lent support to the Big Bang theory and to the idea that there had been a specific beginning of time. Their work culminated in a general theorem of singularities in 1970.

Hawking's work to date had all rested on Albert Einstein's general theory of relativity, a set of laws of physics that prescribe the behavior of gravity on a very large scale. But Hawking's theories soon ran into trouble as he began to look at very small black holes. For these he turned to the laws of quantum mechanics, a branch of physics that describes the behavior of objects on a very small scale—at the subatomic level. The accepted theory, as predicted by relativity, held that the strong gravitational field of black holes prevented any matter from being emitted from them. Yet when Hawking applied quantum theory to minuscule black holes, he determined that they could emit particles—which have since become known as Hawking radiation. This discovery contradicted all that Hawking, as well as other scientists, believed about black holes. While it was almost universally challenged when published in 1974, this view has come to be accepted by most physicists.

In the ensuing years, Hawking has been working to reconcile these contradictions. His goal is what has been called Grand Unification, a single, broad theory that would encompass both relativity and quantum mechanics and that would describe the interactions of all matter. Such a theory might also explain the creation of the universe. Even Einstein spent years trying, without success, to develop a unified theory; and many consider it the most difficult problem facing scientists today.

Developing a unified theory would be a tremendous achievement, of course, but "only the first step," according to Hawking. "My goal is a complete understanding of the universe, why it is as it is and why it exists at all." Just as important, for Hawking, is to share that understanding with as wide an audience as possible, including nonscientists. That is why he wrote *A Brief History of Time* (1988), in which he reviews the history of different theories on cosmology, from Aristotle to Einstein, and describes his own work, including the Grand Unification theory. In his introduction, Hawking described his intent: "Where did the universe come from? How and why did it begin? Will it come to an end, and if so, how? These are questions that are of interest to us all. But modern science has become so technical that only a very small number of specialists are able to master the mathematics used to describe them. Yet the basic ideas about the origin and fate of the universe can be stated without mathematics in a form that people without a scientific education can understand. This is what I have attempted to do in this book. The reader must judge whether I have succeeded." Readers responded with a resounding yes. *A Brief History of Time* spent over a year on the *New York Times* bestseller list and achieved surprisingly strong sales for a science book. Most reviewers seemed to enjoy it too, praising the clear and succinct treatment of the difficult subject matter and the brief but enjoyable glimpses at the personality of its author.

COPING WITH DISABILITY

Hawking has managed to accomplish all this despite the deteriorating physical condition caused by ALS. According to Hawking, "If you are disabled physically, you cannot afford to be disabled psychologically"— and many people marvel at the wit and good humor that he brings to his difficult life. He is only able to control the muscles for two fingers on his left hand, which he uses to control his motorized wheelchair. He lost the ability to speak in 1985, when he had to have a tracheostomy—surgery to provide an opening in the neck to allow breathing—following a bout with pneumonia. Since then, he communicates by using a computerized speech synthesizer mounted on his wheelchair. He is able to create sentences from pre-selected words that appear on a video screen, which are then "spoken" by the computer. It is a slow and laborious process. He is attended by nurses and graduate students, who take care of his personal needs and assist him with his work. With their help he is able to get around surprisingly well, navigating his motorized wheelchair from his home to his office at Cambridge and traveling widely to lecture and participate in scientific conferences. While many people marvel at what he has been able to accomplish despite his physical limitations, Hawking consistently downplays that aspect and refocuses attention on his ideas. As he told an audience at the University of Southern California, "I would like to be thought of as a scientist who just happens to be disabled, rather than as a disabled scientist."

Hawking uses a unique method for his work. Theoretical physicists use complicated mathematical equations to try to describe the behavior of objects in the physical universe. Most develop ideas, then test them by performing the derivations that either prove or disprove their theories. Yet for Hawking, unable to write without assistance, this type of work is phenomenally difficult. He has compensated, though, by developing his own approach: "I tend to avoid equations as much as possible. I simply can't manage very complicated equations, so I have developed geometrical ways of thinking, instead. I choose to concentrate on problems that can be given a geometrical, diagrammatic interpretation. . . .Often I work in collaboration with someone else, and that is a great help, because they can do all the equations." According to the astronomer William Press, what is crucial to theoretical physics is "key overview ideas—great organizational principles, from which the details can follow. And then, of course, working out those details, ultimately to compare them with experiment, with reality—that involves technique and calculation and so forth. That's what Stephen leaves, by both necessity and choice, to his collaborators, and Stephen is the one who tries to come up with the great ideas that make these calculations possible. His track record on that is not just superb. It makes him one of the great physicists of our age."

MARRIAGE AND FAMILY

Hawking first met his future wife at a party in January 1963, just before he was diagnosed with ALS. Jane Wilde was soon to graduate from St. Albans and was planning to attend college in London in the fall to study languages. Their courtship extended over two years, as they visited between London and Cambridge, before they became engaged. According to Hawking, "The engagement changed my life. It gave me something to live for. It made me determined to live. Without the help that Jane has given I would not have been able to carry on, nor have had the will to do so." They were married in July 1965. They have three children: Robert, born in 1967; Lucy, born in 1970; and Timothy, born in 1979. After 25 years of marriage, Hawking left his wife to live with his nurse, Elaine Mason, in 1990. Stephen and Jane Hawking remain separated.

WRITINGS

The Large Scale Structure of Space-Time, 1973 [with G.F.R. Ellis]
General Relativity: An Einstein Centenary Survey, 1979 [editor, with Werner
   Israel]
Is the End in Sight for Theoretical Physics? An Inaugural Lecture, 1980
Superspace and Supergravity, 1981 [editor, with M. Rocek]
The Very Early Universe, 1983 [editor, with G.W. Gibbons and S.T.C. Siklos]
Supersymmetry and Its Applications: Superstrings, Anomalies, and Supergravity,
   1986 [editor, with G.W. Gibbons and P.K. Townsend]

Three Hundred Years of Gravitation, 1987 [editor, with Werner Israel]
A Brief History of Time: From the Big Bang to Black Holes, 1988
Hawking has also written and edited many articles for scientific journals.

HONORS AND AWARDS

Eddington Medal (Royal Astronomical Society, United Kingdom): 1975
Pius XI Gold Medal (Medaglia d'Oro Pio XI, Pontifical Academy of
    Sciences, Vatican City): 1975, "for research concerning black holes"
Hughes Medal: 1976
Maxwell Medal (Institute of Physics): 1976
Albert Einstein Award for Theoretical Physics: 1978
Albert Einstein Medal: 1979
Franklin Medal (Franklin Institute): 1981, "for his revolutionary
    contributions to the theory of general relativity, astrophysics and
    cosmology, and to the dynamics, thermodynamics and gravitational
    effects of black holes"
Commander of the British Empire: 1982
Royal Astronomical Society Gold Medal (Royal Astronomical Society,
    United Kingdom): 1985
Paul Dirac Medal and Prize (American Institute of Physics): 1987
Wolf Foundation Prizes—Physics—with Roger Penrose (Wolf Foundation,
    Israel): 1988, "for their brilliant development of the theory of general
    relativity, in which they have elucidated the physics of black holes"

FURTHER READING

BOOKS

Boslough, John. *Stephen Hawking's Universe: An Introduction to the Most
    Remarkable Scientist of Our Time,* 1984
Contemporary Authors, Vol. 129
Ferguson, Kitty. *Stephen Hawking: Quest for a Theory of the Universe,* 1991
Hawking, Stephen. *A Brief History of Time: From the Big Bang to Black Holes,*
    1988
Simon, Sheridan. *Stephen Hawking: Unlocking the Universe,* 1991 (juvenile)
White, Michael, and John Gribbon. *Stephen Hawking: A Life in Science,* 1992
Who's Who 1992

PERIODICALS

Current Biography Yearbook 1984
Newsweek, June 13, 1988, p.56
New Yorker, June 6, 1988, p.117
New York Times Book Review, Apr. 3, 1988, p.10
New York Times Magazine, Jan. 23, 1983, p.16
Science '81, Nov. 1981, p.66
Time, Feb. 8, 1988, p.58

ADDRESS

5 West Road
Cambridge, England 351905

Hulk Hogan   1953-
American Professional Wrestler

BIRTH

Hulk Hogan was born Terry Jean Bollea in Augusta, Georgia, on August 11, 1953, to Peter and Ruth Bollea. He has an older half brother, Kenneth Wheeler, a retired Air Force colonel; another brother, Allan Bollea, is deceased.

YOUTH

Professional wrestling's lovable giant weighed in at ten pounds, seven ounces at birth and, by the age of twelve, had beefed up to nearly two hundred pounds. He and his family moved to Tampa when he was three, and it was in that northern Florida city that he spent his growing-up years, playing baseball and getting acquainted with the rock music he has loved all his life. Bollea was a star pitcher on Little League and Pony League championship teams until an injury to his right arm ended his participation in that sport when he was fourteen. He turned to guitar and weight lifting and played junior high school football, but his mother's fears that he would be hurt again convinced him to drop that team sport, too. He did, however, become an outstanding bowler during those early years, winning a Tampa junior bowling doubles championship with his friend Vic Petit.

At about this same time, Bollea got mixed up in some street fights, and he was packed off to a session at the Florida Sheriffs' Boys Ranch, where unruly kids were given ample doses of discipline and guidance. There, he became a born-again Christian and, according to a profile in *People,* "emerged headed for the straight and narrow."

Bollea discovered wrestling in high school. As he had always done with any activity that truly interested him, he trained and eventually became obsessed with the sport. Long afterward, he said that he had always dreamed of being a wrestler. But, having watched television in the 1950s and 1960s, he no doubt had in mind the showmanship of professional wrestling more than the ancient sport that was popular in the earliest Olympic games nearly three thousand years ago. Modern professional wrestling is "good theater," explains the book, *Center Stage: Hulk Hogan.* "The wrestlers know who will win before the match begins. They follow a script written by the promoters." The fans don't mind; they love the action and enjoy a sport without too many rules. It's entertainment and business.

EDUCATION

Bollea graduated from Tampa's Robinson High School in 1971. He continued his education at Hillsborough Community College before enrolling at the University of South Florida, where he studied business and music.

FIRST JOBS

Big and strong, and heavily muscled from daily workouts, Bollea left college behind him and turned to the kind of work that often attracts men of his brawn. He took a job as a stevedore, loading and unloading the commercial boats on Florida's docks. Still, his music was not forgotten— he played bass guitar in bands in bars and small clubs, in addition to his daytime job, until a pair of Tampa wrestling promoters, Jack and Jerry Brisco, lured him into the training ring in 1973.

CAREER HIGHLIGHTS

Bollea toured around the "boondocks circuit," earning little more than pocket money for a few years, then moved to Venice Beach, California

191

(known as "Muscle Beach" for the hunks and would-be athletes who hang out there). He began training with onetime wrestler Freddie Blassie and appeared under the names Terry Boulder and Sterling Golden—the latter probably for his silvery blond hair that he kept tied back with a bandanna. He then moved on to the big time, where he acquired a new ring name from the late Vince McMahon, Sr., head of the World Wrestling Federation (WWF), who dubbed him "Hulk" after the TV character, The Incredible Hulk, and "Hogan" for what he said would be Bollea's "Irish" persona. A twist on the new name made him known also as the Hulkster.

It was largely through the marketing skills of Vince McMahon, Jr., a rock concert promoter who succeeded his father in the WWF post, that Hogan became the phenomenon that he is today. Michael Weber, WWF media coordinator at that time, explained in a *Maclean's* story that "Hulk had all the right charisma and the body build...and he and Vince had the right chemistry to put it all together." Hogan became the "good guy" in the ring. Against the blare of rock music, he and the other wrestlers made the showbiz sport fashionable again. The tanned, good-looking Hogan was billed as singer Cyndi Lauper's bodyguard—a move that beefed up the audience of old-time wrestling fans with hordes of rock and roll enthusiasts. These days eight million fans attend WWF contests, not counting the hundreds of thousands who watch the syndicated shows on TV. The Hulkster's personal income from television and arena performances, endorsements, and the sale of products bearing his name is now estimated at between $5 and $10 million a year.

Earlier in his career, Hogan appeared in the films *Rocky III* and *Gremlins II*, and also was seen in the wrestling movie *No Holds Barred*. In 1991, he won a lead role in *Suburban Commando*, an action comedy.

The widespread use of steroids among wrestlers and other athletes has become a serious issue in the past few years, and the WWF was in the news, although not charged, in the mid-1991 trial of a Pennsylvania physician, Dr. George Zahorian III, who had been distributing these drugs to help wrestlers build body mass. Several wrestlers testified about the damage done to their bodies, but Hogan was excused from appearing on the stand. Former wrestling champion Terry Funk was quoted in *Sports Illustrated* as saying that "McMahon [head of the WWF] has made a lot of guys very rich, but he may also be taking years off their lives." Neither the wrestlers nor the WWF were included in the indictment because of a technicality—the sale of steroids was legal until February 1991—but Dr. Zahorian was convicted for dispensing steroids and painkillers for "nontherapeutic" purposes.

Hogan insists that he is careful of what goes into his massive body, telling a *People* interviewer recently that he "briefly used steroids [only] when under a physician's care for injuries."

MARRIAGE AND FAMILY

Home for Hogan is a large, expensive, and traditional two-story house on the Intracoastal Waterway, near Clearwater, Florida. He and his wife, Linda, have two children—daughter Brooke, four years old, and son Nicholas, two. The little blond kids call their daddy "Hulk."

HOBBIES AND OTHER INTERESTS

The affable "Hulkster," who lives a public life surrounded by hype, is generous in the personal time he gives to the Make-A-Wish Foundation. There is no self-promotion in the numerous visits he makes every week to sick and dying children. Friends say that inside that massive body is "a really nice guy with a heart of gold, who has always had a soft spot for kids."

Hogan is more than a superhero to a generation of "Hulkamaniacs" (mostly boys, but some girls too), who are glued to their TV sets for his syndicated shows, who scramble for tickets to his arena shows, and who beg for the Hulk Hogan figures and other toys and gimmicks that have brought millions of dollars to him and to the WWF. By all accounts, his interests lie in being a role model, too. Those who know the real Terry Bollea insist that he is sincere in his warnings against drugs, alcohol, and tobacco. He encourages his young fans to take vitamins, drink milk—and say their prayers.

HONORS AND AWARDS

Gold Belt: WWF World Championship, three-time winner

FURTHER READING

BOOKS

Humber, Larry. *All About Hulk Hogan,* 1991 (juvenile)
Sanford, William, and Carl Green. *Center Stage: Hulk Hogan,* 1986 (juvenile)

PERIODICALS

Maclean's, May 19, 1986, p.34
People, Oct. 14, 1991, p.61
Sports Illustrated, July 8, 1991, p.9

ADDRESS

World Wrestling Federation
P.O. Box 3857
Stamford, CT 06902

Saddam Hussein   1937-
Iraqi President
Commander in Chief of the Armed Forces

BIRTH

Saddam Hussein al-Tikriti was born to peasant parents April 28, 1937, in al-Auja, a village close to the Sunni Muslim town of Tikrit, Iraq, about 100 miles north of Baghdad. His father, Hussein al-Majid, is believed to have died either before, or within a few months after, the child's birth, although it has been suggested that he abandoned his family. Hussein has three half-brothers— Barzan, Sawabi, and Watban Ibrahim—sons of his mother, Subha Talfah (al-Majid), and Ibrahim Hassan, her second husband. The confusion over the names that follow Arab tradition are explained in *Instant Empire: Saddam Hussein's Ambition for Iraq*, by Simon

194

Henderson: sons take the father's given name as their last name and, in Saddam's case, al-Takriti (meaning from Takrit) is his own choice of family designation. Others who use al-Takriti are not necessarily related to him or to one another.

YOUTH

The man who rules Iraq today lived in harsh poverty as a child. There was neither electricity nor water supply in the windowless, single-story house where he spent his earliest years. Worse than the lack of comforts, though, was the abusive treatment he suffered at the hands of his crude, illiterate stepfather, who forced him to steal chickens and sheep for resale, and who tried to deny him a chance to go to school.

Saddam (he still prefers to be called by his given name alone) was ten years old when he finally started school, learning to read and write a full four years behind the town children of Tikrit. He was encouraged in his desire for an education by his maternal relatives, a family of higher social class than that of either his natural father or his stepfather.

EARLY MEMORIES

Information on Saddam's boyhood is sketchy, and often contradictory. But, in *Saddam Hussein and the Crisis in the Gulf,* authors Judith Miller and Laurie Mylroie reveal that in his adult years "Saddam would bitterly recall how his stepfather would drag him out of bed at dawn," screaming at him to get up and look after the sheep. Ibrahim fought over him with Subha (Saddam's mother), grumbling, "He is the son of a dog. I don't want him."

EDUCATION

The first years of Saddam's schooling were in the Tigris River town of Tikrit—a long walk every day for a young boy. When he later moved to Baghdad to live with his mother's brother, Khairallah Talfah, an Arab nationalist and former army officer, he studied at the al-Kharkh Secondary School. However, he spent more of his time as a political activist than as a student.

After being involved in an assassination attempt on Iraq's military dictator, Abdul Karim Kassem (Qassem, in Arabic), Saddam fled to Egypt, where he completed his high school education at al-Qasr al-Anai School in Cairo. He was already twenty-two years old. Saddam enrolled at Cairo University to study law in 1961, but soon returned to Iraq. It was 1970 before he received the law degree he sought, this time from al-Mustanseriya University in Baghdad—the degree, however, was honorary.

CHOOSING A CAREER

Saddam's introduction to politics came while he was still in his teens. He plunged into partisan activities soon after starting high school in Baghdad,

195

although mainly as a street fighter rather than as the hero that his propaganda would have the world believe. He joined the socialist pan-Arab Baath Party (the Arabic term Ba'th means renaissance, or rebirth), and was among the ten militants who tried without success to assassinate General Kassem. Saddam was sentenced to death, but managed to escape across the desert to Syria, and from there to Egypt, where he continued his education.

In 1963, Saddam was back in Baghdad. The Baath Party had formed a new government after overthrowing (and executing) Kassem but, in less than a year, the Baaths were out of power and Saddam was again in hiding. He was found and imprisoned for two years—still planning his political moves and continuing to study law.

CAREER HIGHLIGHTS

A bloodless coup in 1968 brought the Baath Party back to power and Saddam to a position of leadership. By 1979, he had assumed the presidency of Iraq after shamelessly portraying himself as a hero and military man (according to his biographers, poor grades had kept him out of Baghdad Military Academy, and he had never had any military training). Life-size portraits of Saddam Hussein appeared throughout the country —on billboards, in schoolrooms, in every imaginable public place— promoting an image of him as a "father-leader." He appeared on television, in propaganda films, and even had songs and poems written about himself.

But the real Saddam Hussein was creating a brutal dictatorship. He purged or executed those who questioned his authority, and has survived, to this day, numerous threats and attempts on his life by surrounding himself only with close friends and relatives. Yet, in spite of his ruthlessness and the ghastly atrocities connected to his name, few can deny that it is Saddam who thrust a backward nation into the modern age of technology through his ambitious social and educational programs.

In 1980, Iraq invaded neighboring, revolutionary Iran and fought an eight-year war that ended in an uneasy truce negotiated by the United Nations. The original dispute had been over borders and the Shatt al-Arab waterway, but the real objective is said to have been control of the tremendous oil wealth in the region.

THE INVASION OF KUWAIT

In August 1990, Saddam invaded again but, this time, his victim was tiny, oil-rich Kuwait, nestled between Iraq and Saudi Arabia. The powers of the world balked, and a major crisis unfolded early in 1991 in the Persian Gulf. Operation Desert Storm, a U.N. offensive led by more than half a million American troops, was the largest U.S. military action since Vietnam. It was swift and devastating, leaving in its wake an estimated 200,000 dead, uncounted numbers injured, and millions displaced. Added to this was the appalling environmental damage from 600 oil wells that were spitefully torched by the Iraqi armies that occupied Kuwait, as well as from the bombing of Iraq's nuclear, chemical, and biological facilities. The Iraqis were forced to surrender after six weeks of horror. Critics discredit the action as a "war over oil," and one that might have been avoided through less drastic means, including the imposition of economic sanctions.

After the war ended, the United States encouraged the civil unrest that broke out among the Kurdish tribes in northern Iraq and in the predominately Shiite population in the south. No military aid was forthcoming, however, and Hussein brutally crushed these rebellions.

Saddam Hussein has also played a cat-and-mouse game with U.N. inspectors, several times threatening to deny them access to government buildings and to thwart them in attempts to confirm Iraq's observance of cease-fire terms. The U.S., in a reversal of policy, has warned Iraq that failure to comply—or further repression of the Shiites—will lead to military action. The situation remains tense.

MARRIAGE AND FAMILY

Saddam Hussein married his first cousin, Sajida (Khairallah) Talfah, a primary school teacher, in 1963. They have two sons, Udai and Qusai, and three daughters, Raghad (married to Hussein Kamil), Rina (married to Saddam Kamil), and Hala, still a schoolgirl.

Reports are often circulated that Saddam has a second wife, a custom acceptable under Islamic law, but this is not true. The woman in question is Samira Shabandar, who was his mistress and for whom, it is claimed, he once considered either divorcing Sajida or arranging for her to have a fatal accident. No such action took place, but this story recounts only one of the many scandals and family rivalries that surround Saddam Hussein.

FAVORITE MOVIES

Iraq's president is said to be fascinated with *The Godfather*. The authors of *Saddam Hussein and the Crisis in the Gulf* write that it is his favorite movie, and that he has watched it many times over. They refer to him as the "Don from Takrit." The comparison made is that the shrewd, real-life Hussein and the fictional Don Corleone are men of driving ambition and iron will who "both come from dirt-poor peasant villages; both sustain their authority by violence; and, for both, family is...the key to power." The likeness is further noted with the explanation that these men "relish power and seek respect, the more so because each knows what it means to have none."

HOBBIES AND OTHER INTERESTS

Saddam is reportedly an avid reader of history and political theory. However, observers say that his other activities seem to be in a lighter vein; he enjoys the luxuries that his immense wealth has brought—sumptuous living quarters, a yacht, a custom-made wardrobe of suits and uniforms (hundreds, it is said), and a broad range of personal services.

FURTHER READING

BOOKS

Encyclopedia Brittanica Book of the Year, 1989
Henderson, Simon. *Instant Empire: Saddam Hussein's Ambition for Iraq,* 1991
Karsh, Efraim. *Saddam Hussein: A Political Biography,* 1991
Miller, Judith, and Laurie Mylroie. *Saddam Hussein and the Crisis in the Gulf,* 1990
Renfrew, Nita. *Saddam Hussein* (World Leaders Past and Present series), 1992 (juvenile)

PERIODICALS

Current Biography, 1981
Life, Mar. 1991, p.41
New York Times, Aug. 26, 1992, p.A6
Newsmakers, 1991, Issue 1, p.50
Newsweek, Aug. 13, 1990, p.16; Jan. 7, 1991, p.20
People, Jan. 7, 1991, p.54
Rolling Stone, Oct. 18, 1990, p.51
Time, Aug. 10, 1992, p.30
U.S. News and World Report, June 4, 1990, p.38; Aug. 13, 1990, p.20

ADDRESS

Iraqi Embassy
1801 P Street NW
Washington, DC 20036

AUTOBIOGRAPHY

Lee A. Iacocca 1924-
American Business Leader
Retired Chairman of Chrysler Corporation

BIRTH

I was born on October 15, 1924, in Allentown, Pennsylvania. My mother and sister, Delma, still live in Allentown.

YOUTH

When I was growing up our family was so close it sometimes felt as if we were one person with four parts.

My parents always made my sister and me feel important and special. Nothing was too much work or too much trouble. My father might have been busy with a dozen other things, but he always had time for us. My mother went out of her way to cook the foods we loved—just to make us happy. To this day, whenever I come to visit, she still makes my two favorites—chicken soup with little veal meatballs, and ravioli stuffed with ricotta cheese. Of all the world's great cooks, she has to be one of the best.

EDUCATION

School was a very happy place for me. I was a diligent student. I was also a favorite of many of my teachers, who were always singling me out to clap the erasers, wash the blackboards, or ring the school bells. If you ask me the names of my professors in college or graduate school, I'd have trouble coming up with more than three or four. But I still remember the teachers who molded me in elementary and high school.

The most important thing I learned in school was how to communicate. Miss Raber, our ninth-grade teacher, had us turn in a theme paper of 500 words every Monday morning. Week in and week out, we had to write that paper. By the end of the year, we had learned to express ourselves in writing.

I also joined the debate team. That's where I developed my speaking skills and learned how to think on my feet. At first I was scared to death. I had butterflies in my stomach—and to this day I still get nervous before giving a speech. But the experience of being on the debate team was crucial. You can have brilliant ideas, but if you can't get them across, your brains won't get you anywhere.

When kids ask me for advice on how to do well in school, I always tell them: Stop watching so much TV and start reading at night. As head of Chrysler, I don't drive cars and build fancy engines all day. I read memos and reports all day long. In fact, over the years I've become a speed reader. I can usually drink in a memo in one gulp. I've got good comprehension, too, which I attribute to one thing—lots of practice.

FIRST JOBS

In August 1946, I began working at Ford Motor Company as a student engineer. I spent nine months learning different aspects of manufacturing when I decided I was better suited at selling cars than building them. So I switched to a sales job and I've been selling cars ever since.

MARRIAGE AND FAMILY

I got married in 1956 to Mary McCleary, who had been a receptionist at Ford. We dated on and off for several years, but I was constantly traveling, which made for a difficult and extended courtship. But finally we got married and had two wonderful daughters—Kathi and Lia. Kathi now has two wonderful daughters of her own.

All through my career at Ford and later at Chrysler, Mary was my greatest fan and cheerleader. We were very close, and she was always by my side. But Mary had diabetes, a condition that led to other complications. She died in 1983, when she was only 57.

I'm now married to Darrien Earle. I don't want to offend all the bachelors of the world, but I really believe people were made to be together and live together.

CHOOSING A CAREER

I always wanted to work in the auto industry. I drove a beat-up 1938 sixty-horsepower Ford and more than once I'd be going up a hill when suddenly the cluster gear in my transmission would go. I used to joke to my friends: "Those guys need me. Anybody who builds a car this bad can use some help."

MEMORABLE EXPERIENCES

In my life, I've had more than my share of success. But along the way there were some pretty bad times, too. In fact, when I look back on my years in the auto industry, the day I remember most vividly is the day I got fired.

I had worked my way up to the presidency of the Ford Motor Company. When I finally got there, I was on top of the world. But then fate said to me: "Wait. We're not finished with you. Now you're going to find out what it feels like to get kicked off Mt. Everest." So I was fired. I was out of a job. It was gut wrenching.

There are times in everyone's life when something constructive is born out of adversity. That's what happened to me. Instead of getting mad, I got even. I went to work at Chrysler, which at the time was going bankrupt. But with help from a lot of good people, we brought Chrysler back.

WRITINGS

I've written two books. The first, my autobiography, tells how I got fired at Ford and then how I turned Chrysler around. People must like to read about problems because the autobiography became the best-selling general interest nonfiction hardcover book ever. And, if you can believe this, 71,412 people wrote me letters after they read the book.

I was so touched by all that mail that I decided to do one lengthy reply in a second book called *Talking Straight*.

I also write a newspaper column and give five or six speeches every month.

FURTHER READING

BOOKS

Contemporary Authors, Vol. 125
Iacocca, Lee, and William Novak. *Iacocca: An Autobiography,* 1986
Iacocca, Lee, and Sonny Kleinfeld. *Talking Straight,* 1988

PERIODICALS

Business Week, 1991 Business Week 1000 (special issue), p.56
Current Biography Yearbook 1988
Fortune, Aug. 3, 1987, p.43; Apr. 8, 1991, p.56
New York Times, Jan. 11, 1992, p.A1
Time, Apr. 1, 1985, p.39

ADDRESS

Chrysler Corp.
12000 Chrysler Dr.
Highland Park, MI 48288-1919

* UPDATE *

Iacocca retires from Chrysler in December 1992. There has been speculation that he will join the management team of TWA. The airline has had serious financial difficulties, which many hope Iacocca can reverse. In addition, as national head of the PTA, he plans to become involved in education in the U.S.

Bo Jackson   1962-
American Professional Baseball Player
and Former Professional Football Player
Member of the Chicago White Sox Baseball
Team

BIRTH

Vincent Edward (Bo) Jackson was born November 30, 1962, in
Bessemer, Alabama. He was the eighth of ten children of Florence
Jackson Bond, who named him after actor Vince Edwards, the star
of "Ben Casey," a long-running television series of that time. His
father, steelworker A.D. Adams, also was the father of two of Bo's
five sisters, but Adams and Florence never married.

YOUTH

Bo Jackson had an impoverished and troubled youth. He lived

with his mother and eight of his nine siblings in a three-room house in Raimond, a rural community outside Bessemer. His eldest sister had moved away before his baby brother was born. "Sometimes we didn't have anything to eat but grits and margarine," he remembers. "Sometimes we didn't have anything at all." Bo was large and strong for his age. By the time he reached third grade, he was stealing lunch from sixth graders and had become what he describes as a "hoodlum and a bully." His nickname is a shortened version of "boar hog," the wild pig he was compared to by his brothers and sisters.

Frequently teased by other children for his stutter, Bo responded by becoming a tough and mean boy. "I once beat on one of my cousins with a softball bat—one of my girl cousins," he says. "I even hired kids to beat up other kids for me. I didn't have time to beat all of them up myself."

The turning point came at age thirteen, when he and some friends stoned to death several pigs belonging to a local minister. Faced with a choice between reform school or working to pay for the loss of the pigs, a thoroughly frightened Jackson decided to change his ways and to make use of his remarkable athletic ability. He was already playing baseball against grown men in an industrial league, but his decision to harness his skill and to stay out of trouble eventually made him a sports hero and a millionaire rather than the jailbird his mother feared he might become.

EARLY MEMORIES

"I would like to help [kids] avoid some of the mistakes that I made," Jackson once said in explaining why he works with children. Indeed, the mistakes were many and the pleasures few in a childhood marred by poverty and violence. The absence of a father in the home took its toll on both Bo and his mother, who used to whip him in a desperate attempt to keep him in line. He tells about those times in *Bo Knows Bo*, the book he wrote recently with Dick Schaap, saying "I didn't mind the switch and I didn't hear the words. I knew I didn't have a father to answer to."

When reform school, or even prison, became a real possibility, Bo finally woke up. He had to leave his wild ways and his old crowd behind if he wanted to make something of himself. "Sports was my way to be somebody," he told a reporter years later.

EDUCATION

Jackson attended McAdory High School in nearby McCalla, where he excelled in football, baseball, and track. He also studied diligently, especially English, science, and math, his favorite subjects. He had really changed from being "that bad Jackson kid" and now had his eye on going to college and getting away from Bessemer.

At the end of his high school days, Jackson ignored recruiters from far-flung colleges and turned down a $250,000 offer from the New York Yankees, opting instead to attend college in his home state. When he learned that he might not be given any playing time for over a year if he went to the University of Alabama, Bo chose Auburn University. His adviser there assigned him to easy freshman courses, probably concerned about his football eligibility, but Bo wanted more challenge and switched to a heavier and more academic course load the next year. His major was in family and child development. Jackson still is "a handful of credits" short of getting a degree from Auburn, but insists that he will eventually go back and finish. He says that he promised his mother—and himself—that he would get an education.

FIRST JOBS

Jackson had a summer job as a teller in a Birmingham (Alabama) bank between his freshman and sophomore years at Auburn. During his later college days, he worked at the Auburn Child Development Center.

MAJOR INFLUENCES

Bo found what he had always needed in his high-school coach, Dick Atchison. "He was as close as I came to having a father," Jackson says in his autobiography. "I couldn't have become the human being that I am without him. He cared about me. He taught me how to control my temper. . . . Coach Atchison taught me to turn that meanness around, to wait until after school and take that meanness out on running the hurdles or high jumping."

MARRIAGE AND FAMILY

Jackson and his wife, Linda Garrett, met at Auburn University when he was a junior and she was a graduate psychology student. They were married September 5, 1987, in Kansas City, Missouri, during Bo's first full season of play with the Kansas City Royals. The Jacksons have two sons, Garrett (Spud), five, and Nicholas, three, and a daughter, eighteen-month-old Morgan Amanda. The family lives in Burr Ridge, Illinois, near the home base of his new team, the Chicago White Sox.

CAREER HIGHLIGHTS

Jackson's career is divided into two noteworthy parts—collegiate and professional. As a football player, he made an immediate impact at Auburn. He scored the winning touchdown against archrival Alabama in his freshman season, ending a ten-year drought for the Tigers. He led Auburn to a Tangerine Bowl victory against Boston College and, averaging over six yards a carry, this amazing running back was named to the All-Southeastern

Conference Team. Bo led the Tigers to an even better season as a sophomore, helping to beat Alabama again by running for 256 yards on only twenty carries and scoring two touchdowns. Their Southeastern championship gave them a berth in the Sugar Bowl, where they beat the University of Michigan. After missing six games because of a separated shoulder in 1984, Bo stormed back for his senior campaign. He finished that season with 1,786 yards gained on the year, capturing the Heisman Trophy as college football's best player.

As a baseball player, Jackson got off to a slow start at Auburn. In his first season he struck out at each of his first 21 at-bats. Despite 34 total strike outs that year out of 68 attempts, Jackson finished the season with 4 home runs and a batting average of .279. As a sophomore, he skipped the baseball season to concentrate on track. He resumed his baseball career the following year, batting .401 with 17 home runs as a junior and .246 with 7 home runs as a senior.

As his college years drew to a close, Jackson was faced with choosing between professional baseball or football. Scouts for both sports felt that he would be a genuine star, and he received lucrative offers from the Tampa Bay Buccaneers of the NFL (National Football League) and from baseball's Kansas City Royals. Football meant bigger money in the short term, but most felt he opted for the longer, safer career that baseball promised.

In 1986, Jackson's first year in professional baseball was spent mostly with the minor-league Memphis Chicks, the Kansas City Royals' double-A farm team in the Southern League. He was called up to the Royals for a short and unimpressive stint at the end of the season. Still officially a rookie in 1987, Jackson began to show the world why his rifle-like arm and powerful bat had earned such praise. He finished the year with twenty-two home runs, a record for a Royals rookie.

Then, in July 1987, Jackson astonished the sports world by announcing that he had signed a five-year, $7.4 million contract with football's Los Angeles Raiders, and that he would become the first modern player to attempt a two-sport career. Until he was sidelined by a serious football injury in January 1991, Jackson played full seasons with the Royals, joining the Raiders ten days after the completion of each baseball season.

Jackson continued to be plagued with strikeouts, but nevertheless improved as an all-round ballplayer, becoming the first Royal to hit twenty-five homers and steal twenty-five bases in the same season in 1988. He repeated that feat in 1989, and then hit for a career-high .272 average in 1990, all the way thumping "tapemeasure" home runs. The practice and experience needed to become a great major-league player were beginning to pay off.

For the Raiders, Bo was an impact player for four seasons, despite missing the first few games each year playing baseball. He averaged an outstanding

6.8 yards per carry in 1987, falling off slightly the next year. Many felt that he was spreading himself too thin by playing more than one sport, but Jackson proved them wrong in 1989 when he became the first player in NFL history to have two runs from scrimmage of ninety yards or more. He also averaged 5.5 yards per carry, third best in the league.

After a solid 1990 season, Jackson fractured his left hip in an NFL playoff game against the Cincinnati Bengals on January 13, 1991. The injury was thought to be minor, but it led to a diagnosis of avascular necrosis, a degenerative disease caused by blood ceasing to flow to living tissue. The sports world was stunned when the Royals announced two months after the injury that Jackson was being released. However, on the basis of an alternate diagnosis, the Chicago White Sox decided to gamble on Bo's chances of complete recovery, and signed him to a contract.

Many doctors think it highly unlikely that Jackson will make a comeback, but Bo himself is determined to prove the world wrong once more. He is faithfully following a rehabilitation program of swimming and weight training. "I'll be back," he smiles. "I know my body." His now-famous promotional television spots for Nike athletic shoes have a new pitch—this time it's "Bo knows" about rehabilitation, focusing on the road back from his injury. "There's an opportunity in everything," says Nike advertising director Scott Bedbury. "If anybody can make a comeback, it's Bo."

The White Sox and the Raiders both have been firm in the belief that their superstar would shine for them again but, in mid-November 1991, Bo announced regretfully that he would give up football to concentrate on baseball. Bo returned to baseball in the fall of 1991, playing in the last games of the season for the White Sox.

MEMORABLE EXPERIENCES

Even though he has channeled his temper onto the playing field, Bo still knows revenge. An Alabama coach had told Jackson that if he played for Auburn he would have to endure four straight losses to Alabama's powerful Crimson Tide. When he scored in the waning moments of the annual contest to give Auburn a 23-22 victory in his freshman year, Bo remembers glancing up at the Tide coaches as he lay in the end zone. His pride and his judgment had been validated.

HOBBIES AND OTHER INTERESTS

Bo Jackson is a devoted family man who has a longtime interest in child development. To relax, he enjoys hunting, fishing, and archery. He is also fascinated by aviation, and hopes to earn a pilot's license.

WRITINGS

Bo Knows Bo: The Autobiography of a Ballplayer (with Dick Schapp), 1990

HONORS AND AWARDS

All-Southeastern Conference Team (AP, UPI): 1982
Heisman Memorial Trophy: 1985
College Football Player of the Year, *Sporting News:* 1985
Bert Bell Trophy/NFL Rookie of the Year (Newspaper Enterprise Association): 1987
Advertising Age Award: 1989, for star presenter of the year

FURTHER READING

BOOKS

Devanney, John. *Bo Jackson: A Star for All Seasons,* 1988 (juvenile)
Gutman, Bill. *Bo Jackson,* 1990
Hanks, Stephen. *Bo Jackson,* 1990
Jackson, Vincent B., and Dick Schapp. *Bo Knows Bo: The Autobiography of a Ballplayer,* 1990

PERIODICALS

Chicago Tribune, Jan. 4, 1991, IX, p.27
Current Biography, June 1991
New York Times, Nov. 2, 1990, p.B8
New York Times Biographical Service, Jan. 1984, p.76
People, May 20, 1991, p.40

ADDRESS

Chicago White Sox
Comiskey Park
333 West 35th St.
Chicago, IL 60616

Mae Jemison   1956-
American Scientist and Physician
First Black Woman Astronaut

BIRTH

Mae Carol Jemison was born October 17, 1956, in Decatur,
Alabama, the youngest of Charlie and Dorothy (Green) Jemison's
three children. Before she was four, the family moved to Chicago,
the city that she still refers to as her hometown. Jemison's mother
teaches elementary school English and mathematics, and her
father is a maintenance supervisor for United Charities of Chicago.
Her sister, Dr. Ada Jemison Bullock, is a child psychiatrist
in Austin, Texas. Her brother, Charles, is a Chicago real estate
broker.

YOUTH

It may have seemed an unlikely objective to others, but to little Mae Jemison growing up on Chicago's south side in the sixties, space travel was a goal that she saw as entirely within her reach. "It was something I knew I wanted to do," she says now, recalling the fascination she felt in watching the Gemini and Apollo launchings and the moonwalks on television. "I read lots of books about space. I had an encyclopedia about the different phases of Apollo. I don't remember the time I said, 'I want to be an astronaut'; it's just always been there."

There were other interests in Jemison's young life—so many that she wasn't always totally dedicated to school work, although her teachers remember her as a fine student. She loved dancing, drawing, science fiction, and archaeology, and she enthusiastically pursued a number of hobbies that filled her days. Looking back, Jemison says smilingly, "I didn't get straight As, but my sister always did. Maybe the reason I didn't get straight As was that I did stuff because I enjoyed it."

EARLY MEMORIES

Like most small children, Jemison asked about the heavens but, unlike most, she still remembers probing for answers to satisfy her precocious curiosity. "When I was about five or six years old," she related in a recent interview, "I used to look at the stars with my uncle and he would tell me they were just like the sun except they were millions of miles away. That was why they were so small. I have always been interested in astronomy and what goes on in the world. So I guess you could say I've been interested in space travel ever since I can remember."

EDUCATION

A product of Chicago's public education system, Jemison attended Alexander Dumas Elementary School and graduated at the age of sixteen from Morgan Park High School, where she excelled in math and science. Her activities at Morgan Park were diverse enough to also include modern dance and membership on the pom-pom squad. Jemison entered Stanford University in Palo Alto, California, on a scholarship and received a bachelor of science degree in chemical engineering in 1977, at the same time fulfilling the requirements for a bachelor of arts in African and Afro-American studies. Coincidentally, Stanford is also the alma mater of Sally Ride who, in 1983, was the first American woman to travel in space.

Jemison, building on a career plan for biomedical engineering, went on to Cornell University Medical College in New York, earning an M.D. in 1981. During her years at Cornell, she received on-the-job training with the study of social medicine in Cuba and as part of a team providing primary medical care in rural Kenya and in the Cambodian refugee camps of Thailand. Jemison completed her internship at Los Angeles County/ University of California Medical Center in July 1982.

FIRST JOBS

A desire to combine her medical skills with an opportunity to travel led the new young doctor to leave a brief assignment with a medical group in Los Angeles and enter the Peace Corps in 1983. She served for two-and-a-half years as a staff physician in the West African countries of Liberia and Sierra Leone, treating Peace Corps volunteers and State Department employees.

CHOOSING A CAREER

The shuttle program was announced by NASA (the National Aeronautics and Space Administration) in 1977, during Jemison's senior year at Stanford, and it was then that she felt that her longtime dream might possibly come true. "Being an astronaut isn't something you can plan for," she said some years later, "because there is such a small chance of success. I knew I had to have other options. But I also knew I would pursue it when the right moment came in my career."

The right moment for Jemison arrived upon her return from Africa in 1985. She filed an application with NASA but, considering the odds of being chosen quickly, if at all, she returned to medical practice, this time with Cigna Health Plans in Los Angeles. Then the Challenger disaster of January 28, 1986, which cost the lives of seven astronauts and teacher Christa McAuliffe, put the space program on hold. A determined Jemison renewed her application as soon as the selection process was resumed the following October. While she waited, she continued her medical practice and attended graduate classes in biomedical engineering.

In June 1987, the long wait was over. Mae Carol Jemison—chemical engineer and medical doctor, little girl from the black neighborhoods of the south side of Chicago—was one of fifteen candidates chosen from two thousand qualified applicants to begin training in America's space program.

CAREER HIGHLIGHTS

Dr. Jemison underwent an intense, year-long training and evaluation program at the Johnson Space Center before becoming a mission specialist, the title given to scientists and technicians who conduct experiments in flight. It would be four more years, though, until she would be launched into orbit, in September 1992, on the shuttle Endeavor, making history as the first black woman astronaut. The flight was scheduled as NASA's fiftieth mission. Yet at the time of its launching, only four other African-Americans had preceded Jemison in space, and all of these were men— pilot astronauts Guion S. Bluford, Jr., Fred Gregory, and Charlie Bolden, and Dr. Ronald McNair, who perished in the 1986 Challenger explosion.

While Jemison waited for her turn to soar into space, she concentrated on technical assignments, made appearances, and sat for interviews. She was astronaut office representative to the Kennedy Space Center at Cape Canaveral, Florida, a job that involved participating in the processing of the space shuttle for launch. Her particular duties were with the payloads and thermal protection systems and the launch countdown. She also worked in the Shuttle Avionics Integration Laboratory (SAIL), performing verification of computer software.

Jemison says that her excitement about the astronaut program never faded during the long months of preparation for actual flight. Time was spent learning about the shuttle and its operation, studying the response of the body to space travel, taking part in simulated space-walk sessions (in a large tank), learning to fly an airplane and, in general, coming to a basic understanding of the entire program. It was all new, but also a continuation of the plan she had charted years earlier at Stanford. "I think there is an assumption that I have changed careers," she said recently. "My interest is research. People think of space as being all rockets and engines. But actually, anytime you have people involved, you need medicine. Medicine requires research...and my background in biomedical engineering, a combination of engineering and medicine, makes me well suited for space exploration. It's not really a change of careers, it's more of an evolution."

The physician-astronaut began preparations in 1989 for her first flight into space—a cooperative mission between the United States and Japan to conduct experiments in life sciences and materials processing. Part of her training was in Japan, and it was there that she added Japanese to her other foreign language skills, Russian and Swahili.

Jemison and the rest of the seven-member Endeavor crew blasted off from Cape Canaveral September 12, 1992, on their eight-day, 3.3 million-mile journey. The physician's specialties on the mission were the study of space motion sickness, bone cell research, and developmental biology—the latter including the fertilization and hatching of frog eggs. One hundred fifty-five tadpoles were the result of the frog experiment and they are, reports NASA, the first creatures, other than insects, to have been developed in weightlessness. The crew on this laboratory mission broke ground by representing three space firsts: Jemison, the first African-American woman astronaut (she qualifies that by saying, "the first non-white woman"); researcher Mamoru Mohri, the first Japanese citizen to fly the shuttle; and Mark Lee and Jan Davis, the first married couple to travel together in space.

Dr. Jemison urges young blacks to pursue the promising science careers of the future, but is uncomfortable with being considered a role model. What she'd rather be, she insists, is someone who says: "No, don't try to necessarily be like me or live your life or grow up to be an astronaut or a physician unless that's what you want to do."

MEMORABLE EXPERIENCES

When the phone call about her appointment to the space program came on June 4, 1987, Dr. Jemison was on hospital duty. The low-key physician admits being elated, although more restrained than her sister, who started screaming when she heard the announcement on her car radio. "I didn't jump up and down and do a dance," Jemison recalls, "but, yes, I *was* very excited." It was the moment she had waited for since childhood, and had prepared for with diligence and determination. "I just said to myself," she adds, in remembering the impact of the call, "Wow, you asked for it. You got it."

MAJOR INFLUENCES

"My parents have always been supportive of me," is the answer Jemison repeats in her countless interviews since becoming the first black woman astronaut. "When I was a child, they put up with all kinds of stuff, like science projects, dance classes, and art lessons. They encouraged me to do it, and they would find the money, time, and energy to help me be involved."

Jemison also credits the many teachers who nurtured her interests and would let her go off and do things on her own. "One math teacher, David Drymiller, took me and another student aside during our senior year," she recalls, "and taught us solid analytic geometry."

MARRIAGE AND FAMILY

Jemison, who is single, shares her home in a Houston suburb with Sneeze, the white, gray, and silver African wildcat that she brought here as a kitten from Sierra Leone.

Except to note that her busy career has not interfered with socializing and dating, Dr. Jemison will only say, "There are parts of your life that are yours and are very personal. I have to keep mine to myself, because if I don't, they aren't mine any more."

HOBBIES AND OTHER INTERESTS

Jemison's NASA assignments call for long and demanding hours but, just as she did in childhood, she pursues other interests with equal intensity. Her recreational involvements include skiing, traveling, graphic arts, photography, sewing, weight training, foreign languages, and collecting African art. She also has an extensive dance and exercise background and is an avid reader. The reading Jemison speaks of ranges from light to serious and, in recent years, has included the study of economics.

HONORS AND AWARDS

Essence Science and Technology Award (Essence Communications, Inc.): 1988, for extraordinary accomplishments

A Detroit public school was named in the astronaut's honor in March 1992. The Mae C. Jemison Academy emphasizes science, math, and technology at primary-school level.

FURTHER READING

BOOKS

Who's Who among Black Americans, 1992-93

PERIODICALS

Chicago Tribune, July 15, 1987, p.1C; Mar. 8, 1992, p.1CN
Ebony, Oct. 1987, p.93; Aug. 1989, p.51
Harambee, Jan. 1992, p.4
Michigan Chronicle, Sept. 23-29, 1992, p.1
Ms., July/Aug. 1991, p.78
New York Times, Sept. 13, 1992, Sec. 1, p.18
Working Woman, Apr. 1989, p.116

ADDRESS

Lyndon B. Johnson Space Center
Houston, TX 77058

Peter Jennings   1938-
Canadian Broadcast Journalist
Anchor and Senior Editor of
"ABC World News Tonight"

BIRTH

Peter Charles Archibald Ewart Jennings was born July 29, 1938,
in Toronto, Ontario, Canada, to Charles and Elizabeth Ewart
(Osborne) Jennings. He has one sister, Sarah, younger by three
years. Jennings's father, who died in 1973, was a respected radio
newsman and vice president of CBC (Canadian Broadcasting
Corporation); it was his voice that was heard on that nation's first
coast-to-coast hookup in 1936.

YOUTH

The poised, patrician network anchor who graces the ABC television screen each weekday evening has not always been so smooth and in control. As a child he was, by his own admission, "a schlump, bone lazy, and a bit delinquent." His mother is said to have wondered what would become of her errant son. Young Jennings refused to study, read nothing but comic books, taught his eight-year-old sister to smoke (he was eleven at the time), and eventually dropped out of school in the tenth grade because of boredom—a decision he deeply regrets, and one that still embarrasses him. Now self-educated and steeped in the knowledge of world affairs, he projects an image that is no reflection of the irresponsible child he once was.

Peter Jennings grew up in a privileged household. There was great wealth on his mother's side of the family and, through his father's prestige in the CBC, he was exposed to a cultural life that his sister describes in the 1990 Goldberg book, *Anchors,* as a wonderful environment for a child. She tells of their home being filled with "the most talented and interesting and eccentric group of people. There were obscure French horn players, dancers, the people who started Canada's national opera company and the National Ballet."

Young Peter was stimulated by this lifestyle and the other pursuits that often accompany money and social position—travel, riding, skiing, tennis, and cricket. He was an outgoing child who, when he was only nine, hosted a morning radio show for kids on CBC. *Peter's Program* was so popular that Charles and Elizabeth Jennings found themselves answering a flood of fan mail for their little boy.

By all accounts, Peter's teen years were empty of serious goals, a fact that he has never denied. Neither his dashing good looks nor athletic grace, nor even his imposing air of confidence, could mask a distinct lack of interest in academics. He eventually was asked to leave Trinity College School, the upper-crust boarding establishment that had educated his grandfather. The headmaster is quoted in *Anchors* as advising Peter's distraught parents that "this is a great waste of your money and our time."

EARLY MEMORIES

Peter was intrigued with his distinguished father's world from an early age. The elder Jennings was, says his son now, "a very large presence in the family, and a very large presence in the business. . .so I think it was natural" to follow in his footsteps. As a boy, Peter sometimes was allowed to sit in the booth at Massey Hall as his father introduced the Toronto Symphony to Canada's radio audience. He has vivid memories of those heady times, and recognizes that they were his "passport to an even more interesting world."

EDUCATION

The people who have worked with Jennings during his more than a quarter-century as foreign correspondent and network anchor speak far more often of his quest for knowledge than of his skimpy schooling. As an adult, he has read and studied with an obsession—overcompensating, say many associates, for the squandered years.

After leaving Trinity College School, Jennings spent an additional year in public high school in Ottawa, where his family had moved. He later enrolled in night courses at Ottawa's Carleton University, but stayed only a week or two. However, his significant contributions to news gathering and broadcasting in the ensuing years have earned him special academic recognition. He holds an honorary LL.D. (doctorate in law) from Rider College in Lawrenceville, New Jersey, as well as other honorary degrees from Loyola University in Chicago and the University of Rhode Island.

FIRST JOBS

The sons of Canada's well-to-do families often found work in banking circles during the days of Jennings's youth, and he was no exception. Through his father's connections, he spent a brief period in his late teens at the Toronto branch of the Royal Bank of Canada, "cashing people's checks," he says, "and adding sums of figures." It was his first taste of independence, but never a lifetime ambition.

CHOOSING A CAREER

Broadcasting as a profession was always Jennings's dream, but in spite of the obvious talent shown at his auditions, there was an obstacle. The CBC had a rule against nepotism, which is family favoritism in job placement, and this regulation kept him from starting his career at his father's workplace. He found a job of lesser prestige, at the age of twenty, spinning records, announcing, and generally handling operations at tiny CFJR in Brockville, Ontario.

CAREER HIGHLIGHTS

By 1959, Jennings had finally joined CBC Radio in Montreal, doing news and farm reports for its northern service. Soon he moved on to television as a reporter for station CJOH in Ottawa, where he also performed a variety of other duties, among them hosting "Club 13," a dance program for teens. Jaunty and handsome, and possessed of a rich and elegant voice, Jennings quickly won wide recognition in the broadcasting field. He joined Ottawa's CTV Television in 1961 as a reporter and anchor of Canada's first commercial nationwide newscast. His reportorial skills and on-screen presence so impressed ABC (American Broadcasting Company) that he was lured to the States in 1964 to begin work as a national correspondent. His first beat was Mississippi and coverage of the civil rights movement.

Then, in 1965, roving-reporter Jennings was placed in the ABC evening news anchor seat for what he (and others) say now were all the wrong reasons. The network was on a youth kick in those years, and the twenty-six-year-old Canadian with boyish good looks and cultured accent fit their desired image. "I was simply unqualified," he says, thinking back to the three grim years he spent at the anchor desk, resented by more seasoned colleagues and hampered by his scanty familiarity with American culture. He asked to be reassigned as a reporter and is quick to admit that if he hadn't left the anchor desk then, "there's no question they would have fired me." Burned by the unfortunate experience, Jennings was relieved to report from the field again. It was his chance at a new beginning.

Jennings was a national correspondent for more than a year before heading overseas, first to Rome—and then to Beirut for what he called the most exciting time of his professional life. With dedicated study and an unmatched passion for work, he came to know that part of the world as no other broadcast journalist knew it. He filed informed reports and conducted interviews with a special edge that earned him new-found recognition and stature. "Everywhere he went," says a 1989 *Esquire* feature, "he took a book-filled satchel....He talked of nothing but the Middle East." His coverage of the horrifying terrorist attack on the Israeli compound at the Munich Olympics in 1972, continues this article, "enhanced his reputation as a reporter who couldn't be beat on a foreign story." Jennings had put to rest his reputation as a lightweight.

There was a brief assignment in Washington for Jennings in 1976, then ABC named him chief correspondent, based in London, the following year. He also shared the nightly news broadcast during this time on a three-way hookup with Frank Reynolds in Washington and Max Robinson in Chicago. When Reynolds died in 1983, Jennings was brought back to this country to be sole anchor and senior editor of the evening news—once again from New York, the scene of his mediocre performance in the mid-sixties.

Nearly a decade has passed since his return, and "World News Tonight With Peter Jennings" has boosted both man and network to new heights. The crisp composure he projects on camera, however, belies his off-screen intensity and combativeness. He is a perfectionist, setting exacting standards for himself and those around him, yet he is genuinely surprised when his impatience or abrupt criticism is hurtful. Jennings is forever probing and correcting and, as his colleague John McWethy once told *Esquire*, "the things that are a pain...about him also are generally the things that drove him to the top of his profession."

Holding one of the most influential jobs in television, the mellow-voiced Canadian is deemed insightful and believable. His instinct for news is legendary, and, says the *Saturday Evening Post*, he is "brightest in moments of crisis." In live broadcasts or on location when he must depart from prepared text, Jennings speaks with a clarity that is said to impress even his highly competitive peers.

Yet, for all of his accomplishments, and despite the esteem he has earned, a fragment of self-doubt continues to plague him. "I do not think I would measure up well in any comparison test to my father," Jennings said modestly a year ago. "He was a journalist in the truest sense of the word."

MEMORABLE EXPERIENCES

A 1971 incident in a Bengali refugee camp is a memory that haunts Jennings to this day. He tells of being in the midst of teeming thousands, when a weathered old man "dropped to the ground and wrapped his arms around my knees—I panicked. I felt trapped by this sea of humanity. So I asked the camp director to get me out." He realized, too late, that he should have leaned down and comforted the unfortunate man. Now, when covering stories of the homeless or the needy, a mature and more sensitive Jennings still pictures that moment, revealing emotionally that "It's an image that has never left me."

MAJOR INFLUENCES

The public broadcast specials and the community work for which Jennings has become known are, says *Esquire*, "his attempt to honor his father's [lifelong] commitment to public service." Charles Jennings was a man "of high ideals and impeccable morals," says the ABC anchor in remembering his distinguished parent. "I think," he concedes, "I still—to a very great measure—want to impress my father."

Even two decades after the elder Jennings's death, the influence of his father and the imprint of his own early life remain so strong that Peter Jennings clings to his Canadian roots, although his wife and children are American citizens. At least for now, while his mother lives and his father's legacy endures as a driving force in his professional life, he probably will remain a Canadian.

MARRIAGE AND FAMILY

Jennings has been married since September 19, 1979, to Kati Marton, critically acclaimed author and journalist, who came to America as an eleven-year-old in 1957 with her Hungarian parents, Andre and Ilona Marton. The elder Martons had been imprisoned in Budapest for reporting on life under Soviet rule and arrived in the United States to accept the George Polk Award for news coverage of the Hungarian Revolution. In 1990, daughter Kati's book, *The Polk Conspiracy*, would unveil the mystery surrounding the murder of the American reporter for whom that award was named.

Peter Jennings and Kati Marton live in a ten-room apartment above New York City's Central Park with their two children—Elizabeth, twelve, and Christopher, ten. The family also has a home at Bridgehampton, Long Island.

Jennings's marriage is his third. His first wife was Valerie Godsoe, a Canadian; his second, Anouchka (Annie) Malouf, a Middle Easterner whom he met while based in Lebanon. In 1987, Jennings and Marton went through a painful separation after allegations surfaced about her affair with a Washington columnist. Jennings himself had long had a reputation as a ladies' man, and, as his wife said later, the marriage was "on automatic pilot." The couple reconciled within weeks and have rebuilt their relationship into one that is considered steadfast and happy. "When you've been tested by fire," says Jennings, "you discover what is truly meaningful in your life."

HOBBIES AND OTHER INTERESTS

Athletic since childhood, Jennings enjoys an active and exuberant outdoor life. He skis, rides horseback, still plays an occasional game of hockey, and is adept at iceboating and mountain biking. In a recent interview with *USA Weekend,* film director and friend Alan Pakula calls him "an incredibly physical, exhaustingly physical, man...a great big overgrown boy." Jennings walks to his office on most workdays, and usually has a workout there on his exercise bicycle. Friends say that there are no quiet moments in his life except those, when away on assignment, where he often spends hours reading and studying in preparation for his broadcasts.

It is his family, however, that is Jennings' consuming interest. "Fathering is quite possible what I do most naturally and best. It is certainly what I most love," he says with pride. He and his wife share every possible moment with their children—evenings as well as early mornings in their New York apartment, and weekends at their country home on Long Island.

The anchorman who has won many of broadcast journalism's most coveted awards, displays only one in his ABC office—the Father of the Year award he was given in 1985.

WRITINGS

During his years as reporter and anchorman, Jennings has contributed articles to a number of newspapers and magazines, among them the *Christian Science Monitor* and *Maclean's.* He also writes story elements for many of his television documentaries.

HONORS AND AWARDS

George Foster Peabody Award (Henry W. Grady School of Journalism and Mass Communication, University of Georgia): 1974

Emmy Awards (two): 1982; for outstanding coverage of a news story, "Personal Note: Beirut"; and for a ten-part series, "U.S.-U.S.S.R.—A Balance of Powers"

Overseas Press Club of America Awards (three): 1982, for coverage of the assassination of Anwar Sadat, of the Falklands Islands War, and of life in the Soviet Union

Alfred I. DuPont-Columbia University Award in Broadcast Journalism: 1989 and 1991

Bob Considine Award (St. Bonaventure University): 1984, for excellence in news reporting

Father of the Year Award (National Father's Day Committee): 1985

Best Anchor *(Washington Journalism Review):* 1988, 1989, 1990, 1991

Robert F. Kennedy Journalism Award (Robert F. Kennedy Memorial): 1990, First Prize—International, "for a special report on the Khmer Rouge and U.S. policy in Cambodia" [with Tom Yellin and Leslie Cockburn]

George Polk Award for Network TV Reporting (Long Island University Journalism Dept): 1990, "for their report on the U.S. role in the resurgence of the communist-backed Khmer Rouge in Cambodia" [with Tom Yellin and Leslie Cockburn]

Edward Weintel Prize for Diplomatic Reporting (Georgetown University Institute for the Study of Diplomacy): 1991

FURTHER READING

BOOKS

Goldberg, Robert, and Gerald Jay Goldberg. *Anchors: Brokaw, Jennings, Rather, and the Evening News,* 1990

PERIODICALS

Esquire, Sept. 1989, p.158
Good Housekeeping, Apr. 1991, p.46
New York, Nov. 30, 1987, p.50
New York Times Magazine, July 27, 1986, p.12
Rolling Stone, May 4, 1989, p.60
Saturday Evening Post, Nov. 1988, p.42
TV Guide, Jan. 3, 1987, p.27
USA Weekend, Mar. 13-15, p.4

ADDRESS

ABC "World News Tonight"
47 W. 66th St.
New York, NY 10023

Steven Jobs 1955-
American Business Leader
Co-Founder of Apple Computer, One of the
First Companies to Mass Produce Personal
Computers

BIRTH

Steven Jobs (Steven Paul Jobs) was born on February 24, 1955, in
San Francisco, California, and raised by adoptive parents, Paul
and Clara Jobs. He has one sister, Patty.

YOUTH

In 1961, the family moved to the city of Mountain View, south
of Palo Alto. This area, which was starting to be known as Silicon

222

Valley, was becoming a center for electronics. Paul Jobs was a skilled machinist, but he also worked in repossessing and real estate and fixed cars as a hobby. Clara Jobs also held a variety of positions, including working as a babysitter, at the desk of a bowling alley, and as a school secretary. Their son was a bit of a loner as a child, never comfortable with team sports or other group activities. Although he did swim competitively, his true interest lay in electronics. He began to spend a lot of time in the garage workshop of a neighbor who worked at a Hewlett-Packard facility located nearby. Soon Jobs enrolled in the Hewlett-Packard Explorer Club, where company engineers encouraged young scientists and often demonstrated new company products.

EARLY MEMORIES

It was at this club that Jobs saw his first computer: "I was maybe twelve the first time," he once said. "I remember the night. They showed us one of their new desktop computers and let us play on it. I wanted one badly. I thought they were neat. I wanted to mess around with one."

EDUCATION

Jobs attended public schools in Santa Clara County, California. School was not easy for him: he got in a lot of trouble, and he had few friends. He grew to hate it so much that he insisted that he would not return. According to his father, "He came home one day from the seventh grade and said if he had to go back to school there again he just wouldn't go. So we decided we'd better move." The family moved to a new home in Los Altos so Jobs and his sister Patty could attend a better school. He continued to attend the H-P Explorer Club and work on electronic gadgetry. He also met Stephen Wozniak, with whom he would later found Apple Computer.

Jobs graduated from Homestead High School in 1972. He was, in the words of his electronics teacher John McCollum, "something of a loner. He always had a different way of looking at things." Jobs soon headed for Reed College in Portland, Oregon. He dropped out of college after one semester, although he stayed at Reed until 1974. During this time, he experimented with alternative lifestyles, including hallucinogenic drugs, communal living, vegetarianism, Eastern philosophies, and meditation. In 1974 he returned to California. To finance a trip to India in search of spiritual enlightenment, he worked briefly at Atari as a video game designer.

FIRST JOBS

Jobs found one of his first jobs by using the self-confident and brash behavior for which he later became known. While working on a science project in high school, Jobs realized he needed more parts. In his words,

"I picked up the phone and called Bill Hewlett [one of the founders of Hewlett-Packard]. He was listed in the Palo Alto phone book. He answered the phone and he was real nice. He chatted with me for 20 minutes. He didn't know me at all, but he ended up giving me some parts, and he got me a job that summer working at Hewlett-Packard on the line, assembling frequency counters. Assembling may be too strong. I was putting in screws. It didn't matter; I was in heaven."

CHOOSING A CAREER

His professional career got underway in 1975, after his experiences in Oregon and travels in India. Back at the family home in Los Altos, Jobs began attending meetings of the Homebrew Computer Club, a group for computer professionals and hobbyists. He and Stephen Wozniak, also a member, began working on a computer together, designing and building it in the Jobs's family home. To earn enough money to begin producing their new machine, they had to sell their most valuable possessions: Jobs's Volkswagon minibus and Wozniak's Hewlitt-Packard scientific calculator.

Jobs and Wozniak officially founded Apple Computer in 1976. At that time, computers were large and bulky—a whole roomful of machinery—used almost exclusively by businesses and universities. Wozniak and Jobs revolutionized the industry by developing personal computers that were affordable and so easy to use that they could be owned by average individuals. From the beginning, the two played very different roles in the company's development. Wozniak was the gifted engineer, responsible for designing the computer. As Jobs himself once said, "I was nowhere near as good an engineer as Woz. He was always the better designer." Yet it was Jobs who saw the sales potential of the new machine and was able to convince others of its potential—he has been called charismatic and visionary. At a time when he and Wozniak had no resources for creating a new company, he was able to convince others of the ultimate profitability of their idea, securing loans, electrical components, and orders for their new computers.

CAREER HIGHLIGHTS

The original model, the Apple I, was a single circuit board designed for hobbyists, without the accompanying software, video screen, or keyboard. Jobs and Wozniak soon saw a need for a computer for beginners and created the Apple II. It was successful beyond their wildest dreams, and the company earned over one billion dollars in its first five years. With the development of the Macintosh computer, introduced in 1984, Apple cemented its reputation for building computers that could be used by people with absolutely no knowledge or experience of electronic equipment.

As head of Apple, Jobs was recognized not only for the computers he produced but also for the unorthodox way he ran the company. Jobs shunned suits and ties for blue jeans and sneakers and huddled with staff for impromptu brainstorming sessions. His reputation within the industry varied widely: some co-workers considered him charismatic and were devoted to him, while others described him as brash, aggressive, and cocky. He was widely known as a perfectionist and an extremely demanding boss, routinely working 90 hours per week and expecting others to do the same.

Despite Apple's success, the company's rapid growth created problems. There were frequent changes in management, and in 1985, Jobs lost a power struggle with John Sculley, whom he had recruited as the chief executive, and was forced out of Apple.

Since then, Jobs has become involved in two ventures. He founded a new company, NeXT, Inc., in 1985. His goal was to build a new machine that would be as small and simple to operate as a personal computer, but with the power and graphic sophistication of a workstation, used primarily by engineers and scientists. The company began shipping the new computer in 1989, but reviews have been mixed and sales have been slow. In 1986 he bought Pixar, a company created by movie maker George Lucas to develop computer-generated animation and special effects for movies. Pixar has had ongoing financial difficulties, laying off almost half of its employees in February 1991. As Jobs once remarked, "My experience has been that creating a compelling new technology is so much harder than you think it will be that you're almost dead when you get to the other shore."

MARRIAGE AND FAMILY

Jobs was, for many years, involved in an ongoing but intermittent relationship with a woman that began while both were still in high school. A daughter, Lisa, born to his girlfriend in 1978 after she and Jobs had separated, was the object of a paternity suit. Although he denied being the father, a blood test indicated that he was, and he was ordered to pay child support. Since then, Jobs was married on March 18, 1991, to Laurene Powell, a student at Stanford University business school; they recently had a son, Reed.

HONORS AND AWARDS

National Technology Medal (U.S. Department of Commerce): 1985, for "the creation of a cheap but powerful computer" (with Stephen Wozniak)
Jefferson Award for Public Service (American Institute for Public Service): 1987
Entrepreneur of the Decade (*Inc.* magazine): 1989
Lifetime Achievement Award (Software Publishers Association): 1989

FURTHER READING

BOOKS

Aaseng, Nathan. *From Rags to Riches: People Who Started Businesses from Scratch,* 1990

PERIODICALS

Current Biography Yearbook 1983
Forbes, Apr. 29, 1991, p.137
Fortune, Aug. 26, 1991, p.50
Inc., Apr. 1989, p.109
New York Times Biographical Service, Aug. 1989, p.750
Time, Jan. 3, 1983, p.25
Wall Street Journal, June 27, 1991, p.B1

ADDRESS

Allison Thomas Associates
14238 Dickens St.
No. 4
Sherman Oaks, CA 91423

Pope John Paul II   1920-
Polish-Born Head of
the Roman Catholic Church
First Non-Italian Pontiff Since
the Early Sixteenth Century

BIRTH

Karol Jozef Wojtyla (voy-TIL-ah), destined one day to be the
spiritual leader of the estimated 700 million Catholics throughout
the world, was born May 18, 1920, in the southern Polish market
town of Wadowice (va-doe-VEET-suh). He was the second son of
Karol and Emilia (Kaczorowska) Wojtyla; his only sibling was a
brother, Edmund, fifteen years his senior. A daughter also was
born to the Wojtylas, but she died at birth.

YOUTH

Life centered around the 600-year-old Cathedral of St. Mary in Karol Wojtyla's small town, and it was there that he was baptized a month after his birth. He grew up in the shadow of the church, which was next to the building that housed his family's modest apartment. The father's name, which is Polish for Charles, was given to the small boy who came to be known by the affectionate nickname "Lolek." The elder Wojtyla was an administrative officer in the Polish army, assigned to Wadowice, and his wife was a former schoolteacher of Lithuanian descent. Because of his mother, whose family had come from Silesia, the Austrian-occupied part of Poland, young Karol learned to speak German as well as Polish. The natural ability with languages that he has demonstrated in his adult life no doubt had its start in those early years.

The Wojtylas were a deeply religious family who prayed together and went to mass every day. They lived a simple life, as did most of the people in their town, and young Karol divided his time among school, church, and outdoor play. He was an athletic child who loved every imaginable sport, from the street game *palant* (played with two sticks), to swimming and canoeing, to soccer, a game he excelled in—usually as goalkeeper. Lolek's favorite of all sports, though, was skiing, and he practiced on the hills around home until he was old enough to go to the steep slopes of the nearby Tatra mountains. Skiing and mountaineering have held a lifelong fascination for him. George Sullivan, in his book, *The People's Pope,* quotes a friend who once said, "Karol *belongs* with the mountain people. He loves their songs and their poetry; he shares their simplicity, their sense of humor, their independence, their love of freedom. Karol has a lot of mountain man in his makeup. He, too, is in love with freedom."

Lolek's boyhood was marred by sadness. The gentle mother, to whom he bore a striking resemblance in both facial feature and temperament, died when he was barely nine years old. Then tragedy struck again within a few years when brother Edmund, by then a physician, died after contracting scarlet fever from a patient. Father and youngest son were left to fend for themselves. The senior Karol's military background made him a strict parent who expected obedience, but he was a warm and religious man as well. Lolek's friends from those days remember the special bond that loneliness forged between the elder Wojtyla and his young son. The two attended mass every morning and often strolled the streets together after their evening meal. During these years, they lived frugally on a small army pension, with the retired father doing all of the washing, mending, and cooking. He also guided Lolek in his studies and checked the boy's schoolwork each day.

There was nothing unusually pious about the young Karol Wojtyla. Although he led what might be called a spiritual life, he was a normal youth reared in a country whose people are known for their fierce devotion to the Catholic Church. Yet there is no indication that the priesthood was on his mind in those days. He was vigorous and playful and, like boys everywhere, sometimes heedless of danger. A chilling incident, related by Rinna Wolfe in her biography, *The Singing Pope*, points out how close he came to never making a decision about his life's work at all. "When Karol was fifteen," she writes, "and his friend Boguslaw (Bogu) was thirteen, an almost fatal accident happened. Bogu's father kept a revolver in his cafe cash drawer. It belonged to a policeman who knew that when he drank too much he could use it harmfully. So he had left the gun with Mr. Banas for safekeeping. One day the two boys were playing alone in the café. Boguslaw took the revolver from the drawer. Jokingly he pointed it directly at Karol. Standing less than six feet away, he fired at Karol's heart. Somehow the bullet missed. . . . Instead it broke the window behind him."

EDUCATION

Young Karol Wojtyla was a good student from the time he entered primary school at the age of seven, but it was in the upper grades that he excelled. His father chose to send him to the state high school for boys rather than to either of the private schools in Wadowice, partly because of the expense involved, but also because he wanted Lolek to be free of pressure to choose his own career. The private academies were run by religious orders of priests—Pallotine and Carmelite fathers—who often guided their students into the seminary.

The high school years broadened Lolek's interests to include literature and drama, Latin, poetry, and music. He loved acting, too, and his friends and teachers felt that he would one day choose the theater as his profession. The church remained a major part of his life, though, and he continued to serve as an altar boy, as he had done in his very young years, and to head a student religious society. Archbishop Adam Sapieha of Cracow (spelled Krakow in Polish and pronounced "Krakoov") visited the Wadowice school while Karol was a senior and was so impressed with his welcoming speech and obvious intellect that the archbishop asked if young Wojtyla intended to become a priest. When told that the boy was more interested in Polish literature and drama than in religious life, Sapieha is often quoted as replying, "Too bad. He'd make a fine priest. We need someone like him."

After high school, Karol enrolled at Cracow's ancient Jagiellonian University, where the brilliant astronomer Nicolaus Copernicus had studied four centuries earlier. His father moved the thirty-five miles from Wadowice with him, and they shared an apartment in the Debrinki section of the beautiful and historic city. Karol's studies revolved around language and literature, but he also was prominent in a drama group.

WORLD WAR II

His life as a student was interrupted a year later by the beginning of World War II. Germany invaded Poland on September 1, 1939, and soon closed all universities. "The Germans were determined," James Oram explains in *The People's Pope*, "to wipe out all Polish intellectual thought because they saw the Poles only as slaves and there was no room in the plans of the Reich [the Third Reich, the name of the Nazi government] for those who studied, debated and questioned." It would be several years before Wojtyla would return to a formal classroom. He eventually continued his studies at a secret and illegal "seminary" at Archbishop (later Cardinal) Sapieha's palace. He had, by this time, decided to enter the priesthood. Cardinal Sapieha of Cracow certainly played an important role in Wojtyla's early life, making it possible for him to be educated for the priesthood even as the Nazis controlled Poland.

Young Karol had been issued a work card *(Arbeitskarte)* by the Germans after their invasion of his country and had been forced to labor in a limestone quarry belonging to the Solvay chemical works outside Cracow. He spent three years at the backbreaking job, and his meager pay was the only income to support him and his father, whose pension had been cut off when war broke out. During this time, Karol attended informal classes at night wherever young students could hide from the Nazis, and he began to write memorable and touching poetry. He also helped an old friend and designer of stage sets, Mieczyslaw Kotlarczyks, form an underground drama group, the Rhapsodic Theater, which would play to small groups in secret in an effort to keep Polish pride alive.

CHOOSING A CAREER

There are many who say that Karol Wojtyla's vocation for the priesthood began with the unexpected death of his cherished father. The year was 1941 and the horrors of war were everywhere. Innocent people were snatched away in the night, never to be seen again, and rumors had begun about the Nazi gas chambers at Auschwitz, not far from Cracow. Karol himself had survived two serious accidents—first, he was knocked down by a streetcar, then a few months later was nearly crushed by a truck. All of these traumas are said to have influenced him to consider religious life, but one of Wojtyla's oldest friends, who knew him well at this time, also "stressed the importance," writes biographer Lord Longford, "of the depth of Wojtyla's life of prayer." Wojtyla himself has only once been known to speak openly about this period of time, when "the most important questions of my life were born and crystallized," he revealed, "and the road of my calling was decided."

CAREER HIGHLIGHTS

After the war ended, Wojtyla was able to return to his studies. He was ordained November 1, 1946, and sent to study at the Angelicum, or Papal

University, in Rome. From this institute, he received a doctorate of divinity in 1948.

Wojtyla began his priestly duties just as the Soviet-backed Communist Party in Poland replaced Nazi tyranny. He was first assigned to a small village church. Within a year, though, he returned to Cracow to attend the Jagiellonian University, which had reopened after the war, and he was awarded a doctorate in theology that same year and was appointed to the faculty there. Later he would earn a second Ph.D at the Jagiellonian, this time in the field of phenomenology—the study of human consciousness and self-awareness.

In 1954, Wojtyla began to teach at the Catholic University of Lublin, the only Catholic institution of higher learning in Poland that had not been shut down by the Communists; soon he became head of its ethics department. This was a time of government hostility toward religion, and many members of the clergy were imprisoned under trumped-up charges of "disloyalty" to the Polish nation. The popular Stefan Cardinal Wyszynski was among these. It was not until his release in 1956 that he was able to effect a degree of church autonomy unmatched in any other Communist country. He did this by agreeing that the church would not become involved in politics.

Religion in Poland thrived, and it was during these years that Wojtyla began his rise through the ranks of Polish church leaders. He became auxiliary bishop of Cracow in 1958. Two years later, he went to Rome for the Second Vatican Council, the first general assembly of Catholic Church leaders in nearly a century. Here, under the guidance of the beloved Pope John XXIII, modernization and liberalization of church practices began. Here, too, Bishop Wojtyla "first established the international regard and contacts that were to make him pope," said *Time* in a 1978 cover story about his elevation to that office.

More church honors followed. In 1964, Wojtyla was named archbishop of Cracow, and in May 1967, at the age of forty-seven, he became the second youngest cardinal in Vatican history, joining the prestigious ranks of churchmen who elect new popes. An intellectual of note, a man of international reputation who had risen into the hierarchy of the Catholic Church, Wojtyla nonetheless continued to live a simple life. He was enormously popular with younger Poles and with workers—he visited parishes, performed wedding and funeral services, and remained accessible to old friends.

BECOMING THE POPE

As cardinal, he also moved easily in the elite circles of the Vatican, the independent state within the borders of Rome that houses the headquarters of the Catholic Church. He served under Pope Paul VI, successor to John XXIII. Paul had sparked dissent among liberals in the church and, when he died in August 1978, Wojtyla was among those who voted for a new pontiff. The cardinals chose from among themselves the gentle and fragile Albino Luciani, John Paul I, who died after little more than a month. The College of Cardinals convened again and, this time, did the unexpected. They elected the first non-Italian since 1522, Karol Wojtyla, a Pole—and, said *Time*, "the first international pope to lead the global church...a man of extraordinary qualities and experience." Out of respect for the recently deceased pope, and also because of reverence for Paul VI, "who was my inspiration and strength," Wojtyla chose the name John Paul II.

The new pope, schooled in the staunchly conservative Catholic Church of Poland, began his mission, says biographer Timothy Walch, "to solidify the foundations of Catholicism, which he believed were beginning to crumble under the weight of the modern age." After less than three years, the unthinkable happened. On May 13, 1981, an attempt was made on his life as he circled St. Peter's Square in the white vehicle that the press had dubbed "the popemobile." His assailant was Mehmet Ali Agca, a Turk already wanted for murder in his own country. After John Paul recovered, he forgave Agca, who was believed to have been an agent of the Bulgarian government. The pope's unbending stance against Communist repression had nearly ended his life. Security around the pope has been tightened in the ensuing years, but he still defies attempts to keep him from potentially dangerous situations.

In his almost 15 years as pope, John Paul II has traveled the world with his message, including an historic tour of the United States in 1987. He has charmed crowds with his personal warmth and enthusiasm, and has received their outpourings of affection and trust. But his popularity has come into question wherever liberal factions have looked to the church for reform, especially in the U.S. John Paul has stood firmly for traditional authority, by "calling repeatedly," according to Walch, "for a return to traditional Catholic ethical values: he condemned homosexuality as morally wrong; he called on priests to honor their vows of obedience and celibacy; he told the laity that premarital sex, contraception, and abortion were repugnant. . . .and he put severe limits on Catholic academic freedom and theological inquiry." Many Catholics in the U.S. and elsewhere have questioned these teachings, especially his rejection of birth control and his refusal to allow priests to marry and women to become priests. And commentators often discuss his demand for loyalty and intolerance for dissent. Yet they also view him as a champion of human rights and human dignity, a voice for all people throughout the world who are poor, oppressed, victimized, and powerless.

John Paul continues in his efforts to make the Catholic Church the most powerful moral force in the world. Although he puzzles some with his strategies, "even among [his] critics," claims the *New York Times*, "there is acknowledgement that here is a pope who knows exactly where he wants to take his flock; who. . .is many things to many people, but to all he is a leader determined to lead."

MAJOR INFLUENCES

The individual who made the greatest impact on the young man who became John Paul II was a simple tailor and self-styled philosopher. When, as archbishop, Wojtyla spoke of his vocation, he said, "I would be unjust if I failed at this point to recall Jan Tyranowski, an intellectual and at the same time a worker, a man who chose his profession so that he could commune better with God, a man who knew how to exercise an enormous influence on young people. I don't know if my priestly calling is due to him, but, in any case, it was born in his climate, the climate of the mystery of supernatural life he carried with him in his contacts with us. . . ."

MARRIAGE AND FAMILY

Members of the Catholic clergy are not permitted to marry, except for parish priests of the Eastern rites—Byzantine, Chaldean, Armenian, Alexandrian, Antiochene—who share the faith and discipline of Rome. The pontiff's continued defense of this church rule puzzles (and alienates) many Catholics.

John Paul, whose closest living relatives are cousins, lives alone in the papal apartments that overlook St. Peter's Square in the Vatican.

HOBBIES AND OTHER INTERESTS

A man of rural background and simple tastes, the pope has no desire for the luxuries that his position might offer. Whatever spare time is left from his duties is spent either reading or listening to the music he has loved since his youth. Although he was sidelined by abdominal surgery in the summer of 1992, he has recovered well and has resumed mild exercise. He swims daily when he is in residence at Castelgondolfo, his summer home in the countryside near Rome. He has less time and vigor now to pursue the skiing and mountaineering for which he is so well known but, occasionally, he is still seen hiking—even on skis.

SELECTED WRITINGS

Sign of Contradiction, 1976 (collection of sermons, English translation)
The Acting Person, 1979 (translated and revised from the Polish-language publication of 1967; considered John Paul's major philosophical work)

In addition, the pope has authored four scholarly books, more than 500 essays and articles, a play (unpublished), and countless poems. His most widely quoted poem is "The Quarry" (available in translation), which reflects the deep impressions of his days of labor under the Nazi occupation of Poland. Some of his early works, because of the need for secrecy, were published under the pseudonym Andrej Jawien. John Paul also writes encyclicals (papal documents) defining the religious, moral, and political policy of the Catholic Church.

HONORS AND AWARDS

Smithson Medal (Smithsonian Institution): 1979
Olympic Order (International Olympic Committee): 1981

FURTHER READING

BOOKS

Longford (Lord). *Pope John Paul II,* 1982
Oram, James. *The People's Pope: The Story of Karol Wojtyla of Poland,* 1979
Sullivan, George. *Pope John Paul II: The People's Pope,* 1984
Walch, Timothy. *Pope John Paul II,* 1989
Wolfe, Rinna. *The Singing Pope: The Story of John Paul II,* 1980 (juvenile)

PERIODICALS

Christian Century, Oct. 14, 1987, p.876; Oct. 12, 1988, p.887
Commonweal, Oct. 7, 1988, p.516
New York, Oct. 30. 1978, p.93
New York Times Biographical Service, May 1979, p.614; Oct. 1982, p.1331; May 1985, p.549
Newsweek, Oct. 30, 1978, p.78; May 25, 1981, p.24
Time, Oct. 30, 1978, p.84; May 25, 1981, p.10; Jan. 9, 1984, p.27

ADDRESS

His Holiness John Paul II
00120 Vatican City

Magic Johnson 1959-
American Former Professional Basketball Player
Spokesman in the Fight Against AIDS

BIRTH

Earvin (Magic) Johnson, Jr., was born August 14, 1959, in Lansing,
Michigan, to Earvin and Christine Johnson. The fourth of their
seven children, he has two brothers, Quincy and Larry, and four
sisters, Lily Pearl, Kim, and the twins, Evelyn and Yvonne. Earvin,
Sr., is also the father of three older children, one of whom,
Michael, lived with the family part of the time.

YOUTH

The story of Magic's early life in Lansing is one that speaks of
sacrifice, hard work, family devotion, and modest goals. The

236

Johnsons lived in a lower-middle-class neighborhood where the men worked in either the automobile or construction industries, often holding down two jobs. Most of the women also held two jobs—one, raising large families, the other, outside the home, usually in domestic service. Magic's dad (called the Big E) would put in a full shift at the General Motors' Fisher Body plant and then, already weary, would clean the shops and haul rubbish after hours to make extra money. Life was not easy, but there were many simple joys. Family values were strong, and the Johnsons were happy together. Magic often comments that "none of us children presented any serious disciplinary problems." He does smile, though, in recalling the "shouting matches and little fights and tantrums." But, he adds, "overall, we tolerated each other in the worst of times and enjoyed ourselves in the best."

Magic recalls many minor youthful incidents of innocently forgotten chores, basketball smudges on the living room walls, or missing a fifth-grade championship game for failure to turn in a school assignment. But one of his most vivid memories is that of a lesson learned at the tender age of nine, when he was caught stealing candy and balloons from a neighborhood store. His angry and disappointed father turned him over his knee and whipped him with a strap. "Listen," the Big E scolded, "you don't have to steal. If you want something, tell me. I'll get it for you. If I can't, then you know you can do without it." The boy who was to become an idol to a generation of young American sports fans, understood—and has never forgotten.

FIRST JOBS

Even as a young boy, Johnson began to think about earning money and making it work for him. He helped his dad in the after-hours hauling business while he was still in elementary school and started his own small business by cutting lawns and doing errands for neighbors. When he was old enough, he took other jobs, one as a building janitor and one on a soft-drink delivery route. Peter Pascarelli, author of a new biography, *The Courage of Magic Johnson*, tells that the boy who loved basketball also was fascinated with business and "sometimes had two or three jobs going, all fit in between school and basketball. . . .Whether walking or riding his bike, he dribbled his way to work."

EDUCATION

Magic Johnson's formative years were spent in Lansing. As a boy, he attended Main Street Elementary School in his hometown, learning to play basketball as early as third grade. He then moved on to Dwight Rich Junior High, and it was then that he began to be noticed for his expert ball handling and shooting. During those young years, he met another court star, Jay Vincent, and they developed a friendly rivalry that would continue through high school (Magic at Everett, Jay at Eastern), as team-mates at college, and into the NBA (National Basketball Association).

It was at Everett High that Johnson's reputation as a basketball player flourished. Here, too, was where he was given the nickname Magic—a name that has defined his talent, his court instincts, and his charm throughout an astonishing career. In his autobiography, *Magic*, he confesses to an earlier nickname, June Bug, bestowed by his father during his pudgy grade-school years, long before his body lengthened to its present height of six feet, nine inches.

Johnson was pursued by recruiters from all over the country when it was time for college, but he decided on Michigan State University, which was, he said, "just down the road from home."

CHOOSING A CAREER

Street games and sports, and the usual athletic horseplay, were all part of Johnson's growing-up years, as they were for most of the boys in his neighborhood. But it was basketball that captured his mind and his heart. As his skills developed, his interest grew even stronger, until talent was matched with determination. Sports writers often note the similarities in the careers of Magic and the Boston Celtics' Larry Bird—two kids who always knew that basketball was *their* game, and who achieved their goals with a dedication that allowed few intrusions.

CAREER HIGHLIGHTS

Johnson's college and pro-fessional careers have been nothing less than spectacular. The smiling dynamo of the basketball court led the Spartans in 1977-78, his freshman year, to a Big Ten championship—the team's first Big Ten title in nineteen years. Then, as a sophomore, his dazzling court skills and superb team spirit led the Spartans to the NCAA (National Collegiate Athletic Association) championship, capturing for himself the MVP

(Most Valuable Player) award. He left school after his sophomore year to sign a lucrative contract with the Los Angeles Lakers of the NBA.

The $600,000 offer from the Lakers was too good to pass up, so Johnson signed a pro contract in 1979. His rookie statistics broke Lakers records. That season, when the Lakers won the NBA title, he began a decade of phenomenal accomplishments that would forever mark him as a superstar. His second season, however, was blemished by a serious knee injury that kept him out of 46 games; by tension among the team members who resented his unprecedented $25 million, 25-year contract; and by a disagreement with Coach Paul Westhead, which reportedly caused Westhead to be fired. Johnson's popularity fell, but only temporarily. With a new coach, Pat Riley, and somewhat "sobered by his experiences with club politics," he again began to work his brand of magic.

The Lakers moved ahead with their star point guard to five league championships and to NBA championships in 1985, 1987, and 1989. His contributions to his team in twelve years of play, and to basketball in general, are enumerated by biographer Pascarelli. It is not only his size, writes Pascarelli. "He became the first point guard to dominate the game. He made it cool to pass the ball, not just shoot it. . . . He made unselfish play the way to play the game, a legacy that coaches everywhere embraced." Pat Riley, now coaching the New York Knicks, endorses such praise with his own assessment of Johnson's talent. "I spent ten years with the greatest player ever. Earvin [Riley always uses Johnson's given name] was more than a great player, he was a coach on the floor. He has the heart of a great warrior."

The story of an incredible career *seems* to have come to an untimely end with his recent retirement. But Magic Johnson wrote a final chapter by playing in the NBA All-Star game February 9, 1992, and winning, once again, the MVP trophy. He is the first retired player ever to win such an honor, writes Terry Foster in the *Detroit News*, and "probably will be the last—unless he returns to play again. . . . A fairy tale played out on national television. That's what it was."

A postscript will be added to Johnson's story when he represents the United States at the 1992 Summer Olympics. After that, there are career decisions to be made, and no one knows better than Magic himself that basketball is his addiction.

COPING WITH AIDS

In November 1991, Johnson acknowledged to a stunned public that he was infected with HIV, the Human Immunodeficiency Virus that leads to AIDS, Acquired Immunodeficiency Syndrome. He pledged then, in the midst of his personal tragedy, to "stand firm" and to use his celebrity in the fight against the disease. While his message is to *all* young people, he says that his special crusade is "to prevent a generation of black Americans from being devastated" by this terrible illness. He appeared on television's Nickelodeon channel March 25, 1992, answering questions from kids about "his health, his future, and his fears," and telling them what he felt was important to know about AIDS. His talk was straight-forward—even blunt—about sex, intravenous drug use, and death. The show was produced by journalist Linda Ellerbee, and was so successful that it was repeated at designated times over the next weeks so that it could be taped for use in schools.

Johnson's involvement in the AIDS program is sincere. He readily owns up to the mistakes which led to his own tragedy, telling young people, "It was wrong first of all for me to do the things I was doing. I can't correct that. All I can do is try to save your lives."

MAJOR INFLUENCES

All of the sports features and public relations releases about Johnson talk about his impressive passing and rebounding—about his exuberance and charm, too—but there are several people who helped him become the person he is. George Fox, Johnson's Everett High School coach, was the one who taught him to lead and to share the ball, advice that made him more than just a hotshot superstar. The style of play that Fox encouraged became Johnson's trademark as he moved through college and professional basketball. The *New York Times Biographical Service* magazine once praised such generosity on the court: "No player works as hard, or as deftly, to make other players look good."

Another strong influence in shaping Johnson's life was the man he calls Tuck—Charles Tucker, a young high school psychologist and one-time basketball hopeful, who became both friend and mentor. Tuck nurtured Magic's love of the game, lending him his own considerable knowledge and, all the while, providing an example of personal integrity.

The major influence on Johnson's life, however, has been his parents. He tells of his father's love of basketball, shared with him on Sundays as they watched televised games together; of the Big E's strength and honesty and sense of discipline; and of the warmth and spirit of Christine Johnson, the mother who wanted him to stay in college, hoped for him to be a clergyman, but lovingly supported his career decision. Those who know the family say that it is from Mrs. Johnson that Magic inherited his famous and devastating smile. Pictures of the two together leave no doubt.

MARRIAGE AND FAMILY

Magic Johnson and his college sweetheart, Earletha (Cookie) Kelly, were married September 14, 1991, and their son, Earvin III, was born June 4, 1992. They live on an estate in the Los Angeles suburb of Bel Air. As freshmen at Michigan State in 1977, the Johnsons began a fourteen-year romance that was peppered with "a lot of breaking up and getting back together," Cookie revealed recently in an *Ebony* magazine interview. Two earlier marriage dates had been postponed, mainly because of Magic's inability to really commit himself to anything other than basketball. Now, when Cookie says "we have been through everything together," her words take on a deeper meaning than she could have imagined during their dating years.

Johnson has an eleven-year-old son, Andre, who lives in Michigan with his mother. The boy's parents were never married, but Johnson is a caring and involved father who called Andre to reassure him before going public about his HIV infection.

HOBBIES AND OTHER INTERESTS

Most of Johnson's outside interests stem from his preoccupation with basketball. He has endorsement contracts with a number of businesses, including Converse, Spalding, Nintendo, Target Stores, and CBS-Fox Video. He also founded his own sports apparel company, Magic Johnson's T's, and is a general partner with Pepsi in a soft-drink distributorship in Washington, D.C. This world-class athlete, who always has liked the idea of becoming a businessman, would like to own the Lakers someday.

Johnson lends his time and talent to a number of charitable causes, among them the United Negro College Fund, American Heart Association, Boys' Clubs of America, Muscular Dystrophy Association, and the City of Hope. Each year he sponsors the Magic Johnson All-Star Camp (for kids), as well as a one week, money- raising basketball camp in Hawaii for businessmen. To all this activity, he now adds Project 32—for AIDS research and education.

WRITINGS

Magic, with Richard Levin, 1983
What You Can Do to Avoid AIDS, 1992

HONORS AND AWARDS

NCAA Tournament Most Valuable Player: 1979
NBA Playoffs Most Valuable Player: 1980, 1982, 1987
Sporting News Player of the Year: 1987
NBA Most Valuable Player: 1987, 1989, 1990
NBA All-Star Game Most Valuable Player: 1992

FURTHER READING

BOOKS

Goodman, Michael E. *Magic Johnson*, 1988 (juvenile)
Haskins, James. *Sports Great, Magic Johnson*, 1989

Johnson, Earvin, and Richard Levin. *Magic*, 1983
Pascarelli, Peter F. *The Courage of Magic Johnson*, 1991

PERIODICALS

Current Biography Yearbook 1982
Detroit News, Feb. 10, 1992, p.1A
Ebony, Apr. 1992, p.100
Jet, Nov. 25, 1991, p.12
New York Times Biographical Service, Dec. 1987, p.1285; Nov. 1991, p.1187

ADDRESS

10100 Santa Monica Blvd.
Suite 600
Los Angeles, CA 90067

* *UPDATE* *

Magic Johnson announced on September 30, 1992, that he would return to professional basketball with the Lakers. Just over one month later, on November 2, 1992, he announced that he would be retiring again. He says his decision was based on the concern other NBA players had expressed about the possibility of contracting AIDS from Johnson during play, and he believed the controversy would overshadow any contribution he could make to the team.

Michael Jordan 1963-
American Professional Basketball Player
Member of the 1991 and 1992 NBA
Champion Chicago Bulls

BIRTH

Michael Jordan (Michael Jeffrey Jordan) was born on February 17, 1963, to Deloris and James Jordan. There were five children in the Jordan family, including brothers James and Larry and sisters Deloris and Roslyn. Although the family lived in Brooklyn, New York, when Michael was born, they eventually moved to Wallace, North Carolina.

YOUTH

Jordan grew up in Wilmington, North Carolina, where the family

243

settled when he was seven. James worked at an electric plant, starting as a mechanic and eventually becoming an equipment supervisor, while Deloris was employed at a local bank, where she worked her way up from a position as a teller to become the head of customer service. They encouraged their children to succeed, stressed the importance of hard work, and taught them other lessons as well. "My parents warned me about the traps [in life]," Jordan once said, "the drugs, and the drink, the streets that could catch you if you got careless." In addition, his mother taught him to cook, sew, wash clothes, and clean house. From his father he picked up the habit of letting his tongue hang out of his mouth while concentrating, as James used to do when working on cars at the family home, although he did not pick up his father's mechanical abilities.

EARLY MEMORIES

Even as a child Jordan was dedicated to sports. He spent much of his free time practicing basketball, baseball, football, and track, but baseball was his favorite. He once told a reporter, "My favorite childhood memory, my greatest accomplishment, was when I got the most-valuable-player award when my Babe Ruth team won the state baseball championship. That was the first big thing I accomplished in my life, and you always remember the first."

EDUCATION

Jordan's dedication to basketball began while he was still a student. When he entered Laney High School, he hoped to play on the varsity team, like his brother Larry. But at that time Michael was only 5'11" tall, which the coaches considered too short. So he played for the junior varsity team. In his words, "When the varsity team went to the state playoffs, I thought I would be called up. When the team went to the regionals, the coach let me on the bus only because a student manager got sick. I didn't have a ticket to get into the game, so I had to carry the uniform of our star player to get in. I didn't want that to happen again. From that day on, I just worked on my basketball skills."

Jordan's coaches have often commented on his competitive spirit, willingness to practice constantly, and commitment to become the best basketball player that he can be. In high school, though, he began to spend so much time on practice and so little time on his schoolwork that he was suspended three times. His father helped him to understand that he needed good grades in high school to get into college and play for a college team. He continued to practice, but also kept up with his schoolwork. Jordan grew four inches, to 6'3", during the summer before his junior year, and he played successfully for the varsity team for two seasons.

Jordan was offered full scholarships to several schools but chose the University of North Carolina (UNC), a top college basketball team. He was picked for the starting squad in his freshman year, an unusual honor. Again he practiced constantly, and his coach, Dean Smith, later said that his progress that first year was "almost eerie." In the final game of the season, the North Carolina Tar Heels were playing the Georgetown University Hoyas for the National Collegiate Athletic Association (NCAA) championship, the top honor in college basketball. In the last few seconds of a tight game, Jordan sunk a 16' jump shot. That basket clinched the 1982 NCAA title and placed Jordan in the national spotlight.

In 1983 he was named to the United States team for the Pan American Games, and in 1984 he was named co-captain of the U.S. team for the Olympic Games. Both teams won gold medals. He also continued to play well at UNC and was named NCAA Player of the Year for both his sophomore and junior years (1983-84). For three years, Jordan helped the team to a record of 88 wins and only 13 losses. Yet after his junior year he decided to leave college to become a professional basketball player. He later completed his coursework at UNC and received his bachelor's degree in 1986.

FIRST JOBS

All of the Jordan kids worked at a variety of jobs while they were growing up, including cropping tobacco, driving buses, and working at local stores and restaurants—except Michael. He once tried to crop tobacco, like his brothers and sisters, but later said, "I went out there one day, and I swore I wouldn't do it again. It hurt my back too bad." One year, when all his brothers and sisters had summer jobs, his mother encouraged him to work, too. "One summer, my mom said, 'You just got to work,' and she got me a job as a maintenance man in a hotel. Man, I quit that job so quick! I just *couldn't* do it, I could not keep regular hours. It just wasn't me. From then on, I never, *ever*, had another job."

CAREER HIGHLIGHTS

In 1984, Jordan was chosen as a first-round draft pick by the Chicago Bulls, the third pick in the National Basketball Association (NBA) draft that year. At that time the Bulls had had a very poor record for years, and the team looked to Jordan for help. And in his first season, he delivered: he drew lots of fans to the games, who enjoyed his high jumping and high scoring. At the end of the year, having scored more points than any other NBA player, he was named Rookie of the Year. Even Larry Bird, who plays for the Boston Celtics, joked that "Maybe he's God disguised as Michael Jordan."

But during his second year with the Bulls, Jordan broke a bone in his foot during the third game of the season, in October 1985. He was forced to sit out 64 games. Eventually he returned to the team in March, starting out by playing a few minutes each half and gradually working up to more playing time as his foot healed. Since then his skill and expertise have continued to grow, and he continues to set records and win awards. During his third pro season, he became only the second player in NBA history, after Wilt Chamberlain, to score over 3,000 points, which was also the highest single-season scoring record for a guard. The following season, 1987-88, was one of his greatest ever—he won a variety of awards including NBA Most Valuable Player and NBA Defensive Player of the Year. With Jordan the Bulls' record continued to improve. In 1990 he led the team to the Eastern Conference Finals, where they were defeated by the Detroit Pistons, and in 1991 he led the Bulls to the NBA championship against the Los Angeles Lakers.

Jordan is known for a certain style of play that features exuberant leaping, dunking, and scoring, often with his tongue out. His ability to leap and seemingly hang in the air over the basket constantly delights and amazes his fans. But he is also known as an intelligent player, hailed for both his quick thinking and quick reactions. As a master of both offense and defense, he is able to switch his style of play as the game requires. With these skills, Jordan became the first to lead the league in both scoring and steals, a tremendous accomplishment.

MEMORABLE EXPERIENCES

Jordan once told a reporter that his one "memorable game" was the 1982 North Carolina-Georgetown NCAA championship game, which was the beginning of his national reputation as a basketball player. "Everything started with my [winning] shot. That's the game I will always remember because that's when Michael Jordan got his name and started to get the respect of everyone else."

MARRIAGE AND FAMILY

Jordan was married in 1989 to Juanita Vanoy, and they have two sons, Jeffrey and Marcus. He and his family live outside Chicago.

HOBBIES AND OTHER INTERESTS

In addition to basketball, Jordan has had a successful second career doing television commercials, representing such companies as McDonalds, Coca-Cola, Chevrolet, Wilson Sporting Goods, and Nike, which features the Air Jordan product line. He is involved with a number of charities, including the Ronald McDonald Children's Charities, Starlight Foundation, Special Olympics, United Negro College Fund, Sickle Cell Anemia Association, Make-A-Wish, and Best Buddies. He has given both money and time to such causes, participating in celebrity contests and golf tournaments. An avid golfer, he has said that he will play professionally when his basketball career is over: "I'm still learning the game. I've never had the opportunity to play year round, since I don't play during the basketball season. So I don't practice enough. But when I get to the point where I can shoot consistently in the low 70s, I'd like to turn pro. I'm not saying I'm going to win. I'm gonna try. . . . It's not for the money. I should already be financially secure. But it's a challenge, right?"

HONORS AND AWARDS

Co-captain of the United States Olympic basketball team: 1984
NBA Rookie of the Year: 1984-85
NBA All-Star Games: 1985-91
NBA scoring title for five consecutive seasons: 1986-87 through 1990-91
NBA Most Valuable Player: 1988, 1991

FURTHER READING

BOOKS

Berger, Phil, and John Rolfe. *Michael Jordan,* 1990 (juvenile)
Deegan, Paul J. *Michael Jordan: Basketball's Soaring Star,* 1988 (juvenile)
McCune, Dan. *Michael Jordan,* 1988 (juvenile)
World Book Encyclopedia, 1991

PERIODICALS

Current Biography Yearbook 1987
Gentlemen's Quarterly, Mar. 1989, p.319
Jet, Apr. 29, 1991, p.46
New York Times Biographical Service, May 1989, p.479
Sports Illustrated, June 24, 1991, p.38
Time, Jan. 9, 1989, p.50

ADDRESS

Chicago Bulls
1 Magnificent Mile
980 North Michigan Ave.
Chicago, IL 60611

Jackie Joyner-Kersee 1962-
American Athlete
Two-Time Olympic Gold Medalist
in the Heptathlon

BIRTH

Jackie Joyner-Kersee, called the "world's greatest athlete," was born Jacqueline Joyner on March 3, 1962, in East St. Louis, Illinois, a mostly poor community across the Mississippi River from St. Louis, Missouri. She was the second of four children born to Alfred Joyner, a construction worker, and Mary Joyner, a nurse's assistant, while they were still in their teens. They had married when Alfred was 14 and Mary was 16. Jackie's brother, Al, is older, and two sisters, Angela and Debra, are younger.

Jackie was named for then first lady Jacqueline Kennedy by her grand-mother, who said she was destined to "be first lady of something."

YOUTH

Her parents's early marriage and life in poverty in a decaying city did much to shape Jackie. Her mother was determined that Jackie do better in life, that she break the cycle of "children having children" and achieve. Mary Joyner was a tough disciplinarian in a tough town, where violence was a fact of life, with a painful, personal edge. Jackie's dance instructor was murdered when Jackie was 10; she saw a man shot to death when she was 11; and when she was 14, her grandmother was shot to death by her step-grandfather.

The Joyners did their best to raise their kids to value the things they did: honesty, education, and love of family. Even when there was no money for food and they lived on mayonnaise sandwiches, or when they slept on the kitchen floor because the stove provided the only heat in the house, the kids knew their parents loved them and expected alot from them.

EARLY MEMORIES

Across the street from the Joyner home was a youth activity center where Jackie noticed kids enjoying track and field games. She decided to join in and was coached by Nino Fennoy, a man who has devoted himself to aspiring athletes from the ghetto of East St. Louis. When she ran her first race she came in dead last but, according to Nino, with a "big, wide grin." "I can still see her head with pigtails, the little skinny legs, the knees and the smile," he says.

Within a short time, showing the determination and willingness to work hard that has made her such a great athlete, Jackie was winning all her races. She even got her little sisters to help out: they brought sand into the Joyner backyard in potato chip bags so Jackie could have a sand pit for her long jump practice. She began to compete in the five-event pentathlon, combining running, jumping, and hurdles. By the time she was 14, she had begun a four-year streak as National Junior Pentathlon champion.

EDUCATION

Jackie attended John Robinson Elementary School and enjoyed dancing, acting, and cheerleading, as well as academics. She did well in school and clearly excelled in sports. But her mother was adamant about how Jackie was to channel her energies. "Even at 10 or 12 I was a hot, fast little cheer-leader," she says. "But my mother said, with no chance for negotiation, that I was *not* going out with guys until I was 18! So I threw myself into sports and school." She was a star of the Lincoln High School basketball and volleyball teams—her basketball team averaged 50 points more than their rivals her senior year—and was heavily recruited by colleges when she graduated from Lincoln High School in 1980. She chose UCLA (University of California at Los Angeles), where she majored in history and competed in track and field events and in basketball.

During her freshman year tragedy struck: Mary Joyner contracted a rare form of meningitis and died suddenly, at the age of 38. Jackie was devastated, but remained strong for the other family members. "I felt that I was the strong link. If I went back to school and did what I was supposed to do, everyone else would know 'Hey—we're not supposed to sit here and cry'." She didn't allow herself to feel her deep sense of grief until months later. "It hit me. Hard. And I just let it all out, everything I had been holding in. I just exploded." Of her mother's early death, Jackie said this: "It brought about a clearer sense of reality. I knew about setting goals and things, but with her gone, some of her determination passed to me." She used that determination to help her through school. Jackie received her bachelor's degree in history from UCLA in 1986.

MARRIAGE AND FAMILY

When she returned to college after her mother's death, Jackie's coach, Bob Kersee, who had also lost his mother in his late teens, offered her friendship and strength in that difficult time. Kersee had taken an interest in Jackie's training earlier and had approached UCLA's athletic department demanding that he be allowed to help her to develop what he felt was an astounding sports potential. It was Bob, in fact, who encouraged Jackie to compete in the heptathlon, which has become her main sports event.

Although Jackie claims that with Bob "it was athlete at first sight," they began to develop a relationship based on their mutual love of sport. Jackie Joyner and Bob Kersee married in 1986, the year she graduated from UCLA. According to friends, they are able to separate their working and personal lives.

Family also includes other sports champions. Jackie's brother Al, who also coached with Kersee, was a gold medalist in the 1984 Olympics. His wife, Florence Griffith Joyner, another Kersee-coached star, won three gold medals in the 1988 Olympics.

CAREER HIGHLIGHTS

Jackie had a distinguished collegiate athletic career. She was named UCLA Scholar Athlete in 1985, received the Broderick Cup for Collegiate Woman Athlete of the Year in 1986, and was named Most Valuable Player for UCLA's basketball and track and field teams in 1986. And while still in college, she began to realize the dreams she had had as a little girl in East St. Louis: to become an Olympic competitor.

1984 OLYMPICS

The Olympics of 1984 were the first to include the heptathlon for women, a seven-event competition that includes a 200-meter run, 100-meter hurdles, high jump, long jump, shot put, javelin throw, and an 800-meter run. Each activity is scored separately, and an athlete receives a certain number of points for how well she does in each event. The winner is the one with the greatest number of accumulated points. The competition takes place over two days, and it is considered one of the most grueling and demanding sports events. "It shows you what you're made of," Jackie says. "The heptathlon always slaps you back to reality."

Jackie was favored to win the gold medal in the 1984 Olympics. But due to a pulled hamstring, she did not do as well as she thought she would and had to settle for second place and a silver medal. The surprise of the Joyner family was Al, who received a gold medal in the triple jump. But he is best remembered from that Olympics for the encouragement he gave his injured sister in the last leg of her heptathlon race. As Jackie rounded the final turn of the last race, clearly in pain and slowing down, Al ran to the inside track and cheered her on. At the end of the awards ceremony, she collapsed in his arms, crying. "It's O.K.," Al said, trying to comfort her. "I'm not crying because I lost," said Jackie, "I'm crying because you won."

In 1986, Jackie broke the world heptathlon record at the Goodwill games in Moscow and broke her own record one month later at the Olympic Festival Games in Houston. She became the first women ever to break the score of 7,000 combined points in the heptathlon, and the first American woman since Babe Didrikson 50 years earlier to hold a world record in a multievent sport. That year she also received the prestigious James E. Sullivan Award, which is given to the outstanding amateur athlete in the U.S., and rarely given to a woman.

In 1987 she again broke 7,000 points to win the heptathlon at the World Track and Field Championships in Rome, where she also won the long jump. She was ready for Olympic competition again, this time in Seoul, Korea.

1988 OLYMPICS

Jackie qualified and was favored to win the gold medal in both the heptathlon and the long jump, and she met all expectations in this Olympiad, breaking an Olympic record in the long jump. It was also a stunning victory for the other women coached by Bob Kersee, including Griffith Joyner and Valerie Brisco, as they took home more gold medals for the U.S. But it was also an Olympics marred by the controversy over the illegal use of steroids and other drugs by some athletes to enhance performance. At Seoul in 1988, Canadian sprinter and gold-medal favorite

Ben Johnson was disqualified because of drug use. A Brazilian athlete suggested that Jackie and Florence Griffith Joyner had also used drugs, claiming that the way they looked and performed could only be the result of steroids. "Hey, it's sad for me," said Jackie. "I worked hard to get here. I haven't used drugs. It's time and patience and work. So it's just not fair to point fingers, to blame us all."

Injury again prevented Joyner-Kersee from completing the heptathlon competition in the 1991 World Championships in Tokyo, Japan. She strained a hamstring during the 200-meter run and had to leave the stadium in an ambulance.

1992 OLYMPICS

Joyner-Kersee headed to Barcelona in the summer of 1992 determined to win back-to-back gold medals in the heptathlon. "Coming back from the injury was very hard for me to deal with. I'd be running with the other girls in practice and suddenly I'd slow down. I had flashbacks to Tokyo. . . . I guess Tokyo was meant to happen. It helped me put a lot of things in perspective. It motivates me to do better."

All the time spent in physical and mental preparation paid off, as Jackie became the first woman to win the Olympic heptathlon two times. Her point total—7,044—was not her best, but it was good enough to outdistance

her chief rivals, Irina Belova of the Unified Team and Sabin Braun of Germany. "It was tough," Jackie said. "I wanted to psyche myself up and not psyche myself out. . . . It was a feeling of relief and joy when I crossed [the 800-meter finish] line." Back-to-back gold was not to be hers in the long jump, however. She was bested by Heike Drechsler of Germany and Inessa Kravats of the Unified Team and received the bronze medal for third place.

GOALS AND ASPIRATIONS

Joyner-Kersee now looks to the 1996 Olympics in Atlanta to be her last competition. "I would like to stay around until '96 and end my career on American soil," she says. She and Bob would like to start a family, and she would also like to begin a career as a sports commentator. Always the professional, Jackie is practicing speaking and performing with a tutor in front of a teleprompter.

MAJOR INFLUENCES

Jackie names her mother as her most important influence.

HOBBIES AND OTHER INTERESTS

Joyner-Kersee enjoys watching movies and television, as well as shopping, something that her lucrative endorsement contracts allow her to enjoy. She has represented the products of Seven-Up, McDonald's, Primatene Mist, Adidas, and Massengill. Today, she and her husband enjoy their sports cars and remodeling their four-bedroom home in southern California.

She is also very committed to a number of activities to help disadvantaged young people, the homeless, and seniors, traveling often to speak to youth groups. "I realize that I've been blessed to do well in athletics. And I have had a lot of opportunities and a lot of doors have been opened for me. I think being able to share that with someone else is a great satisfaction like winning the gold, being able to give back."

HONORS AND AWARDS

Olympic Heptathlon: 1984, Silver Medal; 1988, Gold Medal; 1992, Gold Medal
UCLA Scholar Athlete Award: 1985
Broderick Cup: 1986
UCLA Most Valuable Player, basketball and track and field: 1986
James E. Sullivan Award: 1986
Jesse Owens Memorial Award: 1986, 1987
Woman Athlete of the Year, *Track & Field News*: 1986, 1987

Associated Press Sports Award Athlete of the Year—Women: 1987
World Track and Field Championships: 1987, First place, heptathlon and
   long jump
Olympic Long Jump: 1988, Gold Medal; 1992, Bronze Medal

FURTHER READING

BOOKS

Who's Who among Black Americans, 1992-93

PERIODICALS

Chicago Tribune, Aug. 3, 1992, p.C8
Current Biography Yearbook 1987
Ebony, Oct. 1986, p.77; Apr. 1989, p.99
Essence, Aug. 1989, p.62
Life, Oct. 1988, p.89
Ms., Oct. 1988, p.31
New York Times Magazine, July 31, 1988, p.15
People, Aug. 29, 1988, p.56; Jan 30, 1989, p.44
Sporting News, June 29, 1992, p.8
Sports Illustrated, Apr. 27, 1987, p.76; Oct. 10, 1988, p.44
Time, Sept. 19, 1988, p.48
Washington Post, Aug. 3, 1992, p.C1; Aug. 8, 1992, p.D1
Women's Sports and Fitness, Jan. 1987, p.38

ADDRESS

JJK & Associates
3466 Bridgeland Dr.
Suite 105
Bridgetown, MO 63044

Spike Lee   1957-
American Filmmaker and Actor
Director of *Do the Right Thing, Jungle Fever,* and
Malcolm X

BIRTH

Shelton Jackson (Spike) Lee was born March 20, 1957, in Atlanta,
Georgia. The Lee family moved to Brooklyn, New York, when
Spike, nicknamed by his mother, was about two years old. His
father, William Lee, is a jazz composer and musician; his mother,
Jacquelyn Shelton Lee, was an art and literature teacher who died
quite suddenly from cancer in 1977, when Spike was in college.
They had five children: Spike was the oldest, followed by Chris,
David, Joie, and Cinque. Lee also has a much younger half brother,
Arnold, from his father's second marriage.

YOUTH

Lee comes from a strong and supportive family that valued education, culture, and their black heritage. His great-grandfather, who graduated from Tuskegee Institute in Alabama, was an author, educator, and disciple of Booker T. Washington; he also founded a school based on Washington's ideas. Both Lee's father and grandfather graduated from predominately black Morehouse College in Atlanta, and his mother and grandmother both attended its sister school, Spelman College.

Though filled with love, Spike Lee's family was certainly not well-to-do. His father's income as a jazz musician was sometimes erratic, and the family often relied on his mother's salary from teaching art at a private school. Yet his parents were able to provide a wealth of artistic and cultural experiences, including many that bolstered Lee's feelings of pride in being black. He visited art galleries and museums, attended plays, read the works of black writers, took piano and guitar lessons, and sometimes accompanied his father to his jobs at jazz clubs and music festivals. As Spike Lee once said, "We were raised in a very artistic family. So he was taking me to see him play at the Village Gate, at The Bitter End, at the Blue Note, when I was four, five years old. See him play with Odetta, Judy Collins, Leon Bibb, Peter, Paul, and Mary."

EARLY MEMORIES

Lee's experiences growing up were unique for his neighborhood, as he recalls: "I remember when my friends would come by the house, and they would say, 'You mean your father lives with you?!' A two-parent household was rare then—and now, and it made a great difference in my outlook on life."

EDUCATION

Lee's strong feelings of racial pride surfaced early. Given a choice between the predominately white private school where his mother taught, or the local public school with its mix of black and white students, Lee chose the latter. In 1975, he graduated from John Dewey High School in Brooklyn. It came as no surprise when Lee, like his father and grandfather before him, decided to attend Morehouse College. Lee has said that his years there, in a virtually all-black environment, had a profound effect on him. In his sophomore year he began, in his own words, "to dib and dab in super-8 filmmaking." By his senior year he had decided to pursue a career in film. He received his B.A. in communications in 1979, then spent the summer doing an internship at Columbia Pictures.

That fall Lee began the master's program in filmmaking at New York University's Tisch School of the Arts. There he met Ernest Dickerson, another black film student, who has worked as cinematographer on all of Lee's films. Dickerson once described how he and Lee felt as film students: "Fever—we all had it *bad*. We were on a mission. We wanted to make films that captured the black experience in this country. Films about what we knew. We just couldn't wait." Despite some difficulties in his early years in the graduate program, Lee's thesis project, entitled *Joe's Bed-Stuy Barbershop: We Cut Heads,* was a great success. The hour-long film tells the story of a Brooklyn barber shop that also serves as a front for a gambling operation. *Joe's Bed-Stuy Barbershop* received a student Academy Award for directing, was the first student film to be featured at a prestigious series at Lincoln Center in New York City, and was shown to great acclaim on public television and at various film festivals. Lee received his master's degree in filmmaking from New York University in 1983.

FIRST JOBS

Despite this success, no job offers awaited Lee after he graduated. As he soon discovered, raising enough money to fund projects is both crucial and difficult for a young filmmaker. While trying to finance what was to be his first feature film, Lee worked cleaning film at a movie distribution house, earning $200 each week. He was able to raise $40,000 to begin filming *Messenger,* the story of a young black bicycle messenger and his relationships with his family. There were pre-production difficulties, though, including a dispute with the Screen Actors Guild and problems with financing, and he was forced to cancel the project.

That experience fueled Lee's desire to work independently. As he later said, "If I had gone to Hollywood for money for [a] film with an all-black cast they'd have said 'Forget it.' I always knew I was going to have to do this on my own." He set out to create a movie that could be made for as little money as possible, with few characters and no elaborate sets or costumes. To fulfill that goal, he wrote the script for *She's Gotta Have It.*

With only an $18,000 grant from the New York State Council on the Arts, Lee and cast and crew shot the movie in an upstairs unventilated apartment in Brooklyn over 12 hot days in the summer of 1985. Every evening, Lee and Monty Ross, his friend from Morehouse and co-producer, would call everyone they knew, trying to raise enough money to continue. The film was produced on a budget of only $175,000, considered phenomenally low by Hollywood standards. Its immediate success, especially considering its low production costs, quickly made Lee into a bankable star.

CAREER HIGHLIGHTS

Lee is an independent filmmaker. Rather than work for a movie studio, he has set up his own production company, Forty Acres and a Mule Filmworks (the name derives from the promise made to the freed slaves after the Civil War). With the staff there, which includes several longtime friends from his days at Morehouse and New York University, Lee writes his own scripts, raises money from investors, and directs his own films.

The issue of race is central to all of Lee's work, and he in turn sees it as the defining feature of American life: "To me, I don't think there's ever going to be a time in America where a white person looks at a black person and they don't see that they're black. That day ain't coming very soon. Don't hold your breath. So that's a given. So why am I going to get blue in the face, worrying about that? For me, that's one of the most important things Malcolm X said: 'What do you call a black man with a Ph.D.? Nigger.' That's it."

Lee has made five films in the past six years. With his pervasiveness in movies, television commercials, music videos, and even books, it's difficult now to believe that in 1986, when his first feature film was released, he was completely unknown. *She's Gotta Have It* (1986) tells the story of an independent young woman with three lovers. In interviews, Lee has discussed two issues he was trying to address in this film: the prevailing sexual double standard about what's acceptable for men and women, and the lack of contemporary romantic movies about blacks: "We wanted to. . .make an intelligent film that showed black people loving each other and black people falling out of love." It was in this film that Lee created the role of the hip, streetwise, fast-talking bicycle messenger Mars Blackmon, a role he has made famous through television commercials for products like Nike athletic shoes. *School Daze* (1988), a musical, depicted two rival groups on a predominantly black campus, the light-skinned Wannabees (for wanna-be-white) and dark-skinned Jigaboos. According to Lee, the film depicts his own college experiences: "The film *is* my four years at Morehouse. But I'm not trying to pick on black colleges. I used black colleges as a microcosm of black society." The film received mixed reviews, and its depiction of prejudice based on color within the black community generated much controversy.

Do the Right Thing (1989) depicts one scorchingly hot summer day in the Bedford-Stuyvesant neighborhood of Brooklyn, New York. A conflict rears up between the white Italian-American owners of a neighborhood pizzeria and the black community members. By the end of the day, a black man, Radio Raheem, has been killed by the police, and the community has erupted into a riot. Lee plays Mookie, who works delivering pizza and tries to mediate during the escalating conflict—although it is Mookie who ultimately touches off the riot by throwing a garbage can through the pizzeria window.

The movie won rave reviews, although many found it controversial. Some critics questioned Mookie's act of violence, which, according to Lee, is understandable, if not defensible, in light of the police brutality that killed a man. Many reviewers questioned Lee's decision to end the movie with a quotation from Malcolm X defending the use of violence. Some went so far as to voice concerns that showing the movie would ignite riots within the audience. Yet Lee, when asked, had a rather different interpretation of the film, one that focused not on the violence, but on the issue of race: "*Do the Right Thing* is about racism, about our own individual prejudices, which I feel are hurtling us as a nation into a descending spiral of hate. There's a character in *Do the Right Thing,* Radio Raheem, who gives a sermon on love and hate and their effects on people. Hate is a bitch. When you're hated as a people, you eventually end up hating yourself. Racism is a bitch."

In his next film, *Mo' Better Blues* (1990), Lee took a break from the issue of racism. The movie has been called a jazz romance, telling the story of a self-absorbed, almost obsessed trumpet player who is sought after by two women—although he ultimately puts his music first. *Jungle Fever* (1991), his most recent release, depicts a relationship between a black architect, who is married, and his white Italian-American secretary. The film was inspired, in part, by the murder of Yusef Hawkins, a black teenager, in Bensonhurst, an Italian-American section of New York City, by a mob who believed that he was dating a white woman. As Lee said, "I thought it was time to go back to the No. 1 problem in America—

racism—but to try to broaden the canvas from *Do the Right Thing*. That was about race alone. This is about race, sex, class, drugs—and that's a more combustible mixture." Critics agreed, praising its inspired technical artistry and compelling treatment of issues; many consider it his best work to date.

Lee's next film is *Malcolm X*, a biography of the activist and leader who was slain in 1965. Due out in late 1992, the film has already generated a lot of heat from those who question how Lee intends to portray him. With his message of black pride and self-determination, Malcolm X has become an important symbol for many blacks. Yet their interpretations of his life vary greatly. According to Alex Haley, the coauthor of his autobiography, "Probably no scriptwriter alive could write a script that would satisfy the diverse groups who feel an ownership of Malcolm, feel a possessiveness of the image of Malcolm." With this film, Lee seems guaranteed to continue to generate controversy, broaden people's awareness, challenge their assumptions, and inspire them to think.

MAJOR INFLUENCES

Lee often cites the influence of several filmmakers on his work, including Martin Scorsese, Akira Kurosawa, and Francis Ford Coppola.

MARRIAGE AND FAMILY

Lee is unmarried. He is said to be dating the model Veronica Webb, who appeared as his wife in *Jungle Fever*, but he refuses to answer interviewers' questions about his personal life. He lives fairly simply in Brooklyn, near his family, to whom he remains close. Indeed, his siblings have done a lot of work for him: Chris handles merchandising at Lee's store, Spike's Joint; David, a photographer, does still shots for the films; Joie has acted in four of his films; and Cinque, who also hopes to become a filmmaker, has videotaped the making of his brother's movies for documentaries. In addition, his father has composed the music for his films.

HOBBIES AND OTHER INTERESTS

Lee has always been more than a filmmaker, interested in disseminating his ideas in other ways too. He markets merchandise from each of his films, has written a book about each film's production, speaks at workshops on entrepreneurship, lectures on Afrocentricity, teaches film courses, and produces commercials as well as music videos for a diverse group of artists including Stevie Wonder, Public Enemy, Tracy Chapman, Anita Baker, Miles Davis, and Branford Marsalis.

He often discusses the need for economic self-empowerment for blacks. As he says, "Without money, you have no control. Without control, you have no power." To that end, he continues to direct resources into the black community: by providing jobs through both his production company and his store, Spike's Joint, located in his Brooklyn neighborhood; by funding a minority student scholarship at New York University's film school; by creating a scholarship fund at Morehouse College; and by contributing to the United Negro College Fund and other charities.

MOVIES

She's Gotta Have It, 1986
School Daze, 1988
Do the Right Thing, 1989
Mo' Better Blues, 1990
Jungle Fever, 1991
Malcolm X, 1992

WRITINGS

Spike Lee's "Gotta Have It": Inside Guerilla Filmmaking, 1987
Uplift the Race: The Construction of "School Daze," 1988
"Do the Right Thing": A Spike Lee Joint, 1989
"Mo' Better Blues," 1990
5 for 5, 1991

HONORS AND AWARDS

Prix de la Jeunesse (Young Director's Prize, Cannes Film Festival): 1986, for *She's Gotta Have It*

FURTHER READING

BOOKS
Encyclopedia Britannica Book of the Year, 1990
Who's Who among Black Americans, 1992-93

PERIODICALS
Current Biography Yearbook 1989
Ebony, Jan. 1987, p.42; Oct. 1989, p.140
Essence, July 1989, p.55
Newsweek, Aug. 26, 1991, p.52
New York Times, May 31, 1992, Sec. II, p.13
New York Times Magazine, Aug. 9, 1987, p.26; also in *New York Times Biographical Service,* Aug. 1987, p.782
People, Oct. 13, 1986, p.67
Rolling Stone, July 11-25, 1991, p.63
Vanity Fair, June 1991, p.70

ADDRESS

40 Acres and a Mule Filmworks
124 DeKalb Ave.
Brooklyn, NY 11217

Mario Lemieux 1965-
Canadian Professional Hockey Player
Member of the Pittsburgh Penguins,
1992 NHL Champions

BIRTH

Mario Lemieux was born October 5, 1965, to Jean-Guy and Pierrette Lemieux. The family lived in Ville Emard, a suburb of the French-Canadian city of Montreal, Quebec. His father worked in the construction business, while his mother stayed at home to care for Mario and his two older brothers, Alain and Richard. The Lemieux family speaks French as their native language.

YOUTH

Winters in Canada are cold, and Montreal is no exception. But children there look forward to winter because they love to play ice hockey, Canada's most popular sport. Like most kids, Lemieux learned to skate on a neighborhood rink when very young, and by the age of six he was playing on an organized hockey team with other kids his age. He got a lot of pointers from his oldest brother, Alain, who went on to play professionally. Mario's father provided encouragement and support, but never pushed—although he did build a hockey rink inside the house, packing snow wall-to-wall so his children could practice indoors.

For Mario, it paid off. By the age of nine he was developing a reputation throughout Montreal for his skill on the ice, his control of the puck, and his size. At the age of 13, as the captain of his bantam team, he scored 130 goals in 32 games. His bedroom, at his parents' home, is filled with trophies from those years. To this day, children walk by the Lemieux home to see where Mario lived.

EARLY MEMORIES

When Lemieux reminisces about his childhood, it's clear that he always knew what he wanted to do with his life. "I started to skate when I was two or three, and played my first game at six. By the time I was twelve, I knew I had a lot of talent."

EDUCATION

Lemieux dropped out of high school at the age of 16. At that point he was playing on a junior league team, and he already knew that he wanted to play professionally. "I quit school when I was 16, in my second year of junior. I wanted to be able to skate in the morning and play hockey at night without being tired for the game. And I figured I could do my learning through living and traveling.

"My father tried to talk me out of it, when I told him during the summer. I told him I was not going back to school. We talked enough and finally he agreed with me that I should concentrate on hockey because I was only two years away from the draft."

CAREER HIGHLIGHTS

JUNIOR LEAGUE

There is nothing in the United States that quite corresponds to the Canadian junior hockey league, where Lemieux was playing when he dropped out of school; it is perhaps closest to baseball's minor league. Lemieux played center for the Laval (Quebec) Voisins of the Quebec Major Junior Hockey League for three seasons, beginning in 1981, while he was still in school. During his first year, he scored 96 points, and the team finished in seventh place. For the next two years, Lemieux led the team to the league championship, finishing with 184 points his second year and an astounding 282 points during his final season, with 133 goals and 149 assists. In the process, he broke all the junior league scoring records. Talent scouts from the National Hockey League (NHL) teams had been watching his progress, and he was the first player selected in the NHL draft in 1984. Lemieux was signed by the Pittsburgh Penguins, a team with a consistently losing record in the mid-1980s.

NATIONAL HOCKEY LEAGUE

It took a while for Lemieux to get adjusted during his first season with the Penguins. He was living with a local family, but he missed his family and friends back home. He spoke and understood little English; according to Lemieux, what little he did know he learned by watching television soap operas. In addition, tremendous expectations were placed on him, and tremendous pressure. With their poor performance, the Penguins were able to sell very few tickets. The team was losing money and was in danger of going bankrupt, being sold, or moving to another city. Team management looked on Lemieux as a savior, created a huge public relations campaign to "market" him to the fans, and sent him out on a round of public appearances to generate interest in the team.

Lemieux got off to a great start with the Penguins, scoring a goal on his very first shot as a professional player. He scored only once during his next twelve games, but he soon returned to his usual form. He finished the 1984-85 season with 43 goals and 57 assists, for 100 points, and was named Rookie of the Year, the first of many such awards. The following year he scored 141 points and was named Most Valuable Player (MVP) by the NHL Players Association. He was well on his way to another outstanding season in 1986-87 when he was sidelined with a sprained knee and bronchitis, finishing the season with 107 points.

In his next season, 1987-88, Lemieux became a hockey superstar. In the Canada Cup tournament in September 1987, he was placed at right wing on a line with Wayne Gretzky, who set up 9 of the 11 goals he scored. By playing with Gretzky, Lemieux learned a lot about the drive and intensity a great player brings to the game. According to Lemieux, "The Canada Cup was the highlight of my career. Watching Gretzky play at the level he does every night and trying to keep up with him showed me what it takes to help your team make it to the top."

In regular season play that year, Lemieux scored 70 goals and 98 assists for 168 points. That earned him the NHL scoring title, which Gretzky had owned for the past seven years, and the Hart Trophy for league MVP, which Gretzky had captured for the past eight years. Lemieux's career-high total of 199 points the following year won him a second scoring title. Initially, 1989-90 looked to be more of the same, until his 46-game scoring streak was stopped by some back trouble. He ended up missing 21 of the last 22 games, finishing the season with 123 points. In July 1990 he had surgery to fix a herniated disk. His recovery was going well, he thought, until he began having new and more severe back pains in late August. He was eventually diagnosed with osteomyelitis, a rare bone infection so severe that his doctors thought he might never play again. After massive doses of antibiotics and a long recovery, he returned to play only 26 games during the 1990-91 season. But even with a shortened season, he scored 45 points, led the Penguins in the championship series against the Minnesota North Stars, and brought home the Stanley Cup for the first time in the history of the Pittsburgh team. For his efforts, Lemieux was named Most Valuable Player of the championship series.

This past season, 1991-92, was difficult for the Penguins. Their popular coach, Bob Johnson, died of brain cancer, the team was sold to a new owner, and several key players were traded. Throughout this string of bad news, the team's performance was erratic, even in the playoffs. Lemieux had to be careful with his back, and he often played in pain. Although he appeared in only 64 regular-season games, he scored 131 points and won his third scoring title. During post-season play, Lemieux missed five playoff games with a broken hand when New York Ranger Adam Graves slashed him with his stick. Lemieux still managed to score 34 points in the playoffs, earning the MVP award for the championship series. The Penguins defeated the Chicago Blackhawks in a 4-0 sweep and won the Stanley Cup for the second year in a row. In Pittsburgh, there's talk of a dynasty.

Comparisons to Gretzky, "the Great One," have dogged Lemieux since his junior league days—an honor, to be sure, but also a burden. Many have described Lemieux's style of play as similar to Gretzky's. Both are said to have great "hockey sense," the ability to forecast the movements of the players and the puck. This special sense allows them to anticipate the play. They seem to know intuitively—almost omnisciently—exactly where each player is, and where all will be moments after the puck is hit. Despite these similarities, there are certainly differences between the two players as well, first and foremost their size. The smaller Gretzky can use speed to finesse his way along the boards or between the opposing players. For Lemieux, at six feet four inches and about 210 pounds, that's impossible. He's known, instead, for his long skating stride, his very long reach, and his powerful, accurate shots. As veteran player Emile Francis described him, "He can thread the eye of a needle with the puck. Mario is one of the best passers I have ever seen."

Lemieux's style of play has earned him some criticism, too. During his early years with the Penguins he was often faulted for lacking intensity, for taking it easy at times during the games. Some of that reputation may have derived simply from his style of play. With his great skating power, he often appears to move effortlessly down the ice. Questioned about this, Lemieux responded, "I skate with a long stride, and that's why I sometimes look slow. But I can skate with all the good skaters in the league. And I don't like to skate for nothing. I look first, and anticipate, and try to be at the right spot at the right moment. That's why a lot of people say that I don't look as though I work hard. But I work my mind. That's a lot better than skating all over the place." John Davidson, former NHL goalie and television commentator, agrees with this assessment. "One of the many things Mario does well is conserve energy," Davidson once said. "He conserves fuel. People think he's lazy, but that's not true. He's just smart." Davidson's comments would earn wide agreement now that Lemieux has led the Penguins to two Stanley Cups, and criticism of his style of play and comparisons with the great Gretzky may have finally come to an end.

MARRIAGE AND FAMILY

Lemieux's steady companion for the past ten years has been Nathalie Asselin. They first met when he was 17 and she was 15 and working as a lifeguard. According to Asselin, a French-Canadian, it was love at first sight: "After the first minute, I knew." They have been living together in a mansion he had built in the wealthy suburb of Mount Lebanon, Pennsylvania, which is just 10 minutes from the Penguins' practice rink. In December 1991, Lemieux and Asselin became engaged.

HOBBIES AND OTHER INTERESTS

Until recently, Lemieux was an avid golfer who dreamed of someday joining the pro circuit, but his back problems have put a kink in that plan. At least for now, he has to be very careful. Fortunately for Lemieux, he can still indulge in the activity he enjoys most: kicking back at home with Nathalie. They are currently buying a second home, in the countryside south of Pittsburgh, where they can keep horses, add to Lemieux's wine collection, and maintain some privacy.

"I've always been quiet," Lemieux once remarked, "and I've always tried to guard my privacy. It was the same when I was very young and, now that I've become a celebrity, it's even more true. It's true I have more money than most people but when I'm in Pittsburgh, I stay at home. I'm happy with Nathalie and I don't want to complicate my life. We have a few favorite restaurants where the people don't bother us even if we are recognized.

"On the road it is just the same. . . .What I like most is just to go have a quiet beer with my teammates and then go to bed. It sounds a little boring, but I'm happy like that."

HONORS AND AWARDS

Calder Memorial Trophy (Rookie of the Year): 1984-85
Lester B. Pearson Award (Most Valuable Player, voted by NHL Players Association): 1985-86, 1987-88
NHL Player of the Year *(Sporting News):* 1987-88
Hart Memorial Trophy: (Most Valuable Player, voted by hockey writers): 1988
Art Ross Trophy (NHL scoring title): 1988, 1989, 1992
Conn Smythe Trophy (Most Valuable Player of playoff series): 1991, 1992

FURTHER READING

BOOKS

The Lincoln Library of Sports Champions, Vol. 10, 1989
Who's Who in America, 1990-91

PERIODICALS

Current Biography Yearbook 1988
Gazette (Montreal, Quebec), Nov. 12, 1983, p.G1
Globe and Mail (Toronto, Ontario), Nov. 30, 1985, p.C1
Hockey News, June 12, 1992, p.3
Macleans, Feb. 20, 1989, p.32
Scholastic Update, Feb. 9, 1987, p.20
Sport, Mar. 1988, p.66; Feb. 1990, p.48
Sporting News, June 8, 1992, p.41
Sports Illustrated, Feb. 6, 1989, p.28; June 8, 1992, p.14

ADDRESS

Pittsburgh Penguins
Civic Arena
300 Auditorium Place
Pittsburgh, PA 15219

AUTOBIOGRAPHY

Madeleine L'Engle 1918-
American Author of Juvenile and Adult Fiction
Writer of *A Wrinkle in Time* and Other Books

BIRTH

I was born in New York City, on the asphalt island of Manhattan, of parents whose friends were artists—opera singers, composers, sculptors, actors, writers. We lived in a small apartment full of books and music. My short cut, when I went to play in Central Park, was through The Metropolitan Museum of Art, in a day when security could be much more casual than it is today. I was a solitary, only child, and read and wrote.

YOUTH

I grew up in New York, France, Switzerland, England. My father's work as a journalist often took us abroad.

EDUCATION

My first recollection of school: empty notebooks to write stories in! Colored pencils to make pictures with. Friends to play with. The first three years of school were wonderful. After that, it was the abyss until I got into high school, where it became wonderful again.

I received an A.B. with honors from Smith. The best thing I learned at Smith was how to do research in any field that interests me, and how to keep on studying and learning all my life. I spent four years living with great writers, the best teachers a learning writer could have.

FIRST JOBS

You don't earn your living by writing novels to start off with, so with less naiveté than it might seem, I worked in the theatre as an actress. My first job was in a play called *Uncle Harry* starring Eva LeGallienne and Joseph Schildkraut.

MARRIAGE AND FAMILY

I met my husband, actor Hugh Franklin, in *The Cherry Orchard* and married him in *The Joyous Season*. We were married until his death, 40 years later. Three children: Josephine; Maria; Bion—all grown and married. I live with my granddaughters, Charlotte and Léna, who are in college in New York.

CHOOSING A CAREER

I wrote my first story when I was five, and have been writing ever since. I learned early that story is the human being's chief vehicle of truth.

MEMORABLE EXPERIENCES

Birthing—children and books.

HOBBIES AND OTHER INTERESTS

Playing the piano; walking with the dog; having friends in for dinner and talking till the candles burn down.

WRITINGS

FOR YOUNG READERS

The Small Rain: A Novel, 1945
And Both Were Young, 1949

Meet the Austins, 1960
A Wrinkle in Time, 1962
The Moon by Night, 1963
The Twenty-Four Days before Christmas: An Austin Family Story, 1964
The Arm of the Starfish, 1965
Camilla, 1965
The Journey with Jonah, 1967
The Young Unicorns, 1968
Dance in the Desert, 1969
Intergalactic P.S. 3, 1970
The Other Side of the Sun, 1971
A Wind in the Door, 1973
Everyday Prayers, 1974
Prayers for Sunday, 1974
Dragons in the Waters, 1976
A Swiftly Tilting Planet, 1978
Ladder of Angels: Scenes from the Bible Illustrated by the Children of the World,
     1979
The Time Trilogy, 1979 (contains *A Wrinkle in Time, A Wind in the Door* and
     A Swiftly Tilting Planet)
A Ring of Endless Light, 1980
The Anti-Muffins, 1981
A House Like a Lotus, 1984
*Trailing Clouds of Glory: Spiritual
     Values in Children's Books,*
     1985
Many Waters, 1986
An Acceptable Time, 1988
The Glorious Impossible, 1990

FOR ADULTS

*18 Washington Square, South:
     A Comedy in One Act,* 1945
Ilsa, 1946
Camilla Dickinson, 1951
A Winter's Love, 1957
The Love Letters, 1966
*Lines Scribbled on an Envelope,
     and Other Poems,* 1969
A Circle of Quiet, 1972
*The Summer of the Great-Grand-
     mother,* 1974
The Irrational Season, 1977

The Weather of the Heart, 1978
The Sphinx at Dawn: Two Stories, 1982
A Severed Wasp, 1983
Walking on Water: Reflections on Faith and Art, 1983
And It Was Good: Reflections on Beginnings, 1984
Dare to Be Creative, 1984
A Stone for a Pillow, 1986
A Cry Like a Bell, 1987
Two-Part Invention, 1987
The Crosswicks Journal Trilogy, 1988 (contains *A Circle of Quiet, The Summer of the Great-Grandmother,* and *The Irrational Season*)
From This Day Forward, 1988
Sold Into Egypt: Joseph's Journey into Human Being, 1988

HONORS AND AWARDS

John Newbery Medal: 1963, for *A Wrinkle in Time*
Hans Christian Andersen Runner-up Award: 1964, for *A Wrinkle in Time*
Sequoyah Children's Book Award: 1965, for *A Wrinkle in Time*
Lewis Carroll Shelf: 1965, for *A Wrinkle in Time*
Austrian State Literary Prize: 1969, for *The Moon by Night*
University of Southern Mississippi Silver Medallion: 1978, for "an outstanding contribution to the field of children's literature"
National Book Award: 1980, for *A Swiftly Tilting Planet*
Smith Medal: 1980
Newbery Honor Award: 1981, for *A Ring of Endless Light*
Sophie Award: 1984
Regina Medal (Catholic Literary Association): 1984
Alan Award (National Council of Teachers of English): 1986
Kerlan Award (Children's Literary Research Collections of the University of Minnesota): 1990

FURTHER READING

BOOKS

Contemporary Authors New Revision Series, Vol. 21
Something about the Author, Vol. 27
Who's Who in America, 1990-91

PERIODICALS

Ms., July/Aug. 1987, p.182

ADDRESS

Farrar, Straus & Giroux
19 Union Square W
New York, NY 10003

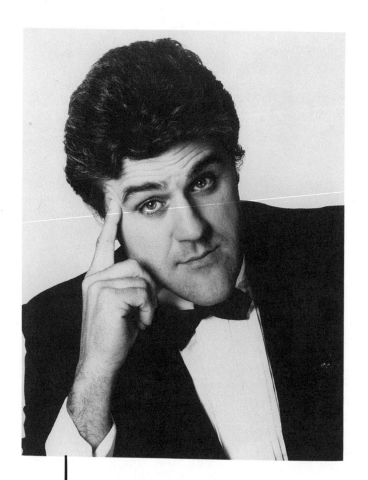

Jay Leno 1950-
American Comedian and Television Personality
Host of "The Tonight Show"

BIRTH

Jay (James Douglas Muir) Leno was born April 28, 1950, in New Rochelle, New York, to an Italian-American father and a Scottish-born mother, Angelo and Catherine (Muir) Leno. Born when his parents were already in their forties, he is younger by ten years than his brother and only sibling, Patrick. The family moved to the northeastern Massachusetts town of Andover when Leno was nine, and it was there that he spent most of his childhood and adolescence.

YOUTH

Jay Leno was a funny kid, just as he is a funny man. He started drawing chuckles when he was in grade school, with his smart quips and disruptive high jinks. In every way, he was the typical class clown. "The things I'd do—flush tennis balls down the toilets, lock dogs in lockers—were not exactly career moves," he says in speaking of those days. Yet, behind all the silliness and the horsing around was a true wit, as well as a developing sense of the ridiculous that has made his adult humor so unique. *Time* explains that "he is always himself. . . .He is the voice of common sense teased out to the absurd."

It is said that comedians often spring from unhappy or luckless childhoods, but Leno cannot make that claim. Jamie (the name his family still uses) grew up happy in a traditional, middle-class household. He absorbed honesty, decency, and respectability in the stable environment provided by his insurance-salesman father and his good-natured, levelheaded mother. His brother, Patrick, educated as a lawyer but now also in the insurance business, was the quiet one and the scholar in the family. Jamie, however, was an indifferent student and athlete, but was popular with his classmates and well-liked by their parents. Even his exasperated teachers appreciated his amiable disposition. He enjoyed life, loved to make others laugh, and never pretended to be anything but what he was—qualities that have clung to him throughout his career.

Leno's love of comedy was, no doubt, inherited from his father, whose delightful sense of humor and skill at telling funny stories brought him requests to entertain at company banquets and sales conventions. "His stories were all true," says the son, "and I used to think the whole thing was kind of neat. That's probably where the interest came from more than anything else."

As for Leno's other early interest—his now-celebrated love of cars and motorcycles—that came from being "a child of the auto culture," according to the *Boston Globe*. He tinkered with engines as a kid, bought his first car (a 1934 Ford pickup with a flathead V8) two years before he was eligible to drive, and worked as a car washer at a dealership during high school. Friends say that he enjoyed the usual pastimes of boyhood in a small town, and lived a normal, spirited youth.

EARLY MEMORIES

Leno talks openly about his young years in Andover, usually poking gentle fun at himself or his family. However, not all of those memories are of jokes and pranks, for when asked recently about his relationship with his parents, he revealed an especially touching incident that explained the depth of their feelings for one another. "We were never one of those [demonstrative] families," he answered. "But we were close. I remember when I was sixteen, I had a '34 Ford truck. I had just had the upholstery all done and I slammed the door one day and broke the window. Didn't have any money to get the window fixed. I drove the truck to school and it was sitting out in the parking lot when it started to rain. I figured my new upholstery was going to get ruined. But I'm looking out the window and I see my mom and dad pull up, and my dad's got a big sheet of plastic and my mom's putting it over the truck. I started to cry. My dad left the office because he knew how much the truck meant to me. We were always close that way."

EDUCATION

Leno's public school years, except for the primary grades, were spent in Andover. He graduated from Andover High School and attended Bentley College in Waltham, Massachusetts, for one year before transferring to Boston's Emerson College, where he earned a bachelor's degree in communications in 1973. A *Saturday Evening Post* feature writer, who attended one of his early professional comedy appearances, quipped later that the wide audience approval for Leno's material and delivery should have earned him, in addition, "a master's in charisma."

FIRST JOBS

Like thousands of teenagers in every city and town across the country, Leno worked for a short time at a local McDonald's. He confesses now, with more than a little embarrassment and shame, to giving away "bags of food" to his friends, but somehow in the telling, it's easy to detect a certain impishness in his admission. "His high school years under the Golden Arches gave Leno his first stand-up experience," says a *Cosmopolitan* article. The monologue he worked up for a company-wide talent contest won him a camera and a vacation trip, but even then there was no master plan, and it wasn't until later that he would seriously consider comedy as his life's work.

While studying at Emerson, Leno worked part-time as a mechanic for a Rolls Royce dealer in Boston. In making overnight deliveries to customers in New York City, he took advantage of a unique opportunity to try out his routines at such popular comedy clubs as the Improv and Catch a Rising Star.

CHOOSING A CAREER

The decision to make a career of comedy began to take shape during Leno's student years at Emerson. There, as frequent master of ceremonies for variety shows in the college cafeteria, he reveled in the audience appreciation of his material. The applause was quick and enthusiastic—and Leno was hooked. He branched out, doing stand-up at local Boston bars and traveling around the East Coast circuit until he finished college. A *New York Times Magazine* profile tells of how "he played everywhere he could: colleges, strip clubs, comedy clubs, a brothel, carnivals—hewing to a basic, simple character: an average Joe looking out at a world that was every day a little more strange than the day before."

CAREER HIGHLIGHTS

In 1975, two years after college graduation, Leno committed himself to comedy by purchasing a one-way ticket to Los Angeles. He had no contacts in the entertainment world, but on his own without a family to support, he was willing to take the considerable risk. His first months in California were a struggle and job offers were spotty, but Leno, who laughingly refers to those days as his "romantic period," hung on, making just enough money in off-beat nightclubs to feed himself and the gas tank of his 1955 Buick Roadmaster. On occasion, he even slept in his car, depending on new-found friends for the use of their bathrooms.

Leno's first break came when he was hired as a writer for comedian Jimmie Walker, then the star of a popular television show called "Good Times." With this measure of economic security, he was able to live a somewhat more normal life. His second break came when he met comic David Letterman, newly arrived from Indianapolis and anxious to be part of the Los Angeles comedy scene. He found Letterman a job on the Walker writing staff, and the two became friends. Years later, it would be through his countless appearances on "Late Night With David Letterman" that Leno would gain national exposure.

Jay Leno's popularity grew slowly but steadily. He was a guest on Johnny Carson's, Merv Griffin's, and Mike Douglas's TV shows, made a few token appearances in small-screen comedies, and became a frequent warmup act for such seasoned (and diverse) entertainers as Perry Como and Tom Jones. All the while, he continued to polish his own material on the road, playing in small towns, on college campuses, and even at shopping malls—he was away from home as many as three hundred nights a year. Finally, by the mid-1980s, Leno had become a hot stand-up comic, headlining at higher-class clubs across the country. He played to a sell-out crowd in a one-man show at New York's Carnegie Hall in 1986. He had arrived.

That same year, he and another popular comic, Garry Shandling, took over as permanent guest hosts on the "Tonight Show," but Leno's wide popularity soon secured for him the solo assignment. He admitted at the time that he hoped to eventually succeed Johnny Carson, although it was generally believed then that David Letterman would be NBC's choice as Carson's replacement. "I would visit every [network] affiliate where I was performing and do promos for them," Leno says honestly and with just a touch of mischief. "Then they would promote me in turn. My attitude was to go out and rig the numbers in my favor." His campaign worked. "Leno became the obvious choice for NBC," wrote *Time* last spring.

"Letterman's pervasive irony seems less suited to the '90s than Leno's sincerity. For NBC, giving Letterman the job was a lose-lose proposition: the network would lose 'Late Night With David Letterman,' the best and most profitable late-late-night show on TV, and it would lose Leno."

Leno's humor is a reflection of his clean and straightforward lifestyle. A big, cheerful guy with a lantern-jawed profile that a casting agent once said would "scare little children," his physical appearance is more accurately described as loose and pleasantly boyish (in spite of his graying hair), and with startling blue eyes. He is a polite, down-to-earth, energetic man who has made it in the entertainment world without sacrificing his own convictions. Racism, prejudice, dirty jokes—none of these are part of his act, say those who know him, any more than they are part of his personal world. His observations on the absurdities of everyday life are sharp, but never cruel, and his audience appeal seems to cross generational lines. If his more gentle form of humor can survive the sniping that has risen in the wake of his good fortune, Jay Leno may settle in for a long run as Carson's worthy successor. He is a "stand-up comic," says *Time*, "who is also a stand-up guy."

MARRIAGE AND FAMILY

Leno has been married since 1980 to former scriptwriter Mavis Nicholson. They had met four years earlier during one of his performances at the Comedy Store, a Hollywood club where struggling artists showcase their talents and where, even today, Leno returns to try out fresh routines. The Lenos live in a comfortable, English-style home in Beverly Hills that is roomy enough for their considerable and vastly different collections— hers, of valuable books, and his, of motorcycles and antique automobiles. The cars and cycles are housed in a two-story garage on the grounds. Leno also keeps an office in the garage and works there on his nightly monologue, which he prepares with the help of a few writer-friends and the studied advice of his wife.

The Lenos have no children but, as told to *Woman's Day* in a recent interview, they share their home with "an independent gray cat called Cheesler, Jay's name for anything cute and little." There is, however, a special child in their life—Sara, the eleven-year-old daughter of Helen Gorman Kushnick, Leno's longtime agent and manager and now executive producer of his new "Tonight Show." An exceptionally close relationship has developed between the two families since the tragic death at the age of three of Sara's twin brother, Sam, who was infected with AIDS through blood transfusions given after his premature birth. The Lenos enjoy the time they spend with Sara and encourage her in her pursuit of horseback riding championships. Helen Kushnick confides that, seeing them together, it's sometimes hard to tell who is the biggest kid—Sara or Jay.

MAJOR INFLUENCES

Leno never fails to credit his parents for their lasting influence on his personal life, nor his managers (Kushnick and her late husband, Jerry) for their loyalty and direction in his career, but he is basically a self-made man. His wife is quoted in *TV Guide* as saying that he is "amazingly self-produced—his outlook and talents he came up with on his own."

HOBBIES AND OTHER INTERESTS

Other than his family and his work, Leno's consuming interest is in vintage cars and motorcycles. He maintains a huge storage garage on his property and slips into coveralls at every free moment to tinker with the nineteen autos and approximately forty cycles he has acquired in the past several years. Among these is the Buick Roadmaster that served as sleeping quarters when he first arrived in California to jump-start his career. Leno admits that he devours "every car magazine published," and he has been known to ride out miles from home in search of just the right part for a given engine. His collection is not just for show, either—he drives his exotic classics to and from the studio and on short leisure excursions.

WRITINGS

Headlines, 1989
More Headlines, 1990
Headlines Three: Not the Movie, Still the Book, 1991
Headlines IV: The Generation, No. IV, 1992

All royalties from these collections of weird and amusing headlines are donated to the Samuel Jared Kushnick Foundation to raise funds for pediatric AIDS programs.

FURTHER READING

PERIODICALS

Cosmopolitan, Sept. 1989, p.210
Current Biography, 1988, p.235
Newsweek, June 29, 1992, p.56
New York Times Magazine, Feb. 26, 1989, p.26
Redbook, July 1992, p.48
Rolling Stone, Nov. 2, 1989, p.47
Saturday Evening Post, Mar. 1988, p.32
Woman's Day, Mar. 10, 1992, p.38
Time, Mar. 16, 1992, p.58; Aug. 17, 1992, p.62

ADDRESS

"The Tonight Show"
3000 W. Alameda
Burbank, CA 91523

Yo-Yo Ma 1955-
American Musician
Cellist

BIRTH

Yo-Yo Ma, considered the finest cellist of his generation, was born in Paris, France, on October 7, 1955, to Hiao-tsiun and Marina Ma. He was the second of two children. His sister, Yeou-Cheng, is four years older. His first name, "Yo," means "friendship" in Chinese.

YOUTH

Ma's parents, both musicians, had emigrated to France from China. His father was born in a town near Shanghai and moved to France in 1936, where he continued his musical studies and made his living as a musicologist, composer, and music teacher, specializing in instructing gifted young musicians. Ma's mother was raised in Hong Kong and moved to Paris in 1949, where she continued her career as a classical singer. Ma has talked about how his parents spoke different dialects of Chinese and had distinctly different attitudes toward music: he calls his father "analytical, technical, and intellectual," and describes his mother as "more emotional" and "less the pedagogue." Both these sides contributed in molding a prodigious talent in a young man whose cheerful, patient, and unruffled temperament make him one of the most delightful, as well as talented, of modern musicians. As Bernard Holland of the *New York Times* described him, "he is much as he plays—graceful, lyrical, thoughtful, and generous."

EARLY MEMORIES

Yo-Yo began lessons with his father at the age of four, in both cello and piano. He wanted something that was bigger than the violin, which his sister was playing at the time, so his father put a viola on an end-pin, and the young boy began to play on this makeshift "cello" while sitting on a stack of telephone books.

His father's method of teaching music offered Yo-Yo an exceptional opportunity to develop his young talent. He memorized two measures of music each day. But it wasn't two measures of a simple piece or a selection written for children: it was from a Bach suite for unaccompanied cello, music of great difficulty and complexity even for adult players. Yo-Yo was able to master these pieces at an astonishingly young age, and by the time he was five, he knew three of the Bach suites by heart and had performed one of them at a recital at the University of Paris. The world-renowned violinist Isaac Stern remembers hearing Ma play at that time: "The cello was literally larger than he was. I could sense then, as has now been confirmed, that he has one of the most extraordinary talents of this generation."

EARLY TRAINING

When Ma was seven, the family moved to New York City. Yo-Yo began to study with Janos Scholz, who remembers his young pupil with fondness: "He learned with lightening speed. He was everything one could wish for as a student, and the last I ever took." When he was eight, he appeared on television with Leonard Bernstein on the American Pageant of the Arts, which gave him national exposure as a child prodigy. By the age of nine, he was studying with Leonard Rose, one of the finest cellists of the modern era, at the Julliard School of Music. Under his teaching, Ma's talent flourished. "He may have one of the greatest techniques of all time," says Rose. "I'm always floored by it." Ma made his Carnegie Hall debut at nine.

EDUCATION

He attended school in New York City, and it was his experience in the American educational system that first brought him face to face with the clash of Chinese and American cultures that was to pose problems in his young years. "One of the duties of an Oriental child is unquestioning obedience to the parents," he recalls. "At home, I was to submerge my identity. . . . At school, I was expected to answer back, to reveal my individuality." By the time he was in the fifth grade, he began cutting classes. He later attended the Professional Children's School in New York, but he continued to skip classes. His teachers placed him in an accelerated program, and he graduated at 15, but the rebelliousness continued. The summer after graduation, he went to summer music camp at Meadowmount and really "went wild," in his own words. He drank, left his cello out in the rain, slept on tables, played pranks.

Back in New York, Ma entered Columbia University, which didn't turn out well. He dropped out, not telling his parents, and spent most of his time at Julliard. One day, he got drunk and passed out in a rehearsal room and had to be taken to the hospital. His parents were deeply shamed by the incident, and Ma himself is still rather embarrassed by his youthful indiscretions.

Ma and his sister, Yeou-Cheng, who is now a pediatrician, have always been close. While a student at Radcliffe College, she combined her academic work with continued studies in music. On a visit to her at Cambridge after he'd dropped out of Columbia, Ma decided to enroll at Harvard for his undergraduate degree. It proved to be a pivotal choice in his life. At Julliard, the stress had always been on his skill and development as an instrumentalist; at Harvard, his teachers tried to reach and develop the whole musician: "You know, I went to Harvard as a budding cellist. And they all started getting down on me, saying, 'You play very well, but if you only knew what you were doing.'. . . And I fought that for a long time, because I was scared of it. Because you hear of people who are very gifted when they're young, and then suddenly they become conscious of what they're doing and lose their natural ability. But finally, after about two years, I began to appreciate their advice." Ma also studied a range of subjects, from literature to philosophy to anthropology, indulging his fascination and curiosity with the wide world beyond music.

Yet it is certainly his musical education and the self-knowledge that he achieved at Harvard that he remembers. "What the people at Harvard gave me was a way of looking at things so that I could continue on my own— sort of training the mind to search for the meaning behind the notes."

MARRIAGE AND FAMILY

Ma met his future wife, Jill Horner, when he was sixteen, while she was a student at Mount Holyoke and he was at Harvard. Their friendship developed when they met again at the Marlboro Music Festival in Marlboro, Vermont, and continued long-distance during Jill's junior year abroad. When they married in 1978, their marriage put a strain on Ma's relationship with his parents. Because Jill was not Chinese, the elder Mas felt she posed a threat to the highly structured unit that typifies the traditional Chinese family. Yet they eventually accepted Jill as part of the family, and they take great delight in their grandchildren, Nicholas, born in 1984, and Emily, born in 1986.

CAREER HIGHLIGHTS

It is difficult to focus on highlights in the life of a young virtuoso who began playing solo concerts at five and had played Carnegie Hall at nine. He claims that his success took both him and his wife by surprise, for after he graduated from college his career took off, with a demanding performing and recording schedule that has only slowed in recent years to accommodate the needs of his family. He has played and recorded all the major pieces for cello, and his experience is distilled not only in performance, but also in his articulate response to the works of the great masters. Of Bach, one of his very favorites, he says: "Bach takes you to a very quiet place within yourself, to the inner core, a place where you are calm and at peace."

Ma's brilliant career was once in jeopardy because of a serious health problem. He was suffering from scoliosis, or curvature of the spine, and had to have an operation in his early twenties to correct a curve that formed an "s" in his back. The operation could have ended his cello playing because of potential nerve damage. He and Jill were both aware of the risks, yet with characteristic optimism, going into the operation Ma said: " 'Look, if I come out of this alive but not able to have control of my fingers, I will have had a very fulfilling life in music.'" The operation was a complete success, and he went on to even greater musical achievements.

Ma loves to play chamber music, music written for small groups of instrumentalists to perform. His frequent partner in this field is the American pianist Emanuel Ax, and their collaboration reflects a depth of training, talent, and sympathetic understanding that goes to the root of the chamber music experience. They have recorded the complete cello sonatas of Beethoven and Brahms, as well the Rachmaninoff and Prokofiev sonatas. As a reviewer in the *Los Angeles Times* wrote: "In the best ensemble tradition, they listen to each other, they watch each other, and minds and hearts become as closely attuned as bow and fingers." The two have also performed and recorded with Isaac Stern, who has been a great mentor to both of them.

Ma has also explored the realm of modern music, commissioning works from contemporary composers. Another recent departure for him is a foray into jazz, an often perilous field for a classically trained musician who has not been encouraged to improvise, which is the very soul of jazz. These new interests have led him to perform and record with the great jazz violinist Stephane Grappelli, and to collaborate with jazz vocalist Bobby McFerrin, which has resulted in a new recording, "Hush."

Ma enjoys teaching and devotes a good portion of his busy schedule to giving masters classes at the Tanglewood Music Festival in the Berkshires of Massachusetts. He is concerned about the current cutbacks in arts education. "The arts are always the first thing to go," he says. "That's the biggest problem we have in developing musicians and listeners. I'm very aware of our aging audiences. That's why I appear on programs like *Sesame Street* and *Mister Rogers Neighborhood.*"

Ma never plays the same concert twice and always tries to develop and grow with the pieces he plays. "You have to be within a piece of music, and then things become really exciting. You have to open yourself up to the audience. . . .What people call my exuberance comes from wanting to share what I've gained from a piece with my listeners. I hope I'll always do that."

INSTRUMENTS

Ma said recently that the cello is still his favorite instrument because it "has the exact range of the human voice, from basso profundo to soprano.

So in that sense, it's a very human instrument." He has played three different cellos during his career, all with a distinguished history, and each with its own tonal gifts. One is a Matteo Goffriller, made in Venice in 1722. Nicknamed "Sweetie Pie," this cello once belonged to the world-renowned cellist Pierre Fournier. The second instrument is a 1733 Montagnana. The third, and perhaps the most precious, is a Stradivarius, built in 1712. This instrument was once played by the great nineteenth-century cellist Davidoff and most recently by the late Jacqueline du Pre, a greatly gifted cellist whose brief, meteoric career was cut short by multiple sclerosis. The Strad has been made available to Ma for his lifetime and will presumably pass on to another accomplished player.

Travel is a constant reality in the life of a performing musician, and Ma frequently takes his cello with him on airplanes, buying it a ticket and putting up with the surprised stares and bureaucratic red tape with humor and patience: "Good morning. This is my cello. It's 250 years old. I have a ticket for it and myself."

MEMORABLE EXPERIENCES

Ma was part of the all-star group of musicians who helped to celebrate the 100th anniversary of Carnegie Hall in 1991, an event he marked with a performance of the six Bach Suites for cello, the pieces he had learned at the age of four, playing all of them in a single evening.

MAJOR INFLUENCES

His family and his music provide the greatest influences on Ma. "Fame and success are always being dangled before you," he says. "You can easily become a slave to your desire, become an addict. But you have to choose your drugs carefully. I have yet to find something that beats the power of being in love, or the power of music at its most magical."

HOBBIES AND OTHER INTERESTS

Ma enjoys playing chess, practicing calligraphy, reading, and jogging to relax.

SELECTED RECORDINGS

Haydn: Cello Concertos in D and C Major, 1981
Beethoven: Sonatas #1 and 2 for Cello and Piano [with Emanuel Ax], 1982
Shostakovich/Kabalevsky: Cello Concertos, 1982
Bach: Suites for Unaccompanied Cello, 1983
Brahms: Cello and Piano Sonatas in E Minor and F Major [with Emanuel Ax], 1984
Beethoven: Cello and Piano Sonata No. 4 in C/ and Variations [with Emanuel Ax], 1985

Elgar: Cello Concerto/Walton: Cello Concerto, 1985
Dvorak: Cello Concerto, 1986
Boccherini: Concerto for Cello and Orchestra/J.C. Bach: Symphonie Concertante, 1987
Brahms: Double Concerto/Piano Quartet #3 [with Isaac Stern, Jaime Laredo, and Emanuel Ax], 1988
Schumann: Cello Concertos/Fantasiestucke/ 5 Stucke in Volkston, 1988
Barber: Cello Concerto/Britten: Symphony for Cello and Orchestra, 1988
R. Strauss and B. Britten: Sonatas for Cello and Piano [with Emanuel Ax], 1989
Anything Goes [with Stephane Grappelli], 1991
Hush [with Bobby McFerrin], 1992
Brahms: Sextets [with Isaac Stern, Cho-Liong Lin, Sharon Robinson, Jaime Laredo, Michael Tree, and Emanuel Ax], 1992

HONORS AND AWARDS

Avery Fisher Prize: 1978
Grammy Award: 1984, for *Bach: Suites for Unaccompanied Cello;* 1985, for *Elgar: Cello Concerto & Walton: Cello Concerto;* 1985 for *Brahms: Cello and Piano Sonatas* [with Emanuel Ax]; 1986, for *Beethoven: Cello and Piano Sonata No. 4 in C/ and Variations* [with Emanuel Ax]; 1989, for *Barber: Cello Concerto & Britten: Symphony for Cello and Orchestra*

FURTHER READING

PERIODICALS
Current Biography Yearbook 1982
The Economist, Feb. 15, 1992, p.107
Los Angeles Times, Apr. 9, 1992, p.F6
Musical America, May 1990, p.23
New York Magazine, Mar. 28, 1988, p.31
New York Times Biographical Service, Apr. 1979, p.503; May 1981, p.683
New Yorker, May 1, 1989, p.41
Stereo Review, Apr. 1990, p.71

ADDRESS

ICM Artists Ltd.
40 W. 57th St.
New York, NY 10019

Nelson Mandela 1918-
South African Political Leader
Released in 1990 After Twenty-Seven Years
in Prison

BIRTH

Nelson Rolihlahla Mandela was born July 18, 1918, in Umtata,
Transkei, South Africa. His father, Henry, was a Tembu tribal
counselor; his great-great-grandfather had been a Transkeian king.
His mother, Nonqaphi (also known as Nosekeni and Fanny), was
the third of Henry's four wives. Nelson Mandela has three sisters
and numerous half-brothers and sisters.

YOUTH

Nelson Mandela (whose tribal name, Rolihlahla, means in the

Xhosa language "one who brings trouble upon himself") led a rustic early life, working as a herdboy in the Eastern Cape area. By night, he developed an interest in tribal law while listening to his elders speak of politics. This continuing fascination later led one of his lawyers to complain that Mandela spent too much of his time resolving vague legal issues for visiting chiefs.

When Henry Mandela died, twelve-year-old Nelson was sent to live in the court of his uncle, the Tembu paramount chief. Here, his studiousness, self-confidence, and intelligence marked him as the man who would eventually rule the tribe. The rigorous education that his mother provided him through church schools allowed Mandela to develop his intellect in a way that is denied to South African black youths, who are forced into inferior schools by the South African authorities.

While tradition has played a great role in Mandela's life, he balked at a marriage his uncle had arranged for him, fleeing to Johannesburg in 1941.

EARLY MEMORIES

Nelson Mandela's early, and deeply influential, memories are of the childhood he spent tending pastures and looking after cattle, of the thatched hut near the Bashee River where he grew up, and of the self-governing, relatively open society around him in his youth. His royal background gave him access to tales of his beautiful kingdom before it was blighted by the white conquerors—and of the great black national heroes who continue to inspire him. On trial for treason, and facing life imprisonment, he was to say that those memories are what have "motivated me in all that I have done."

EDUCATION

Mandela was sent to the Headtown Methodist Boarding School, from which he was graduated in 1937. From there, he went to Fort Hare University College, a black school, where his political studies introduced him to Marxism (the theory and practice of socialism). He was expelled from Fort Hare in 1940 for his activities in promoting a strike that protested the limitations imposed on the power of the student council. Mandela later completed his undergraduate studies through correspondence courses at Witwaterstrand University and received his law degree from the University of South Africa in 1942.

FIRST JOBS

After leaving his tribal homeland, Mandela worked briefly as a guard in a Transvaal gold mine. It was here that he met lifelong colleague Walter Sisulu, who found a job for him as a law clerk and encouraged him to finish his undergraduate degree and pursue a career in law.

CHOOSING A CAREER

With his law partners Sisulu and Tambo, Mandela began to consider what course his political activism should take. While at first he was moved toward the ideas of Indian revolutionary leader Mohandas Gandhi, he later came to accept the belief that violent acts were appropriate against a state that was violently depriving blacks of their rights.

Mandela was aware that his unbending activism against a brutal and repressive state would cause deprivation, imprisonment, and possibly death. "Sometimes I feel," he wrote to Winnie from prison, "like one who is on the sidelines, who has missed life itself."

CAREER HIGHLIGHTS

In 1944 Mandela, Tambo, and Sisulu founded the Youth League of the African National Congress, and began cooperating with the Communist party. Six years later, Mandela became the league's president, putting him on a collision course with the ruling National Party. He and Sisulu were given nine-month suspended sentences in 1952 for holding "communist" meetings.

Late in 1956, 156 activists, including Mandela, were arrested and charged with treason for encouraging resistance to the "pass laws" of apartheid (racial segregation). These laws restricted the movements of blacks and forced them to carry documents at all times. The trial, one of the longest in South African legal history, dragged on until 1961. When the defendants were cleared for lack of evidence, it hardly mattered, as the government had banned the ANC.

Mandela went underground and founded the ANC's armed wing, Umkhanto we Sizwe ("Spear of the Nation"). As commander in chief, he was the most wanted man in the country, escaping capture by travel and disguise. After seventeen months, he was arrested near the seaport city of Durban and sentenced to five years for leaving the country illegally. Security police soon raided ANC headquarters and discovered the group's plans to destabilize the government. Mandela was on trial for eighteen months and, at the end, was sentenced to life imprisonment. His four-and-a-half hour plea in his own defense made no apologies, and set the stage for his twenty-seven years as the world's most famous political prisoner. "I have cherished the ideal of a democratic and free society," he concluded, "in which persons live together in harmony. It is an ideal which I hope to live for and achieve. But if needs be, it is an ideal for which I am prepared to die."

Nelson Mandela spent twenty years on harsh, isolated Robben Island, in the South Atlantic Ocean off Capetown. At first, he was forced to dig in a lime quarry. When a new young group of activists began to appear after the 1976 Soweto riots, the prison became known as "Nelson Mandela University" because of his influence on the young prisoners. This fact, along with growing international pressure, led to Mandela's transfer to Pollsmoor Prison in 1982. After being diagnosed with tuberculosis in 1988, he was taken to the hospital, then to Victor Verster Prison, where he lived in the deputy governor's bungalow.

Fearing the negative effects of Mandela's possible death in prison, the government began to offer him his freedom in exchange for conditions—renouncing violence or going into exile. Mandela, stubborn and patient as he has been throughout his life, refused *any* conditions. Finally, in February 1990, he was released without restrictions.

He now faces what is for him an unprecedented task: as a national and international hero, he is expected to bring South Africa into the future while avoiding civil war. He is a man born at about the same time as John F. Kennedy, and the expectations are no less daunting than those placed on the American president who was assassinated the year after Mandela was given his life sentence.

MEMORABLE EXPERIENCES

As might be expected of anyone who spent over twenty-seven years in prison, Mandela's release and subsequent world tour were the crowning moments of his life. Despite his suffering, though, he has no regrets: "It is an achievement for a man to do his duty on earth irrespective of the consequences."

MAJOR INFLUENCES

While Mandela professes great admiration for such international black leaders as Martin Luther King, Jr., Paul Robeson, W.E.B. DuBois, and Malcolm X, his influences are closer to home. Oliver Tambo and Walter Sisulu, with whom he formed the Youth League of the African National Congress (ANC) in 1944, were his early allies and law partners—the men remain very close. In addition, Mandela singles out the heroes of the South African Communist Party, for decades the country's only multiracial political group. Joe Slovo, its longtime secretary general, has been an important associate.

With Mandela, however, it is impossible to neglect the influence of family. He holds that Winnie, his wife, gave him the strength to continue his struggle during his twenty-seven years in prison. His friend and biographer Fatima Meer claims "his two great passions are his people and his family; the first is an extension of the second."

MARRIAGE AND FAMILY

Nelson Mandela has been married twice. He first married Evelyn Ntoko

Mase (Walter Sisulu's cousin) in 1944, a nurse with whom he had two sons, Thembi (who died in a 1969 car crash) and Makaatho, and a daughter, Maki (another daughter died as an infant in 1948). This marriage became troubled when Evelyn asked Nelson to renounce his radical activism, and ended when it became clear that he was committed to the struggle for racial equality.

In 1958, he married Nomzamo Winnie Madikileza, a social worker, with whom he has two daughters, Zenani and Zindziswa. Winnie, a formidable and controversial figure in her own right, was his strongest supporter through years in prison. "Had it not been for your visits, wonderful letters, and your love, I would have fallen apart many years ago," he wrote to her in 1979. For her part, Winnie claims one of her most painful experiences was to take their elder daughter to meet her father for the first time, during his imprisonment, when she was nearly an adult.

Since Mandela's release from prison in 1990, the two now enjoy their first real time together. "This is a lot of fun," Winnie says. "I am learning the tricks of married life."

HOBBIES AND OTHER INTERESTS

Nelson Mandela's continuing passion is his recently rediscovered family. Intellectually, he retains his interest in tribal law. For recreation, he keeps himself fit and has always loved boxing.

WRITINGS

No Easy Walk to Freedom, 1965
Nelson Mandela Speaks, 1970
The Struggle Is My Life, 1986

HONORS AND AWARDS

Jawaharlal Nehru Award for International Understanding (India): 1980
Bruno Kreisky Prize for Human Rights (Austria): 1981
Simón Bolívar International Prize (UNESCO): 1983

FURTHER READING

BOOKS

Contemporary Authors, Vol. 125

Meer, Fatima. *Higher Than Hope: The Authorized Biography of Nelson Mandela,* 1990
Steffof, Rebecca. *Nelson Mandela: A Voice Set Free,* 1990
Vail, John. *Nelson and Winnie Mandela,* 1989 (juvenile)
World Book Encyclopedia, 1991

PERIODICALS

Current Biography Yearbook 1984
Ebony, June 1990, p.98
Essence, June 1990, p.49
Nation, Feb. 11, 1991, p.151
Newsweek, Feb. 19, 1990, p.44
People, Feb. 19, 1990, p.56; Feb. 26, 1990, p.77
Time, Feb. 26, 1990, p.28

ADDRESS

President, African National Congress
Shell House
Johannesburg 2000
Republic of South Africa

* UPDATE *

After two years of increasing political and personal differences, Nelson and Winnie Mandela are separating, although there are no fixed plans to end their 35-year marriage at this time.

Wynton Marsalis   1961- ·
American Musician and Composer
Jazz and Classical Trumpeter

BIRTH

Wynton Marsalis was born October 18, 1961, in New Orleans,
Louisiana, to Ellis and Dolores Marsalis and grew up in the
neighboring town of Kenner. He is the second of six boys. His
older brother, Branford, is also an accomplished musician (a
saxophone player and musical director), as are younger brothers
Jason (drums) and Delfeayo (trombone). Another brother, Ellis III,
is a computer consultant, and Mboya is autistic and lives at home
with his parents.

YOUTH

Wynton was born into a tremendously gifted musical family. His father is a graduate of Dillard University and is head of jazz studies at the University of New Orleans. His mother is a former jazz singer and teacher.

Ellis Marsalis was playing in the band of trumpeter Al Hirt when he asked for an advance to buy his second son a trumpet. Hirt gave Wynton one of his own, instead. By the time he was eight, he was playing in the Fairview Baptist Church marching band. "But," he says, "I was the saddest one in the band. We played at the first New Orleans Jazz and Heritage festival, but I remember I didn't want to carry my trumpet because it was too heavy."

EARLY MEMORIES

Growing up in New Orleans was of great importance to Wynton: "Once I got serious about music, the best thing about New Orleans for me and other young musicians is that we had a generation of older musicians, maybe seven or eight people, who loved music so much they would do anything for us, because we were trying to actually play it." One of these was John Longo, Wynton's first trumpet teacher, and like his most famous pupil, Longo also played both classical and jazz music. Longo used to give him "two and three-hour lessons, never looking at the clock."

Excelling in two fields of music was a challenge that Wynton met with enthusiasm. "It's harder to be a good jazz musician at an early age than a good classical one," he says. "In jazz, to be a good performer means to be an individual, which you don't have to be in classical music. Because I've played with orchestras, some people think I'm a classical musician who plays jazz. They have it backwards! I'm a jazz musician who can play classical music."

EDUCATION

Wynton attended Benjamin Franklin High School and took classes in music theory at the New Orleans Center for the Creative Arts. When he was in the eighth grade, he formed a funk band with his brother Branford, called "The Creators." He played first trumpet in the New Orleans Civic Orchestra while still in high school, and was also a member of the New Orleans Brass Quintet.

Wynton says he was a "wild kid" in school, but maintained a 3.98 grade point average. He has always been extremely sensitive to the racial tensions that affected his life. He went to a chiefly white school and excelled academically, but refused to behave according to what was expected. He recalls that he was "the best English student they had, but that was only on tests. I never spoke English correct."

Although he was one year younger than the official application age, Marsalis was accepted into the summer music program at the Berkshire Music Festival at Tanglewood when he was 17, where he won the top award for brass players. He was a National Merit finalist during his senior year in high school and received offers from a number of top colleges, including Yale, but he chose the prestigious Julliard School of Music instead. During his first year at Julliard, he also played in the pit orchestra for the Broadway musical *Sweeney Todd* and with the Brooklyn Philharmonic.

FIRST JOBS

During the summer after his freshman year, Marsalis received an offer to play with the band of Art Blakey and the Jazz Messengers, and he soon became their musical director. Back at Julliard, Marsalis became discouraged by the condescending attitude he felt many at the school had toward jazz music. "When you play jazz at Julliard, people laugh; it's like the darkies cracking jokes, man." Throughout his career he has fought the perception that jazz is not "real music," kept "in a position of subservience." He left Julliard in 1981, without finishing his degree.

His next important experience came in the summer of 1981, when he toured with Herbie Hancock and his V.S.O.P. quartet. The band was made up of Hancock on piano, Tony Williams on drums, and Ron Carter on bass. These players had all performed with jazz trumpeter Miles Davis in the 1960s, a musical giant whose "cool school" of acoustical jazz—jazz played without amplifiers or electrified instruments—was the main force in jazz music for a generation. Marsalis recorded with both the Blakey and the Hancock group, appearing on *A La Mode* with the Messengers in 1982 and on *Quartet* with V.S.O.P. in 1981.

CAREER HIGHLIGHTS

In 1982 he formed his own group, with his brother Branford on sax, Kenny Kirkland on piano, Jeff Watts on drums, and Phil Bowler and Ray Drummond on bass. Their first recording, *Wynton Marsalis*, was produced by Herbie Hancock, and it won Marsalis his first of eight Grammys to date.

The group's next recording, *Think of One*, which Marsalis produced, was released in 1983 at the same time as his first classical recording, *Trumpet Concertos by Haydn, Hummel, and L. Mozart*. These two recordings won him two more Grammys, and he became the first artist ever to win in both a classical and jazz category in the same year. In accepting the awards, Marsalis said: "I'd like to thank the great masters of American music, Charlie Parker, Louis Armstrong, and Thelonius Monk, all the guys who set a precedent in Western art, and gave an art form to the American people that can't be limited by enforced trends or bad taste."

In 1984 the group released *Hot House Flowers*, a collection of jazz tunes featuring string accompaniment, and Marsalis furthered his dual career with the classical release of *Wynton Marsalis Plays Handel, Purcell, Torelli, Fasch, Molter.* These two recordings won Marsalis two more Grammys, again in two categories, an unprecedented accomplishment in the musical world.

Black Codes (From the Underground), released in 1985, was another Grammy winner and the last recording of the group that included Branford Marsalis and Kenny Kirkland. They had decided to join the rock star Sting to form a new group, and Wynton was forced to rethink the direction of his musical career. The effect of the breakup on the relationship of the two brothers has been much discussed in the press, but it clearly established a new path for each. Branford played with Sting for several years, and has performed jazz with other groups as well, keeping up a rigorous touring schedule. He is now the musical director of "The Tonight Show," with new host Jay Leno.

Wynton found his new focus in 1986 with a group featuring the astounding talents of Marcus Roberts on piano. Blind since childhood, Roberts is known as a major force in the new generation of jazz musicians. Also in the group are Robert Leslie Hurst III on bass and Jeff Watts on drums. Their first recording, *J Mood,* earned another Grammy for Marsalis. His classical recording career continued with the release of *Tomasi/Jolivet: Trumpet Concertos.*

In 1987, the group released *Marsalis Standard Time, Vol. 1*, a collection of "standards," favorite pieces from the world of jazz music written by such greats as Duke Ellington and George Gershwin, as well as original tunes by Marsalis. Another Grammy award was added to the list. On the classical side, Marsalis recorded *Carnaval* with the Eastman Wind Ensemble. 1988 saw the release of *Wynton Marsalis Quartet Live at Blues Alley* and *Baroque Music for Trumpet*. *Crescent City Christmas Card* was Marsalis's jazz offering for 1989, named for the "Crescent City" of New Orleans. He also appeared as guest soloist on a classical recording of Aaron Copland's *Quiet City*.

The *Standard Time* series continued in 1990 with the appearance of *Standard Time Volume 3: The Resolution of Romance*, a recording featuring the playing of his father, Ellis. 1990 also marked a new departure for Marsalis: he composed the score for *Tune in Tomorrow*, a film set in New Orleans and starring Barbara Hershey, Peter Falk, Keanu Reeves, and John Larroquette, and featuring a cameo appearance by Wynton himself.

Marsalis has always been outspoken and articulate, speaking often and at length on a number of issues of concern to him, including the importance of jazz education in the U.S. and the need to recognize the intellectual and emotional depth of the music. "My music is a very intellectual thing—we all know this—art music, on the level we're attempting. Sonny Rollins, Miles [Davis], Clifford Brown, Charlie Parker, . . . [Thelonius] Monk, Duke Ellington, Louis Armstrong. These were extremely, extremely intellectual men. Whoever doesn't realize that is obviously not a student of their music, because their intellect comes out in that music."

In 1983, he began to hold workshops for elementary and high school kids to introduce them to the scope and importance of jazz, and to encourage them to learn to play it and play it well. "You don't just hit a chord 'cause you feel like hitting it—you got to understand the logic of the progressions of the harmonies—the logic of sound, the logic of drums, the logic of how bass parts should go." To Liane Hansen of National Public Radio, he explained it this way: "It's a combination of understanding what that experience is about and developing the technique to express that through music and through art. And I really won't rest until I see high school bands playing Duke Ellington's music and I hear an actual improvement in our musicians around the country as a result of coming into contact with the music of this great genius."

In 1987, he founded the Classical Jazz at Lincoln Center Series, which he also headed until 1990. Calling jazz "the ultimate twentieth-century music," Marsalis finds the art a symbol of democracy: "In terms of illuminating the meaning of America, jazz is the primary art form, especially New Orleans jazz. Because when it's played properly, it shows you how the individual can negotiate the greatest amount of personal freedom and put it humbly at the service of a group conception."

He has also been an outspoken critic of pop music. "Coming out of a heavy pop area, it's hard to play jazz—because a lot of pop music addresses teenage and adolescent emotions, and jazz addresses adult emotions." Of styles like rock 'n' roll and rap, he says: "It's like a toy train. You don't try to put people in there. It's like what Louis Armstrong told Dexter Gordon: 'Don't bring a hamburger to a banquet.' It's not that a hamburger is bad. A hamburger is good sometimes, but don't turn it into a cultural statement."

MEMORABLE EXPERIENCES

"The biggest honor I ever had is for me to play with the musicians I've played with," says Marsalis. "To stand on-stage with Ron [Carter] and Herbie [Hancock] and Tony [Williams], Sonny Rollins, Dizzy Gillespie, to have the opportunity to talk with them and have them teach me stuff."

MARRIAGE AND FAMILY

Marsalis is married to Candace Stanley, and they have two sons, Wynton Jr., and Simeon.

MAJOR INFLUENCES

Performing with the great jazz giants of an earlier era had a great influence on Marsalis. He admires their "ability to be individuals every second that they're playing. *Every* second. All my biggest influences had that in some way—Clifford Brown, Louis Armstrong, Don Cherry, Miles Davis, Freddie Hubbard, Wood Shaw, Fats Navarro. Some set standards in sound and conception, some in virtuoso techniques. But they all provided so much quality."

HOBBIES AND OTHER INTERESTS

Marsalis loves basketball, and sees parallels between jazz and his favorite sport: "Basketball moves so fast and requires such improvisational skills that it's an extremely beautiful game to watch. That's why the game works like a jazz quintet—with spontaneous creativity. The guards are soloists, the center is the bass player, and the forwards are the drum and piano players."

He is also committed to a number of charities, and has offered his talents to raise money for a number of scholarship funds, including the United Negro College Fund, as well as the Red Cross, Muscular Dystrophy Association, National Urban Coalition, Center for Battered Women, Thelonius Sphere Monk Jazz Center, National Guild Community Schools of the Arts, and the National Rehabilitation Hospital. He is also co-chairperson for the Martin Luther King, Jr., Federal Holiday Commission, National Youth Committee.

SELECTED RECORDINGS

Wynton Marsalis, 1982
Think of One, 1983
Trumpet Concertos by Haydn, Hummel, and L. Mozart, 1983
Wynton Marsalis Plays Handel, Purcell, Torelli, Fasch, Molter, 1984
Hot House Flowers, 1984
Black Codes (From the Underground), 1985
J Mood, 1986
Marsalis Standard Time, Vol. 1, 1987; *Vol. 2*, 1991; *Vol. 3*, 1990

HONORS AND AWARDS

Grammy Award: 1983, for *Think of One* and *Trumpet Concertos*; 1984, for *Wynton Marsalis Plays Handel, Purcell, Torelli, Fasch, Molter* and *Hot House Flowers*; 1985, for *Black Codes (From the Underground)*; 1986, for *J Mood*; 1987, for *Marsalis Standard Time, Vol. 1*.

FURTHER READING

BOOKS

Current Musicians, Vol. 6
Haskins, James. *Black Music in America: A History through Its People*, 1987
Who's Who in America, 1990-91

PERIODICALS

Current Biography Yearbook 1984
Down Beat, July 1984, p.17; Sept. 1990, p.16; June 1991, p.17
Ebony, Mar. 1983, p.29
The Instrumentalist, Nov. 1984, p.10
Maclean's, Mar. 26, 1984, p.49
Rolling Stone, Nov. 8, 1984, p.37
Time, Oct. 22, 1990, p.64
Times-Picayune (New Orleans), Nov. 15, 1991, p.19

OTHER

"Weekend Edition," Jan. 26 and Feb. 2, 1992, National Public Radio

ADDRESS

CBS Records, Inc.
51 West 52nd Street
New York, NY 10019

Thurgood Marshall   1908-
American Jurist and Lawyer
Former Associate Justice, United States
Supreme Court

BIRTH

Thurgood Marshall (born Thoroughgood Marshall), the great-grandson of a slave, was born on July 2, 1908, in Baltimore, Maryland. His father, William, worked as a waiter in the dining car of a train and later as a steward at a prestigious all-white private club; his mother, Norma, was an elementary school teacher. Thurgood Marshall was their second child, following an older brother, Aubrey.

YOUTH

When Marshall was young, many laws and customs were very

different from those today. Blacks had been freed from slavery only about fifty years earlier, and they were still treated as second-class citizens. Most of the country, and especially the South, was segregated by race. That meant that blacks and whites lived, worked, and went to school separately, and the housing, jobs, schools, and other facilities available to blacks were consistently second-rate. Blacks were openly treated as inferior and were expected to show respect for whites at all times. It was during this era, too, that members of the Ku Klux Klan and other all-white groups could beat and kill blacks without fear of the police.

Marshall grew up in a comfortable neighborhood in Baltimore. As a child, he often got in trouble at school. As punishment, he was made to memorize sections of the United States Constitution, the document written by our nation's founders that describes the basic principles of our legal system. It is the job of our judges to decide exactly what the Constitution means and to determine how its rules should be applied to current situations. "Before I left that school," he once said, "I knew the whole thing by heart"—although he certainly never realized that he would grow up to interpret it as a judge on the nation's highest court, the Supreme Court.

EARLY MEMORIES

Marshall's parents valued education. They encouraged him and his brother to study, to ask questions, and to think. Marshall once recalled how his father helped him learn to reason: "He never told me to become a lawyer, but he turned me into one. He did it by teaching me to argue, by challenging my logic on every point, by making me prove every statement I made." Yet the senior Marshall also emphasized self-respect: "Son," his father would say, "if anyone calls you a nigger, you not only got my permission to fight him—you got my orders to fight him."

EDUCATION

Despite his fun-loving behavior in school, Marshall graduated with honors from Douglas High School. When he decided to attend college, his parents supported him enthusiastically. His brother was already a medical student who eventually became a well-known surgeon. Their mother hoped that Marshall would become a dentist, a secure, well-paying profession. As a black high school senior in 1925, Marshall had only a few choices about where to attend college—most U.S. universities were exclusively white. He was accepted at Lincoln University in Pennsylvania, then one of the nation's best all-black schools. He worked throughout college to pay for his tuition, holding jobs in a grocery store, dining car of a train, and bakery. At first, Marshall spent much of his time playing cards and meeting with friends. In his second year, though, he was briefly suspended from school, and after that he became a more serious student.

It was during Marshall's college years that he began seriously considering the role of blacks in society. This was the time of the Harlem Renaissance, a period when many notable blacks began writing about their heritage and their experiences. Marshall began reading their works. He was especially interested in W.E.B. DuBois's *The Souls of Black Folk,* a collection of essays on life for blacks. Marshall also joined the debate team and discovered that he had a talent for persuading others. He abandoned his mother's plans for dentistry and decided to study law.

Marshall had help with that decision. He had recently met Vivian Burey at a church social. They soon fell in love. Buster, as Marshall called her, was a student at the University of Pennsylvania. According to their friends, she inspired him to work hard and encouraged him to study law. They married on September 4, 1929, just before the start of his senior year. Marshall received his B.A. degree in 1930 in the humanities, with honors.

Marshall first applied to law school at the highly respected University of Maryland, then an all-white school. He was rejected. He then applied to and was accepted by Howard University in Washington, D.C., an all-black school. At Howard, according to Marshall, "for the first time, I found out my rights." The university had recently hired the civil rights attorney Charles Houston as vice-dean of the law school. Houston was also active in the National Association for the Advancement of Colored People, or NAACP. He believed that the law could be used to change society, and he intended to train lawyers at Howard to fight discrimination.

Marshall was a dedicated law student. He lived with his wife at his parents' home in Baltimore and traveled to Washington every day by train. He spent the day at school, returned home to his part-time job, and studied every evening. Marshall became Houston's star pupil and graduated first in his class in 1933.

MARRIAGE AND FAMILY

The Marshalls remained happily married until 1955, when Buster died of lung cancer. He got married again later that year to Cecilia Suyat, or Cissy, a former secretary with the NAACP. They have two sons, Thurgood, Jr., and John.

FIRST JOBS

Marshall's legal career began in Baltimore in 1933, when he set up a law practice specializing in civil rights and criminal cases. At first business was terrible. Few people were willing to hire a black lawyer, and the Great Depression had forced many people out of work and into poverty. Although many of his clients couldn't afford to pay him, he turned no one away. And even non-paying work gave him a chance to practice his courtroom skills. As Marshall won many of these early cases, his reputation grew, and he gradually picked up some paying clients, too. He continued his law practice until 1936.

Meanwhile, in 1934, he began preparing civil rights cases for the NAACP. In one of his first important cases, he represented a black student who wanted to enter the University of Maryland law school, the same school that had rejected Marshall. He won the case and forced the school to admit black students. In 1936, Charles Houston, former dean of Howard University and now chief counsel for the NAACP, offered him a position as assistant special counsel at the main office in New York. Even though he was told that the work would be frustrating, low-paying, and dangerous, Marshall jumped at the offer. When Houston left the NAACP in 1938, Marshall was named special counsel, the top attorney responsible for the organization's national legal strategy.

CAREER HIGHLIGHTS

Throughout his career, Marshall showed his passionate commitment to two principles: he believed that all people were guaranteed equal rights under the Constitution, and he believed that blacks and others could use the American legal system and many existing laws to achieve those rights. Yet when Marshall began working for the NAACP, blacks had a long way to go to achieve equality. They were discriminated against in all areas of life, including housing, schools, jobs, voting rights, transportation, public facilities, and the criminal justice system.

In many cases this discrimination was founded on the legal doctrine of "separate but equal." The United States Constitution guarantees equal protection for all citizens. But the Supreme Court ruled in 1896 that equal protection could mean separate but equal facilites. This meant, in theory, that separate facilities could be provided for blacks as long as they were equal to the facilities for white Americans. In reality, it meant that states and cities could create a wide range of laws that required segregation by race. The result was that most blacks lived in rundown housing and attended overcrowded schools with few supplies. They were forced to ride at the back of the bus or train. They were barred from using whites-only bathrooms, drinking fountains, and restaurants. Although called equal, these separate accomodations were consistently inferior to those used by white Americans.

With the staff of the NAACP, Marshall set out to challenge these discriminatory laws. During over twenty-five years with the organization, he worked to integrate schools and transportation, to secure voting rights for all citizens, and to protect the rights of people accused of a crime, including black servicemen. He traveled extensively, mostly throughout the South, taking cases that would challenge segregation. It was dangerous work, and he was often threatened. When he lost in the local, or lower courts, he would appeal the decision in a higher court, and continue his appeals to the Supreme Court. Of the 32 cases throughout his career that he argued before the Supreme Court, he won 29.

Although he had many successes, each one applied to only a small area of the law—until his most important case, known as *Brown v. Board of Education.* (Law cases are named after the two opposing sides, here Oliver Brown versus the Board of Education of Topeka, Kansas.) Marshall and the NAACP staff had been looking for a case that they could bring before the Supreme Court that would directly challenge the doctrine of separate but equal. They particularly wanted to eliminate segregated schools because they believed that a good education was crucial to blacks' success in other areas. In *Brown v. Board of Education,* which brought together five separate cases that challenged segregated education, Marshall led the NAACP attack. He argued that segregated education was unequal because it destroyed black children's self-esteem, motivation to learn, and future prospects.

In 1954, in a monumental decision, the Supreme Court found in favor of Marshall and the NAACP. Because segregated education created a feeling of inferiority in black children, the justices called it inherently unequal and therefore unconstitutional. The decision generated shock waves throughout the country. The ruling didn't eliminate racial prejudice or immediately abolish school segregation—it took years for many states to comply. Yet it marked the end of legal segregation and allowed for the creation of new laws that prohibited discrimination in all areas of life.

After working as a lawyer for the NAACP for over twenty-five years, Marshall went on to fight injustice in an even longer career as a public servant. In 1961 he was appointed to the U.S. Court of Appeals, Second Circuit, by President John F. Kennedy. Marshall ruled on 98 cases on the Circuit Court, all of which were upheld by the Supreme Court. In 1965 President Lyndon B. Johnson named him Solicitor General, the third-highest position in the U.S. Justice Department. The Solicitor General represents the U.S. government before the Supreme Court. During his two years in that position, Marshall won 14 of the 19 cases he argued. One of his most important victories was the Court's approval of the Voting Rights Act of 1965, which guaranteed that every citizen would have the right to vote. In 1967 he was appointed by President Johnson to the Supreme Court, the first black ever to become a Supreme Court justice. He remained in that position until his retirement in 1991 at the age of 82.

During his years of public service, and especially during his later years on the Supreme Court, Marshall was known for his often liberal positions. In the area of criminal law, he opposed the death penalty and worked to uphold the rights of those suspected of a crime. He fought improper detentions, searches, and questioning of suspects. In addition, he supported free speech, affirmative action, and the rights of welfare recipients. In general, Marshall continued to demonstrate his concern for the rights of individuals, especially minorities, in their quest for equal protection under the laws of the land.

HONORS AND AWARDS

Springarn Medal (NAACP): 1946, "for his distinguished service as a lawyer
  before the Supreme Court and inferior courts"
Freedom Medal (Franklin D. and Eleanor Roosevelt Institute): 1991

FURTHER READING

BOOKS

Aldred, Lisa. *Thurgood Marshall: Supreme Court Justice,* 1990 (juvenile)
Encyclopedia Britannica, 1991
Hess, Debra. *Thurgood Marshall: The Fight for Equal Justice,* 1990 (juvenile)
Who's Who in America, 1990-91
World Book Encyclopedia, 1991

PERIODICALS

Current Biography Yearbook 1954; 1989
Ebony, May 1990, p. 68; Nov. 1990, p.216
New York Times, June 28, 1991, p.A1; June 29, 1991, p.A15
Newsweek, July 8, 1991, p.24
People, July 15, 1991, p.34
Time, July 8, 1991, p.24

ADDRESS

U.S. Supreme Court
Supreme Court Bldg.
1 First St. NE
Washington, DC 20543

Ann M. Martin   1955-
American Author of Juvenile and
Young Adult Books
Creator of "The Baby-sitters Club" Series

BIRTH

Ann Matthews Martin was born August 12, 1955, in Princeton, New Jersey. Her father, Henry Martin, was a cartoonist for the *New Yorker* magazine, while her mother, Edith (Matthews) Martin, worked as a nursery school teacher. Ann has one younger sister, Jane.

YOUTH

Martin grew up in Princeton, a suburban, middle-class community that has been compared with Stoneybrook, the fictional setting for the Baby-sitters Club series. Her town, Martin has said, was "a neighborhood in the true sense of the word. When I was growing up, there were kids up and down the street. We played in the street and school was within walking distance. I was a good student but didn't particularly like school."

Despite this typical-sounding childhood, Martin describes her early home life as "a fantasy world" created for her and her sister by their imaginative parents. According to Martin, her parents loved fantasy and children's literature, encouraged creativity, and filled their home with books and art supplies. As she later recalled, "I was moody and temperamental, but those were very happy years because I had parents who would read to us, take us to circuses, teach us magic tricks and roast marshmallows in the woods with us. They never cared if we made a mess. My mother called our playroom 'toy soup'."

Two of Martin's childhood interests remain to this day. She has always loved to read, either by herself or listening to stories her parents would read aloud. She even liked to wake early and read in bed before school! Some of her early favorites were stories about Dr. Doolittle, Mary Poppins, Nancy Drew, and horse stories by Marguerite Henry. In addition, Martin also enjoyed babysitting: "I think I was good at it," she has said. "I spent time with the kids. I didn't watch TV until they were in bed."

EDUCATION

Martin graduated with honors from Smith College in 1977. She majored in two subjects, psychology and early childhood education. She also worked during the summer teaching autistic children.

CHOOSING A CAREER

After college, Martin taught fourth and fifth grade for one year at an elementary school in Noroton, Connecticut. Although she enjoyed teaching, she began to feel that she wanted to work with children's books. In 1978, Martin left teaching to work in publishing. She worked as an editor of children's books for several publishing companies, and in about 1979 began writing children's books of her own. She left publishing to write full-time in 1985.

CAREER HIGHLIGHTS

Martin wrote several books before beginning the "Baby-sitters Club" series. Her first, *Bummer Summer*, was published in 1983. In this story, the character Kammy has to learn to deal with two difficult experiences at the same time: remarriage of a widowed parent and summer camp. Some of Martin's other stories also deal with serious problems, including peer pressure and living with a handicapped sibling in *Inside Out*, sibling rivalry in *Me and Katie (the Pest)*, the serious illness of a parent in

With You and Without You, and dyslexia in *Yours Turly, Shirley.*

After several years of writing these stories, Martin was approached by Jean Feiwell, the editor-in-chief at Scholastic Books. Feiwell had noticed that books about babysitters and books about clubs both sold very well, and she had the idea to create a series combining the two. Feiwell discussed the idea with Martin and asked her to write what was expected to be a mini-series of four books. In about 1985, Martin began creating the characters and plots for the Baby-sitters Club series. The first book, *Kristy's Great Idea,* was published in 1986. This title, along with the next three, were moderately successful, and they decided to publish two more. The sixth title, *Kristy's Big Day,* was the first big hit: it shot to the top of the best-sellers list. Since then, most of the Baby-sitters Club titles have routinely made the best-seller list; to date, there are over forty-four million copies in print. These stories are so popular, in fact, that a new television series called "The Baby-sitters Club," a spin-off from Martin's books, debuted on HBO in September 1991. With the success of the original titles, Martin created a second series, the "Baby-sitters Little Sister" books, for readers aged seven to nine.

The Baby-sitters Club books all revolve around a group of eighth-grade girls who have formed a baby-sitting cooperative. The group, originally four girls but now increased to seven, live in the fictional town of Stoneybrook, Connecticut. According to Martin, the outgoing leader of the group, Kristy, is patterned after her best friend from childhood, Beth Perkins, while shy and quiet Mary Anne is based on Martin herself. Each book focuses on the experiences of one or more of the girls as they wrestle with problems, both large and small. Stories explore the types of problems that her readers often confront, including divorce, sibling rivalry, peer pressure, race and ethnic issues, stepparents, and the death of a grandparent. Reviewers often comment on her insight into the thoughts and feelings of pre-adolescent girls. According to Martin, that insight comes from memories of

Baby-sitters' Island Adventure
Ann M. Martin

her own childhood: "Some of my books have been based on past experiences, although very few of them have been based on actual events in my childhood. But I would say that while I write any book, I'm remembering how I felt when I was a kid. Those feelings definitely go into the books." In addition, reviewers often praise the Baby-sitters Club books because they are well-written and fun to read, because they contain believable characters and interesting plots, and because they encourage kids to read.

Martin is a very disciplined writer. She gets up at 5:30 A.M., spends the morning writing, and then spends the afternoon editing manuscripts and reading letters from her fans. Even with this demanding schedule, Martin writes two books each month—with the exception of one month each year, when Martin takes a well-earned vacation and another writer pens the stories from her outlines and notes.

Despite the success of her books, Martin lives modestly, preferring to spend her money to help others: she donates toys to needy children, sponsors a student at Princeton University, and supports a dance program at a public school in New York City. As she says, "I don't feel any different now than I did at seven. I don't want success to change things in any way. I'm very happy to get up on a particular day and know it will be the same as the day before. I want all my old friends and all my familiar things around me, just as I did when I was a kid."

MARRIAGE AND FAMILY

Martin lives with her two cats, Mouse and Rosie, in an apartment in New York City. She is unmarried. Asked about having children of her own, she once said, "I really enjoy other people's kids. Right now there is not enough room in my life for one child and fifteen books a year."

HOBBIES AND OTHER INTERESTS

"My hobbies are reading and needlework, especially smocking and knitting," Martin has said. "I like being with people, but I am very happy alone, and prefer quiet and solitude to noise and excitement. I love animals and have [two cats]. . . . I usually put cats in my books, and plan to write a book from a cat's point of view."

SELECTED WRITINGS

Bummer Summer, 1983
Just You and Me, 1983
Inside Out, 1984
Stage Fright, 1984
Me and Katie (the Pest), 1985
Missing Since Monday, 1986

With You and Without You, 1986
Just a Summer Romance, 1987
Slam Book, 1987
Fancy Dress in Feather Town, 1988
Ten Kids, No Pets, 1988
Yours Turly, Shirley, 1988
Ma and Pa Dracula, 1989
Moving Day in Feather Town, 1989
Eleven Kids, One Summer, 1991

"Baby-sitters Club" Series, 50 titles to date, 1986-
"Baby-sitters Little Sister" Series, 21 titles to date, 1988-

FURTHER READING

BOOKS

Contemporary Authors New Revision Series, Vol. 32
Something about the Author, Vol. 44

PERIODICALS

New York Times Book Review, Apr. 30, 1989, p.42
People, Aug. 21, 1989, p.55
Time, Jan. 28, 1991, p.89
Wall Street Journal, Nov. 22, 1989, p.A11

ADDRESS

Scholastic Books
730 Broadway
New York, NY 10003

OBITUARY

Barbara McClintock 1902-1992
American Biologist
Winner of the Nobel Prize for
Her Work in Genetics

BIRTH

Barbara McClintock, called a "giant figure in the history of genetics" and the "most important figure there is in biology," was born June 16, 1902, in Hartford, Connecticut. She was the third of four children born to Thomas Henry and Sarah Handy McClintock; her sisters Marjorie and Mignon were older, and her brother, Malcolm Rider, called Tom, was younger. The McClintocks named their third daughter Eleanor, which they felt was a very "feminine" name. But as her lively and strong-willed personality emerged, they decided to change her name to Barbara, which they felt was more "masculine."

YOUTH

Barbara's mother had come from a wealthy and influential family, and Sarah McClintock found the responsibilities of raising four young children too much sometimes. She sent young Barbara to live with her paternal aunt and uncle in rural Massachusetts for extended periods during her youth, which Barbara enjoyed very much. She was a solitary but happy child. The family moved to Brooklyn, New York, in 1908, where Thomas McClintock became a doctor for the Standard Oil Company, treating the men who worked on the company's oil rigs. The family spent summers at Long Beach, where Barbara loved to swim and to run.

EARLY MEMORIES

Barbara McClintock was raised in a family that valued and encouraged independent thinking, activity, and confidence. Dr. McClintock told his children's teachers that his children would not do homework, that they needed to get outdoors and explore their world instead. Her parents would allow Barbara to miss school whenever she wished, sometimes a day, sometimes whole semesters, to skate, to play, and to explore.

She also loved to read, and to sit just "thinking about things." Her solitary, intense nature sometimes worried her mother, who, although she respected her daughter's intelligence and drive, never quite gave up her expectations for Barbara to be a more conventional girl.

Always independent in her thinking, Barbara found long hair hot and messy, so she kept her own short; and she thought dresses were confining, so her mother had a tailor make her pants to wear under her dresses so she could climb, jump, and play "like a boy."

EDUCATION

Barbara attended P.S. [Public School] 139 in Brooklyn, where, despite her many absences, she made the honor role. She graduated from Erasmus Hall High School with honors at the age of 16, and wanted very much to go on to college. Her father was in Europe at the time, attending the men wounded in World War I (1914-1918), and her mother thought that college would hurt Barbara's chances of finding a husband. American society had profoundly different expectations and limitations for women when McClintock was young; most young girls were raised to confine their ambitions to becoming wives and mothers. To Barbara McClintock, this made no sense. But because of her family's difficult financial situation, she took a clerical position in an employment agency. She spent her evenings and weekends in the library, determined to continue her education.

From a very young age, Barbara McClintock knew she was different from other children, but she knew that she had to follow the path she had chosen for herself. "I found that handling [my difference] in a way that other people would not appreciate, because it was not the standard conduct, might cause me great pain, but I would take the consequences. I would take the consequences for the sake of an activity that I knew would give me great pleasure. And I would do that regardless of the pain—not flaunting it, but as a decision that it was the only way that I could keep my sanity, to follow that kind of regime. And I followed it straight through high school, and through college, through the graduate period and subsequently. It was constant. Whatever the consequences, *I had to go in that direction.*"

When her father returned home at the end of the war, he could see that Barbara's thirst for knowledge deserved to be satisfied. Besides, she had found a college with free tuition: the School of Agriculture at Cornell University in Ithaca, New York. She began her college studies in the fall of 1919. "I was entranced at the very first lecture I went to," she recalled. "I was doing now what I really wanted to do, and I never lost that joy all the way through college."

McClintock excelled academically and also enjoyed the social aspects of college life. She went on dates, played banjo in a band, and was elected president of the women's freshman class. She was also asked to join a sorority. She turned down the offer, though, because her Jewish friends had specifically been excluded. "I just couldn't stand that kind of discrimination," she said. "It was so shocking that I never really got over it."

McClintock took courses in genetics—the study of heredity—in her junior year of college, and her life-long fascination with the subject began. She was such an outstanding student that she began to take graduate courses in genetics in her junior year, and she received her B.S. (Bachelor of Science) degree in 1923. She continued her graduate studies at Cornell in botany rather than genetics because the department did not admit women. Her area of specialization in biology was "cytology"—the study of the way that cells work. Genetics was truly in its infancy when McClintock came to study at Cornell, where many of the pioneers in the field were teaching. She received her M.A. (Master's degree) from Cornell in 1925, and began work on her Ph.D (doctorate), which she received in 1927.

FIRST JOBS

McClintock's first academic job was as a botany instructor at Cornell, a position she held from 1927 to 1931. She also taught as a visiting scholar at the California Institute of Technology during this time. As the recipient of a Guggenheim Fellowship in 1933, she traveled to Germany to study at the Kaiser Wilhelm Institute. She was shocked and frightened at the rise of Nazism, however, and left Germany before her fellowship was over, returning to Cornell. She then taught at the University of Missouri at Columbia from 1936 to 1941.

CAREER HIGHLIGHTS

Realizing that her future as a research professor was dim due to the prevailing attitude toward women, she joined the staff of the Carnegie Institute's Cold Spring Harbor Laboratory on Long Island, New York, in 1941, where she remained for more than 50 years. It was at Cold Spring that her most important discoveries took place.

THE NATURE OF HER DISCOVERY

All living things are made up of cells, and all living things reproduce, passing on certain characteristics—the color of eyes and hair in humans, for example, or the size and shape of kernels in a corn plant. Cells pass on this information through a part of the cell called a "gene," which is the root of the word "genetics." The study of genetics really began with the work of Gregor Mendel, a Russian monk who lived in the mid-nineteenth century. Mendel studied peas and discovered a pattern in the way that certain characteristics—size, shape, and color—of peas were passed on from parent to offspring in the plant. In the late nineteenth and early twentieth century, the American scientist Thomas Henry Morgan, who studied fruit flies and the way in which the shape and color of the eyes of the flies were passed on, provided the next most significant contribution to the study of genetics. At the time McClintock began her research, scientists were quite sure that genes behaved in a predictable, set way. But her research was to change all that, and to establish her as one of the most important figures in the history of biology, called one of the "Three M's" for her contribution to the study of genetics.

McClintock's lifelong study of the way cells pass on their genetic information was based on the study of corn, specifically maize, or Indian corn, the multicolored vegetable that is often used in harvest or Thanksgiving celebrations. The color, shape, and size of the kernels of maize reflect inherited traits. In her first year of graduate studies in the early 1920s, she developed a method for identifying the 10 different chromosomes—the parts of the gene that contain its information—of maize. McClintock began to see that the genetic material being passed on did not behave in the predictable way that scientists believed. Instead, she discovered that the genes appeared to move randomly, or "jump," during the breaking, rearranging, and joining of the reproductive process. She knew that what she had discovered would not be readily accepted by traditional scientists, and she was right. She was ignored, and even scorned by fellow scientists. While early in her academic career she had published a number of scientific papers, in the 1940s and 1950s McClintock fell silent, but was determined to continue her research and wait for the world to catch up. Her work even predated the discover of DNA—deoxyribonucleic acid—the molecular basis of heredity.

McClintock was a woman of profound intellect, great powers of concentration, and physical strength. She raised the corn she used for her studies herself, planting, pollinating, and harvesting it, and always keeping exact notes and records on the "parent" and "offspring" ears of corn. She always worked alone, without even a lab assistant.

In the 1960s and 1970s, the scientific world began to come around to McClintock's way of thinking. In the 1970s, molecular biologists—scentists who examine life on the level of molecules—began to discover that the way bacteria and other forms of life behave mirrored what McClintock had been saying about corn—that the genes passed on their information randomly, and not with the certain, predictable pattern they had assumed. McClintock began to be seen as a prophet, almost a mystic, and the praise and prizes began to come her way. In 1981, she became the first MacArthur Laureate Award winner, which included a grant of $60,000 a year for life. That same year she received the Albert Lasker Basic Medical Research Award, one of the more prestigious awards in science, and Israel's Wolf award, as well. The publicity and attention that came with the awards were surprising and somewhat annoying to this solitary scientist, who really just wanted to be left alone to continue her work.

THE NOBEL PRIZE

McClintock received the Nobel Prize for physiology and medicine in 1983 at the age of 81, nearly forty years after her ground-breaking research. The award committee cited "her discovery that genes can move from one spot to another on the chromosomes of plants and change the future generations of plants." She was the first women ever to win an unshared Nobel in the category and only the third woman to win an unshared Nobel (Marie Curie, who won the prize in 1911, and Dorothy Hodgkin, who won in 1964, are the others; both won in chemistry).

In the words of Nobel Laureate James Watson, the co-discoverer of DNA and McClintock's colleague at Cold Spring Harbor: "She is a very remarkable person, fiercely independent, beholden to no one. Her work is of fundamental importance."

When asked why she felt recognition for her work had taken so long, McClintock said this: "When you know you're right, you're right. You don't care. You can't be hurt. You just know that sooner or later it will come out in the wash."

MARRIAGE AND FAMILY

McClintock never married. Her life was solitary by choice, and even as an undergraduate she realized that close, emotional attachments were not to be part of her life. "There was not that strong necessity for a personal attachment to anybody. I just didn't feel it. And I could never understand marriage." She worked seven days a week, sometimes 12 hours a day, until shortly before her death. She lived in an apartment over her lab for many years, until she won the Nobel, when she bought a car, got a telephone, and moved to an apartment overlooking the harbor. She died of natural causes on September 3, 1992.

HOBBIES AND OTHER INTERESTS

McClintock's daily routine almost always included a long walk in the woods around the grounds of the Cold Spring Harbor labs. Her research schedule was very demanding, but she always had time to respond to the letters that came from scientists and students, who wrote for autographs, pictures, and for help with questions.

HONORS AND AWARDS

National Medal of Science (National Science Foundation): 1970
Lewis S. Rosentiel Award for Distinguished Work in Basic Medical Research (Brandeis University): 1978
Albert Lasker Basic Medical Research Award: 1981
MacArthur Laureate Award: 1981
Wolf Foundation Award: 1981
Nobel Prize for Physiology and Medicine: 1983

MEMBERSHIPS

National Academy of Sciences, 1944
Genetics Society, President, 1945
American Academy of Arts and Sciences
Royal Society of England

FURTHER READING

BOOKS

Dash, Joan. *The Triumph of Discovery: Women Scientists Who Won the Nobel Prize,* 1991
Keller, Evelyn Fox. *A Feeling for the Organism: The Life and Work of Barbara McClintock,* 1983
Kittredge, Mary. *Barbara McClintock,* 1991 (juvenile)

PERIODICALS

Current Biography Yearbook 1984
New York Times, Jul. 26, 1992, p.LI:3; Sept. 4, 1992, p.A1
Newsweek, Nov. 30, 1981, p.74
Time, Nov. 30, 1981, p.84; Oct. 24, 1983, p.75

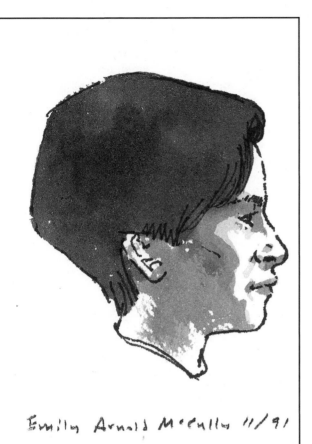

Emily Arnold Mcculle 11/91

Emily Arnold McCully   1939-
American Illustrator of over 100 Children's
Books
Author of Books for Both Adults and
Young Readers

BIRTH

Emily Arnold McCully was born July 1, 1939, in Galesburg, Illinois,
to Wade E. and Kathryn (Maher) Arnold. Her mother had been
a talented actress and singer, although she never pursued it as
a career. Her father had been a writer and producer for radio
shows in New York City, before he moved back to Galesburg,
home of Knox College. Both parents were alumni of Knox, and
Wade Arnold had agreed to return and produce the college's
centennial celebration. Emily was born there in 1939, and her
sister, Becky, was born the following year.

315

YOUTH

World War II soon intruded on the family's plans. Shortly after Becky's birth, Wade Arnold moved to Washington, D.C., to work for the Office of War Information. The rest of the family stayed behind, and Emily had a pleasant early childhood growing up in a college town. In 1945, after the war's end, Wade Arnold took a job as a documentary scriptwriter and producer for NBC in New York, and the family went to join him there. They moved to Garden City, a suburb on Long Island, where Emily and Becky continued their childhood games: cowboys and Indians, hide and seek, playacting, riding bikes, playing ball, and climbing trees. As she grew older, she began to decorate sets for school plays and became active in student government. While she was a senior in high school, McCully's parents divorced, after several years of difficulties.

EARLY MEMORIES

McCully loved to read and draw throughout her youth, and her skill was recognized early and encouraged. "Drawing was my talent and therefore to be developed. My mother noticed when I was three or so that I drew from observation, and so she had me practice until I mastered ears, hands, feet, and so on. Soon I was making up little stories and binding them in books, complete with copyright pages."

EDUCATION

McCully selected Pembroke College, now part of Brown University in Providence, Rhode Island, because students there were able to take courses at the renowned Rhode Island School of Design (RISD). After two semesters there, including a course in illustration, she withdrew from RISD; after that, she did very little art work in college. Instead, she began writing and became active in the theater—in fact, she met her future husband when he came backstage to congratulate her on her performance in a Tennessee Williams play. She received her B.A. in art history in 1961.

MARRIAGE AND FAMILY

The early 1960s was an era vastly different from our own, especially for women. This was an era in which women were encouraged to pursue marriage and children, rather than education and careers. As McCully explained, "It's hard to remember how different society was for young women in 1961 and how differently society perceived us. We were not allowed to wear pants to class. Most girls dressed according to a formula; there was little variation, and despite the fact that this made fashion totally predictable, people passed judgment on others according to the correctness of their attire. Professors could ridicule women in class and get away with it. Brown students married Pembrokers, but not until after they had heaped scorn on them with the contempt bred of familiarity, not to mention availability. . . . Young women did not necessarily contemplate careers, and an education by no means led to one. We were years away, in 1961, from 'The Sixties'. "

For McCully, and many of her classmates, the end of college meant the beginning of a new life. She was married on June 3, 1961, one day before her college graduation, to George E. McCully, her admirer at Brown. They had two sons, Nathaniel, born in 1968, and Thaddeus (Tad), born in 1971. McCully went through a period of personal upheaval during the 1970s, including problems with alcoholism, hospitalization for detoxification, divorce, and temporary loss of custody of her sons.

CHOOSING A CAREER

According to McCully, "I was groomed from early childhood to be an illustrator. My mother wanted me and my sister to be independent women, or at least self-supporting, and my talent seemed marketable. Illustrators were glamorous figures in American life then, and I loved stories, hence I chose illustrating a text over fine art from the start."

FIRST JOBS

After graduating from Pembroke, McCully went to work for a tiny advertising firm in New York City, and then worked for the art department of a large advertising agency. In both jobs she was stymied by the era's expectations of women: she was prevented from doing any interesting work and from advancing, even as she saw the men around her being promoted. When she quit her second job, she pulled together her portfolio and began showing her work to "as many art directors at publishing houses, ad agencies, magazines, and newspapers as would see me." A few freelance assignments began to come in, designing book jackets and some advertisements. Still frustrated, and afraid, as she says, "that my brain was atrophying," McCully decided to enroll in the master's program in art history at Columbia University. While there she was able to spend one year doing research in Europe, with the help of a fellowship granted to her husband, also a graduate student. After completing her master's degree in 1964, she continued her career as a freelance artist.

CAREER HIGHLIGHTS

McCully came to children's books in an indirect way. For a radio advertisement, she had prepared some posters that showed children at play. In 1966, a children's book editor saw one of the posters in the New York subway and contacted McCully to see if she would be interested in illustrating a children's book. McCully agreed, and has since illustrated over 100 books for children. Her approach to her work is fairly consistent. When she receives a manuscript to illustrate, she first reads through it to decide how to divide up the story, which events to depict, and what the characters should look like. She then makes a series of rough sketches.

With pen and ink, she next does line drawings on tracing paper. Using a light table, McCully then traces the line drawings onto heavy paper, which she paints with water colors. She often works on several books simultaneously, alternating among the illustrations for the different texts. In addition to pen and ink and watercolors, McCully has also used tempera, woodcuts, and rice paper and ink.

In the mid-1980s, McCully moved from illustrating works by others to creating her own books. She is now the author of over ten books for young readers, some consisting solely of pictures, and others consisting of both text and illustrations. In addition to these books for young readers, McCully has written two novels and a short story for adults.

MEMORABLE EXPERIENCES

"So many compete for attention," according to McCully: "My first day in Paris long ago, the births of my sons, the day I learned that my first (and only) published short story had been selected for the *O'Henry Collection: Best Short Stories*. This encouraged me to go on writing and led to the publication of two novels: *A Craving* and *Life Drawing*."

FAVORITE BOOKS

"As a child," McCully has said, "I loved *Stuart Little, Mary Poppins*, the Tunis sports books, Howard Pease's sea adventures, and every sort of illustrated book. Now my favorites are too numerous to mention. I read a lot of fiction."

HOBBIES AND OTHER INTERESTS

According to McCully, "I still love athletics and play squash, swim, and ride a bicycle. I attend the theater often, read, write, and follow politics closely. I have homes in two places, each of which satisfies a different inclination: one is a loft on the edge of Soho, in Manhattan, with Greenwich Village right around the corner. The other is an eighteenth-century house in the New York Berkshires, where I garden and cook and swim in the most exquisite of ponds! In short,I still do the things I began to do when I was a child, or dreamed of doing."

WRITINGS

FOR YOUNG READERS (WRITTEN AND ILLUSTRATED BY McCULLY)
Picnic, 1984
First Snow, 1985
School, 1987
The Show Must Go On, 1987
The Christmas Gift, 1988
The Grandma Mixup, 1988
New Baby, 1988
You Lucky Duck! 1988
Zaza's Big Break, 1989
The Evil Spell, 1990
Grandmas at the Lake, 1990
I & Sproggy, 1990
Speak Up, Blanche! 1991

FOR ADULTS
O'Henry Collection: Best Short Stories, 1977 [contributor]
A Craving, 1982
Life Drawing, 1986
Emily Arnold McCully has also illustrated over 100 books for young readers.

HONORS AND AWARDS

National Book Award: 1969, for *Journey from Peppermint Street* [as illustrator]; National Book Award (finalist): 1982, for *A Craving*
Best Books of the Year *(School Library Journal):* 1984, for *Picnic*
Christopher Award: 1985, for *Picnic*

FURTHER READING

BOOKS
Something about the Author, Vol. 50
Something about the Author Autobiography Series, Vol. 7

PERIODICALS
Language Arts, Oct. 1979, p.824

ADDRESS

Macmillan Publishers
Children's Marketing Dept.
25th Floor
866 3rd Ave.
New York, NY 10022

Antonia Novello   1944-
American Physician
First Female Surgeon General of the
United States

BIRTH

Antonia Coello Novello was born August 23, 1944, in Fajardo,
Puerto Rico, to Antonio and Ana Delia (Flores) Coello. She has
one brother, Tomas.

YOUTH

Novello's father died when she was eight. Her mother remarried,
and the family remained in Fajardo, a small city southeast of
Puerto Rico's capital city of San Juan. Although Novello's mother
was an educator, principal of the local Antonio Valero de Bernabe

Intermediate School, and Novello's stepfather, Ramon Flores, was an electrician, the family was "far from rich."

"Tonita" was plagued by illness throughout her childhood and teen years. She was born with a congenital megacolon, which is an abnormally large, distorted colon that causes pain and swelling of the abdomen. "I was a sick kid," she says now, but there was more than chronic illness to her young life. She managed to rise above the pain and embarrassment of what she calls "those big bellies" that came and went, and to join in activities with other young people. She played softball, sang lead soprano in the high school chorus, was elected president of her class, and one year was chosen as queen of the town's patron-saint festival.

At eighteen, after high school, she made a decision to do something about her intestinal problem. Complications that arose after the first surgery sent her to the noted Mayo Clinic in Rochester, Minnesota, where she helped pay for the treatment by caring for her physician's children and teaching them Spanish. It was three more years, however, before Novello was completely well.

EDUCATION

Novello graduated in 1965 from the University of Puerto Rico (UPR) at Rio Piedras with a bachelor's degree in biology. After earning a medical degree at UPR in San Juan in 1970, she spent the next several years at the University of Michigan Medical Center in Ann Arbor, where she was an intern and resident physician in pediatrics and served a fellowship in pediatric nephrology (kidney specialty). Novello then moved to Washington, D.C., as pediatric nephrology fellow (1974-75) at Georgetown University Hospital. She earned a master's degree in public health in 1982 from Johns Hopkins University in Baltimore, Maryland.

In addition, in the summer of 1987, Novello completed a program for senior managers in government at Harvard University's John F. Kennedy School of Government.

CHOOSING A CAREER

Antonia Novello often tells of being hospitalized for at least two weeks every summer when she was growing up, and of having to wait until she was a young adult to have corrective surgery. Her colon should have been repaired years earlier, but as she explains, "the university hospital was in the north, I was 32 miles away, my mother could only take me on Saturday, so the surgery was never done. . . . I thought, 'When I grow up, no other person is going to wait eighteen years'." The kindness of the doctors who treated little Tonita, and the fact that she felt that she had spent "all my life" in the hospital, helped to plant the seed of a medical career. Her dream was to help kids in her hometown.

CAREER HIGHLIGHTS

Novello entered the U.S. Public Health Service (PHS) in 1978 after a brief stint in the private practice of pediatrics and nephrology. Until her appointment in 1990 as surgeon general, her entire PHS career was spent at the National Institutes of Health (NIH), where she quickly rose through the ranks. In 1986, she was appointed deputy director of the National Institute of Child Health and Human Development. She remembers thinking then that she probably would retire from that post. "The biggest jobs were held by men," she says. Novello's responsibilities covered a broad range of programs and research projects, among them pediatric AIDS, women's health issues, and the direction of a special work group planning the reorganization of the PHS. She also served as a legislative fellow for the U.S. Senate Committee on Labor and Human Resources in 1982-83; it was in that position that she worked on a major organ-donation and transplant law and drafted warning labels concerning the health risks of cigarette smoking. The anti-smoking issue would become one of her most ardent missions.

In March 1990, Antonia Novello became a "doctor for all Americans" when she was sworn in as the nation's fourteenth surgeon general. The first woman and the first Hispanic ever to hold the position, she advises the public on AIDS, diet and nutrition, sex education, the dangers of smoking, environmental health hazards, and the importance of immunization and disease prevention. In the two years since her surprise appointment—"I never dreamed I would get to this level. Ever, ever, ever"—she has emerged as a worthy successor to the outspoken Dr. C. Everett Koop, who was surgeon general for seven years. Her manner is more laid-back than his, but there's no mistaking her purpose as she fights for a healthier America.

Novello has declared war on teenage drinking and presses, too, for a smoke-free society. "My style is as forceful as Dr. Koop's," she says laughingly. "The only difference is that now sometimes [the work] will be done in Spanish." Her quick wit, her diplomacy, and her modesty, in particular, are traits seldom seen in people who hold high office. Although she wears the uniform of the PHS and holds the prestigious rank of vice admiral, friends say neither military garb nor office of authority can hide her natural warmth. David Sundwall, a former assistant surgeon general under Koop, told the *Chicago Tribune* soon after Novello's appointment, "She comes across as a real person. She's not going to be a stuffy bureaucrat." Her mother added, "I always tell her to be humble and talk to everyone. Because if you forget where you came from, the thump will be loud when you fall."

In addition to being surgeon general, Novello holds a clinical professorship of pediatrics at Georgetown University School of Medicine, and at

Uniformed Services University of Health Sciences.

MAJOR INFLUENCES

Novello spoke at length about the positive influences in her life when she was profiled in 1990 by *Balance,* a magazine for women physicians. "She says," wrote the interviewer, "her first role model was her mother, a professional woman, principal of the local school. After that, because of the career path she had chosen, female mentors were rare." One of those rare persons of her own gender, though, was Dr. Ruth Kirchstein, director of the Institute of General Medical Sciences at NIH. "I learned from her," says Novello.

The mentors were mostly male—Dr. Duane Alexander, for example, whom Novello credits with "nurturing me to grow up as simply me." Now, the first female surgeon general hopes to be a role model to other women, as well as to Hispanics, and to career public health officers who, she says, should be given the opportunity to contribute their knowledge and experience.

MARRIAGE AND FAMILY

There are two Doctors Novello in the surgeon general's household— Antonia, and the man she married May 30, 1970, the day after her graduation from medical school. Joseph R. Novello, a naval officer and physician stationed in Puerto Rico at the time of their marriage, is a child psychiatrist and television personality in Washington. The Novellos went to Ann Arbor together early in their marriage to pursue their separate medical specialties, and then returned to the Washington area, where they now have a home in the Georgetown section of the city. They have no children.

An interesting note about the Novellos is that Joe's brother, comedian Don Novello, is the gossipy Father Guido Sarducci of "Saturday Night Live" fame. Until recently, he was the one in the family with the widest recognition. The chain-smoking aspect of his act does not amuse his sister-in-law, but a *People* article tells that they approach the portrayal in reasonably good humor—always the comedian, Don Novello says that he's *thinking* of giving up cigarettes now that Antonia is surgeon general. "For now, though," he teases, "I'm switching to menthols. I heard they have more Vitamin C." In real life, he does not smoke.

HOBBIES AND OTHER INTERESTS

Her daily schedule is so demanding, and her public health mission so intense, that Novello finds little time for outside interests. She makes an effort to fit in aerobic walks around her Georgetown neighborhood a few times a week, and she enjoys listening to classical music or watching videos during quiet hours at home. She also collects French antiques. An endearing part of Novello's personality is her relationship with her mother, whom she still refers to as Mommy. Novello herself is called Toni by her family and friends.

WRITINGS

Dr. Novello is the author or co-author of more than seventy-five scientific papers on pediatric nephrology and public health.

HONORS AND AWARDS

Intern of the Year: 1971, University of Michigan, Department of Pediatrics
Woman of the Year: 1980, Distinguished Graduates, Public School System, San Juan
Public Health Service Commendation: 1983, Health and Human Services (HHS)
Public Health Service Citation: 1984, HHS
Public Health Service Outstanding Medal: 1988, HHS
Surgeon General's Exemplary Service Medal: 1989
Certificate of Commendation: 1989, HHS

FURTHER READING

BOOKS

Encyclopedia Britannica, 1991
Who's Who Among American Women, 1991-92

PERIODICALS

Chicago Tribune, June 3, 1990, p.4
Miami Herald, Mar. 20, 1990, p.1C
Newsday, Apr. 28, 1992, p.39
People, Dec. 17, 1990, p.109
Saturday Evening Post, May/June 1991, p.38
USA Today, Apr. 30, 1991, p.D4

ADDRESS

Office of the Surgeon General
200 Independence Avenue, SW
Washington, DC 20003

Sandra Day O'Connor   1930-
American Associate Justice,
U.S. Supreme Court
First Woman on the U.S. Supreme Court

BIRTH

Sandra Day O'Connor was born Sandra Day on March 26, 1930, in El Paso, Texas, to Harry A. and Ada Mae (Wilkey) Day. Her family owned a cattle ranch, the Lazy B, on the Arizona-New Mexico border. O'Connor's grandparents had bought the 300-square-mile desert spread in the 1880s, and years later they left the ranch to their youngest son, Harry Day. Forced to give up his dream of attending college, he returned to run the ranch. Harry met his future wife, Ada Mae, on a trip to El Paso while buying a herd of cattle from her father. After several months of courtship across 200 miles, they were married in 1927. Life was very hard on the ranch then: there was no indoor plumbing, running water, telephones, or electricity, and the four ranch hands shared their small adobe home. Because there were no doctors nearby, Ada Mae briefly returned to her family's home in El Paso when she was ready to give birth to their first child, Sandra.

YOUTH

Much of O'Connor's character and personality is said to derive from her experiences growing up on the ranch. As her brother explained years later, "We all have deep ties here," referring to the family and cowboys who work there. "This dried up-old piece of desert is what we are." Life on the ranch fostered certain qualities, like perseverance, dedication, and a willingness to work hard. There were no neighbors nearby, and no children to play with, but O'Connor kept very busy. As she later said, "It is very different from growing up in a city. When you grow up on a ranch, you tend to participate along with everyone else in whatever the activity is that's going on around you. If there's a roundup, then everyone gets involved in working on the roundup. If there's a fence to be fixed, or if there's a gate, or a well to be repaired, then everybody participates." O'Connor often tagged along with her father and the cowboys who worked on the ranch, riding horses, mending fences, fixing windmills, and taking care of the cattle. By age eight, she learned how to drive a truck and how to use a gun. But O'Connor also spent time on indoor activities, playing with dolls, learning to cook, and listening to her mother read her stories from an encyclopedia, the *Saturday Evening Post,* and *National Geographic* magazine. O'Connor loved the time she spent at the Lazy B.

O'Connor was a bright child; she even learned to read by the age of four. Her parents wanted her to attend a school that would match her intellectual abilities, but that was impossible in such a remote area. When Sandra was six, they decided to send her to live in El Paso with her maternal grandparents. As her mother described it, "We missed her terribly, and she missed us, but there was no other way for her to get a good education." Her grandfather was ill and died shortly afterward, but her grandmother, Mamie Scott Wilkey, was a self-sufficient woman who managed the household and carefully supervised young Sandra's education.

Wilkey enrolled her young charge at the Radford School for Girls, an exclusive private school. O'Connor did very well in her classes and enjoyed living with her grandmother, but she still missed her family. She returned to the ranch each summer, but her departure at the beginning of each school year was always hard—and it became especially difficult after the birth of her sister, Ann, when O'Connor was eight, and her brother, Alan, two years later. For one year, during the eighth grade, O'Connor stayed at the ranch and attended the local school. Because of the distance, she had to leave the house before sunrise and didn't return until sunset. Ultimately, the long bus ride proved too tiring, and she returned to the Radford School for one more year. She then skipped a grade and moved on to Austin High School. She was placed in honors classes yet still completed all the credits for her diploma a year early. She graduated from Austin High at age sixteen, in 1946.

MAJOR INFLUENCES

O'Connor has described her grandmother Mamie Scott Wilkey, with whom she lived as a girl, as one of her greatest influences. "She was a wonderful person—very supportive of me. She would always tell me that I could do anything I wanted to do. She was convinced of that, and it was very encouraging."

EDUCATION

Determined to attend college, O'Connor applied only to Stanford University, the school her father had hoped to attend. At that time, shortly after the end of World War II, colleges were flooded with applicants. It seemed unlikely that a 16-year-old, and a girl at that, would be accepted to such a renowned school. Yet to her family's surprise, she was accepted. O'Connor did well at Stanford. As one of her roommates once said, "Even though she was younger than us, she always seemed to handle it. She never got upset. She never went into a panic about anything. She was easy to get along with and she was fun." O'Connor led an active social life, but also earned good grades in her classes. She majored in economics, looking forward to the day when she would return to the Lazy B or run her own ranch. Yet her courses in business law intrigued her, and she decided to attend law school.

At that time, Stanford had a "three-three" program in which a student could complete both their undergraduate and law degrees in six, rather than seven, years. In 1950, O'Connor received her bachelor's degree in economics with high honors, having already completed one year of her law courses. She did exceptionally well in law school. She was elected to a prestigious honorary legal society and chosen to work on the *Stanford Law Review.* Student editors of these legal publications typically select and edit articles prepared by legal professors and practicing lawyers. For a law student, it is considered a great honor to be selected to work on a review. In the spring of 1952, O'Connor completed her law degree, graduating third in her class.

MARRIAGE AND FAMILY

O'Connor gained more than just legal experience while working on the law review—that's also where she met her future husband, John Jay

O'Connor III. They first met in the law library, where they discovered that they were both assigned to check the same article. After finishing their work, they decided to continue their conversation at a restaurant. As he remembers it, "We liked each other immediately. We went out the next two or three nights, and then one night I asked for dates for the next five nights. She agreed. We ended up going out the next forty-two nights in a row! Neither one of us went out with another person after we met each other." They dated for two years, and were married at the Lazy B ranch on December 20, 1952, after Sandra had graduated from law school, and just one semester before John O'Connor would complete his degree. The O'Connors now have three grown sons, Scott, Brian, and Jay. To date, they have one grandchild.

FIRST JOBS

Despite O'Connor's excellent academic credentials, it proved very difficult for her to find her first job. With her new husband still completing his final year at Stanford Law School, she began interviewing with law firms in California. Yet at that time in the United States it was very rare for a woman to seek out a professional career; most remained at home, taking care of children and domestic responsibilities. As O'Connor later explained, "I interviewed with law firms in Los Angeles and San Francisco, but none had ever hired a woman before as a lawyer, and they were not prepared to do so." She did, finally, receive one offer from a law firm—to work as a legal secretary. She shifted her focus to public service positions, or governmental jobs, and soon went to work as a deputy attorney for San Mateo county.

CAREER HIGHLIGHTS

EARLY CAREER

O'Connor has worked in a variety of positions, both paid and unpaid, during her career, changing jobs to accommodate the needs of her family and her own evolving interests. She left her job with San Mateo county in 1953, when her husband was drafted into the army and they moved to Germany. There she worked as a civilian attorney for the Quartermaster Corps, which buys supplies for the army. They were able to spend their free time touring European capitals and skiing in the Austrian Alps.

STARTING A FAMILY

After John O'Connor's army duty ended in December 1956, they moved to Phoenix, Arizona. There Sandra O'Connor had their first child, Scott, in 1957. As she later explained, "There was never a doubt in my mind about wanting to have a career as well as a family. Life is just more interesting if one is engaged in intellectually stimulating work." She began looking for part-time work, and ended up setting up a new firm with another young attorney. With the help of a wonderful babysitter, she was able to spend mornings at work and afternoons with her new son. As she once said, "Many women are happier juggling various roles than not having the opportunity. I'm like that."

After a while, though, the juggling became too hard. After the departure of her babysitter and the birth of her second son, Brian, in 1960, O'Connor decided to leave work for a while to be a fulltime homemaker. A third son, Jay, was born two years later. During this time she took care of her children, her home, and an increasing array of volunteer responsibilities. She was active with many local organizations and especially with the Republican party. After five years at home, O'Connor returned to her law career.

COMBINING FAMILY AND CAREER

Since that time, O'Connor has worked in a series of governmental positions. From 1965 to 1969, she worked as an assistant attorney general for the state of Arizona and continued her activities with the Republican party. That allegiance was rewarded in 1969, when she was appointed to fill a vacant seat in the Arizona state senate; she ran for election and won the seat in 1970 and 1972. Previously, as a lawyer and part of the judicial branch of government, she had seen how the law works in the courtroom; now, as a senator and part of the legislative branch, she had the opportunity to actually write the laws that the courts are charged with enforcing. Because of her competence, diligence, thorough preparedness, and ability to win compromises, she was elected majority leader of the Arizona senate in 1973, the first woman in the United States to hold such a position.

By 1974, though, O'Connor was ready to leave congress and return to the judicial branch of government. She ran for election, and won, as an Arizona Superior Court judge for Maricopa County. While on that court from 1974 to 1979, she heard cases involving offenses against state law, including both criminal and civil trials. In 1979, she was appointed to the Arizona Court of Appeals. After a trial, if one party wants to contest (or appeal) the decision, the case then goes before the Court of Appeals. The appeals (or appellate) court judge is responsible for reviewing the lower court's decision and either sustaining or overturning it. O'Connor served as an appeals judge for two years. As a judge on both the Superior and the Appeals courts, she developed a reputation among attorneys as fair-minded but tough. O'Connor was always very thoroughly prepared for each case brought before her, and she expected lawyers in her courtroom to know every detail of their cases, to be familiar with all aspects of the appropriate laws, and to represent their clients' interests diligently.

SUPREME COURT APPOINTMENT

On July 7, 1981, President Ronald Reagan appointed O'Connor to the United States Supreme Court. The Supreme Court is the highest court in the land, the final court of appeals as well as the group charged with interpreting and upholding the U.S. Constitution. Supreme Court justices are appointed to that position for life. It is an extremely important position in the government, and appointees are the subject of much national scrutiny. By law, they must be confirmed by the U.S. Senate, which voted to confirm O'Connor 99-0. Many Americans were delighted that, for the first time in U.S. history, a woman had been selected for the court. As O'Connor herself described it, "I had no idea when I was appointed how *much* it would mean to many people around the country. It affected them in a very personal way—people saw the appointment as a signal that there are virtually unlimited opportunities for women. It's important to mothers for their daughters and to daughters for themselves." It was also important to O'Connor's family—they were thrilled with her achievement. As her husband, John, explained, "[I am] not only happy for Sandra because she is so competent and so deserving, but I am happy for myself and my family because all our lives have become more interesting. Sandra's accomplishments don't make me a lesser man; they make me a fuller man." O'Connor took the oath of office as a U.S. Supreme Court Justice on September 25, 1981. She has served consistently since that time, taking only a few weeks off in 1988 after a diagnosis of breast cancer, a mastectomy, and a round of chemotherapy.

Since she joined the court, O'Connor has occupied a centrist position among justices with widely divergent views, often casting the deciding vote on a divided court. She is considered generally conservative, but also an independent thinker who follows no set judicial or political ideology. She respects legal precedent, favors judicial restraint, and defends states' rights over the rights of the federal government. Court observers describe her as hardworking, open-minded, conscientious, and a meticulous legal thinker whose viewpoints are difficult to categorize and impossible to predict. In particular, many are uncertain about her opinions on the divisive issue of abortion, which will continue to receive much attention and analysis as additional cases are brought before the court. As the first woman on the Supreme Court, her role in history is undisputed. Yet after only ten years there, her ultimate impact is still unclear. As O'Connor herself once suggested, "History will have to determine that."

HOBBIES AND OTHER INTERESTS

In addition to her heavy work load, O'Connor enjoys reading, tennis, skiing, golf, and traveling. She and her husband, John, also frequently attend parties on the Washington social circuit. Her approach to the game of golf shows the type of dedication and perseverance she brings to all activities, both work and play. She first took it up while the family was still living in Phoenix. She signed up for golf lessons at a country club and every Saturday she hit buckets of balls on the driving range. O'Connor did this every week for two years before she finally played a game of golf—and then, of course, she shot under 90 on her first game.

HONORS AND AWARDS

Service to Democracy Award (American Assembly): 1982
Jane Addams Medal (Rockford College): 1987

FURTHER READING

BOOKS

Gherman, Beverly. *Sandra Day O'Connor: Justice for All,* 1991 (juvenile)
Greene, Carol. *Sandra Day O'Connor: First Woman on the Supreme Court,* 1982 (juvenile)
Huber, Peter. *Sandra Day O'Connor,* 1990 (juvenile)
Who's Who in America 1990-91
Woods, Harold, and Geraldine Woods. *Equal Justice: A Biography of Sandra Day O'Connor,* 1985 (juvenile)

PERIODICALS

Current Biography Yearbook, 1982
Newsweek, May 1, 1989, p.35
People, Oct. 21, 1981, p.46
Saturday Evening Post, Sept. 1985, p.42
Scholastic Update, Jan. 26, 1990, p.4, 14
Time, July 20, 1981, p.8; July 9, 1990, p.27
Washington Post Magazine, June 11, 1989, p.21

ADDRESS

U.S. Supreme Court
Supreme Court Bldg.
1 First St., NE
Washington, DC 20543

Rosa Parks 1913-
American Civil Rights Activist
Known for Her Pivotal Role in the Montgomery
Bus Boycott

BIRTH

Rosa Parks was born Rosa Louise (or Lee) McCauley on February 4, 1913, in Tuskegee, Alabama. Her father, James McCauley, was a carpenter, and her mother, Leona (Edwards) McCauley, was a teacher. Parks had one younger brother, Sylvester.

YOUTH

The family started out in Tuskegee. When Rosa was two years old, her parents split up and she, her mother, and her brother moved to her grandparents' farm in nearby Pine Level, Alabama. Her grandparents were one of the few black families in the area to own their own land, rather than work for someone else. Although they were poor, they were able to raise enough food on the small farm for all. As a child, Parks often worked alongside her grandfather in the fields, harvesting vegetables or picking cotton.

For Parks, and for all blacks living in America during the first half of this century, skin color affected every part of their lives. The South, in particular, was segregated by race. Slavery had been abolished only some fifty years earlier, and blacks were still hated and feared by many whites.

One result of these attitudes was the legal doctrine known as "separate but equal," which created the segregationist laws known as Jim Crow. Although the United States Constitution guarantees equal protection for all citizens, the Supreme Court ruled in 1896 that equal protection could mean separate but equal facilities. While the justices of the Supreme Court may have envisioned separate facilities for blacks and whites that were truly equal, the reality was appalling. Blacks were made to feel inferior to whites in every way. They were restricted in their choices of housing and jobs, were forced to attend segregated schools, and were prohibited from using many restaurants, movie theaters, and other public accommodations. The facilities available to blacks were consistently substandard. Often prevented from voting, blacks were discriminated against in the legal system as well. It was at this time, too, that hate groups like the Ku Klux Klan could beat and kill blacks without fear of retribution from the all-white judicial system. As Parks herself said, years later, "Whites would accuse you of causing trouble when all you were doing was acting like a normal human being, instead of cringing. You didn't have to wait for a lynching. You died a little each time you found yourself face to face with this kind of discrimination."

This segregated way of life meant, for Parks, attending a poor, one-room school, with few books or supplies; not being able to stop on her way home from school for a soda at a whites-only lunch counter; being prohibited from using whites-only restrooms or drinking fountains; watching at all times for the "colored-only" sections of movie theaters, restaurants, trains, and buses—and even then being forced to give up her place if any white asked for it; entering a bus in the front, paying the fare, then exiting and reentering by the rear door, to avoid walking through the whites-only section; always taking care to avoid giving offense to whites; and always living in fear of the Ku Klux Klan.

EARLY MEMORIES

Parks has written movingly, in her autobiography *Rosa Parks: My Story* and elsewhere, of lying in her bed at night while still quite small, listening to the hoofbeats of the horses as the Ku Klux Klansmen rode by the windows, and wondering if they would stop at her home that night. Her grandfather, she knew, waited by the door with a rifle. But he would be no match for the Klan. "Back then," as Parks tells it, "we didn't have any civil rights. It was just a matter of survival;...of existing from one day to the next. I remember going to sleep as a girl hearing the Klan ride at night and hearing a lynching and being afraid the house would burn down."

EDUCATION

Rosa's mother, Leona McCauley, worked as a teacher, and the whole family knew the value of education. But for Rosa, that would be hard to achieve. She attended the local black elementary school, where her mother was the only teacher. When she graduated, the family worked hard to save enough money to send her to a private school for black girls. At the age of 11 she began to attend Montgomery Industrial School for Girls, known as Mrs. White's School for Girls, which stressed self-worth. At the age of 13, she started at Booker T. Washington Junior High, a black public school in Montgomery. Yet when she graduated two years later, no public high schools in Montgomery were open to black students, who were then forced to abandon their education. The McCauley family was determined that Rosa would succeed, and they worked together to raise enough money to send her to Alabama State College to finish her high school classes. When Parks was close to graduating, though, the family fell on hard times and could no longer afford the tuition. Her grandfather had died a few years earlier, and her grandmother became ill. Parks decided to leave school for a while to help care for her and to help out on the family farm. Her grandmother died soon after, and then her mother also became ill. Parks was forced to abandon her classes for good—or so she believed then.

MARRIAGE AND FAMILY

In 1931, Rosa met and fell in love with Raymond Parks, a barber who was active in civil rights causes; they were married in 1932 and settled in Montgomery. Raymond Parks encouraged Rosa to finish her education, and she received her high school diploma from Alabama State College in 1933.

FIRST JOBS

After her marriage, Rosa Parks worked at several different jobs, as an insurance saleswoman and as a seamstress, doing alterations either in a shop or in people's homes. Throughout the Depression, both Parks and her husband were fortunate to be able to find regular work.

CAREER HIGHLIGHTS

While Parks continued to support herself by sewing, she also became active in civil rights and community work. She was inspired, in part, by an event she witnessed while on a Montgomery bus. A young black soldier celebrating his release from the hospital stepped off the curb in front of the bus. The white driver got off and beat the soldier with a metal ticket puncher until he bled so heavily that he had to return to the hospital. Infuriated, Parks attended the bus driver's trial. He was fined $24 for assault and battery, but he didn't lose his job.

Soon after, Parks joined the National Association for the Advancement of Colored People, or NAACP. Founded in 1910, the purpose of the NAACP is, to this day, "to promote equality of rights" and to eliminate racial prejudice. Parks first joined the organization in 1943 and soon became the secretary, using some of the skills that she had learned in high school, but which she was unable to use to find a decent job. With the NAACP she was able to do more interesting and rewarding work, arranging meetings, lining up speakers, helping other blacks to register to vote, and working as an advisor to youth groups. Although Parks was dedicated to the work, she began receiving hostile and threatening phone calls. It was during this time, also, that Parks attended workshops at the Highlander Folk School, where people from all over the United States gathered to share their experiences in fighting segregation.

THE MONTGOMERY BUS BOYCOTT

The action that would forever link her name with the cause of civil rights in the U.S. came on Thursday, December 1, 1955. Returning home from work as a department store seamstress at the end of the day, Parks boarded the bus and took a seat in the first row behind the whites-only section. Coincidentally, the bus driver was James Blake, who twelve years earlier had removed Parks from his bus for refusing to enter by the rear door. At the next stop, a white man entered and found all the seats full. The driver told the black passengers in Parks's row to stand—at that time, a black couldn't sit in even the same row as a white, and the driver had the right to change the boundary of the whites-only section as needed. Although they hesitated, the other three passengers in the row stood up. But Parks felt both tired and insulted, and she refused. "I had had enough," she later explained. "I wanted to be treated like a human being." The driver again ordered her to move, and then threatened to call the police. Parks told him to go right ahead. The police came, arrested her for violating racial segregation laws, and took her to jail. She was released on bail and returned home with E.D. Nixon, president of the Alabama chapter of the NAACP.

Nixon saw her arrest as an opportunity to challenge the laws requiring segregation on public transportation. Parks was well known and respected among Montgomery blacks for her work with the NAACP and with youth groups, and Nixon believed that the black community would support her. He asked her to appeal her case the following Monday in court. Raymond

Parks urged her to refuse, warning "The white folks will kill you, Rosa." Although she knew it would be risky, Parks agreed.

Throughout the weekend, leaders in the black community planned the strategy to challenge Parks's arrest. To protest the unfair treatment and to show their strength, they decided to stage a one-day boycott of the city's buses on the coming Monday. As Nixon said, "The only way to make the power structure do away with segregation is to take some money out of their pockets"—and considering that 70 percent or more of the Montgomery bus riders were black, they were in a position to do just that. Ministers of black churches were soon involved in the planning, including Rev. Ralph Abernathy and Rev. Martin Luther King, Jr., both of whom became leaders in the civil rights movement. King, then young and virtually unknown, was asked to lead the boycott, which soon brought him to the forefront of national attention.

The boycott was a phenomenal success. Parks was delighted to see the buses virtually empty of black passengers, and even more heartened to find 500 supporters at the courthouse for her trial, where she was found guilty and then appealed. The boycott was so effective that first day—90 percent of blacks refused to ride the buses—that leaders decided to continue the boycott until they received better treatment. It required a great deal of effort for all. Most blacks had no cars and little money. Many had to walk to work, while others were able to ride in car pools set up by the churches, or in

black-owned taxis. Parks, along with other organizers, traveled around the country to raise support for their cause and money for the car pools. Everyone who participated was harassed by the police, city officials, and other segregationists: King was arrested and jailed, and his home and others were bombed. In the face of all this, the protesters maintained their nonviolent stance. Finally, on December 20, 1956, the United States Supreme Court ruled that segregation on public transportation was illegal—and the bus boycott, originally planned for one day and extended to over a year, finally came to an end.

Parks was made to pay heavily for her role in instigating the Montgomery bus boycott. Both she and her husband lost their jobs and were unable to find work. They frequently received hateful and threatening phone calls, and they worried constantly that the violent threats would come true. Raymond Parks suffered a nervous breakdown from all the stress. As their situation worsened, Rosa Parks decided in 1957 that she and Raymond, with her mother, should move to Detroit, Michigan. Her brother Sylvester lived there, and Parks, like many other Southern blacks before and since, hoped to find steady work and a new life there. Initially, it was very tough. Both her mother and her husband were too sick to work, and at one point Parks was hospitalized with stomach ulcers. Eventually she found a job as a seamstress, joined a church, where she became a deaconess, joined the local chapter of the NAACP, became active again with youth groups, and took part in ongoing civil rights activities. In 1965, Parks was hired by a newly elected black congressman, John Conyers, Jr., to work in his Detroit office, and her days as a seamstress were finally over. She continued working in his office until her retirement in 1988. In 1986, she was elected to the Board of Directors of the NAACP.

In recent years, Parks has become something of a celebrity. As her role in the civil rights movement has been recognized, she has been sought after for public speeches and received numerous awards. Today, Parks is widely respected for the great strength, dignity, and courage she showed in refusing to give up her seat on that Montgomery bus. A seemingly small event, perhaps, but one that galvanized blacks, inspired them to work together, and ultimately helped the civil rights movement win equal rights for black Americans. A few lines from an American Public Health Association citation aptly summarizes her importance: "There are rare moments when just one individual's action can change the course of history, mobilizing great numbers of people in a worthy cause. . . . Such a moment occurred. . .when one brave woman challenged a civil evil and set into motion a series of world-shaking events that ultimately changed longstanding patterns and discriminatory traditions in the United States."

HOBBIES AND OTHER INTERESTS
Although Parks and her husband had no children, young people have always had a special place in her heart. In addition to her ongoing work

with youth groups, in 1987 she founded the Rosa and Raymond Parks Institute for Self-Development to teach young people history, communication and leadership skills, political awareness, and how to work for social change. One program offered by the Institute is the Reverse Freedom Tour, in which a group of teenagers travel by bus to the major landmarks of the civil rights struggle, learning about the history and the people that fought for their rights.

WRITINGS

Rosa Parks: My Story, with Jim Haskins, 1992 (juvenile)

HONORS AND AWARDS

Springarn Medal (NAACP): 1979, "for the quiet courage and determination exemplified on December 1, 1955, when she refused to surrender her seat on a Montgomery, Alabama, bus to a white male passenger. Her defiance of a demeaning situation brought about desegregation of buses in Montgomery. In recognition of her personal dedication since that time to the cause of civil rights and particularly to the youth of the Detroit area to whom she is dedicated to help grow, develop, and reach their full potential."

Martin Luther King, Jr., Nonviolent Peace Prize: 1980

Martin Luther King, Jr., Leadership Award: 1987

Roger E. Joseph Prize (Hebrew Union College—Jewish Institute of Religion): 1987, " 'the mother of the modern freedom movement' and a national civil rights activist."

Adam Clayton Powell, Jr., Legislative Achievement Award: 1990

FURTHER READING

BOOKS

Celsi, Teresa. *Rosa Parks and the Montgomery Bus Boycott,* 1991 (juvenile)
Friese, Kai. *Rosa Parks: The Movement Organizes,* 1987 (juvenile)
Parks, Rosa, with Jim Haskins. *Rosa Parks: My Story,* 1992 (juvenile)
Who's Who among Black Americans, 1992-93

PERIODICALS

Current Biography Yearbook 1989
Ebony, Sept. 1977, p.54; Feb. 1988, p.68
Newsweek, Nov. 12, 1979, p.18.
Senior Scholastic, May 1, 1981, p.5

ADDRESS

Rosa and Raymond Parks Institute for Self-Development
65 Cadillac Square
Suite 3200
Detroit, MI 48226

Jane Pauley 1950-
American Television Newswoman
Former Co-Anchor of the "Today" Show

BIRTH

Margaret Jane Pauley was born in Indianapolis, Indiana, on October 31, 1950, to Richard (Dick) and Mary (Patterson) Pauley. She has one sister, Ann, older by two years. The senior Pauleys moved to Florida several years ago after Dick retired from a longtime sales career with Dean Foods.

YOUTH

The shy little girl from the Midwest who grew up to be a television news superstar had what her parents called "a typical normal" upbringing. She and her sister, best friends throughout their childhood (and now as adults, too), produced plays in their garage, led cheers in grade school and junior high, went to church on Sundays, and spent happy weekends on their maternal grandparents' farm in Hurricane, Indiana. There were unspoken expectations for the girls to bring home good grades, which they did, but family members and friends who watched the Pauley sisters grow up say that there was unconditional love and the rules were never overly rigid. The standards were high, however, and both Jane and Ann were able to meet them without sacrificing the exuberance of childhood.

Several stories about Jane Pauley's childhood emerged soon after she won the choice role of co-anchor on NBC's "Today" show in 1976. Now, poised and professional and the respected survivor of a TV news controversy that erupted in 1989, she was so timid as a little girl that she was called "Margaret" throughout second grade because she was too meek to tell the teacher that her family chose to use her middle name instead of her first. Tales of her embarrassment about being born on Halloween or about breaking out in hives are stories that she "delights in telling with typical self-deprecating wit," says an *Indianapolis News* article. "Her mother toted her youngest daughter to a specialist who announced that Jane was a nervous child, and would have to be careful her whole life." Pauley is noted for the self-assurance she projects today on live TV, but realizes that she sees in her own kids that "it's possible to be both shy and want to be noticed. I had the same simultaneous, contradictory impulses."

EDUCATION

Pauley was educated in the public schools of Indiana from early childhood through college. She attended Eastridge and Moorhead elementary schools and Woodview Junior High, all in the greater Indianapolis area. At Warren Central High School, where she was a prize-winning public speaker and debater, she represented her school as governor of Girls' State and, later, as an elected delegate to Girls' Nation. Among her toughest competitors in statewide high school debates was a Fort Wayne student who also would gain television celebrity—actress Shelley Long of "Cheers" fame.

Pauley's college years were spent at Indiana University in Bloomington, earning good grades, but also taking time for a social life in her sorority, Kappa Kappa Gamma. She completed credits for her degree in political science a semester early. With the thought of eventually returning to enroll in law school, she joined the 1972 presidential campaign of New York City Mayor John Lindsay, working as an aide in Arizona. When Lindsay's primary bid folded, Pauley returned to Indianapolis for a staff job with the Indiana Democratic Central Committee.

CHOOSING A CAREER

Law school had lost its appeal in the months that Pauley was out in the working world. Away from the classroom less than a year, and with no television or news credentials, she applied for and won a job with WISH-TV, the CBS affiliate in her hometown. She was co-anchoring a midday broadcast and anchoring the weekend newscasts within fifteen months. Pauley eventually caught the eye of an NBC network official, who suggested that she try out for an opening at WMAQ-TV in Chicago. "I was twenty-four and I thought, '*No way* are they going to hire a woman my age,' " she said in an interview a couple of years later, when she had already moved on to national recognition. "Being confident that they were not going to consider me seriously, I was completely relaxed," she explained. "I had nothing to lose. And I'm sure that showed in the audition. I simply was not afraid."

Pauley spent an uneasy year at the Chicago station, fending off the critics' arrows and the skepticism of her fellow reporters. She was resented for her youth and lack of experience in such a high-profile job—that of first female evening newscaster in the city. Although the barbs hurt, Pauley took them in stride and struggled to establish herself. *Time* quotes a former WMAQ staff member as saying that "she didn't know the first thing about reporting. But her on-camera presence was incredible."

CAREER HIGHLIGHTS

In 1976, Jane Pauley was swept away from the anxieties of her year at WMAQ. Her professional career began in earnest when she was chosen from a field of veteran reporters to replace the respected Barbara Walters as co-anchor on NBC's "Today" show. The selection was a surprise to nearly everyone involved, especially to Pauley herself, who felt that she had been given the chance to try out for the job merely as a courtesy to her Chicago affiliate. After the auditions, however, viewers in major television markets were polled on their impressions and Pauley, the indisputable favorite, was chosen for the "Today" show.

Only twenty-five years old and with a world of potential, if not experience, the poised young woman who had survived Chicago's harsh judgment took her place beside Tom Brokaw and learned the craftsmanship of television. "It was the only way someone of my age could have gotten away with it—to be anchored to someone with his credibility," admits Pauley. "Critical acceptance was a while in coming, probably until I had the good sense to turn thirty."

Pauley eased into a comfortable role on "Today," appealing to a nation-wide audience with her natural good looks and an unspoiled freshness seldom seen in the heady world of big-time TV. She interviewed celebrities and politicians, covered two British royal weddings, had a private audience with the pope, was beamed into American living rooms from the 1988 Seoul Olympics, and still remained the level-headed Jane Pauley from Indianapolis—uncorrupted by the glamour and prestige surrounding her.

There were many times, though, throughout her thirteen years in the early morning slot when she felt that she was being taken for granted. Bryant Gumbel, the show's current host, replaced Brokaw in 1982, and Pauley made the case then that she and former sportscaster Gumbel had comparable experience, and that she was the one with seniority on the show. She took it as a vote of no confidence about women in television. Nevertheless, she chose not to make waves, since she knew that there was "tremendous impact for Bryant to be the first black member of the cast, let alone host. To cry sexism," she said, "would pale against the thirty years of racism."

Gumbel and Pauley played well off one another, due in large part to the latter's good nature and well-documented willingness to be a team player. Witty and articulate, a competent writer, and a hard-working broadcast journalist, she had won the respect of her peers—and the affection of millions of viewers. But change came in September 1989 when, in an attempt to boost its ratings with a younger audience, NBC added thirty-one-year-old Deborah Norville to the main desk at "Today." Pauley concluded that her place on the show was in jeopardy and that the time had come to move on. "I. . .wasn't figuring in anyone's strategic plans," she says now. "It seemed pretty simple to me—I'd just leave." With her departure, there was an outcry by viewers who deluged the network with calls and letters—and worse—who stopped watching. The consequences were a public relations disaster, and the producer who had created the controversy in the first place was forced to make a public apology and to give up control of the program.

Pauley was now a genuine celebrity. Her courage to stick up for her convictions showed the toughness that had always lay beneath her agreeable exterior; it rose to meet her redefined identity. With new-found clout, she renegotiated her contract and began preparations for what turned out to be a smash prime-time special, "Changes: Conversations with Jane Pauley." Next on her agenda was a newsmagazine program called "Real Life with Jane Pauley." She wrote and co-produced "Real Life," and the early episodes dominated the ratings during their time slots. The show floundered in its second season, though, and ultimately failed.

In the spring of 1992, NBC introduced still another newsmagazine, "Dateline NBC," pairing Jane Pauley with Stone Phillips, a competent reporter recruited from ABC. The show appears infrequently, and in the meantime, Pauley does frequent duty as a deputy anchor for Tom Brokaw on "NBC Nightly News," and enjoys a normal daily routine that allows her to spend more time with her family. She was gracious enough earlier this year to return briefly to the "Today" set but, this time, she was sitting in for the host—a notch up from her old supporting role.

MAJOR INFLUENCES

Although she gives herself credit for making good choices and for knowing her own priorities, Jane Pauley is quick to acknowledge those who have inspired her. She remembers the high expectations of her father—a gracious man who taught his children to always do the honest and decent thing—and friends say now that Pauley absorbed his goodness and warmth. She denies being "a pathologically nice person" like her dad, saying earnestly and with good humor, "Nice implies a selfless quality I just don't have."

Pauley also cites the special influence of her sister, who is now an engineering manager in the nuclear-safety division of Westinghouse in Pittsburgh. "Ann. . .was both an inspiration and a pacesetter for me," says Pauley. "I grew up trying to keep up with my sister. Whatever I accomplished, she had done it first." Pauley goes on to say, however, that there never was any sibling rivalry between them, and that they were—and are—best friends.

MARRIAGE AND FAMILY

Jane Pauley has been married since June 14, 1980, to Garry Trudeau, the political satirist whose "Doonesbury" cartoon strip has influenced a generation of readers. They live in a spacious apartment on Central Park West in New York with their nine-year-old twins, Ross and Rachel, and six-year-old son, Thomas. Many family weekends are spent at their country house, where they are able to live quietly and in privacy.

Pauley and Trudeau "have never allowed their high-profile careers to interfere with their family life," said a *New York* feature written soon after Pauley left "Today." The magazine quotes journalist and friend Linda Ellerbee, who talks of the low-key life led by the two celebrities—the bright and eager Midwesterner who has earned her place as one of America's favorite newswomen, and the Yale-educated Easterner from a privileged background whose brilliant satire has merited a Pulitzer prize. Says Ellerbee, "Their household is as normal a place as you will ever be in the city of Manhattan. It's an island of sanity. . . . It's not that they are unaware of the extraordinary position they are in. They've thought about it a great deal and made conscious choices to raise their children the way they were raised, which is a pretty good way."

HONORS AND AWARDS

Media Award for Television News (American Association of University Women): 1980-81
Spirit of Achievement Award (National Women's Division of the Albert Einstein College): 1982

Broadcaster of the Year Award (International Radio and Television Society):
  1986 (co-recipient with Bryant Gumbel)
Woman of the Year Award (*Glamour* magazine): 1990 (with nine others)

FURTHER READING

BOOKS

Jacobs, Linda. *Jane Pauley: A Heartland Style,* 1978 (juvenile)
Who's Who among American Women, 1991-92

PERIODICALS

Cosmopolitan, June 1991, p.232
Good Housekeeping, Feb. 1990, p.46
Ladies Home Journal, July 1990, p.87
New York, July 23, 1990, p.25
People, Nov. 13, 1989, p.114; Aug. 13, 1990, p.67
Redbook, Sept. 1991, p.89
Time, Aug. 20, 1990, p.76
TV Guide, Mar. 14, 1992, p.8

ADDRESS

NBC News
30 Rockefeller Center
New York, NY 10020

H. Ross Perot 1930-
American Business Leader
Former Presidential Candidate

BIRTH

Henry Ross Perot was born in Texarkana, Texas (on the border between Texas and Arkansas) on June 27, 1930. His parents, Gabriel Ross Perot and Lulu May Perot, had lost their first child, Ross, Jr., to spinal meningitis. Doctors warned Lulu May Perot that having other children would carry a risk, but she went ahead anyway, giving birth to a girl, Bette, and then Henry Roy Perot, whose name they changed to "Ross" when he was in the fifth grade.

YOUTH

Growing up in east Texas in the 1930s and 40s, Ross learned much from his father, a trader in cotton and horses. Starting at the age of six, he helped his father to break in horses for riding, earning a dollar or two per horse. While doing that work, Ross twice broke his nose in falls, marking his appearance for life. As a child he also sold used saddles, magazine subscriptions, and garden seeds.

When he was 12, at a time of prejudice against blacks, particularly in the South, Ross offered to deliver the Texarkana *Gazette* newspapers to the black slum community of New Town. To do that he demanded—and received—70 percent of all the money he collected, instead of the usual 30 percent given to other newsboys. Each day he awoke in the darkness at 3:30 A.M. and, on horseback, delivered newspapers to families nobody else had been willing to serve. Soon he was receiving so much money that attempts were made to cut his commissions. But young Ross appealed directly to the publisher, saying they had a deal that should be kept. The publisher agreed. From that time on, Perot later declared, he "always went straight to the top with a problem."

EARLY MEMORIES

Well after his childhood, Ross remembered the poverty of his family and neighbors during the Depression of the 1930s. Tramps, out of work and hungry for food, knew that by coming to the Perot house they could count on being fed by his mother. Nor, as Ross later recalled, did she feel it necessary to tell her neighbors what she had done; she just did it. Young Ross also remembered that, often to the horror of their white neighbors, his father would sit side by side with local blacks on their porches or load them into his car for visits to the county fair.

Because of hard times, even the Perots, living in a paid-up home, were sometimes short of money. Ross vividly recalls one Christmas when his father had to sell a horse he very much loved in order to have enough money for Christmas presents and a Christmas dinner for the family.

Once asked on a nationwide TV interview what had been most important in shaping his life, Perot answered without hesitation. Undoubtedly, he said, it was his family.

Perot insists even today that the high point in his entire life was the day when, as a Boy Scout, he attained the rank of Eagle Scout. Such scouting ideals as "For God and Country" also helped to shape his personality.

EDUCATION

After graduating from high school, Perot attended Texarkana Junior College while persistently trying to win admission to the United States Naval Academy. After finally winning appointment to Annapolis, he achieved only moderate academic success, ranking in the middle of his class. But in his junior and senior years he was elected class president. Unlike many of the other cadets, he refused to smoke or drink alcohol and made it a point to be neat and physically fit. Although he never had seen a ship or the ocean before arriving at Annapolis and stood only five feet six inches tall, his classmates elected him "best all around midshipman" at the Naval Academy.

MARRIAGE AND FAMILY

While at Annapolis, Perot had a blind date with Margot Birmingham, a student at a nearby college. In 1956 they married and since have had a son, Ross, Jr., and four daughters, Nancy, Suzanne, Carolyn, and Katherine. They have four grandchildren, and two more are on the way. To Perot, a stable marriage and close-knit family are goals he considers necessary for American society, along with such traditional virtues as hard work, ambition, and reverence for religion. At the same time, he understands that not everyone in today's diverse world agrees with him. As a result, Perot takes pride in his own tolerance. Still, he has been quoted as saying that, "If I could do one thing, I would try to construct a strong family unit for every family [in America]. . . . All the other problems then would disappear."

MAJOR INFLUENCES

Along with his childhood in Texarkana, his family, and his Naval Academy experience, Perot has been deeply influenced by major figures in the history of American patriotism. Some visitors have remarked that his corporate office resembles a patriotic museum. There are pictures of George Washington, bronze statues of the American west by Frederick Remington, and throughout the office American eagles—some carved, some in bronze.

Perot also points to the enormous influence on his life of Winston Churchill, Prime Minister of Great Britain during the darkest hours of World War II. Of all historical personalities it is the courageous Churchill whom Perot most admires, so that he includes in almost all of his speeches Churchill's deeply felt statement: "Never give in. Never give in. Never. Never. Never." In thinking about running for president, Perot is motivated by the belief that someone must do for America today what Churchill did during Britain's greatest crisis: mobilize the nation's will.

CHOOSING A CAREER

After graduating from Annapolis in 1953, Perot went to sea. As he later put it, "I loved the Navy, loved the sea, loved ships." What he did not like, however, was that to advance in rank he had to wait in line instead of being judged by his own performance. In 1957 he decided to return to civilian life. He took a job with IBM (International Business Machines Corporation), selling computers in Dallas, Texas.

As an IBM salesman he proved astonishingly successful. In his fifth year with the company he met his sales quota for the entire year by January 19, less than three weeks after the year had begun. Once, while waiting for a haircut in a barbershop, he read a line quoted from Henry David Thoreau's *Walden:* "The mass of men lead lives of quiet desperation." At that moment, he later said, he decided not to accept IBM's offer of an administrative position, but instead to strike out on a career of his own.

CAREER HIGHLIGHTS

In June 1962, Perot founded Electronic Data Systems (EDS), using only a $1,000 personal check for seed money. During his years as an IBM salesman he had seen that many companies did not know how best to use the computer equipment they were buying. His company was organized to design, install, and then help in the operation of electronic systems. From the very beginning, he declared that "I want [to hire] people who are smart, tough, self-reliant, have a history of success since childhood, a history of being the best at what they've done, people who love to win."

By 1969-70, the price of EDS stock had risen to $150 a share. H. Ross Perot had become incredibly wealthy. But for him, "The day I made Eagle Scout was more important to me than the day I discovered I was a billionaire."

In the years that followed he gave vast amounts of money to Dallas public schools to help inner city black children. He gave money to the Boy Scouts, the Girl Scouts, the Salvation Army, and the Dallas Symphony Orchestra. He bought one of only four existing copies of the British Magna Charta from England for $1.5 million and then donated it to the National Archives in Washington, D.C. By 1988 he had given away more than $120 million.

During the Vietnam War Perot became concerned that American prisoners were being brutally treated. For Christmas 1969, he rented two enormous jets and had them filled with food, medicine, and letters from the prisoners' families. The Vietnamese refused to allow the planes to land in Hanoi, but in the neighboring country of Laos, Perot dramatically shouted into a bullhorn, "Let us have our men!" Eventually the Vietnamese improved the conditions of the prisoners and permitted more mail to be received. While the action made him a hero for some Americans, many officials within the administration of then-President Richard Nixon were not pleased with Perot's willingness to take things into his own hands.

In 1978 during revolutionary turmoil in Iran, two EDS executives were imprisoned in Teheran. Perot personally visited the executives. Then, unable to buy their freedom with money, he arranged for some of his company executives and a former U.S. commando leader to aid an Iranian revolutionary mob in storming the prison. The result was freedom for some 11,000 friends of the revolutionaries, as well as for the two Americans. Again Perot emerged as a hero to some members of the American public, but his actions clashed with the objectives of the U.S. State Department and the administration of President Jimmy Carter.

In 1984, Perot sold EDS to General Motors for $2.5 billion—$1 billion of that paid directly to him in cash. Although GM then owned the company, Perot stayed on as an executive. The arrangement, however, was a failure for all concerned. Just as Perot had been unable to change the U.S. Navy or IBM into "his kinds" of organizations, he could not change GM. In public statements he expressed irritation about the company's posh executive dining rooms, the use of uniformed chauffeurs for company managers, the large bonuses received by executives, and the quality of cars that GM was manufacturing.

By 1986, the other GM board members were so unhappy with Perot's criticisms that they voted to pay him $700 million for his remaining share in EDS. It was their way—an expensive way—of finally getting him to leave the company. Perot soon started a new company, Perot Systems Corp., which eventually went into open competition with EDS.

This outspoken American recently took part in the race for President of the United States. With the singular fervor of commitment that has marked all of his career, Perot burst upon the political scene in early 1992 and galvanized a significant number of the American electorate with his message: "We own this country. Government should come from us. In plain Texas talk, it's time to take out the trash and clean out the barn, or it's going to be too late." He claimed that the current government was not addressing the key issues of concern to the American people and that he offered a distinct alternative to the political establishment. He had organizations active in all 50 states and said he would run as an independent if he was able to get enough signatures to get on the ballot in all the states.

Perot's showings in the polls were significant: in early June 1992, he was running ahead of incumbent president George Bush and Democratic candidate Bill Clinton. His candid, singular approach to life, work, and politics was scrutinized in the media, and many aspects of his past and personality were closely examined; his percentages in the polls began to slip. But loyal supporters and political pundits alike were shocked when Perot suddenly withdrew from the race on July 16, 1992, without ever formally announcing his candidacy. Citing a "revitalized" Democratic party

349

and claiming that "our objective is to improve our country, not disrupt the political process," Perot concluded that he could no longer win the election. At press time, Perot's plans as either a political figure or a business leader were uncertain.

MEMORABLE EXPERIENCES

To Ross Perot, despite all of his wealth and fame, it is still memories of his childhood and family background that move him most deeply. For that reason he headed a state commission in 1984 to improve the public schools in Texas. He recommended smaller classes, competency tests for teachers, and a rule that failing students would lose their eligibility for such extra-curricular activities as football. "We've turned our schools from places of learning into places dedicated to play," said Perot. "Organized sports, the marching band, the pep squad, the 4-H groups dominate some of our schools, and any time left over is devoted to learning." Many of the changes Perot suggested eventually were approved by the state.

HOBBIES AND OTHER INTERESTS

Since his years in the Navy, boats have been Ross Perot's special fascination. He has three racing boats, one of them driven by jet engines, as well as a 45-foot cabin cruiser. At his home he has a pool, gymnasium, tennis court, and stables for his horses. As he once declared, "My dream is to die dancing with my wife, Margot, when I'm 94. Ninety-four or beyond."

HONORS AND AWARDS

Perot has won hundreds of awards and received many honors, including:
Horatio Alger Award: 1986
Thomas Jefferson Award for Greatest Public Service Performed by a Private
    Citizen: 1986
Raoul Wallenberg Award for Humanitarianism: 1987

FURTHER READING

BOOKS

Follett, Ken. *On Wings of Eagles,* 1983
Levin, Doron. *Irreconcilable Differences: Ross Perot Versus General Motors,* 1989
Mason, Todd. *Perot: An Unauthorized Biography,* 1990

PERIODICALS

Current Biography Yearbook 1971
Dallas Morning News, Mar. 22, 1992, p.9
Inc., Jan. 1989, p.54
National Review, Apr. 27, 1992, p.39
New York Times, May 10, 1992, p.A1; May 12, 1992, p. A1; May 26, 1992, p.A1

New York Times Biographical Service, Apr. 1986, p.546
Texas Monthly, Dec. 1988, p.98
Washington Post Magazine, Apr. 12, 1987, p.24; Apr. 19, 1987, p.24

ADDRESS
777 Main Street
Fort Worth, TX 76102

* UPDATE *

After leaving the race in July, Perot decided to rejoin the run for the presidency on October 1, 1992. Saying that neither Bush nor Clinton was addressing the "mess" the government was in, Perot became an active and aggressive candidate, buying large blocks of television time and taking part in three televised debates with the Republican and Democratic challengers. His showing in the election was stunning: he captured 19% of the popular vote, more than any other independent candidate in this century since Theodore Roosevelt.

Luke Perry 1964- [date uncertain]
American Actor
Plays Dylan McKay on "Beverly Hills, 90210"

BIRTH

Luke Perry (Coy Luther Perry III) was born in Mansfield, Ohio, on October 11—this much is clear. But the year of his birth is less certain, probably either 1964 or 1966. Those associated with the show "Beverly Hills, 90210" would prefer to keep their star's age a mystery, hoping to maintain the illusion that Perry is still a teenager like Dylan McKay, the character he plays. As Perry once joked with a reporter, "I could tell you how old I am, but then I'd have to kill you."

YOUTH

Perry was born in Mansfield but grew up in Fredericktown, a

small, rural community about an hour from Columbus, Ohio. Although the family lived on a farm, his father, Coy Sr., also worked in the steel industry, while his mother, Ann, stayed home to care for Luke, older brother Tom, and younger sister Amy. When Luke was just six, his parents divorced. Perry was not on good terms with his father, who died in 1980. When Luke was twelve, his mother married Steve Bennett, a construction worker with a daughter, Emily, from a previous marriage. Perry became very close to Bennett, whom he calls "the greatest man I know."

EARLY MEMORIES

Perry decided when he was very young to become an actor. "When I was a kid," according to Perry, "my mom had this thing for Paul Newman, and when I was like four years old I saw this movie of his called *Cool Hand Luke*. I saw my name on TV, I saw Luke on TV, I'd never seen it written before. Then I watched the movie. After that I couldn't imagine my life being about anything else. I couldn't imagine not being an actor." Despite this decision, Perry was hesitant to confide in anyone about his acting ambitions. In his community, most kids wanted to become farmers, and he worried that few would understand his desire to perform.

EDUCATION

Fredericktown High School was, for Perry, quite different from West Beverly Hills High, the fictional school he attends as Dylan McKay: "My high-school experience was so hugely different," he has said. "We had classes on giving birth to cows and driving tractors." Perry was not a very dedicated student, but he did have one special subject: he was voted Biggest Flirt in his senior year! He also played on the baseball and tennis teams. He tried to get some acting experience, but his school's small drama department put on the same play three years in a row. By the time he graduated in 1984, he had had enough of school: "I didn't even bother applying to colleges," Perry has said. "I didn't want to go to school anymore. I was really sick of it. Besides, I'm one of those people who learned everything he needed to know in kindergarten." He decided then to head for Hollywood, hoping to break into show business.

FIRST JOBS

In California, Perry enrolled in acting classes and worked in different jobs to support himself, spreading asphalt, painting parking lots, selling shoes, cooking, and working in a factory. He also began auditioning for parts in television shows, commercials, and movies. He was not very successful, but he was persistent: he spent three years going on 216 auditions without ever once landing a part. Finally, on audition number 217, he was selected for the part of Ned Bates on the soap opera "Loving." Because that show and most other soap operas are filmed on the East Coast, Perry moved to New York City. He continued to take acting classes there. After about a year, though, his part was written out of "Loving." He managed to work in New York for about two more years. He landed a brief role on the soap "Another World," did some jeans commercials, and got a couple of parts in some off-Broadway theatrical productions. He even landed small roles in two movies, *Terminal Bliss* and *Scorchers.* Although he didn't know it, Perry was on the brink of his big break.

CAREER HIGHLIGHTS

Perry returned to the Los Angeles area in late 1989 and resumed auditioning for various roles. The following spring, the Fox Broadcasting Company announced that it would be creating a new series about high-school life in Beverly Hills. Along with a lot of other young hopefuls, Perry showed up to try out for a part. He auditioned first for the role of Steve Sanders—at that point, the role of Dylan McKay hadn't yet been created. Although Perry knew he wasn't right for the Steve Sanders character, he hoped that by frequent auditioning he would become known throughout the industry. And, in fact, his hard work paid off: that summer, when the role of Dylan McKay was created, the Fox casting team remembered him from his earlier audition and asked him to come back in. After six separate auditions, Perry, elated, won the part.

"Beverly Hills, 90210" focuses on the lives of a group of teenagers at the fictional West Beverly Hills High School. The show centers on Brandon and Brenda Walsh, sixteen-year-old twins who have recently moved to Beverly Hills with their parents, Cindy and Jim, following the father's job transfer from Minneapolis, Minnesota. The Walsh family provides the moral center for the show. Many of the stories highlight the differences between their down-to-earth values and the faster, looser, and wealthier lifestyles in Beverly Hills. This framework allows the show to explore many issues that confront teenagers today, including sexuality, divorce, adolescent rebellion, date rape, AIDS, alcoholism, and drug abuse. The show has been praised for its strong writing, fine acting, truthful portrayal of sensitive issues, and, above all, for taking the concerns of teenagers seriously.

Broadcast at the same time as the ever-popular show "Cheers," "90210" initially had poor ratings after its debut in October 1990. Yet the show gradually established itself with the teenage audience. The decision to air new shows during the summer of 1991, instead of showing reruns like the other networks, brought in a host of new viewers. In fact, when Perry made a promotional appearance at a Florida mall in August 1991, 10,000 fans showed up. In the resulting crush, twenty-one people were injured, and Perry was forced to give up such appearances. Today, he receives two thousand fan letters each week.

The role of Dylan McKay, the best friend of Brandon and boyfriend of Brenda, has been steadily developing during the series from a minor to a central character. Dylan is an appealing character to many. He is intelligent and good-looking, but also blunt, cynical, rebellious, brooding, vulnerable, and distant, a loner who has battled an alcohol problem and learned to live without his absent parents. According to Perry, he and Dylan are not much alike: "Dylan's angry and he has a dark side. Me, I don't think I'm an angry guy at all. I'm pretty happy."

Despite their differences, Perry loves the role: "What attracted me to Dylan is that he's from one of the richest families in Beverly Hills, but he's totally avoided all the trappings of wealth. Monetarily, he has everything a kid could want...but he's not much into the life-style. Dylan's literate, articulate, and a staggering intellect. He's rebellious and intimidating, but most of all he's smart. Myself, I'm in awe of intelligent people. Before this, I never had the chance to play someone that smart. This is a dream role for me."

MARRIAGE AND FAMILY

Perry lives in a modest two-bedroom home in Hollywood, California. He is unmarried, but he has a rather unusual live-in companion—a Vietnamese potbelly pig named Jerry Lee (after Jerry Lee Lewis, one of Perry's favorite singers). Despite his current success, Perry lives simply. "I don't prize possessions, I prize *people*," he has said. "My friends are the most valuable things in my life."

FAVORITE TELEVISION SHOWS, MOVIES, MUSIC, AND BOOKS

Some of Perry's favorite things include watching the television shows "Starsky & Hutch," "S.W.A.T.," and "Jeopardy"; seeing the movies *Cool Hand Luke* and *The Pope of Greenwich Village*; listening to classical music or the singers Jerry Lee Lewis, Harry Connick, Jr., Billy Joel, and B.B. King; and reading biographies and autobiographies.

HOBBIES AND OTHER INTERESTS

Perry enjoys tinkering with cars, cooking, fishing, spending time in the country, and designing and building furniture. He supports environmental causes and has also been involved in promotional work for several charities.

FURTHER READING

BOOKS

Cohen, Daniel. *"Beverly Hills, 90210": Meet the Stars of Today's Hottest TV Series*, 1991 (juvenile)

Mills, Bart, and Nancy Mills. *"Beverly Hills, 90210": Exposed!,* 1991 (juvenile)

Reisfeld, Randi. *The Stars of "Beverly Hills, 90210": Their Lives and Loves,* 1991 (juvenile)

Rovin, Jeff. *Luke-Mania! Jason-Fever!,* 1991 (juvenile)

PERIODICALS

New York Times, Aug. 4. 1991, II, p.29
People, Aug. 26, 1991, p.38; Sept. 9, 1991, p.81; Nov. 4. 1991, p.96
Rolling Stone, Aug. 8, 1991, p.81

ADDRESS

Fox Broadcasting Company
P.O. Box 5600
Beverly Hills, CA 90209

Scottie Pippen 1965-
American Basketball Player
All-Star Forward for the Chicago Bulls

BIRTH

Scottie (Scott) Pippen was born September 25, 1965, in Hamburg, Arkansas, a small town in the southeastern part of the state. He is the youngest of twelve children born to Preston and Ethel Pippen. His father, now deceased, worked at the local paper mill.

YOUTH

Pippen grew up on the playgrounds of Hamburg, where he and his five brothers functioned as a team, often holding the basketball court for hours. Despite his ambition to play the game, Scottie had little hope of fulfilling that dream. At the age of fifteen, he was still no taller than his mother, who is six feet tall. "Everyone in our family is tall," he told *Sports Illustrated* shortly after breaking into the NBA. "Being the size I was then, I didn't have any big plans for basketball." Pippen was happy to be an equipment manager for his high school football team and didn't count on any more exalted position in athletics.

Scottie suffered a shock when he was a freshman in high school—his father had a severe stroke, confining him to a wheelchair for the rest of his life. The loss of their only breadwinner put the large, poor family in dire financial straits, and not until the youngest son became a basketball star eight years later would they breathe easily.

EDUCATION

Pippen attended Hamburg High School, where he warmed the bench for the basketball team for his first three years. He was so discouraged that he skipped the off-season conditioning program between his sophomore and junior years to concentrate on his football-equipment duties. Coach Donald Wayne was prepared to kick Pippen off the team until the other players intervened. As a senior, he finally was given the opportunity to start at point guard—the crucial position that involves distributing the ball and running the offense. At about six feet tall, and 150 pounds, he was hardly a college prospect and did not receive a single scholarship offer.

Coach Wayne, believing that Pippen needed an education, convinced University of Central Arkansas coach Donald Dyer to give him a government grant and a work-study job as team equipment manager. He majored in industrial education, expecting to manage a factory after college, and spent two summers working in furniture plants. Before Pippen left school a few credits short of his degree, he had undergone a growth spurt, earned a basketball scholarship, and become the best player in the small-college National Association of Intercollegiate Athletics (NAIA).

CHOOSING A CAREER

Although Pippen was an NAIA All-American in his junior year, Central Arkansas was so small that an NBA future was by no means assured. His unhappy experience working in furniture plants, however, made him dedicate himself to basketball. In his senior year, he got the attention of NBA scouting director Marty Blake, who contacted several teams about the young prospect. The Chicago Bulls sent a scout who was duly impressed, despite the poor quality of Pippen's opposition. Scottie's senior campaign was brilliant, as he averaged 26.3 points and ten rebounds per game, connecting on nearly 60 percent of his shots.

Also impressive was Pippen's versatility—he played all five positions at various times, confounding the opposition with his ability to score, pass, rebound, defend, block shots, and steal the ball. He was a far cry from the six-foot tall high school boy of a few years earlier, having grown to nearly his current size, 6'7" and 210 pounds.

CAREER HIGHLIGHTS

When it came time for the NBA draft in 1987, the Bulls had hoped to sneak Pippen past their unwary opposition and select him in the second round, but Scottie ruined their game plan. He excelled in post-season exhibitions for scouts, playing for the first time against top-caliber competitors. So obvious were his multiple skills that the Bulls expected him to be gone by the time they made the eighth pick in the first round. Jerry Krause, the team general manager, was undeterred. He struck a deal with the Seattle Seahawks, trading up to fifth in the drafting order. The Bulls drafted Pippen and signed him to a six-year, five million dollar contract.

Pippen played well in the 1987-88 season, his rookie year. A dislocated thumb and a herniated disc limited his effectiveness after mid-season, but the Bulls still saw the potential greatness that had so excited them a year earlier.

After successful off-season surgery, Pippen returned in 1988-89 to become a starter and the team's second force after Michael Jordan, the shooting guard who is often described as the world's best player. Playing small forward with occasional stints at point guard, Scottie averaged 14 points, six rebounds, three-and-a-half assists, and nearly two steals per game. Pippen had arrived, thrusting the Bulls—previously criticized as a one-man team—into the league championship picture.

Despite a 4-2 loss in the Eastern Conference final series to the league-champion Detroit Pistons at the end of the 1988-89 season, things were looking up for Pippen and the Bulls. Scottie improved every aspect of his game in 1989-90, averaging over 16 points and nearly seven rebounds. The Bulls made the conference finals again, this time taking their arch-rival Pistons to a seventh and deciding game. Here Pippen hit the low point of his career and gained a label as a choker, which has dogged him to this day. Just before the final game, he was stricken with a blinding migraine headache. The Bulls lost badly, 93-74, as Pippen went one-for-ten from the field and managed only two points and four rebounds in 42 minutes.

The 1990-91 season was payback time, and Pippen again took his game to a higher level. He was denied an All-Star spot during that season, however, which he felt could be attributed to his awful seventh-game performance against Detroit. By late in the season, he was playing as never before, but gaining a reputation for bitterness. When general manager Krause began wooing Croatian star Tony Kukoc before negotiating

Pippen's contract, Scottie became enraged. "I'll finish the season...but my heart won't be in it," he told a reporter. "I can't guarantee what kind of effort they'll get out of me because I am really upset."

By the time the playoffs rolled around, Pippen had forgotten those words. He averaged nearly 22 points and nine rebounds as the Bulls took the championship while losing only two playoff games. The sweetest revenge came in a four-game sweep of the hated Pistons. "Scottie's breakthrough was the Detroit series, no question," teammate Jordan later told the *New York Times*. "He dominated them. He made them respect him."

In 1991-92, Pippen helped Chicago to its second straight championship, but not without controversy along the way. After returning to the All-Star team in a season that saw his scoring average breaking 20 for the first time, Pippen was inconsistent early in the playoffs. He seemed befuddled by the defensive pressure applied by the New York Knicks and the Cleveland Cavaliers, which renewed the dreaded criticism that he choked in important games. That seemed academic, however, once the Bulls defeated Portland to win the title, largely because Pippen outplayed the Blazers' star forward, Jerome Kersey.

Scottie Pippen was named to the United States basketball team for the

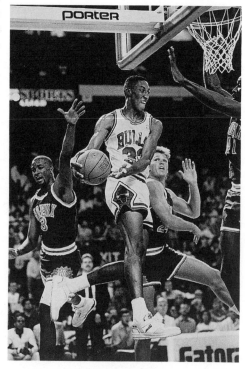

1992 Olympics, solidifying his standing as one of the world's best players. He and the other eleven athletes, known as the Dream Team, cruised to the gold medal while winning their games by an average of 44 points.

At 27, Pippen still has room to improve. "He is just coming into that age range... when players are at the top of their game," Krause told *Sports Illustrated* this year. Many sports followers, especially Bulls fans, hope it's true.

MEMORABLE EXPERIENCES

Scottie Pippen's father was paralyzed from the time he suffered his stroke until his death in 1990, and never saw his son play until the family showed him a videotape of Scottie's first professional game. "The stroke even took away his speech," Pippen quietly told *The National*. "But my mom told me he cried."

MARRIAGE AND FAMILY

Pippen married Karen McCollun in 1988. They divorced in 1990. He has one son, Antron, from this marriage. Antron lives in Chicago with his mother.

HONORS AND AWARDS

NAIA All-America: 1985-86 and 1986-87
NBA All-Star Team: 1989-90 and 1991-92
All-Defense Second Team: 1990-91
Member of NBA Championship team: 1990-91, 1991-92
All-NBA Second Team: 1991-92
All-Defense First Team, 1991-92
Olympic Basketball: 1992, Gold Medal

FURTHER READING

BOOKS
Smith, Sam. *The Jordan Rules*, 1991

PERIODICALS
Newsmakers, Issue 2, 1992, p.88
New York Times, May 11, 1992, p.B9
Sport, Feb. 1992, p.66
Sporting News, Feb. 24, 1992
Sports Illustrated, Nov. 30, 1987, p.67; May 20, 1991, p.26; Feb. 24, 1992, p.74

ADDRESS

Chicago Bulls
1 Magnificent Mile
980 N. Michigan Avenue
Suite 1600
Chicago, IL 60611-9739

Colin Powell 1937-
American Army General
Chairman, Joint Chiefs of Staff

BIRTH

Colin Luther Powell was born April 5, 1937, in the Harlem section
of New York City to Theopolis and Maud Ariel (McKoy) Powell,
immigrants to the United States from Jamaica. He has one sister,
Marilyn.

YOUTH

With his parents and Marilyn, he moved to the South Bronx
during his childhood. In those years, the neighborhood was a
place where people watched out for one another. "We could

never get into trouble," says his sister (now Marilyn Berns, a bilingual teacher of advanced primary school students in Santa Ana, California). "Everywhere we went, there were forty pairs of eyes watching us." Powell grew up surrounded by a closely knit family. He and Marilyn and their many cousins were raised in an atmosphere of hard work and solid expectations. Demonstrating a willingness to work and to sacrifice was the parents' way of setting an example for the children. Powell, recalling those days, told an interviewer how they all got together on weekends and "somehow, over time, they made it clear to us that there were certain expectations built into the family system. It was unthinkable not to be educated, get a job, go as far as you could, whether it meant becoming Chairman of the Joint Chiefs or having a good job as a nurse." His own parents, a shipping clerk and a seamstress, had dropped out of high school to work, and they wanted more in life for their children. While many in the now dangerous and desolate South Bronx never "got out," most of Powell's family did. He has cousins who are business leaders and prominent members of government; one, Arthur Lewis, is a former ambassador to Sierra Leone.

EARLY MEMORIES

Powell freely admits that he was only a so-so student. His sister was more interested in learning and was always asking their mother to read street signs and to spell words. When telling about their differences as children, she says with amusement, "Colin could not have cared less. But look at us now—I guess he was a late bloomer." Growing up, young Colin played stickball (a game that city children play in the streets, using a broomstick and a lightweight ball), was an acolyte at St. Margaret's Episcopal Church on 151st Street and, later, worked part-time in a baby furniture store near home. He recalls that he never thought of himself during those years as a member of a minority. People in his neighborhood were either black, Puerto Rican, Jewish, or of some vague (to him) European extraction.

EDUCATION

After graduating from Morris High School in the South Bronx, but still unsure of what he wanted in life, Powell entered the school of engineering at City College (now City University) of New York, where the tuition at that time was an unbelievable $10 a year. He is quoted as saying that he joined the Reserve Officers Training Corps (ROTC) because he liked the uniform, but it was in this program that the otherwise C student earned straight A's. He graduated at the top of his class and decided then on an army career. Years later, Powell settled down again to serious study and, in 1971, earned a master's degree in business administration from George Washington University. He also has a diploma from the Army Command and General Staff College at Fort Leavenworth, Kansas, where he finished second in his 1976 class.

FIRST JOBS

Commissioned as a second lieutenant in the Army after his 1958 graduation from City College, Powell served in what was then West Germany and next had an assignment at Fort Devens, Massachusetts.

MARRIAGE AND FAMILY

Powell met Alma Vivian Johnson, the daughter of an Alabama educator, on a blind date during his early career assignment at Fort Devens. They were married August 24, 1962, a few months before he was sent to Vietnam for the first time. Their son, Michael, was born the next year while Powell was on patrol in the jungle, but the news did not reach him for two weeks. Now Michael and the couple's other children, daughters Linda and Annemarie, are grown, and Michael has a small son of his own—Jeffrey, born in 1989. The senior Powells live in a Virginia suburb of Washington, D.C.

CHOOSING A CAREER

Now a four-star general, Colin Powell looks back on his choice of career and is convinced that his special interest in history has given meaning to his profession. He feels that with each step up in rank, he has gained a better understanding of the policy "in which national security and military matters operate." He makes it clear that the message of his experience is to work hard and to learn lessons from the past, "so that we can do things better in the future."

CAREER HIGHLIGHTS

In his nearly 34 years of Army service, Powell has risen through the ranks to the highest military position in the land, that of Chairman of the Joint Chiefs of Staff. He had two tours of duty in Vietnam (1962-63 and 1968-69), and was wounded twice, the second time as he rescued his troops after a helicopter crash. He later had a command post in Korea (1973-74), after taking time out for graduate study at George Washington University, and to fill a White House Fellowship at the Office of Management and Budget in Washington. Powell was a Pentagon staff officer during the years between 1975 and 1981, serving as a military defense assistant and as executive assistant to the Secretary of Defense.

During the 1981-83 period, he was back on active military duty as assistant commander of the Fourth Infantry Division at Fort Carson, Colorado. His recall to Washington surprised no one, since he had won such widespread admiration for his work in advisory and policymaking posts. For three years, he was senior military assistant to the Secretary of Defense, and then served as National Security Council Advisor before President George Bush named him, in August 1989, to head the Joint Chiefs of Staff. According to U.S. law, the Chairman of the Joint Chiefs is the "principal military advisor" to the President, the Secretary of Defense, and the National Security Council.

Powell came to the attention of the general public after the invasion of Kuwait by Iraq's forces on August 2, 1990. As Chairman of the Joint Chiefs, Powell advised President George Bush and oversaw the activities of all branches of the United States' armed forces in Desert Shield and Desert Storm—the deadly six-week war that forced Saddam Hussein and his army to surrender and leave Kuwait.

MEMORABLE EXPERIENCES

The turning point in Colin Powell's life, an honor that led him to political power, came when, at the age of 35, he was chosen to receive a White House Fellowship. The appointment eventually took him through several Pentagon assignments to his present post as Chairman of the Joint Chiefs of Staff. He is the youngest chairman ever and also is one of only three persons in that job who did not attend one of the service academies.

MAJOR INFLUENCES

As an adult and a successful career officer looking back on his youth, Colin Powell seems to give the most credit for his achievements to his parents and his extended family. They provided the home life and the opportunities that made him want to do well. The military discipline of his ROTC years also has been a strong influence on a personal level.

FAVORITE BOOKS

Powell is a great student of history and most of his limited leisure reading time is spent on that subject.

HOBBIES AND OTHER INTERESTS

Talking to and encouraging minority students is one of Powell's chief interests. Whenever his busy schedule permits, he is willing to share with them his views on hard work, persistence, and the pursuit of excellence. He tells them that "they must be ready for opportunity when it comes." Some of Powell's spare time at home is spent rebuilding old cars but, most of all, he enjoys being with his family.

HONORS AND AWARDS

Purple Heart medals (two, for wounds suffered in action in Vietnam)
Bronze Star for Valor
The Soldiers Medal
The Legion of Merit
Distinguished Service Award
Congressional Gold Medal: 1991

FURTHER READING

PERIODICALS

Current Biography Yearbook 1988
Ebony, July 1988, p.136
New York Times, Aug. 15, 1989, I, p.18
People, Sept. 10, 1990, p.52
Reader's Digest, Dec. 1989, p.121

ADDRESS

Joint Chiefs of Staff
Pentagon
Room 2E-857
Washington, DC 20318-0001

Jason Priestley   1969-
Canadian Actor
Plays Brandon Walsh on "Beverly Hills, 90210"

BIRTH

Jason Bradford Priestley was born August 28, 1969, in Vancouver, British Columbia, Canada, into a show-business family: his grandfather was a circus acrobat, his father was at one time a set builder (although he has also worked in several other jobs), and his sister, Justine, eighteen months older than Jason, was a model and actress. His mother, though, was the real professional in the family: using the stage name Sharon Kirk, she worked as a dancer, choreographer, actress, and singer. "She even danced at two command performances for the Queen," Priestley proudly recounts. After snapping a hamstring muscle while dancing,

Sharon Kirk retired from show business and now works in real estate; Lorne Priestley, Jason's father, is a manufacturer's representative for a furniture company.

YOUTH

Although he always enjoyed a lot of typical childhood activities, especially sports like rugby and hockey, Priestley was interested in acting from a very young age. He and Justine sometimes accompanied their mother to the set—in fact, he got his first job at age three months in one of his mother's films—and soon he wanted to act, too. His mother refused at first, but relented and allowed both brother and sister to sign with an agent when Priestley was just five. He began with commercials for all types of products. At age eight, he won his first real role, a part in the Canadian television movie *Stacey*. He began taking acting lessons as well.

Yet throughout this time, according to Priestley, he had a normal childhood. "I was Joe Average. I played sports, went to school, always in the classroom, never on the set." But he also quickly learned some fairly difficult lessons. "As a six-year-old I learned this: you always had to be a professional. If you weren't, if you just acted like a kid at any time, it was 'see ya, kid,' and you're out the door." Probably his most difficult experience from his young years was his parents' divorce when he was seven; both remarried a few years later, and Priestley gained two step-sisters, Christine and Karen.

Priestley quit acting rather abruptly when he was in junior high school. He has mentioned several reasons for quitting—trouble finding good parts, being ostracized by his friends at school—but he now says, "Mainly I quit because I just wanted to be a teenager. I didn't want to worry about how I looked—did I look right for this part or that part?" In fact, he had very firm ideas about how he wanted to look: "I jumped on the tail end of the punk movement. I was into chains, black jeans, combat boots. You know how everyone's shaving stripes into their hair now? I was doing that back in 1980, shaving stripes, mohawks, everything into my head. And I didn't want to worry, 'Oh, if I cut my hair this way I'm going to lose out on this or that part in a movie.' Spare me that! I just suddenly wanted to be a kid. And I was, I was a kid."

Even after he quit acting Priestley continued to take acting classes, and by age sixteen he was back in the business. He started out with school and community theater and quickly landed roles in a range of productions, including a couple of television series, some TV movies, and some stage productions, all based in Vancouver. In 1987, after finishing high school, he moved to Los Angeles.

FIRST JOBS

At first, following his move, Priestley had great success. He quickly won two successive roles on "21 Jump Street," which brought him recognition and work on such series as "Beans Baxter," "Airwolf II," and "Quantum Leap," as well as the lead role in the Disney movies *Teen Angel* and *Teen Angel Returns*, which were shown in fifteen-minute segments during episodes of the new "The Mickey Mouse Club." But he also had some lean times when no work appeared, and at one point he briefly returned home to Vancouver. In 1989 his luck changed, though, when he was cast in "Sister Kate," a weekly situation comedy about a nun who comes to live with a group of seven rebellious orphans. Priestley's character, Todd Mahaffey, was usually described as a nice guy, but not too bright—in his words, "My character has the IQ of a bag of dirt." The cancellation of that series, after just a few months, proved to be his best luck yet.

CAREER HIGHLIGHTS

Unbeknownst to Priestley, he was being considered for a role on a new series on the Fox Broadcasting Network originally called "Class of Beverly Hills" (later "Beverly Hills, 90210"). The producer was Aaron Spelling, known for the hit series "Charlie's Angels," "Love Boat," "The Mod Squad," and "Dynasty." He and his team had auditioned hundreds of young actors, but none seemed right for the role of Brandon Walsh. His daughter, Tori Spelling (who plays Donna Martin), had developed a crush on Priestley from watching "Sister Kate," and she suggested to her father that he audition Priestley for the role of Brandon—after also suggesting Shannen Doherty for the part of Brenda. Priestley auditioned on a Thursday, won the role, and was on the set by the following Monday.

"Beverly Hills, 90210" is a weekly, one-hour dramatic series about a group of friends at fictional West Beverly High School. A set of twins, Brenda and Brandon Walsh, are part of the group. Their recent move from Minnesota to southern California with their parents, Cindy and Jim, is often used to highlight the differences between the glamorous lifestyle of Beverly Hills and the Walshes' emphasis on family ties and solid Midwestern values. As such, the Walsh family represents the moral center of the show. Over time, Brenda and Brandon—as well as their friends— have come to appreciate the love, attention, and guidance that the Walsh family has to offer. "Beverly Hills, 90210" has explored many issues of concern to teens, including drug and alcohol use, date rape, sexuality, peer pressure, divorce, homosexuality, and teenage pregnancy. The show's debut in October 1990 received lukewarm ratings and little attention from the press. Yet it soon became a must-watch show for many young viewers, who have come to expect the honesty, forthrightness, and respect for teens that have won it such a devoted audience.

Priestley describes Brandon as "a normal guy thrust into the glamorous, fast-paced lifestyle of Beverly Hills. He wants to fit in, but he's secure enough with who he is not to let go of his Midwestern values and morals."

369

The character has changed somewhat since the show began, becoming less moralistic, less perfect—as seen, for instance, in the episode in which Brandon gets arrested while driving drunk and faces up to the consequences. Asked about the role, Priestley once responded, "I'm very different from Brandon. To play him, I found that little piece of Brandon within me. That piece is inside everyone. It's that sliver of sincere morality in there." In fact, Priestley is usually described as quite different from the character. He's known as fun-loving, adventurous, playful—the one member of the cast who is always joking around, keeping the atmosphere on the set relaxed when pressures build. His enthusiasm for his work shines through when asked how he sees his future: "I just can't see myself sitting behind a desk all day, so I think I will always do something creative. Hopefully, if acting didn't work out for me, I could get into something else in entertainment like directing or writing. I just love this business too much to even think of doing anything else."

MARRIAGE AND FAMILY

Priestley lives alone outside Los Angeles. He is said to be dating the actress Robyn Lively, recently seen on "Doogie Howser, M.D."; they met when co-starring in *Teen Angel Returns*.

HOBBIES AND OTHER INTERESTS

Priestley's favorite pastimes are sports, especially hockey, his first love, but also golf, tennis, skiing, and bungee jumping. He also participates in charity events to benefit poor and sick children. Priestley spends a lot of time hanging out with fellow cast-members Luke Perry and Ian Ziering.

FURTHER READING

BOOKS

Catalano, Grace. *Just Jason*, 1991

Mills, Bart, and Nancy Mills. *"Beverly Hills, 90210" Exposed!*, 1991

Reisfeld, Randi. *The Stars of "Beverly Hills, 90210": Their Lives and Loves*, 1991

PERIODICALS

Interview, Feb. 1992, p.124
People, May 20, 1991, p.48; Sept. 9, 1991, p.80
Rolling Stone, Aug. 8, 1991, p.81; Feb. 20, 1992, p.22
Sassy, Nov. 1991, p.52

ADDRESS

Fox Broadcasting Company
P.O. Box 5600
Beverly Hills, CA 90209

Queen Latifah   1970-
American Rap Singer
Recording Artist Whose Works Include *All Hail the Queen* and *Nature of a Sista*

BIRTH

The rap star now known as Queen Latifah [Lah-TEE-fah] was born Dana Owens on March 18, 1970, in Newark, New Jersey. Her father, Lance Owens, was a policeman, and her mother, Rita, later became a teacher. She has a brother, Lance Jr., who is two years older.

YOUTH

"Latifah" means "delicate and sweet" in Arabic, and the name was given to the future queen of rap by a Muslim cousin when she was eight. She added the Queen later: "not to denote rank, but to acknowledge that all black people come from a long line of kings and queens that they've never really known about. This is my way of giving tribute to them."

Her parents, who had separated when she was five, were divorced when she was eight, and Rita Owens was forced to move her family into a housing project in East Newark. "It wasn't as bad as you might imagine," Latifah says. "But a project can only get so good, because you're dealing with people with a different mentality, who may not care as much." Her family was "somewhere between some money and no money," she says, yet she really didn't think of herself as poor. But Rita Owens vowed to get them out, and she worked two jobs and went to college—taking her young children with her to class—to do so. After she completed her degree, she moved her family into a house.

EDUCATION

Education was very important to Latifah's family, so when Dana's teachers determined that she was gifted during her second grade year, her mother made the necessary sacrifices to send her daughter—and son—to a parochial school, Saint Anne's Roman Catholic School in Newark.

Although she first began singing at Shiloh Baptist Church, it was at Saint Anne's that Latifah first took to the stage: she played Dorothy in a school production of *The Wiz*, and according to her mother, Latifah brought the house down. "When she sang 'Home,' people were crying," she says.

Latifah started rapping at 16, while attending Irvington High School in Irvington, New Jersey, where her mother taught art. She and her friends would rap in the bathrooms and locker rooms of the school. Trying to sound like the Fat Boys, Latifah took the part of the human beat box. "I'd do the beat box and I'd be beatin' on the stalls," she remembers. Soon Latifah and friends Tangy B and Landy D formed a rap group, Ladies Fresh, and competed against other girl groups in high school talent shows.

She and her friends used to hang out and talk about serious things, too, like apartheid, drugs, and racism—things she would rap about in her later songs. She was voted Most Popular, Best All Around, Most Comical, and Best Dancer during her senior year: "In high school I was popular but I wasn't the type of popular other people were. I was popular for being me. I was popular with the coolest people and the nerds and the introverts."

She was also an outstanding basketball player for Irvington High, and her team won two state championships. Her rap talents were put to use on the court, too. "During rest periods, I'd say, 'Dana, give us a little rap and cheer us up'," says her former coach, Vinny Smith.

373

FIRST JOBS

It was her mother's search for the right DJ for a high school dance that brought Latifah to the attention of record companies. "I knew not to get a square DJ but one who really pumped it," recalls Rita Owens. "I heard Mark James (now known as DJ Mark the 45 King) play for another class and I just loved what he did." DJ Mark made some demos with Latifah and took them to Fred Brathwaite, known as Fab 5 Freddy, the host of *Yo! MTV Raps*, who played them for executives at Tommy Boy records. They signed Latifah to a contract in 1988, when she was only 17.

CHOOSING A CAREER

"I was attracted to the sound and the content and the freedom of rap," says the Queen. "To me, it's like a free art form. It flows—it's smooth. It can be anything you want it to be—harsh, bitter, funny, you name it. I used to write poetry when I was younger. Rap was just reciting my poetry to music."

CAREER HIGHLIGHTS

Although she had started to study journalism at Manhattan Community College, Latifah now devoted herself to her career as a rap artist, coming out with her first album, *All Hail the Queen*, in 1989. It included her singles "Wrath of My Madness" and "Dance with Me," and "Ladies First," a rap duet with fellow star Monie Love. Both "Dance with Me" and "Ladies First" were made into videos, which spread her music to the MTV audience. On her first album, Latifah performs the raps to a variety of background music, including reggae, house, jazz, and vocal choruses. *All Hail the Queen* sold 400,000 copies and reached No. 6 on *Billboard's* black music list.

Latifah is one of a growing number of female rap artists, including M.C. Lyte, Yo-Yo, Salt-N-Pepa, and Monie Love. But what sets her apart is her message: she talks about self-respect and pride, and she is clearly anti-drug. As she says: "we're the only ones who actually try to tell kids, don't do drugs and get an education, use contraception to not get pregnant or catch a disease, and have a conscience, and look around you and know yourself and know where you come from, and be proud of who you are." She avoids the feminist label often placed on her by others who feel that her raps about taking pride in being a black woman come from that specific social and political point of view: "What I have is common sense," she states, saying she believes in "womanism—feminism for black women, to be natural, to have her sisterhood." Neither she nor the women who appear on stage with her dress in the revealing outfits so often worn by women in rap videos and concert tours. "Sex sells; that's common sense. A lot of women sell their bodies—without *selling* them. It shows you're lacking in talent. Positivity takes a bigger push." She prefers African-style dress, and dashikis, kufi hats, turbans, and loose, billowing skirts and pants have become her trademark.

She has strong feelings about the anti-female lyrics of some male rappers, like Ice Cube and N.W.A., known as "gangstas": "They may say they're talking only about certain women but I don't buy that. They don't stop to think about the women they're offending....These guys have that negative streak in them regarding women. That's why they say those nasty, vicious things."

On the other hand, she is strongly anti-censorship, and believes that rap lyrics express an attitude toward life that needs to be heard. "This is not a fair country in a lot of ways, and you have to be black to completely understand that."

Latifah's second album, *Nature of a Sista*, was released in 1991. Featuring songs like "How Do I Love Thee," "Fly Girl," and "Nuff of the Ruff Stuff," the record shows off Latifah's talents as a rapper *and* a singer. "I've become more creative with melodies and things like that," she says of this record. "I am singing more and this album is really rhythmic." She also produced one of the songs.

Recently, Latifah has broadened her entertainment base by appearing on television, in episodes of "Fresh Prince of Bel Air," "In Living Color," and as a guest on the Arsenio Hall Show. She's also made her movie debut: she played a waitress in Spike Lee's *Jungle Fever* and had roles in the recent *House Party 2* and *Juice*.

Latifah now heads an enterprise known as Flavor Unit Management, a group made up largely of family and old high school friends. They edit her lyrics, appear on stage during performances, and help in finding and developing new talent, including the management of 10 bands. She remains positive about the power of rap and her role in the world of music: "When you can get a 50 percent black audience, 20 percent Spanish and the rest white, together, to listen to music from a black artist—no fighting, a lot of partying, a lot of fun going on—and then to have the artist tell them some things to bring them even closer, to tell them they need not be racist, they need to fight racism and things like that, to bring them closer together without a fight, then we're making the world a better place."

MARRIAGE AND FAMILY

Latifah is unmarried, and currently lives in a new home with her mother and brother.

MAJOR INFLUENCES

Latifah's mother, Rita Owens, is now a vice president of Flavor Unit Management, and has always been a great influence on her daughter. "Any person who can take two kids, basically without any support from their father and put them through Catholic school, because she felt they deserved a better education, is doing all right," she says. "She put us into a decent home, and gave us decent living conditions within the house. And watched us graduate from high school and do some college and become professionals."

HOBBIES AND OTHER INTERESTS

Latifah has been active in fundraising for AIDS research and other causes.

RECORDINGS

All Hail the Queen, 1989
Nature of a Sista, 1991

FURTHER READING

PERIODICALS

Chicago Tribune, July 4, 1990, VII, p.13
Christian Science Monitor, Nov. 4, 1991, p.10
Los Angeles Times, Sept. 8, 1991, p.G6
Mother Jones, Oct. 1990, p.36
New York, Dec. 3, 1990, p.125
New York Times, Sept. 15, 1991, p.B35
Philadelphia Inquirer, Sept. 18, 1991, p.D1

ADDRESS

Tommy Boy Records
1747 1st Ave.
New York, NY 10128

Yitzhak Rabin   1922-
Israeli Military Leader and Politician
Prime Minister and Head of the Labor Party

BIRTH

Yitzhak Rabin [YIT-sock rah-BEAN] was born March 1, 1922, in
Jerusalem, in what was then Palestine. His parents, Nehemiah
and Rosa (Cohen) Rabin, were both Russian immigrants who had
met and married in Jerusalem. Yitzhak's only sibling, Rahel, was
born three years after her brother.

YOUTH

Modern-day Israel only came into being in the late 1940s, after
years of struggle between the Arabs, Palestinians, and immigrant

Jews who fought, through political and military channels, to claim Jerusalem and the surrounding lands as their own. The early 1920s, when Rabin was born, was an era of great civil unrest between the various factions. Under the directive of the League of Nations, England had been given the task of governing Palestine and trying to keep the peace among the warring factions.

The Rabins, both political activists, were brought together by their common commitment to the labor movement and their determination to build a Jewish state in Palestine. Nehemiah Rabin, who had been born in Kiev (Ukraine), and later fled the Czarist police for the United States, came to Palestine in 1918 as part of the Jewish Legion, a military unit under British command. Rosa Cohen, from a wealthy Russian family, was a strong, opinionated woman, dedicated to her political and social ideals. She and her husband represented a determined group of Zionists, a worldwide movement of Jews whose goal was the creation of a separate Jewish state.

The parent's dedication to their political beliefs molded the way of life in the Rabin household. The family lived in a two-room apartment that the later Prime Minister called "spartan," and he grew up in an atmosphere where a life in public service was encouraged. "One did not work merely to satisfy material needs," he recalls, "work was valuable in itself."

EARLY MEMORIES

Nehemiah was a worker at the Palestine Electric Corporation and active in labor organizations. Both parents were involved in the Haganah, the underground military force of the Zionists, and Rosa had been named its first commander in 1922. Yitzhak and Rahel were expected to help with the upkeep of the house, and Rabin remembers "making beds, washing dishes, sweeping floors." They often spent days alone when their parents were busy with their political activities. When Rabin was only seven, the Arabs began the first concentrated attacks on Jewish settlements. According to a profile of Rabin by the Israeli writer Amos Elon, the "Rabin bathroom was turned into a secret military arsenal" at this time.

Rosa Rabin suffered from a heart ailment and later from cancer. When she died in 1938, Yitzhak was only 16; some say that this intensely shy man turned ever more inward from this point.

EDUCATION

Rabin went to the School for Workers' Children in Tel Aviv. His first experiences there were difficult, and he remembers feeling "confused and on the brink of tears. My character (which I seem to have inherited from my mother) always showed a tendency toward withdrawal, but soon I was deeply involved in school—though then, as now, I did not show my feelings or share them with others." Because his parents were so busy, Yitzhak would spend eight hours a day at the school, six days a week. He was a good student and very interested in sports, especially football. He also enjoyed tending the school's garden and taking care of the school donkey.

He later attended school on a kibbutz, a settlement where a group of people live and share the tasks of developing the area for farming. Yitzhak originally wanted to go into agriculture, and he graduated with honors from the prestigious Kadourie Agricultural School in Kfar Tabor in 1940. He had applied for a scholarship and planned to attend the University of California at Berkeley to continue his studies, but those plans were cut short by the outbreak of World War II (1939-1945).

FIRST JOBS

In 1941, Rabin was living on a kibbutz near Haifa when he met Moshe Dayan, who would later distinguish himself as a military commander in Israel. It was Dayan who persuaded Rabin to join the Palmach, the commando unit of the underground Jewish defense forces in Palestine. Their goal was to undermine the efforts of the pro-Nazi French government controlling Syria and Lebanon at that point in the war. Rabin's first job as a member of the Palmach was to cut telephone lines in Lebanon. Thus his 26-year military career began.

CAREER HIGHLIGHTS

MILITARY CAREER

Rabin was part of the Palmach throughout the war, even fighting against the British. Although they were part of the Allies, the British also helped determine the future of Palestine, including limiting the number of Jews who could emigrate from Europe. In 1945, Rabin was part of a group that attacked a British detention camp near Atlit to free Jews who had tried to enter Palestine illegally and who had been captured and detained by the British. Rabin was later arrested with other members of the Haganah as part of a conspiracy responsible for blowing up a series of bridges under British protection. He spent six months in a British prison camp.

Weary of their mandate, the British gave up their command in Palestine in 1948, and the United Nations (U.N.) declared a Jewish State in Palestine, thereby creating Israel. This act triggered the Israeli War of Independence, as the surrounding countries of Egypt, Syria, Lebanon, and Jordan went to war to reclaim land they thought was rightfully theirs. Rabin was named commander of the Harel Brigade, directing the defense of Jerusalem and fighting the Egyptians in the Negev region.

After the War of Independence, Rabin continued his career in the military, moving ahead swiftly as Israel continued to be involved in border skirmishes with their hostile neighbors. He was recognized as a superb technician and a strong leader. Furthering his military education, Rabin took a one-year course at the British Staff College, graduating in 1953. In 1964, he was named Chief of Staff, and in that position he headed the armed forces from 1964 to 1967. He put together the military plan that led to the decisive victory for Israel in the Six-Day War of June 1967, in which Israel decisively defeated their neighbors, annexing the Sinai from Egypt and the Golan Heights from Syria. These two territories have been fought over for years and continue to be a source of contention in the continuing debate on the future of the Mideast.

POLITICAL CAREER

In 1968, Rabin retired from the Army and was named Israeli Ambassador to the United States, a position he held until 1973. His goals as ambassador were to improve relations between his country and Washington, to secure increased military aid from the U.S. to Israel, and to further his own belief that Israel should withdraw from some of the land they had seized in the Six-Day War, a position that distanced him from conservative members of the Israeli government. He developed a close relationship with Henry Kissinger, then an advisor to President Richard Nixon, and was criticized for his outspoken support of Nixon at the time of his bid for re-election in 1972. Rabin claimed that he was misinterpreted in his words of praise for Nixon, whom he considered a good friend of Israel.

In March of 1973, Rabin returned to Israel and was elected to the Israeli Parliament, called the Knesset [kuh-NESS-it], as a member of the Labor party. In October of that year, Syria and Egypt launched a surprise attack on Yom Kippur, the Jewish Day of Atonement and an important holy day. The Yom Kippur War, as it became known, lasted 17 days, and Israel suffered heavy casualties. The government of Golda Meir, then Prime Minister of Israel, was criticized for being unprepared for the attack, and she and her coalition, which included Defense Minister Moshe Dayan, began to lose credibility and power. In March of 1974, Meir named Rabin Minister of Labor, and in May, she resigned. Despite his lack of political experience, Rabin became a Labor party candidate for Prime Minister. In May, he was elected the fifth Prime Minister of Israel. At 52, he was the youngest person ever elected to the post, and the first native-born Israeli.

Throughout his three-year term as Prime Minister, Rabin worked for greater peace in the Mideast. He often had the help of then U.S. Secretary of State Henry Kissinger, who devoted a good deal of his time to "shuttle diplomacy," flying back and forth from Washington to the Mideast to hammer out negotiations between Israel and her restive neighbors. In negotiations with Egypt, then under the rule of the late Anwar Sadat, Israel agreed to leave the oil-rich area of the Sinai they had held since 1967, and Egypt agreed to allow U.N. and American troops into the area to monitor the peace. Egypt also allowed Israel to use the Suez Canal, a vital trade link for goods passing from the Mediterranean Sea, through the Red Sea, and on to the Indian Ocean.

In July 1976, Palestinian terrorists hijacked a French airliner carrying many Israelis to Entebbe, in Uganda. Rabin orchestrated their release through the use of Israeli commandos who stormed the plane and freed the hostages. Called "one of the most daring, spectacular rescues of modern times" by *Time* magazine, the raid on Entebbe did much to restore Israeli self-confidence in military matters.

The Entebbe raid proved to be a high point for Rabin in an otherwise embattled term as Prime Minister. Growing pressure from right-wing parties and dissent within his own Labor party prompted him to call for a general election in 1977. In April of that year, one month before the elections, Rabin was forced to resign as revelations about his finances came to light. He and his wife had held two U.S. bank accounts with amounts higher than they had originally declared, in violation of Israeli law.

Out of office and power, Rabin spent the next four years in the shadow of Shimon Peres, a lifelong adversary, who became acting Prime Minister and head of the party after the scandal. The two remained bitter rivals, and their fighting seriously damaged the Labor party's strength and appeal in the eyes of many Israelis.

In 1984, Rabin became Minister of Defense in the coalition government of Labor and the Likud party, a right-wing group. As head of Defense, Rabin formulated the Israeli response to the *intifada*, the uprising by the Palestinians to protest Israel's continued occupation of the West Bank and the Gaza strip. His handling of the demonstrations and strikes of the Palestinians was popular in Israel, but sparked world-wide criticism as he sought to realize his country's policy of "might, power, and beatings" against the demonstrators. This aggressive stance also seemed to contradict Rabin's earlier commitment to ensure greater autonomy for the Palestinians and peace for the area.

In February of 1992, Rabin was elected to lead the Labor party, and in June was once again elected to the position of Israeli Prime Minister. It was a decisive victory of Labor over the Likud, the conservative hard-liners. Rabin's priorities include working for Palestinian self-rule in the Gaza and West Bank, an end to Israeli settlements in the area, and an improvement in Israel's relations with the U.S. Cautious, pragmatic, and willing to negotiate, Rabin begins a second term determined to bring peace to his embattled homeland.

MARRIAGE AND FAMILY

Rabin has been married since 1948 to the former Leah Schlossberg. She is from a wealthy German family, and the two met as members of the Palmach. They have two children, Dalia, born in 1949, and Yuval, born in 1956.

HOBBIES AND OTHER INTERESTS

Rabin enjoys photography, collecting art, and sports, particularly soccer and tennis. This quiet, reserved man is also an avid reader. Not one for small talk and pleasantries, Rabin is known for his intensely private nature.

WRITINGS

The Rabin Memoirs, 1979

FURTHER READING

BOOKS

Current Biography 1974
Encyclopedia Britannica, 15th ed.
International Who's Who, 1991-92
Rabin, Yitzhak. *The Rabin Memoirs,* 1979
Reich, Bernard, ed. *Political Leaders of the Contemporary Middle East and North Africa,* 1990
Slater, Robert. *Rabin of Israel,* 1977

PERIODICALS

New Republic, May 17, 1975, p.17
New Statesman, Feb. 28, 1992, p.23
New York, Feb. 13, 1978, p.50
New York Times, June 25, 1992, p.A1, A14; June 28, 1992, Sec. IV, p.1
New York Times Magazine, May 14, 1975, p.11
Newsweek, July 4, 1977, p.51; July 6, 1992, p.46
Time, May 6, 1974, p.33; July 12, 1976, p.21; Apr. 18, 1977, p.54; Feb. 11, 1985, p.44
Washington Post, Sep. 16, 1992, p.A24

ADDRESS

Prime Minister's Office
Qiryat Ben Gurion
Jerusalem, Israel 91919

Sally Ride 1951-
American Astronaut
First American Woman to Travel in Space

BIRTH

Sally Kristen Ride was born May 26, 1951, in Encino, California, a suburb of Los Angeles, to Dale Burdell and Carol Joyce (Anderson) Ride. She has a younger sister, Karen, whom she called "Bear," a nickname that has remained in adult life.

YOUTH

Ride was reared by educated parents in a household that allowed the children freedom to develop at their own pace. There was little pressure put on the girls, except to study hard and do their best in school. Some years ago, in an interview, Dale Ride said, "We might have encouraged, but mostly we let them explore." Young Sally was an athletic child, playing rough team sports with the neighborhood boys. Her sister, now Karen Ride Scott, a Presbyterian minister, tells that "when the boys chose up sides, she was always first." When Ride was about 10, she discovered the less hazardous game of tennis, and took to it as if she were on a special mission. She was trained by the famous champion Alice Marble and, by her teen years, had become a nationally ranked amateur. Ride was headstrong and sometimes an indifferent student, but her extraordinary skill at tennis won her a partial scholarship to a private girls' high school that challenged her quick mind and her imagination. Growing up, Sally Ride did a lot of reading, often science fiction, but also lighter, more popular books. There was little in her early life to suggest that she would someday be America's first woman astronaut. The only faint clue might have been her enthusiasm for what she once called her favorite childhood gift—a telescope to watch the stars. Friends say now that she never felt a need to follow in anyone's footsteps. It is generally agreed that she always set and lived up to her own standards.

EDUCATION

After her 1968 graduation from the exclusive Westlake School for Girls in suburban Los Angeles, where she first became interested in science, Ride enrolled as a physics major at Swarthmore College, near Philadelphia, Pennsylvania. She continued to play competitive tennis and dropped out of school after three semesters to return to California and give full attention to her game. World-famous tennis star Billie Jean King advised her to stick with tennis, but Ride felt that she was not quite good enough to be a professional player. She returned to college, this time closer to home, at Stanford University in Palo Alto and was graduated with a double major in English literature and physics. She once told Susan Okie, a friend and former schoolmate who wrote a lengthy feature story about her for the *Washington Post,* that she enjoyed studying Shakespeare because "It's kind of like doing puzzles. You had to figure out what he was trying to say and find all the little clues inside the play that you were right." Ride's logical thinking obviously was shown in literary subjects as well as in science.

Although she briefly considered English Literature for graduate study at Stanford, her preference for science won out, and Ride finally decided on astrophysics. She earned a Ph.D degree in that field in 1978.

CHOOSING A CAREER

Before she left Stanford, and while looking for a job in her profession, Ride happened to see an announcement in the university newspaper that NASA (the National Aeronautics and Space Administration) was interested in young scientists for future flights. She applied on a whim, saying later that she was not sure why she wanted to do it, and had never really had any "burning ambition" to be in the space program. So began a unique career that may have surprised even Sally Ride at the time but, looking back, would not have seemed out of the ordinary to family and friends of the little girl who once had her heart set on being a professional football player.

CAREER HIGHLIGHTS

A new world opened up to the bright young scientist when she arrived at the Johnson Space Center near Houston, Texas, in 1978. Her training was both rigorous and exciting. She learned skills for ground support as well as for actual flight and rehearsed in a simulator, "sometimes for as many as fifty-six hours straight." Ride was part of a team that spent two years developing a robotic "arm" to place and restore satellites in space; she eventually was able to help put that design to successful use in flight. Ride also served three times as capsule communicator, or capcom, relaying instructions from the ground to the crew of the space shuttle *Challenger* in orbit.

In all, Sally Ride was given more than four years of preparation for her first mission, and on June 18, 1983, the space shuttle lifted off from Cape Canaveral, Florida, on its seventh flight, this time with a woman crew member on board. Two Russian women had already traveled in space— Valentina Tereshkova in the early sixties and Svetlana Savitskaya in August 1982—but Ride's six-day flight marked a special moment in the history of the United States' space program.

America's first woman to travel beyond the Earth's atmosphere made a second shuttle flight in October 1984, and one of the other astronauts on the mission was Kathryn D. Sullivan, who had been a grade-school classmate of Ride in California. During that flight, Sullivan became the first American woman to walk in space. The space program remained active until the tragic explosion of the *Challenger* on January 28, 1986, when all seven crew members lost their lives. Ride was named to a presidential panel to investigate the accident. She left NASA the following year for a fellowship at Stanford's Center for International Security and Arms Control. Since June 1989, she has been a professor of physics at the University of California, San Diego. Ride also spends part of her time in La Jolla as director of the California Space Institute.

MAJOR INFLUENCES

Throughout her adult life, Ride has given credit to a woman named Elizabeth Mommaerts for introducing her to the logic of science. The former professor at UCLA (University of California at Los Angeles) had come to Westlake to teach physiology, and the two became not just teacher and enthusiastic student, but devoted friends as well. After Ride was chosen for the space program, she grieved at being unable to share the news with Mommaerts (who had committed suicide in 1972), and told Susan Okie that "She was the one person in the world that I wanted most to call."

MEMORABLE EXPERIENCES

There could hardly be any other answer than the one Ride gave in 1983 to an interviewer who asked what was the greatest moment in her life. She said, "The shuttle flight. Absolutely. The engines light, the solids light, and all of a sudden you know you're going. It's overwhelming."

Ride became an unwilling celebrity after she was chosen for her first mission, with newspaper and television reporters making constant demands on her time. Never one to explain herself, she did not like personal questions. According to her sister, she showed "an obvious impatience" when asked about her private life, or about being a woman in what was then considered a "man's world." However, she was a good sport about appearing professionally as a spokesperson for the space program.

MARRIAGE AND FAMILY

Sally Ride has been divorced since early 1987 from fellow astronaut Steven Alan Hawley, whom she married July 26, 1982. They had no children.

HOBBIES AND OTHER INTERESTS

Sally Ride is, her friends say, energetic and fun-loving, and has not lost her taste for sports. Besides tennis, she has, at various times, enjoyed volleyball and jogging and is licensed to fly a plane, something she learned to do during her training as an astronaut. She is interested in the education of young people and said recently, in speaking about the future of the space program, that she is concerned that not enough is done to make science and mathematics attractive to children.

WRITINGS

To Space and Back (with Susan Okie), 1986

HONORS AND AWARDS

Member, Presidential Commission on the Space Shuttle: 1986

FURTHER READING

BOOKS

Behrens, June. *Sally Ride, Astronaut: An American First,* 1984 (juvenile)
Hurwitz, Jane, and Sue Hurwitz. *Sally Ride: Shooting for the Stars,* 1989
   (juvenile)
O'Connor, Karen. *Sally Ride and the New Astronauts,* 1983 (juvenile)
Ride, Sally, and Susan Okie. *To Space and Back,* 1985 (juvenile)

PERIODICALS

Current Biography Yearbook 1983
Ms., Jan. 1983, p.45
Newsweek, June 13, 1983, p.36
New York Times Biographical Service, June 1983, p.729
People, June 20, 1983, p.83
San Jose Mercury News, Mar. 30, 1990, p.F1
Time, June 13, 1983, p.56
Washington Post, May 8-11, 1983, p.A1

ADDRESS

UCSD
Director
California Space Institute
9500 Gilman Dr.
La Jolla, CA 92092-0221

Pete Rose 1941-
American Athlete
Former Professional Baseball Player
and Manager

BIRTH

Peter Edward (Pete) Rose was born April 14, 1941, in Cincinnati,
Ohio, to Harry Francis and LaVerne Bloebaum Rose. He was the
third in a family of four children that included sisters Caryl and
Jackie and a brother, David.

YOUTH

Pete Rose grew up in the western section of Cincinnati, close to
the Ohio River. He ran with the neighborhood kids, played ball

388

after school and after supper, fished and swam in the river, "dodged trains," and watched his dad play rugged semipro football. His days, except during school hours, were unprogrammed, but not without limits. The family was close in those early years. They all loved sports of almost any kind, and played to have fun, but "always to win." The competitive streak ran strong in the family, no doubt inherited from Harry Rose, who worked in a bank to support his wife and children, but was regarded as the most famous athlete ever to play in Cincinnati's local football leagues.

Some memories of Rose's teen years were not so happy. He was small for his age, although tough and aggressive, and had been playing pickup football with the same passion he gave to every sport. However, when he failed to make the high school football team in his sophomore year, he was so devastated that he hardly ever went to class and, as a result, flunked his courses. He recalls now that he was "hanging out and doing nothing. . .it was a bad time." Rose finally pulled himself together, returned to school (although he lost a year of football eligibility), and helped his team win a co-championship in the public high school league.

EARLY MEMORIES

When Pete Rose was helping to prepare his autobiography a few years ago, he talked about the things that most people do when they look back on their childhood. But, when the story went to print, it was evident that sports, above all else, dominated those early days. He either played sports or watched them on the family's little seven-inch television set. He remembers playing with his little brother—sports again—and the good games he and his friends got up in the old neighborhood.

Other people's memories of Rose paint a picture that still fits the man of today: street smart and brash. Bill Staubitz, well-known journalist and onetime deputy sheriff in the Cincinnati area, is quoted as saying, "You have to picture Pete as this bumpy little guy. . .the way small kids do, he acted tough. But with Pete it wasn't just acting. He *was* one tough little athlete."

EDUCATION

Rose's formal education ended with graduation from Western Hills High School. He gave momentary consideration to a football scholarship at Miami University in Oxford, Ohio, but what he really wanted then was a professional sports career. Now, wishing that he had paid more attention to his studies, he says in his book, *Pete Rose: My Story*, "One thing in my life, if I could do differently, I would have concentrated more on getting educated."

FIRST JOBS

Rose was never urged by his parents to find a job when he was a teenager.

They, and especially his father, were anxious for him to be involved in sports. Nevertheless, like most boys his age, he liked having pocket money. During one period in those years, he worked part-time as a ticket-taker on the ferry that crossed the Ohio River to the open-gambling spots in Kentucky. There are those who say that this may have been Rose's introduction to betting, but he had seen "numbers running" on the streets at home long before he took the job. Sadly, it would be gambling that would ban him from baseball and put an end to his fabulous career.

During the off-season of 1960, his first baseball job was with the Geneva Red Legs team of the Cincinnati Reds organization. Rose had another short-term job, this time unloading box cars so that he could build up his physique. He was successful—he gained twenty pounds and grew two inches in height.

MAJOR INFLUENCES

Harry Rose was his famous son's hero. "Big Pete," as he was known in Cincinnati, was liked and admired by all who knew him, and always was the dominant character in his own family. Even today, more than twenty years after his father's sudden death, Pete Rose shows uncharacteristic emotion in remembering the man who "loved his kids and treated us all the same." He was a hard-working man who encouraged his sons to participate in sports and worked with them from an early age to develop their talent. David, the younger son, might have furthered his own baseball career, which had a start in high school and in the Appalachian League, but a motorcycle accident put an end to those particular hopes.

Without question, Pete Rose considers his father to be the greatest influence in his life. Other people were important to him—Fred Hutchinson, his first major league manager, attorney and good friend Reuven Katz, former Reds manager George "Sparky" Anderson—but "only one person *really* influenced me," he told author Roger Kahn, "and that was my dad."

CHOOSING A CAREER

With Rose, there never was any other career in mind except one associated with sports. Knowing that professional football was probably out of the question for a player of his size, he tells now of begging for a chance with the Cincinnati baseball organization. An uncle, who was an unsalaried scout for the Reds, pleaded his case for him and, in June 1960, Pete Rose joined the farm team in Geneva, New York. He went from there to Tampa and then to Macon, scrambling then, as later, for every play, and finally was called to Cincinnati in 1963.

CAREER HIGHLIGHTS

The glory years began. He played for the Reds from 1963 until 1978, and again as player-manager (after stints with the Philadelphia Phillies and the Montreal Expos) from 1984 through 1987, amassing records unequalled in the history of baseball. It was early in his career that he was christened "Charlie Hustle," a lasting nickname given him by Yankees pitcher Whitey Ford, who watched with amazement in spring training as Rose *ran* to first on a "walk," and charged full speed around the bases and into the dugout.

Pete Rose took part in nearly two thousand victories with three major league clubs, and three times led the National League in batting. He had ten seasons with 200 hits (a major league record), and in 1978 had a hitting streak of 44 consecutive games. News profiles tell of how he holds the record for playing more than 500 games in five different positions, covering first, second, and third base, and left and right field. Rose was on the National League All-Star teams in 1965, from 1967-71, 1973-79, and 1980-81. In addition, he played in thirty-four World Series games. In 1985, with the 4,192d hit of his career, Pete Rose broke the renowned Ty Cobb's major-league record, which had stood for fifty-seven years. His lifetime batting average is .303.

Rose's aggressiveness and single-mindedness made him a hero on the field, although he often was criticized for "unnecessary roughness." But it was his indiscreet personal life that brought him the greatest criticism— his serious gambling, the flaunting of his numerous affairs, and, eventually, a paternity suit that was settled out of court. Then, in 1989, after two seasons as manager of the Reds, baseball's "winningest player" was banned forever from the sport that was his life. The late A. Bartlett Giamatti, who was baseball commissioner at that time, charged that he had violated rules by gambling on baseball games. Rose vigorously denied those charges, although he admitted betting heavily on other sports. After a long investigation and much coverage by the media, he pleaded guilty to income-tax evasion connected to the charges and was given a prison sentence and a fine. His career was over.

Since completing his sentence, he is trying to restore his image and to repair the strained relationships with the children of his first marriage. In a July 1991 television interview on NBC's "Real Life With Jane Pauley," he said that one good thing about not being in baseball is, "I'm going to have time to see these youngsters [his small children] grow up." He is fighting his compulsive-gambling problem and, little by little, getting back into the public eye. He dreams that someday, if he can establish a more normal life, he will be reinstated to baseball and find a place in the Baseball Hall of Fame.

MEMORABLE EXPERIENCES

Pete Rose's greatest moment came September 11, 1985, in an evening game against the San Diego Padres, when he singled into left field to break the long-standing record of the legendary Ty Cobb. Remembering it, he says "Man. Fireworks light up the sky. . . .Up above, a Goodyear blimp hovers with blinking lights that say: Pete Rose, 4,192. . . .It's *my* moment."

MARRIAGE AND FAMILY

Pete Rose has been married twice. His first marriage, to Karolyn Ann Englehardt in 1964, produced a son, Peter Jr., and a daughter, Fawn. Both are now grown, and Petey plays in the minors. In 1984, about three-and-a-half years after a stormy divorce, Rose married Carol Woliung, and they have two small children, Tyler and Cara. In the summer of 1991, when Pete Rose had completed the term of his much-publicized prison sentence for tax fraud, he and his new family moved from Cincinnati to Boca Raton, Florida.

HOBBIES AND OTHER INTERESTS

For a while during his baseball years, Rose hosted a weekly radio program on WCKY in Cincinnati. His interests always revolve around sports. He has golfed, bowled, played tennis—and is good at most of these. In *Pete Rose: My Story*, he says, "Put me head to head with anyone in a pressure situation, and I'll win."

WRITINGS

The Pete Rose Story: An Autobiography, 1970
Charlie Hustle (with Bob Hertzel), 1975
Winning Baseball (with Bob Hertzel), 1976
Pete Rose: My Life in Baseball, 1979
Pete Rose: My Story (with Roger Kahn), 1989

HONORS AND AWARDS

National League Rookie of the Year: 1963
National League All-Star team: 1965, 1967-71, 1973-79
National League Player of the Year, *Sporting News:* 1968
National League Most Valuable Player: 1973
Most Valuable Player, World Series: 1975
Ball Player of the Decade: 1979

FURTHER READING

BOOKS

Aaseng, Nathan. *Pete Rose: Baseball's Charlie Hustle*, 1981
Contemporary Authors, Vol. 113
Reston, James, Jr. *Collision at Home Plate*, 1991

Rose, Pete, and Roger Kahn. *Pete Rose: My Story,* 1989
Sorolove, Michael Y. *Hustle: The Myth, Life, and Lies of Pete Rose,* 1990
Who's Who in America 1990-91
World Book Encyclopedia, 1990

PERIODICALS

Gentlemen's Quarterly, Apr. 1989, p.274
New York Times, Jan. 11, 1991, p.4
New York Times Biographical Service, Aug. 1989, p.812
People, Sept. 2, 1991, p.47

ADDRESS

Hit King Enterprises, Inc.
243 NE 5th Ave.
Delray Beach, FL 33483

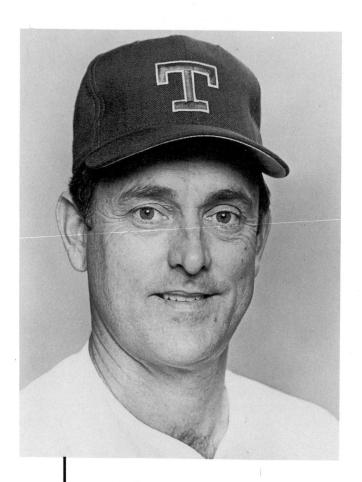

Nolan Ryan   1947-
American Baseball Pitcher with the
Texas Rangers
300-Game Winner and Career Strikeout
and No-Hit Leader

BIRTH

Lynn Nolan Ryan, Jr., was born January 31, 1947, the youngest
of six children of Lynn Nolan Ryan, Sr., and Martha (Hancock)
Ryan. His birthplace was Refugio, a small town in southeastern
Texas about 38 miles north of Corpus Christi. The Ryans moved
to nearby Alvin when he was six weeks old. His father worked
there for Stanlon Oil Company (now Pan American Petroleum)
and also as a distributor of the *Houston Post*. Ryan has four sisters,
Lynda, Mary Lou, Jean, and Judy, and one brother, Robert.

YOUTH

Nolan Ryan took up baseball early, playing throughout the summer on the sandlots of Texas. Taught to pitch by his brother, Bob, he quickly became aware of his ability to throw the ball past opposing batters. When the opportunity to play Little League came, he relished the chance to compete on a real diamond, wearing a uniform—"the only place you could pretend to be a big leaguer and really look the part," as he remembers in his autobiography. Ryan pitched and played infield, consistently making the All-Star team.

Aside from baseball, the young Nolan Ryan had a passion for animals. "He bought a calf when he was a little boy and he kept it in a pasture near town," his mother remembered in telling of those early days. "When we had hurricane threats around here, he'd take that calf into our garage, make a bed for it there, and feed it milk from a baby bottle." While cattle ranching eventually became an adult pursuit for Ryan, it is his ability to throw a ball that has made him a household name.

EARLY MEMORIES

Ryan recalls that, without air conditioning or television, he and his friends would play ball from sunup to sundown, leaving their makeshift diamond only when it was too dark to see. He believes that this experience, now rare but once almost the norm, improved the skills of his generation. "You got used to the ball," he says. "Your brain recorded angles and bounces and hops and even sounds."

FIRST JOBS

All was not play during Nolan's youth. Ryan started working in second grade, helping with his dad's newspaper distributorship. At first, he would help roll the papers to be delivered; as he got older, he drove over the back roads in the small hours of the morning before getting ready for school and baseball practice. He kept at that job until he graduated from high school. Today, Ryan credits his late parents for instilling in him a strong work ethic and value system.

EDUCATION

Biographies of Nolan Ryan, and even his own autobiographies, rarely mention his classroom experiences at school. Instead, they focus almost exclusively on his athletic pursuits. Even Ryan himself once said, "My attitude at that time was that I went to school to play sports. Now I wish I had paid more attention to my studies."

Ryan attended public schools in Alvin, Texas. At six-foot two, he played center on the high school basketball team, which had a record of 27-4 two years in a row. But his real love was baseball, and by the time he reached high school his skill had already begun to bring him notoriety. "I was wild in those days," he later said, "and I didn't have a curve ball because nobody in town knew how to throw one." What he did have, according to his high school coach, was "a fireball. I swear that ball jumped eight inches when it reached the plate." Ryan compiled a 20-4 record as a senior while batting .700 in the state tournament. That same year, he was picked for the All-State team and was named Outstanding Athlete at his school. Ryan graduated from Alvin High School in 1965.

It was on the local baseball diamond that Ryan met his future wife, Ruth Elsie Holdruff. They first went out on a date when they were teenagers and then stayed together through high school and beyond. According to Ruth, "There was never anybody else for either of us."

After high school graduation, Ryan enrolled at Alvin Junior College, but his education was interrupted by his baseball career.

CHOOSING A CAREER

Red Murff, a Mets scout, began watching Ryan when he was a high school junior in 1964; by the following year, Murff suggested that the Mets sign the young pitcher. "The first time I saw Nolan throw," said Murff, "I watched about four pitches and said, 'Am I really seeing this?' He was throwing 100 miles per hour. He didn't have any upper-torso strength except in his arm." Despite Murff's interest, the young ballplayer didn't believe that he had much chance of ever making the majors. He had a tendency to throw wild, and he pitched a poor game when Murff and Mets general manager Bing Divine came to watch. But the Mets did choose him in the draft—as the 295th player—and they thought highly enough of him to offer a $20,000 signing bonus. Feeling that the money would pay for college should he fail in baseball, Ryan signed with the Mets on June 26, 1965.

CAREER HIGHLIGHTS

NEW YORK METS: 1965-1971

Ryan has had an amazingly long and productive career in baseball. When he started out over 25 year ago in the minor leagues, on a rookie-class farm team in Marion, Virginia, he had a reputation as a powerful thrower. During his first two seasons, 1965 and 1966, he moved up through the Mets' farm teams and made his major league debut with the Mets at the end of the 1966 season. Although he was inconsistent in his early years, he showed flashes of the brilliant pitcher he would become. He had an amazing fastball that overpowered hitters, but his pitches were erratic and wild. This poor control, coupled with injuries and Army Reserve duty in 1967, prevented him from becoming a mainstay of the Mets' staff.

During his years with the Mets, he lost more games than he won. The Mets' 1969 postseason, however, was a triumph. Relieving Gary Gentry in the League Championship Series, Ryan gained the victory and the pennant for his team. The victory by the Mets, long an underdog team, surprised everyone. Then, in the World Series, he preserved Gentry's victory in game three, helping the Mets to their first world championship.

CALIFORNIA ANGELS: 1971-1979

Ryan was traded to the California Angels after the 1971 season, and he left New York determined to make the Mets regret the trade. And surely he succeeded: he learned how to throw a curveball, started to develop his reputation for strikeouts, threw four no-hitters, and averaged at least 17 wins a year with the Angels, although he never won more than 10 games in a season with the Mets. But equally importantly, in his view, Ryan discovered the weight room, and he credits his training there for his strength and longevity.

During his first year in California (1972), he pitched 20 complete games, going 19-16 with a 2.28 ERA (earned run average) and 329 strikeouts. He set an American League record by striking out eight Boston Red Sox players in a row on July 9. Over the next two seasons, Nolan Ryan would win 43 games and strike out more than 700 batters, establishing himself as one of the game's premier pitchers. He also threw three no-hitters, two of them exactly two months apart late in 1973. Ryan broke two records held by Hall-of-Famer Sandy Koufax in that year by striking out ten or more batters twenty-three separate times, with a total of 383 for the season. In 1974, his fastball was timed at 100.9 miles per hour, making him the hardest thrower ever. The next year saw Ryan tie Koufax's record of four career no-hitters when he shut down the Baltimore Orioles on June 1, 1975.

All was not well, however. Late in 1975, Ryan was sidelined for the year with bone chips in his elbow. He came back strongly the next season, though, winning 17 games and striking out 327 hitters. In 1977, he led the league in strikeouts (341) for the fifth time in six years while winning nineteen games, and was named American League Pitcher of the Year by the *Sporting News*. Ryan continued to pitch well over the next two seasons, 1978 and 1979, but Angels general manager Buzzie Bavasi felt that he was not worth the money it would take to re-sign him. Hurt by comments Bavasi had made, Ryan began talking to other teams.

HOUSTON ASTROS: 1979-1988

In 1979, Ryan signed a three-year contract for $3 million with the Houston Astros, based just one-half hour from his home and family. He knew that the contract was huge for its time and would bring pressure. But at age 32, he thought he was nearing retirement, and he wanted to finish his career near home. Ryan had a rocky first year in Houston, going 11-10 and pitching poorly in the League Championship Series against Philadelphia. The 1981 players' strike took a bite out of his statistics and his income, but Ryan still reached a milestone. At the age of 34, he pitched his record-breaking fifth no-hitter against the rival Los Angeles Dodgers. He finished the year 11-5, with a league-leading 1.69 ERA. The following season, 1982, saw a 16-12 record for a declining Astros team, win number 200, and 245 strikeouts. This last count left Ryan 15 short of Walter Johnson's career strikeout record. He broke that record in Montreal in his fourth start of the next year. But Ryan was becoming disillusioned with the Astros' management because of its failure to promote his accomplishments or to recruit the players necessary to win a championship.

Despite the team's divisional title in 1986—due largely to his good year and the emergence of pitcher Mike Scott—Ryan remained unhappy. He felt that he was being treated as an aging pitcher who was no longer of much use, despite his increasing ability to control the ball. After leading the league in strikeouts in both 1987 and 1988, Ryan was determined to make a move.

TEXAS RANGERS:
1988-PRESENT

Ryan negotiated with several teams, including the Tokyo Swallows of the Japanese league. But in the end, Ryan decided to stay near home and signed with the American League's Texas Rangers. That team has been rewarded handsomely for signing him. On June 29, 1989, Ryan notched his 5,000th career strikeout. He finished the year with sixteen victories and a league-leading 301 strikeouts. He again led the league in 1990 with 232, but that was hardly the highlight of the season. On June 11, 43-year-old Nolan Ryan amazed the baseball world by recording his sixth no-hitter, becoming the oldest pitcher ever to accomplish that feat. He won his 300th game on July 31, removing any doubt that he would join the Hall of Fame. The next season saw Ryan win 12 games, only the sixth time a player of his age had ever done so. Even more impressively, he pitched his seventh no-hitter against the Toronto Blue Jays on May 1. He has called this his most gratifying no-hitter of all. His longevity continues to astonish observers of the game. As early as 1986, the Houston pitching coach told *Sports Illustrated*, "How many pitchers have thrown that hard for that long? The answer is none."

In 1992, his most recent season, Ryan's skills seemed to decline as he posted a 5-9 record with a 3.72 ERA. But he still had his customary strikeout ability, getting 157 batters in as many innings. For the first time in his career, he was ejected from a ball game when plate umpire Rich Garcia ruled that he intentionally threw at Willie Wilson in an August game against Oakland. The harsh words he had for Wilson during and after the game contrasted sharply with his usual low-key approach. At press time, Ryan has announced plans to retire after the 1993 season, at the age of 46.

Five years after retiring, Ryan is expected to enter the Baseball Hall of Fame at Cooperstown, New York, with career records for both no-hitters and strikeouts. It is unlikely, according to baseball analyst Bill James, that the latter record will be broken in the foreseeable future. "I just don't believe that we are likely to see anyone else who has his *combination* of abilities," James wrote in 1991. "Ryan's strikeout record, I think, would be much, much more difficult to break than Aaron's homerun record, Rose's hit record, or Joe DiMaggio's hit streak. It may be more difficult to break than Cy Young's win record. It's going to be around awhile."

MAJOR INFLUENCES

Ryan first met Hall-of-Famer Tom Seaver at minor league spring training in 1967. While Nolan still did not see a clear chance for stardom and was merely trying to throw hard, Seaver had his mind on bigger things. It was from Seaver that Ryan learned how a thinking pitcher works, absorbing much of the game that he had yet to master. The two remain friends.

MARRIAGE AND FAMILY

Nolan Ryan married his high school sweetheart, Ruth Elsie Holdruff, on June 26, 1967. They have three children, Robert Reid, Nolan Reese, and Wendy Lynn. Reese and Wendy are now in high school; Reid attends the Texas Christian University, where he pitches for the baseball team. In 1991, Nolan and Reid Ryan, then a freshman at the University of Texas, had the opportunity to pitch against each other in an exhibition game between the Rangers and the Longhorns. The elder Ryan held the Longhorns to 5 hits and 3 runs, and the Rangers won 12-5.

A devoted family man, Ryan looks forward to spending more time at home after his retirement. "My family has always been my strength," he recently said. "They've always been supportive and understanding of my life. It has always been my goal to raise kids in the same kind of atmosphere I grew up in—a family doing things for each other and loving each other."

HOBBIES AND OTHER INTERESTS

The Ryan family lives on an 82-acre ranch outside Alvin, where he grew up. He also leases 3000 acres nearby, where he keeps cattle. About 150 miles west of there they also have a second ranch, some 2000 acres where they have another herd of cattle. Ryan enjoys the physical labor—when the baseball season is over, he can be found "getting kicked, stomped, and hooked." Meticulous in his ranching work and in his business dealings as well, Ryan has no intention of "coasting" after his baseball days are over. He says he will continue his hands-on approach to managing his property.

WRITINGS

Nolan Ryan: Strike-Out King (with Steve Jacobson), 1975
Nolan Ryan: The Other Game (with Bill Libby), 1977
Pitching and Hitting (with Joe Torre), 1977
Throwing Heat: The Autobiography of Nolan Ryan (with Harvey Frommer), 1988
Nolan Ryan's Pitcher's Bible (with Tom House), 1991
Kings of the Hill: An Irreverent Look at the Men on the Mound (with Mickey Hershkowitz), 1992
Miracle Man: Nolan Ryan, the Autobiography (with Jerry Jenkins), 1992

HONORS AND AWARDS

American League All-Star Team: 1972-73, 1975, 1979, 1989
Sporting News American League Pitcher of Year: 1977
National League All-Star Team: 1981, 1985
Texas Baseball Hall of Fame: 1987
Sporting News Man of the Year Award: 1990
Peter McGovern Little League Museum Hall of Excellence: 1991

FURTHER READING

BOOKS

Encyclopedia Brittanica, 1988
Libby, Bill. *Nolan Ryan: Fireballer,* 1975 (juvenile)
Lincoln Library of Sports Champions, Vol. 16, 1989
Rappoport, Ken. *Nolan Ryan,* 1992 (juvenile)
Ryan, Nolan, and Jerry Jenkins. *Miracle Man: Nolan Ryan, the Autobiography,* 1992

Ryan, Nolan, and Henry Frommer. *Throwing Hard: The Autobiography of Nolan Ryan*, 1988
Who's Who in America, 1990-91
World Book Encyclopedia, 1991

PERIODICALS

Boys' Life, Apr. 1991, p.18
Current Biography 1970
Sport, Apr. 1990, p.21
Sporting News, Jan. 7. 1991, p.24
Sports Illustrated, Sept. 29, 1986, p.84; Aug. 13, 1990, p.18; Apr. 15, 1991, p.120
Time, June 25, 1990, p. 68

ADDRESS

Texas Rangers
Arlington Stadium
P.O. Box 90111
Arlington, TX 76004

H. Norman Schwarzkopf 1934-
American Army General (Retired)
Commander of Desert Shield and Desert Storm Forces during the Persian Gulf War

BIRTH

H. Norman Schwarzkopf was born August 22, 1934, in Trenton, New Jersey, to Herbert Norman and Ruth (Bowman) Schwarzkopf. He was the only son in a family that included two older sisters, Ruth Ann and Sally Joan. Schwarzkopf was named for his father, except that the "H" in his name is an initial only, and does not stand for Herbert, a name his father detested and seldom used.

YOUTH

Young Schwarzkopf spent his childhood in the Trenton suburb

of Lawrenceville, although the family had been living in nearby Pennington at the time of his birth. His father, a West Point graduate and cavalry officer during World War I, was the New Jersey State Police superintendent who led the investigation into the sensational Lindbergh case of that era. The baby son of aviator hero Charles Lindbergh had been kidnapped and murdered, and the senior Schwarzkopf oversaw the conviction and controversial execution in 1936 of Bruno Hauptmann for "the crime of the decade." Little Norm was unaware of his father's celebrity then, or even afterward, when Norman Sr. hosted the old-time radio show "Gangbusters."

Life was normal for Norman Schwarzkopf, Jr., in those early years—palling around with his tomboy sister Sally, playing cowboys and Indians, riding a bus to school, dabbling in amateur magic—but things changed dramatically when he was twelve. He went alone to Iran to join his father, who was there on U.S. Army assignment to train that country's police. Norm's mother and sisters arrived in the Middle East six months later, and the family began a long absence from home. By his mid-teens, the globe-trotting young Schwarzkopf had lived a year in Iran, another in Switzerland, two years in Germany, and a half-year in Italy. (The senior Schwarzkopf would go back to Iran some years afterward to help organize the CIA-directed overthrow in 1953 of Prime Minister Mohammed Mossadegh and the return to power of Shah Mohammed Reza Pahlavi.)

Schwarzkopf was a fun-loving and outgoing youngster and knew all along that he would follow in the career footsteps of his father. One story that has been repeated often concerns the boy's choice of a class picture for his first military-school yearbook: he picked a solemn pose rather than a smiling one, explaining, "Later on when I'm a general, I want them to know I'm serious." He went on to prove himself a leader, both in upper school at Valley Forge Military Academy, and later at the United States Military Academy at West Point. The tall, burly cadet excelled academically and in sports (football and wrestling), conducted the West Point choir, and "dreamed of glory in battle." A former West Point roommate says that Schwarzkopf felt, even then, that one day he would lead a major American army into combat in a battle "decisive to the nation." Thirty-five years later, Operation Desert Storm would confirm that prediction.

EARLY MEMORIES

Many memories of his colorful youth remain fixed in Schwarzkopf's mind, but one particular incident pops up whenever he talks of those days. At an official function he attended with his father in Iran, sheeps' eyes were served on a platter, and Schwarzkopf *still* remembers looking to his father for help in what to do, and "seeing in his [father's] eyes that the dish must be eaten, and eaten with a smile."

Stories of Schwarzkopf's life usually mention that special time that he spent in the Middle East. A feature article appearing last year in *U.S. News & World Report* tells of the long letters sent home by the senior Schwarzkopf, "filled with fascinating accounts of the culture, art, and politics of Iran and Saudi Arabia." The father sent for young Norm, "plucking him out of Trenton, N.J., and permitting him for one glorious year to live the adventures of those letters in Tehran."

EDUCATION

Public school in Princeton, New Jersey (close to his home in Lawrenceville), was Schwarzkopf's first brush with the classroom but, by the age of ten, he was sent to nearby Bordentown Military Institute. After his return from Europe, he enrolled at Valley Forge Military Academy in Wayne, Pennsylvania, on a football scholarship, and it was there that his considerable leadership in almost every field singled him out for success. He graduated at the head of his class. Years later, he would write that "Valley Forge prepared me for life."

Schwarzkopf went on to graduate (in 1956) from the United States Military Academy at West Point, New York, and was commissioned a second lieutenant in the infantry. During his military career, he attended Basic and Advanced Infantry Officer Training School at Fort Benning, Georgia; the Command and General Staff College at Fort Leavenworth, Kansas; and the Army War College at Carlisle Barracks, Pennsylvania. He also holds a master's degree in missile engineering from the University of Southern California.

MARRIAGE AND FAMILY

Norman Schwarzkopf and Brenda Holsinger, a TWA flight attendant from Timberville, Virginia, were married July 6, 1968, in the chapel at West Point. They have two daughters, Cynthia and Jessica, and a son, Christian. The family home is in Tampa, Florida, near MacDill Air Force Base, where the now-retired general maintains an office.

MAJOR INFLUENCES

Schwarzkopf speaks of "my dad" as one of the great influences in his life. In a recent interview, the general lists other heroes too—the great humanitarian Albert Schweitzer, as well as U.S. Army Generals Ulysses S. Grant, William Tecumseh Sherman, and Creighton Adams. But he points to his father, who rose to the rank of major general, as the one who "really did give me a set of moral and ethical standards by which I try to live my life today."

The horrors of war in the jungles of Vietnam also made a lasting impression on Schwarzkopf. His sister Sally recalls: "After the first tour, he lost his youth...this light wonderful youth that young men have." Then, during his second Vietnam tour of duty in 1969 and 1970, he began to feel the bitter criticism of men who served under him. While they recognized his abilities in the field, many resented his hot temper, his endless drills, and his tough discipline—heaped upon the brutal conditions they already faced every day in battle.

A tragic incident, in which two soldiers in Schwarzkopf's command were killed by American artillery fire, worsened an already ugly situation. The parents of Sergeant Michael Mullen, one of the dead soldiers, had been so angered by official indifference to their tragedy that they blamed Schwarzkopf personally for helping to cover up this, and untold numbers of other, accidental casualties. Research eventually cleared Schwarzkopf of blame, but the soldier's parents could not forgive. Mrs. Mullen still maintains that her son's commander went to Vietnam the second time not to save lives, as he claimed, but "to boost his rank." The Mullen story was dramatized in *Friendly Fire,* a book by C.B.D. Bryan, and later made into a television movie.

Schwarzkopf won a third Silver Star for heroism during those terrible months, but returned home deeply disillusioned about the whole war experience. He said that it was there he saw the worst: his superiors "living in luxury" while he took his totally unprepared battalion into battle. He even considered resigning his commission, but finally decided to stay with the career he was trained for. Nevertheless, the nightmare of Vietnam remains with him to this day.

CAREER HIGHLIGHTS

During his years of service, Schwarzkopf commanded army units from platoon through corps level. He served two combat tours in Vietnam, the first as a task force advisor with the Vietnamese Airborne Division, and the second as commander of the First Battalion, Sixth Infantry, 23rd Infantry Division. He was sent to Fort Richardson, Alaska, in 1974 as deputy commander of the 172d Light Infantry Brigade, and two years later was made commander at Fort Lewis, Washington. From there he was assigned to a job in military planning and policy for the Pacific Command at Camp Smith, Hawaii, and then, in 1980, to (West) Germany as assistant commander of the Eighth Infantry Division.

An assignment at the Pentagon followed before Schwarzkopf was transferred to a command post at Fort Stewart, Georgia, in mid-1983. The autumn after his arrival at Fort Stewart, he was named deputy commander of a Joint Task Force to invade Grenada. The United States had been asked by the Organization of Eastern Caribbean States (OECS) to take part in an operation whose stated purpose was to restore democracy and to eliminate Cuban interference in the West Indian island's politics.

In 1986, Schwarzkopf was promoted to the rank of lieutenant general and chosen to command I Corps at Fort Lewis. He returned to the Pentagon in 1987, and the following year, with a fourth star (as full general), he was appointed commander in chief of U.S. Central Command, or CentCom, at MacDill Air Force Base in Tampa.

The event that brought Norman Schwarzkopf to the attention of the general public was the invasion of Kuwait by Iraq's forces on August 2, 1990. Before the month was out, Schwarzkopf was in the Persian Gulf, directing an allied operation that came to be known first as Desert Shield and, in January 1991, as Desert Storm—the deadly six-week war that forced Saddam Hussein and his army to surrender and leave Kuwait. Schwarzkopf's skilled and hard-charging command was widely recognized, and he returned to the United States a hero. However, he was quick to credit his troops—those from the U.S., Great Britain, France, Italy, and the supportive Arab countries—with the "real heroism it takes to go into battle."

Schwarzkopf is known for his explosive temper which, he claims, dates from the dark days of Vietnam. His nicknames are "Stormin' Norman" and "Bear" (the latter meaning grizzly, not teddy, bear). He insists that his show of anger is never at people, only at "things that happen. . . betrayal of trust, lack of consideration for [my] soldiers." Those who know him best say that he has fierce loyalty and affection for his troops, a sharp sense of humor, and, in spite of his legendary temper, never holds a grudge.

Norman Schwarzkopf, the "soldier's soldier" and modern-day warrior, retired from service in June 1991. He is in the process of writing his autobiography (for an estimated sum of $5 million), to be published by Bantam Books in the fall of 1992.

HOBBIES AND OTHER INTERESTS

From sports to the performing arts, Schwarzkopf is a man of varied interests. He enjoys hunting, fishing, physical workouts, and skeet and trap shooting, but also is a fan of opera and the ballet. Country music, folk singing, westerns—he likes them all, and he has not lost his zest for the magic tricks that were his boyhood hobby.

HONORS AND AWARDS

Distinguished Service Medal, with Oak Leaf Cluster
Silver Star, for heroism (three)
Defense Superior Service Medal
Legion of Merit
Distinguished Flying Cross
Bronze Star, with "V" device (three)
Purple Heart (two, for wounds suffered in action in Vietnam)
Combat Infantryman Badge
Master Parachutist Badge
Congressional Gold Medal: 1991

FURTHER READING

BOOKS

Anderson, Jack, and Dale Van Atta. *Stormin' Norman: An American Hero,* 1991

Bryan, C.B.D. *Friendly Fire,* 1976

Cohen, Roger, and Claudio Gatti. *In the Eye of the Storm: The Life of General H. Norman Schwarzkopf,* 1991

Pyle, Richard. *Schwarzkopf: The Man, the Mission, the Triumph,* 1991

Stefoff, Rebecca. *Norman Schwarzkopf,* 1991 (juvenile)

Valentine, E.J. *H. Norman Schwarzkopf,* 1991 (juvenile)

Who's Who in America, 1990-91

PERIODICALS

Current Biography, May 1991

New Republic, Mar. 11, 1991, p.20

New York Times Biographical Service, Jan. 1991, p.72

People, Mar. 11, 1991, p.35; May 13, 1991, p.42

Time, Oct. 22, 1990, p.23

U.S. News & World Report, Feb. 11, 1991, p.32

ADDRESS

Gen. H. Norman Schwarzkopf (Ret.)
MacDill Air Force Base
Florida 33608-7001

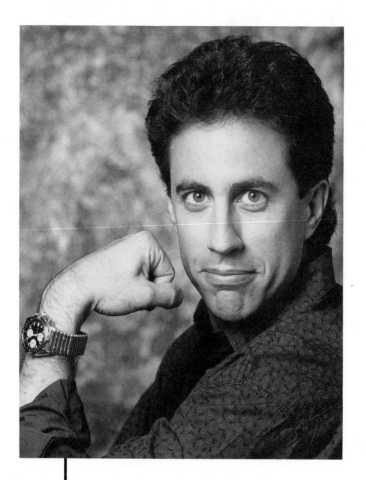

Jerry Seinfeld 1954-
American Comedian
Co-Creator and Star of NBC's "Seinfeld"

BIRTH

Jerry Seinfeld, the only son of Kalman Seinfeld, owner of a commercial sign business, and Betty Seinfeld, a homemaker, was born in Brooklyn, New York, on April 29, 1954. He has an older sister, Carolyn Liebling.

YOUTH

Jerry grew up in Massapequa—"it's an old Indian name that means 'by the mall,'" he says—a Long Island suburb of New York City. Nothing was particularly unusual about his childhood except, perhaps, the fact that his parents had grown up without parents of their own, passing on to their children the resulting independence. Jerry's mother remembers him as a television addict. "At one point, I had to get rid of [the TV set]," she said. "I couldn't stand it." Her ploy failed when Jerry simply went next door to watch his favorite programs. Carolyn remembers the same obstinacy. On his third birthday, Jerry wanted the entire cake instead of a mere slice. When refused this request, he chose to eat no cake at all rather than back down.

EARLY MEMORIES

Jerry's father, Kal, was known as the family comic, while Jerry seemed quiet and introverted. Apparently, though, such was not the case inside his mind. He wanted to be Superman. "I may look meek and mild," he says, "but inside there's a raging super power." Failing to develop any extraordinary physical skills, Jerry remembers looking inward. "When you retreat from contact with other kids, your only playground left is your own mind. You start exploring your own ability to entertain yourself."

EDUCATION

Seinfeld graduated from Massapequa High School in 1972. He earned a bachelor of arts degree from Queens College of the City University of New York in 1976, with a double major in theater and communications.

CHOOSING A CAREER

"I knew I was going to be a comedian at a very young age," Seinfeld claims. "I remember one time I made a friend laugh so hard he sprayed a mouthful of cookies and milk all over me and I liked it. That was the beginning." At the age of eight, Jerry was studying the techniques of comics on television and receiving continual inspiration from his cut-up father.

College only reinforced his choice. "I went from course to course going, 'I can't do this. I hate this.'" Then, sitting on a ledge in Manhattan one day, he observed people scurrying to and from their jobs. "Right then," he says, "I decided I never wanted to have a job. I wanted to do something I was really in love with, and that was more important than a job."

FIRST JOBS

Earning little or nothing performing at comedy clubs, Seinfeld was forced to work odd jobs to support himself. He purposely took the worst opportunities so that he would "never have anything to fall back on." He swept floors, waited tables, hawked umbrellas on New York sidewalks, and— his favorite—sold lightbulbs over the telephone. This last he has described as a tough job, joking "there aren't a lot of people sitting home in the dark saying 'I can't hold out much longer.'" He reduced his expenses during these lean years by living on the greasy food offered at comedy clubs and wearing the T-shirts sold there. He also dispensed with socks and a belt.

CAREER HIGHLIGHTS

Jerry Seinfeld is known as one of the masters of "observational humor," the art of seeing everyday experiences from a fresh perspective. He honed this technique through a decade of working in comedy clubs, starting in his native New York City. Success was by no means immediate—when he first got on stage, he was so paralyzed with fear that he was almost unable to speak. He conquered his nerves and became a regular on the club scene.

At a time when most comedians were leading overindulgent lives and verbally assaulting their audiences, Seinfeld worked clean and told jokes without gimmicks. His audiences recognized his topics from their own lives. "All this education and conversation and parental guidance that you've had in your life does not prepare you for a huge number of things that come up," he told Tom Shales of the *Washington Post*. His skills in dissecting the pitfalls of life come from hard work (he still writes jokes every day) and from an attitude. "All comedians have an essential crankiness if they're funny at all. . . .Just being easily annoyed is kind of the early impetus for being a comedian," he says.

The only detour off course in his career came when Seinfeld decided to try his luck in Los Angeles. Down to his last twenty dollars, he landed a supporting role in the situation comedy "Benson." He played a joke writer for the show's bumbling governor—a bad joke writer. "They thought that would be funny," he explains, "but bad jokes aren't funny." Jerry was fired after only three episodes, making him realize what was unique about his niche in show business. With stand-up, "I have a job in show business that I have complete control over. So I said, 'From now on, I'm not doing anything unless it's mine.'"

In May 1981, Seinfeld got the break that most comedians only dream of. At only 27, he was booked for an appearance on the "Tonight" show, then hosted by the venerable Johnny Carson. He has called the pressure of that experience "like being on your dad's show." Nevertheless, he successfully put his five years of work into a five-minute performance that turned heads. Jerry was off and running, "lifted from the pack." He would appear on Carson's show over twenty more times before Johnny yielded his desk to Seinfeld's close friend Jay Leno. "Next year, when it'll really be Jay's show," Jerry joked in 1991, "[it] really won't be much of a thrill, because I don't have a lot of respect for him."

The rest of the decade saw Seinfeld undertake what would be a back-breaking schedule for almost anyone, tackling 300 nights of stand-up a year in venues ranging from tiny clubs to huge auditoriums. He steadily built a following with his droll observations about such mysteries as dry cleaning ("What the hell is dry-cleaning fluid? It's not a fluid if it's dry"); parakeets ("Even if he thinks the mirror is another room, why doesn't he avoid hitting the other parakeet?"); and—a crowd favorite—detergents that remove blood stains ("If you've got a T-shirt with blood stains on it, maybe laundry is not your biggest problem right now").

"SEINFELD"

In 1988, NBC offered Seinfeld the opportunity to do a series. In search of a novel approach to TV comedy, he contacted his friend Larry David. A coffee-shop meeting between the two, which has been parodied on the program, produced the premise of the show—the everyday life of a comedian in search of material. To Seinfeld and David's surprise, the network bought the idea and hired them to create the show. After two years of time-slot moves and on-and-off production, "Seinfeld" became a hit. Importantly, the show attracts a loyal following of 18-to-39-year-old viewers that advertisers covet.

Jerry, playing himself, is joined on the show by George, a hyper-neurotic friend based on Larry David and played by Broadway veteran Jason Alexander. They, with crazy neighbor Kramer (Michael Richards) and Jerry's ex-girlfriend Elaine (Julia Louis-Dreyfus), negotiate the perilous path of single men and women in New York City. The plot lines are purposely thin (one episode features, in real time, the four waiting in line at a Chinese restaurant) and are punctuated by clips from Jerry's stand-up routine that comment on the issues raised. "Seinfeld" explores the inner workings of a mind stimulated mostly by minor irritants. The show also has a strict rule against moral lessons or character development—"no hugging, no learning"—that all connected with it continually espouse.

Critical reaction to "Seinfeld" has been largely positive, focusing on the show's unique qualities. " 'Seinfeld' doesn't feel like sitcom television," says New York magazine's Chris Smith. "[It] feels more like a conversation with your funniest friends." While the accolades don't surprise the show's creators, the approval of the network and mass audience do. "We figured we'd do six shows and that would be it," Seinfeld says. "We wanted to be a legend, the show they should have left on."

Skeptics remain. Lawrence Christon of the Los Angeles Times, one of the country's most powerful comedy critics, complains that Seinfeld is "expressive. He's clear. And he's completely empty. . . . Seinfeld pays homage to insignificance, and he does it impeccably." Christon later said, less unkindly: "He is funny, but after a few minutes you want more. It's like eating cotton candy. There's nothing very nutritious." Most, however, see the focus on trivia as the very strength of Seinfeld's comedy. "If he were a superhero," claims Larry Charles, a writer and producer for the program, "he'd be Microscope Man."

In addition to his careful work habits, Jerry has a reputation for being obsessively neat. His trademark jeans are always pressed and creased, his Nike shoes ("Air Seinfeld") always a blinding white. Colleagues torture him with threats of dropping muddy leaves on his Porsche. And he insists that he can always tell when someone has moved something in his apartment, even if the object has been returned to its original place. He eats health food, abstains from alcohol and cigarettes, and practices yoga. He is also said to be a follower of Scientology, the cult-like religion created by science-fiction writer L. Ron Hubbard. Seinfeld counters that he merely took a couple of courses offered by the church, which he says helped him in his career and personal life. "There are things in yoga that I don't agree with and I don't do," he says. "I go to get what I need. And that's the way I approach everything."

On breaks from production, Jerry continues to perform stand-up comedy. He doesn't worry about the show's ultimate cancellation—he'll just go back to the old 300-nights-a-year routine. Jerry explains: "I remember reading something somewhere about some comedian and he was saying, 'I don't want to be fifty-something, getting up on a Tuesday night in Milwaukee,' and I thought, 'Boy, I'd love to be getting up on a Tuesday night in Milwaukee when I'm fifty-something.'"

MARRIAGE AND FAMILY

Although he has never been married, Seinfeld has no shortage of opinions on the subject. "I'm a single guy. I date," he wrote in *Redbook*. "I think I enjoy it. For me, nothing caps off a week like four hours of solid tension." He worries that no woman could put up with his obsessive devotion to his career, and comments: "Even Superman can't make a commitment. Why give me a hard time?" And while he says that he gets a "domestic fix" when he sees his six-year-old nephew on Long Island, he insists, "I've hit my biological snooze alarm."

MEMORABLE EXPERIENCES

Seinfeld says that the biggest satisfaction of his career was being credited with a great line. After hearing about Kirk Gibson's game-winning home run for the Dodgers in the World Series, he was treated to hearing the announcer quote one of his own stories, relating that that day in sports might be one of the things we could tell our grandchildren about—things Seinfeld had worried would be missing. "How can the world change that much again that we can blow kids away with stories like the ones our parents told us, about the war and the Depression, when milk was a nickel and cars were a quarter? What will we say? 'When I was a boy, dogs didn't have the vote. They had no say in the world at all. In fact, we kept them on leashes.'" Hearing himself thus quoted on radio, Seinfeld says, "was the biggest boost I'd ever had. That, to me, is the coolest thing you could do on this planet."

MAJOR INFLUENCES

"When men are growing up and reading about Batman, Spiderman and Superman, these are not fantasies, these are options," Seinfeld wrote in *Redbook*. Among mortals, he found fewer role models. While he acknowledges Bill Cosby as a youthful idol, he seems to have gotten the most inspiration from Robert Klein. "He shattered my image of a stand-up," Seinfeld says. "He wasn't distant or pretentious; he made it seem accessible, like something I could do."

Among his peers, he particularly enjoys the comedy of close friends Jay Leno and Larry Miller, and that of David Letterman, whom he describes as having the funniest show on television. "I've never once seen the Letterman show and not laughed out loud," he says. "He's my idea of funny."

HOBBIES AND OTHER INTERESTS

Among the few things that interest him outside of his career are expensive watches and sports cars. He also enjoys baseball and plays outfield ("because it takes less skill") on Sundays in the Comics' Softball Game.

HONORS AND AWARDS

American Comedy Awards (George Schlatter Productions): 1988, for Funniest Male Comedy Club Stand-Up
Best Male Comedy Club Performer: 1988 (voted by nightclub regulars)

FURTHER READING

PERIODICALS

Boston Globe, Dec. 1, 1991, p.A2
Current Biography, Aug. 1992, p.44
Gentlemen's Quarterly, May 1992, p.137
New York, Feb. 3, 1992, p.33
Redbook, Feb. 1991, p.62
TV Guide, May 23, 1992, p.10
Us, Apr. 4, 1991, p.16
Washington Post, Apr. 22, 1992, p.G12

ADDRESS

Jonas Public Relations
417 South Beverly Drive
Suite 201
Beverly Hills, CA 90212

OBITUARY

Dr. Seuss (Pseudonym of Theodor Seuss Geisel)
1904-1991
American Author and Illustrator of
Juvenile and Adult Fiction
Writer of *The Cat in the Hat, Green Eggs*
and Ham, Oh, the Places You'll Go!
and Other Books

BIRTH

Theodor Seuss Geisel (GUYS-ell), known to millions of readers
as Dr. Seuss, was born March 2, 1904, in Springfield, Massachusetts, to Theodor Robert and Henrietta Seuss Geisel. He was their
only child.

414

YOUTH

Seuss grew up in Springfield, where his father ran a brewery until Prohibition—a time in the 1920s when the sale of alcohol was against the law. His father later became superintendent of the Springfield Park system and expanded the local zoo, which became a favorite place for his son.

EARLY MEMORIES

During World War I (1914-1918), Seuss, whose last name—Geisel—is German, experienced the prejudice some Americans felt against people of German backgrounds. He stated that he "sometimes fled home with coals bouncing off my head," and was called "Kaiser" (for Kaiser Wilhelm, the German leader) or "Drunken Kaiser," because of his father's job in the brewery.

EDUCATION

Seuss went to public schools in Springfield and was an early and avid reader. He had read some of the works of Jonathan Swift, Charles Dickens, and Robert Louis Stevenson by the time he was six. He loved to draw, but was discouraged by his first art teacher in high school, who told him he would never learn how. After high school he attended Dartmouth College, where he majored in English. He became the editor of the campus humor magazine, *Jack-O'-Lantern*, which published his early illustrations and stories. He first used the pseudonym of Seuss for these works, hoping to use the name Geisel for the adult fiction he planned to write. After Dartmouth, Seuss continued to study at Lincoln College, part of Oxford University in England, and at the University of the Sorbonne in Paris. While at Oxford, he met another American student, Helen Palmer, who later became his wife. He tired of the idea of an academic career and began to write a novel, which he described as "very long, and mercifully never published."

FIRST JOBS

In the late 1920s, Seuss and his wife returned to the United States, and he began writing and illustrating ads for a variety of products. He was also writing humorous articles for magazines like *Vanity Fair, Liberty,* and *Judge,* but it was an ad for insect spray with the line: "Quick, Henry, the Flit!" that first brought him recognition as a writer.

CAREER HIGHLIGHTS

The success of the "Flit" campaign led Seuss to the vocation that would make him famous. The contract he signed with the company that produced the ad did not allow him to write for anyone else—anyone else, that is, except children. So in 1936, he began *And to Think That I Saw It on Mulberry Street.* But even this part of his career path was not easy: the book was rejected by twenty-nine publishers before it was finally published, in 1937, by Vanguard Press. It was immediately successful, and the characteristic

Seuss style—with its unique rhyme pattern and illustrations—was born. Seuss claimed that the pattern of the verse was influenced by the rhythmic clang of the engines on the ocean liner he was riding when the book idea first came to him.

During World War II (1939-1945), Seuss's career as a children's author was briefly interrupted when he began his military service as a member of the Army Signal Corps in Hollywood. There he worked under the famous American film maker Frank Capra and was awarded the Legion of Merit for the films he made about the war. His films won him three Academy Awards, and he later used what he had learned to adapt his children's works for television.

After the war, Seuss's involvement with children's literature made him interested in what made kids want to read. The "Dick and Jane" readers, or primers, of the 1950s were boring to him—and to a generation of would-be readers. In a 1954 article in *Life* magazine, the author and educator John Hersey made the suggestion that Seuss try to develop a reader for the young. The suggestion was inspired: Seuss got the list of words used in primers, chose 220 of them, and wrote *The Cat in the Hat*, surely the most famous reader of all time. Seuss started a new publishing house, Beginner Books (later part of Random House), which he headed until his death. This company published such Seuss favorites as *Hop on Pop* and *Green Eggs and Ham*, the best-selling children's book of all time. Of his influence on the reading education of children, he said: "That's what I'm proudest of; that I had something to do with getting rid of Dick and Jane."

Seuss's illustrations won him three Caldecott Honor awards, a prestigious prize given to illustrators of children's books. His artistic style is unmistakable: using bold, heavy black strokes he created an array of creatures who have been described as fantastic, bizarre, even surreal.

Despite their obvious delight in sheer nonsense, Seuss's books often carry a serious moral message. For *Horton Hears a Who* Seuss drew on memories of a trip to the Japanese city of Hiroshima, which had been devastated by an atomic bomb at the end World War II. The threat of nuclear war also inspired *The Butter Battle Book*. *The Lorax*, which Seuss claimed was his favorite book, features a world where the environment is being ruined in the name of progress. *The Sneetches* takes on the problem of prejudice, and *You're Only Old Once*, supposedly for adults, but enjoyed by children as well, is about the problems of growing old.

At the time of his death on September 24, 1991, Seuss had written forty-seven books, which have sold over 200 million copies worldwide, and his popularity shows no sign of slowing. His most recent book, *Oh, the Places You'll Go!* remained on the best-seller list for more than two years. Although his appeal is first and foremost to the young (Seuss once called adults "obsolete children"), a recent ad for his books indicated that they are intended for "Ages 3 to 93." He and his wife never had children of their own—"You make 'em, I'll amuse him," he said—yet his works provide an uncanny insight into what challenges and delights the young reader. The millions of children throughout the world who learned to love words and reading through his books cherish the memory of the man who had infinite respect for young people and their needs. Their affection spans generations and borders, and they are a faithful tribute to this beloved author.

MAJOR INFLUENCES

One of the most important influences in Seuss's life was his father, Ted, and he dedicated two of his books, *If I Ran the Circus* and *McElligot's Pool*, to him. He thought his father inspired in him the desire to work hard and to always do his best.

MARRIAGE AND FAMILY

Seuss met his first wife, Helen Palmer, while a student at Oxford. They married in 1927. She was an early and eager supporter of his plans to become an author and illustrator. The two co-authored the Academy Award-winning documentary *Design for Death*. After his success as a children's writer, she became his business manager and edited some of his books. She also published children's books under her maiden name. Helen Geisel died in 1967.

In 1968 Seuss married Audrey Stone Dimond and became stepfather to her two children, Lea and Lark.

SELECTED WRITINGS

FOR YOUNG READERS

And to Think That I Saw It on Mulberry Street, 1937
The Five Hundred Hats of Bartholomew Cubbins, 1938
Horton Hatches the Egg, 1940
McElligot's Pool, 1947
Thidwick, the Big-Hearted Moose, 1948
Bartholomew and the Oobleck, 1949
If I Ran the Zoo, 1950
Horton Hears a Who! 1954
On beyond Zebra! 1955
If I Ran the Circus, 1956
The Cat in the Hat, 1957
The Cat in the Hat Comes Back, 1957
How the Grinch Stole Christmas, 1957
Yertle the Turtle and Other Stories, 1958
Happy Birthday to You! 1959
Green Eggs and Ham, 1960
One Fish, Two Fish, Red Fish, Blue Fish, 1960
The Sneetches and Other Stories, 1961

Dr. Seuss's Sleep Book, 1962
Dr. Seuss's ABC, 1963
Hop on Pop, 1963
Fox in Socks, 1965
I Had Trouble Getting to Solla Sollew, 1965
Mr. Brown Can Moo! Can You? 1970
The Lorax, 1971
Marvin K. Mooney, Will You Please Go Now? 1972
Did I Ever Tell You How Lucky You Are? 1973
Oh Say Can You Say? 1979
The Butter Battle Book, 1984
Oh, the Places You'll Go! 1990

FOR ADULTS

The Seven Lady Godivas, 1939

You're Only Old Once! 1986

The Tough Coughs as He Ploughs the Dough: Early Writings and Cartoons by Dr. Seuss, 1987

Seuss also wrote under the pseudonym of Theo LeSieg.

HONORS AND AWARDS

Academy Award: 1946, for *Hitler Lives;* 1947, for *Design for Death* [written with Helen Palmer Geisel]; 1951, for *Gerald McBoing-Boing*

Caldecott Honor Book Award: 1947, for *McElligot's Pool;* 1949, for *Bartholomew and the Oobleck;* 1960, for *If I Ran the Zoo*

Peabody Award: 1971, for television specials "How the Grinch Stole Christmas" and "Horton Hears a Who"

Emmy Award: 1977, for television special "Halloween Is Grinch Night"

Pulitzer Prize: 1984, "for his contribution over nearly half a century to the education and enjoyment of America's children and their parents"

FURTHER READING

BOOKS

MacDonald, Ruth K. *Dr. Seuss,* 1988

Something about the Author, Vol. 28

PERIODICALS

Current Biography Yearbook 1968; obit. Nov. 1991

Hornbook, Sept./Oct. 1989, p.582

Life, July 1989, p.104

New York Times, Sept. 26, 1991, p.A1

Newsweek, Oct. 7, 1991, p.69

Parade Magazine, Feb. 26, 1984, p.4

Parents Magazine, Sept. 1987, p.116

Time, Oct. 7, 1991, p.71

Gloria Steinem 1934-
American Writer, Editor, Lecturer, and Feminist
Political Activist and Leader in
the American Women's Movement

BIRTH

Gloria Marie Steinem was born in Toledo, Ohio, on March 25,
1934, to Leo and Ruth (Nuneviller) Steinem. Both families had
objected to the marriage because of the difference in religions: Leo
was Jewish, while Ruth was Christian. Gloria's father, who died
in 1962, was a charming, carefree, financially irresponsible man
who worked as a traveling antiques dealer and as a summer resort
operator. He took great pride in never working for anyone else.
"He was always going to make a movie, or cut a record, or start
a new hotel, or come up with a new orange drink," according to

420

Steinem. Her mother, who died in 1980, had been a teacher and journalist in the early days of her marriage. But Gloria never got to know this competent, confident woman. Ruth was able to juggle her beloved career and motherhood for several years after the birth of her first child, Susanne, in 1925. But when Susanne was five, Ruth suffered a nervous breakdown and was hospitalized for several months. From that time onward she suffered periods of depression and delusion, and her mental stability never returned. Years later, Steinem would attribute her mother's emotional illness, in part, to social pressures on women.

YOUTH

Steinem had an unconventional and difficult childhood. When she was young, each year was firmly split into two parts. During the winter, her family traveled to Florida or California. They lived out of a trailer while Leo Steinem bought and sold antiques. They moved about frequently, and young Gloria was never able to develop lasting friendships or attend school on a regular basis.

During the summer, the family lived in Clark Lake, Michigan. There Leo owned and managed an entertainment hall, the Ocean Beach Pier. He had big plans to turn that isolated spot into a fancy resort that would attract the dance bands that were so popular during the 1930s and 1940s. Gloria loved her summers at Clark Lake, whiling away the hours swimming, meeting the musicians and dancers, taking her first dance lessons, and dreaming of becoming a performer. The resort was never very successful, though, and conditions worsened when gasoline rationing during World War II limited family travel. The resort closed when Gloria was about ten.

Soon after, her father left the family and moved to California to continue his antiques business. He never returned to live with the family, and Leo and Ruth eventually divorced. Gloria's sister, Susanne, had left for college some two years earlier, and at first Gloria and her mother moved to Massachusetts to be near her. The following year, however, the two moved back to Toledo, Ohio, Ruth Steinem's childhood home. They lived at first in a basement flat, then in an old, rundown farmhouse that Ruth inherited from her family, where they were able to rent out the downstairs apartments.

The years in Toledo were extremely difficult for Gloria and her mother. Although she had periods of lucidity, most of the time Ruth was acutely depressed, anxious, and fearful. Without medication, she was terrorized, delusional, and unable to sleep, but with medication, her movements were clumsy and her speech was slurred—people thought she was drunk. She was unable to work or to manage even the most basic household tasks. Many days she could not even get out of bed. Gloria tried, without much success, to take care of her mother and the house. They were desperately poor.

Gloria dreamed of creating a different life for herself. She took music and dance lessons, lost herself in books, and pretended that she had been adopted, that Ruth was not her real mother. The two of them went on like this until several things happened. Their old furnace was condemned by the Health Department, their rat-infested, dilapidated house became unfit to live in, and the church next door offered to buy the land. Gloria's sister convinced their father to take care of Ruth for one year so that Gloria could move in with her in Washington, D.C. Leo agreed, and Gloria spent one "normal" school year. She was elected vice-president of her senior class and graduated from Western High School in 1952.

EARLY MEMORIES

Years later, Steinem gave readers a glimpse of her early life, and her experiences with her mother, in a powerful and moving essay entitled "Ruth's Song (Because She Could Not Sing It)," published in *Outrageous Acts and Everyday Rebellions* (1983): "She was just a fact of life when I was growing up; someone to be worried about and cared for; an invalid who lay in bed with eyes closed and lips moving in occasional response to voices only she could hear; a woman to whom I brought an endless stream of toast and coffee, bologna sandwiches and dime pies, in a child's version of what meals should be. She was a loving, intelligent, terrorized woman."

EDUCATION

Steinem applied to Smith College in Northampton, Massachusetts, a top women's college and her sister's alma mater. Although she didn't have top grades in high school, her counselor's glowing recommendation and her high test scores won her a place at that prestigious school. Her family decided to use the money from the sale of the Toledo house toward her tuition, and Ruth went to live with Gloria's sister. Steinem loved life at Smith; she has said that she "couldn't understand the women who were not happy there. They gave you three meals a day to eat, and all the books you wanted to read—what more could you want?" Despite the differences between her background and that of her wealthier classmates, Steinem became part of the community at Smith in every way. She worked her way through school, but still found plenty of time to study and to lead an active social life. She also spent one year studying in Geneva, Switzerland. She won numerous awards in college, including being chosen senior class historian and being elected to Phi Beta Kappa, an academic honors society. She graduated magna cum laude (with high honors) from Smith College in 1956 with a major in government.

Most young women at that time, including many of her classmates, planned to get married after college. And while Steinem was engaged to her college boyfriend, she felt unprepared for marriage. But she was uncertain what to do instead—until one of her professors suggested she apply for the Chester Bowles Asian Fellowship. Steinem received the award and was able to spend 1957-58 in India, studying at the universities in Delhi and Calcutta. She also joined in the movement for land reform. At that time, as she learned, many Indian peasants worked on land that did not belong to them; they had to pay rent to wealthy owners to farm the land. Steinem joined a great march to convince landowners to give land to the poor. During her stay there she published a few freelance articles in Indian newspapers and was commissioned by the government to write a guidebook for American tourists, *The Thousand Indias*. After seeing the depth of poverty in India, Steinem was determined to work with oppressed people.

FIRST JOBS

Returning to the United States in 1958, she planned to live in New York City and work as a political writer. But at that time, women were rarely given such writing assignments. Many of the male editors Steinem encountered were patronizing and condescending. A woman wasn't intellectually capable of writing about serious issues, they thought, and women wouldn't be interested in reading about them. Instead, Steinem was offered pieces on so-called women's topics—fashion, makeup, caring for children and the home. Steinem then left New York to take a position in Cambridge, Massachusetts, as co-director of the Independent Research Service, where she worked to encourage democratic ideals, especially among youths in Communist countries.

CAREER HIGHLIGHTS

EARLY CAREER

Determined to win respect as a serious journalist, Steinem returned to New York in 1960. She got her start working on *Help!*, a new magazine of political satire. Through that position she met many writers and editors and began to develop a freelance career. Her first major piece in a national magazine was "The Moral Disarmament of Betty Coed," a discussion of the sexual revolution that was published in *Esquire* magazine in 1962.

That piece eventually led to an assignment for an article on Playboy Bunnies. These young women worked as waitresses and hostesses in Playboy clubs, semi-private men's clubs that were owned by the company that puts out *Playboy* magazine. At that time, working for a Playboy club was supposed to be an honor and an adventure for a young woman, "the chance of a lifetime." It was also supposed to be well paying. Steinem went undercover to work at the club, wearing a skimpy costume, bunny ears and tail, and shoes with three-inch heels that permanently enlarged her feet. Her expose showed the ways in which the Playboy clubs exploited women: the jobs were demeaning, the costumes were degrading and painful to wear, the women poorly paid and dreadfully overworked, and the customers boorish. While none of this sounds very surprising today, it was a revelation in 1963, when "I Was a Playboy Bunny" appeared in *Show* magazine. Steinem got a lot of recognition for that piece, but it was not all positive. Many missed the point entirely, ignoring her findings about the Playboy organization and focusing instead on the fact that she had worked as a bunny. From that point onward she received lots of assignments, although much of the subject matter was rather frivolous. She did quite a few interviews with celebrities, and in the process she became a minor celebrity herself.

That all began to change in 1968, when she co-founded *New York* magazine with Clay Felker. As an editor on the new magazine, she was able to decide what stories would be covered in each issue. She often wrote a column entitled "The City Politic" covering political and social issues in the city and around the country. The year 1968 was a time of tremendous upheaval, as the country dealt with such divisive issues as the Vietnam War, the demonstrations and police brutality at the Democratic convention in Chicago, race riots, and the assassinations of Martin Luther King, Jr., and Robert Kennedy. It was a difficult time in American history, but, for Steinem, a fascinating time to be a journalist. She also became active then as a volunteer in political and social causes, including the farm workers' strike in California. Finally, she was doing important and rewarding work.

A POLITICAL AWAKENING

Steinem's life changed dramatically that same year. She attended a meeting of the Redstockings, a radical women's group, to gather information for an article. At that meeting, women were discussing their experiences with abortion, then illegal throughout the United States. Steinem herself had an abortion shortly after college, and the anger, desperation, and helplessness these women suffered spoke directly to her. That night, Steinem had a sudden and profound understanding of sexual politics. A double standard, which encouraged men to do interesting work but kept women in low-paying, entry-level positions, became obvious to her. And she saw that the situation affected not only her, but was part of a larger political and social issue—discrimination against women solely on the basis of their sex. Steinem did eventually publish an article, "After Black Power, Women's Liberation," her first openly feminist piece, which won the Penney-Missouri Journalism Award. But perhaps more importantly, the experience changed the whole direction of her life.

Since that time, Steinem has been active in the feminist movement. Although she was not one of the movement's pioneers—Betty Friedan and her book *The Feminine Mystique,* along with other women, usually receive that credit—Steinem quickly became one of its most visible leaders. She started reading feminist pieces and continued writing her own. Along with

Friedan and Congresswomen Shirley Chisholm and Bella Abzug, she founded the National Women's Political Caucus (NWPC) in 1971. NWPC, which encourages women to run for political office, is still an important organization today. Steinem also started traveling around the country organizing events and giving lectures, despite her profound fear of public speaking. She was also active in the fight for the Equal Rights Amendment (ERA).

Ms. MAGAZINE

Steinem's travels around the country made it clear to her and others that there was widespread interest in feminist issues. They began planning a new type of magazine, the first of its kind, completely owned and operated by women. They named it Ms., after the feminist courtesy title used to avoid labeling women by their marital status. The first issue of Ms. was published as an insert in New York magazine in December 1971. Response was so positive that they published the first full issue the following month. To their amazement, 300,000 copies sold out nationwide within ten days. The letters section soon offered convincing testimony on how important the magazine's singular viewpoint was to its readers, who were angry and frustrated by their own daily experiences with sexism. The magazine has had its ups and downs, both editorially and financially, since that time.

For the issue dated July/August 1990, Steinem wrote a piece titled "Sex, Lies & Advertising" that illuminated the magazine's financial difficulties. Magazines rely heavily on advertisements to pay their costs, and in this area she uncovered a widespread double standard. Unlike general interest publications, Ms. and others for women were expected to provide a "supportive editorial atmosphere" for the products advertised in their pages; in other words, recipes should be placed near food ads, fashion pieces near clothing ads, beauty tips near makeup ads. Without this "complementary copy," companies would not place their ads in Ms.; in addition, many other types of companies, like those for cars and electronic equipment, refused to advertise because they did not believe that women made their own decisions to buy such products. Because the staff refused to change the magazine's editorial content to comply with the wishes of the advertisers, the magazine ultimately foundered. Due to financial losses, Ms. was sold in 1987 to an Australian communications conglomerate, John Fairfax, Ltd.; they then sold it in 1989 to magazine publisher Dale Lang. Today, Ms. magazine is reader supported; they accept no advertisements, and the subscription price covers its full cost. Ms. is currently published bimonthly, and Steinem serves as consulting editor.

For over twenty years, Steinem has been a writer, editor, and political activist in the movement for full equality for women. She has worked tirelessly for social change. But in her new book, *Revolution from Within: A Book of Self-Esteem* (1992), she takes a new direction. In it she focuses on the inner life, identifying poor self-esteem as an internal barrier to change and suggesting ways to overcome it. The book is a mixture of her own experiences and philosophy combined with politics, history, sociology, and psychology. This exploration of personal issues is widely viewed as a departure for Steinem. This derives, she has said, from feelings of exhaustion, vulnerability, and depression after a diagnosis of breast cancer in 1986 (she is cancer-free now, following a lumpectomy), the sale of *Ms.* magazine in 1987, and the end of a romance that same year.

MARRIAGE AND FAMILY

Steinem lives in an apartment in New York City. She has never married nor had children. Steinem once suggested that her early experiences taking care of her mother were perhaps the reason she chose not to have children: "It may be true that since I had taken care of my mother for so many years that I felt I had done that already. I had already fed and looked after and nurtured another human being." She has had several serious relationships with men. Her most recent, with wealthy real-estate tycoon Mort Zuckerman, was the subject of a great deal of publicity, in part because of the perceived differences in their values and because of the many references to a recent failed relationship in her book.

MAJOR INFLUENCES

In response to a question about who has inspired her, Steinem once cited the courage of Robert Kennedy, Bella Abzug, and Alice Walker. She praised Kennedy for his willingness to speak in public even when afraid, Abzug for her dedication and ability to face conflict, and Walker for her deep empathy for others.

WRITINGS

The Thousand Indias, 1957
The Beach Book, 1963
Outrageous Acts and Everyday Rebellions, 1983
Marilyn: Norma Jeane, 1986
Revolution from Within: A Book of Self-Esteem, 1992

Steinem has also edited and contributed articles to various anthologies.

HONORS AND AWARDS

Chester Bowles Asian Fellow in India: 1957-58
Penney-Missouri Journalism Award: 1970, for "After Black Power, Women's Liberation"
McCall's Woman of the Year: 1972

Ohio Governor's Award for Journalism: 1972
Bill of Rights Award, American Civil Liberties Union (ACLU): 1975
Woodrow Wilson International Center for Scholars Fellow: 1977
Ceres Medal (Agricultural Organization, United Nations): 1975, for her
    contribution to the women's movement
Front Page Award (Newswomen's Club of New York): 1980
Clarion Award (Women in Communications, Inc.)

FURTHER READING

BOOKS

Cohen, Marcia. *The Sisterhood: The True Story of the Women Who Changed the World*, 1988
Contemporary Authors New Revision Series, Vol. 28
Daffron, Carolyn. *Gloria Steinem*, 1988 (juvenile)
Encyclopedia Americana, 1990 ed., Vol. 25
Encyclopedia Brittanica, 1991 ed., Vol. 11
Henry, Sondra, and Emily Taitz. *One Woman's Power: A Biography of Gloria Steinem*, 1987 (juvenile)
Hoff, Mark. *Gloria Steinem: The Women's Movement*, 1991 (juvenile)
Who's Who of American Women, 1991-92
World Book Encyclopedia, 1991 ed., Vol. 18

PERIODICALS

Cosmopolitan, Jan. 1989, p.60
Current Biography Yearbook 1972, 1988
Mother Jones, Nov./Dec. 1990, p.32
People, Jan. 27, 1992, p.47
Vanity Fair, Jan. 1992, p.88
Washington Post, Oct. 12, 1983, p.B1
Working Woman, Jan. 1992, p.66

ADDRESS

Ms. Magazine
230 Park Ave.
New York, NY 10169

Clarence Thomas 1948-
American Jurist and Lawyer
Associate Justice, United States Supreme Court

BIRTH

Clarence Thomas was born to M.C. and Leola Thomas on June 23, 1948, in Pin Point, Georgia, a small, marshland community seven miles from Savannah. One of three children, he has an older sister, Emma Mae (Martin), and a younger brother, Myers, who was not yet born when the father abandoned the family. His mother, now Leola Williams, still lives in Pin Point.

YOUTH

When Clarence was seven, he and his brother were sent to live with their grandparents in Savannah. His sister stayed with their mother who was, by then, remarried. Grandfather Myers Anderson made a decent living as a fuel and ice dealer, and he and his wife were able to give the little boys a better start in life. They stressed discipline, self-reliance, and hard work, teaching the children that they must "follow a straight and narrow path" if they were to rise above their dependence on white society.

"Of course, I thought my grandparents were too rigid and their expectations too high," Thomas revealed many years later in writing to the *Wall Street Journal*. "I also thought they were mean at times. But. . .they wanted to raise us so that we could do for ourselves, so that we could stand on our own two feet."

EARLY MEMORIES

The pressure to do well in school is one of the things from his youth that Thomas remembers well. He tells of times when his "unlettered" grandfather would take him to meetings of the local NAACP (National Association for the Advancement of Colored People) and proudly stand to read his grandson's grades aloud. Even for a serious student eager to excel, these expectations from home were so great that Thomas has never forgotten them.

Other memories stay with him as well, and some of them are bitter. He has spoken about the discrimination he felt as a black child, and about the racial slights that prompted him to leave the seminary where he was studying for the Roman Catholic priesthood.

EDUCATION

Thomas's early education began at St. Benedict the Moor School on East Gordon Street in Savannah. He was taught by white Franciscan nuns, who often were belittled for mingling with their black students outside the classroom. Thomas continued his education at Savannah's St. John Vianney Minor Seminary and was the only black in his 1967 graduating class. With intentions of becoming a priest, he enrolled at Immaculate Conception Seminary in northwestern Missouri, but left after a year. He later said that he felt and saw evidence of racism there, and could not stay "at a school that did not practice what it preached."

The disillusioned seminarian transferred to Holy Cross College in Worcester, Massachusetts, a traditionally Irish Catholic school that was then in the midst of change. He was a founding member of the college's Black Student Union, and according to friends from those days, emerged as a leader and a fiercely independent thinker.

Thomas was graduated from Holy Cross in 1971. Three years later, he earned a law degree from Yale University in New Haven, Connecticut.

MAJOR INFLUENCES

A grandfather's guidance and a strict Catholic education are the elements that Thomas speaks of as being his strongest influences. He says that the philosophy that shaped his life was rooted in faith, discipline, and hard work. His success, he acknowledges, is due to his grandfather's insistence that he receive a good education, even though that man could barely read himself.

Thomas has named other personal heroes—Abraham Lincoln, Martin Luther King, Jr., St. Thomas Aquinas, and Thomas Jefferson. But radical and controversial figures also have made an impact on the thinking of Clarence Thomas, who now embraces conservative Republican views. He was openly sympathetic toward the black nationalism movement during college and law school, reading Malcolm X and expressing admiration for the Black Panthers.

His system of beliefs is complex, yet a recent profile in the *Detroit News* argues that Thomas finds no real conflict in the widely different theories that have formed his personal philosophy. Friends say that his current conservative views are more an outgrowth of his strict upbringing and religious education than loyalty to party politics.

FIRST JOBS

When Clarence Thomas left Yale in 1974 with his new law degree in hand, he was determined not to involve himself again in racial issues. He was tired, he said, of "having to prove himself as a black." He accepted a job as an assistant to Missouri Attorney General John Danforth (a Republican, and now that state's senior U.S. senator), and worked mainly on tax and environmental issues. In 1977, he became an in-house lawyer for Monsanto Chemical Corporation, but returned to government service two years later when Danforth took him to Washington as a legislative aide.

CAREER HIGHLIGHTS

The work that Thomas was doing for Senator Danforth brought him to the attention of the Reagan administration, then in power, and he was given his first major appointment in 1981 as assistant secretary in the Department of Education. His division dealt with civil rights, which are the rights of personal liberty as guaranteed by the Constitution and by acts of Congress.

The following year, Thomas became chairman of the Equal Employment Opportunity Commission (EEOC), the federal agency charged with enforcing laws against discrimination. There was much controversy over his opposition to affirmative action—an active effort to improve the employment or educational opportunities of women and members of minority groups—and his outspoken view that it produced the "feeling that blacks are inferior, so let's help them." His conservative guidelines on the rights of minorities offended traditional civil rights groups. They felt that he had distanced himself from his roots and was increasingly anxious to please his patrons in the administration, especially the right-wing members who opposed federal involvement in promoting social welfare. Thomas's detractors further accused him of substituting his own personal beliefs—against abortion, school desegregation, and minority hiring goals—for the law. Some even said that because he had made it on his own, he felt that others should be able to do the same. This theory, though, seemed to deny the fact that he, himself, had enrolled at Yale under an affirmative-action program.

In March 1990, Thomas was appointed by President Bush to the Court of Appeals for the District of Columbia as a federal judge, a job he held for fifteen months. The cases he ruled on during that time were mainly routine, and, except in judiciary circles, he was not a widely known figure.

Then, in July 1991, President Bush nominated Thomas to the Supreme Court to replace retiring Justice Thurgood Marshall, a long-time champion of civil rights for blacks in America. The long confirmation process ended in an uproar when Anita Hill, a former Education Department and EEOC assistant to Judge Thomas, accused him of sexual harrassment. Nationally televised hearings were conducted by the Senate Judiciary Committee, and the testimony given by Hill, a black Oklahoma law professor, was descriptive and sensational. Thomas denied the charges and angrily denounced the public hearings as a national disgrace and racist in nature. Both the accuser and the accused were supported by articulate and believable character witnesses; in the end, Thomas was confirmed by the Senate on October 15, 1991, in a 52 to 48 vote. His oath of office was administered in a private ceremony October 23, with formal investiture held the following week. Clarence Thomas is the 106th justice on the U.S. Supreme Court. As only the second black in history to serve on the Court and one whose conservative opinions represent a striking change from the liberal views of the civil rights pioneer whom he succeeds, Thomas has received much scrutiny and analysis in the press.

MARRIAGE AND FAMILY

Clarence Thomas has been married since 1987 to Virginia Bess Lamp, a Nebraskan who works in the congressional liaison office of the U.S. Labor Department. Their home is in the Washington suburb of Alexandria, Virginia. Thomas has raised his son, Jamal, who was born in 1973 to him and his first wife, Tracey Ambush.

HOBBIES AND OTHER INTERESTS

The Supreme Court's newest justice, once a high school quarterback, now follows a program of physical exercise that includes weight lifting. He also enjoys spectator sports. His other absorbing interest is reading, particularly books on political philosophy.

FURTHER READING

BOOKS

Who's Who among Black Americans, 1990-91

PERIODICALS

Detroit News, Sept. 8, 1991, p.A14
Newsweek, Sept. 16, 1991, p.18
New York Times, July 2, 1991, p.A1; July 3, 1991, p.D18
People, July 22, 1991
Time, July 15, 1991, p.18; Sept. 16, 1991, p.25
Wall Street Journal, Feb. 20, 1987, p.A21

ADDRESS

U.S. Supreme Court
Supreme Court Bldg.
1 First St. NE
Washington, DC 20543

Chris Van Allsburg 1949-
American Writer and Illustrator of
Children's Books, and Artist
Author of *The Polar Express, Jumanji,* and
The Garden of Abdul Gasazi, among Others

BIRTH

Chris Van Allsburg was born on June 18, 1949, to Richard Allen
and Doris Marie (Christiansen) Van Allsburg. The family lived in
Grand Rapids, Michigan. Young Chris was occasionally allowed
to help his father and uncles in the family business, a dairy that
purchased raw milk from local farmers and turned it into cottage
cheese and ice cream.

YOUTH

The Van Allsburg family lived on the outskirts of town, and his descriptions of his childhood sound almost idyllic: "There were open fields, trees, wandering dirt roads. The houses weren't big—they were nice, small houses for families of four or maybe five. There were still places nearby where I could catch tadpoles, there were places to go sledding, there were fields where you could play baseball—not someplace surrounded by a fence, just open fields. And I rode my bike to school." He also enjoyed building model cars, trucks, planes, and boats. And he became quite adept at drawing cartoon characters. Dagwood Bumstead was his specialty, but Pluto and Mickey impressed his friends the most. Soon, though, succumbing to peer pressure, Van Allsburg began to concentrate on sports rather than art. As he tells it, "Rumors circulate around the schoolyard: kids who draw or wear white socks and bring violins to school on Wednesday might have cooties."

EARLY MEMORIES

For a time, though, during elementary school, art classes were the high point of his week. "I loved those days," Van Allsburg once said. "Children often use a slight fever as an excuse to stay home from school, drink ginger ale, and eat ice cream in bed. Once, in the second grade, I felt feverish at breakfast but concealed it from my mother because it was an art day. Midway through the morning art class, my teacher noticed that I looked a little green. Ordinarily it wasn't unusual, but paint wasn't being used that day. She took me out in the hall where we children left our coats and boots, and asked if I felt OK. I said I felt fine, then threw up into Billy Marcus's boots. I was profoundly embarrassed. The teacher was very comforting. She took me to the nurse's office, and my mother was summoned. I went home, drank ginger ale, and ate ice cream in bed."

EDUCATION

Van Allsburg attended the University of Michigan at Ann Arbor with a vague plan to study law. During his freshman year, though, he enrolled in a course listed as "Fgdrw" [figure drawing]. "I did not know what Fgdrw meant," Van Allsburg confessed, "but the materials required were newsprint and charcoal. I went to the appointed room and was surprised to see an older woman wearing a terry-cloth robe and slippers. I thought, 'What? Does she live here or something? Maybe we're here too early, and she hasn't had time to dress.' Then she took off her bathrobe, and I deduced the meaning of Fgdrw."

The class rekindled Van Allsburg's interest in art, and he soon decided to study sculpture; as he later said, "When I studied three-dimensional art it reminded me so much of building models when I was a little kid.

I thought it was great that I was going to get a college degree for doing the same thing I did when I was six years old." He received his Bachelor of Fine Arts degree at Michigan in 1972. Van Allsburg then attended graduate school at the Rhode Island School of Design (RISD) in Providence, Rhode Island, one of the finest art schools in the country, where he received his Master of Fine Arts degree in sculpture in 1975.

CHOOSING A CAREER

In 1977, Van Allsburg began exhibiting his sculpture at the Alan Stone Gallery in New York City, where his pieces met with great success. Since then, his work has been shown at the Whitney Museum of American Art, the Museum of Modern Art, and the Schiller-Wapner Gallery, also in New York. Many depict a precise moment in time, capturing some event in progress: a coffee cup tipping, its contents frozen in air; a recreation of the Titanic, in the process of sinking; a tall obelisk being buffeted by a wind storm, its bricks exploding outward. His sculpture is known for its expert craftsmanship, intricate detail, offbeat humor, skewed perspective, and sense of the surreal. These qualities also mark his fine-art illustrations. Like his sculpture, these pencil drawings are a little offbeat. In one, a fish jumps out of a large tureen of soup; in another, an impatient dinner guest bites into an empty dinner plate, glass pieces flying, as his startled hostess looks on.

In addition to his artwork, Van Allsburg began teaching both sculpture and illustration at RISD. There he became friends with David Macaulay, who wrote and illustrated *The Way Things Work* as well as several children's books on architecture. After seeing Van Allsburg's drawings, Macaulay encouraged him to consider illustrating a book. Van Allsburg's wife, Lisa, an elementary school teacher at the time, showed him some of the standard picture books she used in teaching, which Van Allsburg considered simplistic and naive. She then submitted several of her husband's drawings to publishers, and their favorable reactions inspired Van Allsburg to begin work on his first book, *The Garden of Abdul Gasazi*.

CAREER HIGHLIGHTS

Since his writing career began in 1979, Van Allsburg has published twelve books that have garnered praise from reviewers, won numerous awards, and delighted readers, young and old. Like his other artistic creations, Van Allsburg's books engage the imagination by showcasing the unexpected. As he once explained, "To puzzle children is more interesting to me than to educate or frighten them. I like to plant a seed that will start a mental process, rather than present my own."

A feeling of mystery and uncertainty pervades the stories. Often, the reader is left with unanswered questions at the end—what really happened, and how? The illustrations reinforce this feeling, combining reality with fantastic elements, depicted from odd angles, to underscore the skewed point of view. His drawings typically combine several features: they are narrative, designed to tell a story; parts are realistic, depicting life as it is, but often with some unexpected twist; they use varied perspectives to show sometimes surprising viewpoints and to increase the dramatic quality of each scene; and they use strong contrasts in color, either through complementary colors or black and white. With these qualities, Van Allsburg has created drawings that are original, enchanting, intelligent, and quite sophisticated. Indeed, some critics feel that his illustrations are far more engaging than the stories that accompany them.

In Van Allsburg's first book, *The Garden of Abdul Gasazi* (1979), a mischievous dog, Fritz, runs into a forbidden garden. Chasing him, eight-year-old Alan finds not Fritz but Abdul Gasazi, magician and owner of the garden, who seems to turn Fritz into a duck, which then flies off with Alan's hat. Dejected, he returns home, but finds Fritz there playing with his hat—leaving the reader uncertain what exactly did happen. With its intriguing text and illustrations, *The Garden of Abdul Gasazi* won instant acclaim for Van Allsburg and was cited as a Caldecott Honor Book, a runner-up for the Caldecott Medal. The Caldecott Medal, given annually by the American Library Association to the best illustrated book of the year, is the highest

THE POLAR EXPRESS

award for illustrated children's books, and a Caldecott Honor is a rare achievement for an author's first book.

Jumanji (1980), his second book, tells the story of two bored children left on their own one afternoon. They find a board game in the park, and return home to play. Its instructions include this warning: ONCE A GAME OF JUMANJI IS STARTED IT WILL NOT BE OVER UNTIL ONE PLAYER REACHES THE GOLDEN CITY. And with that the two children enter a world where fantasy and adventure abound: monkeys tear apart the kitchen, rhinoceroses stampede through the living room, monsoons flood the house, and volcanoes spill lava throughout. As soon as they finish the game, though, the house returns to normal. They quickly take the game back to the park, leaving it for some other children to find. The book won several awards, including the Caldecott Medal.

In *The Mysteries of Harris Burdick* (1984), Van Allsburg tried a new approach—this book contains fourteen unrelated drawings, each accompanied by just a title and a brief caption. The introduction claims that the author, Harris Burdick, left the drawings with a publisher, promising to return the next day with the stories to accompany them. But the author never returned, and many years later Van Allsburg found the pictures. The pictures defy categorization; they are all different and rather odd. The book is designed to inspire the imagination, to challenge the reader to create stories to accompany the drawings. Van Allsburg has received hundreds of stories from children who have taken up the challenge.

The Polar Express (1985), Van Allsburg's best-known and most acclaimed book, won for the author his second Caldecott Medal. In this fable about the power of belief, which Van Allsburg says is about his own life, a young boy takes a train trip one Christmas Eve to the North Pole. Santa Claus allows him to pick the first gift of the season, and he chooses a bell from Santa's sleigh. Yet when he returns home, the bell is missing. The next morning, the bell is under the Christmas tree with a cryptic note: "Found this on the seat of my sleigh. Fix that hole in your pocket, Mr. C." He and his sister think the bell has the most beautiful sound, but his parents can't hear it and believe it must be broken. Over time, his sister and his friends lose the ability to hear the bell chime, but not the boy: "the bell still rings for me, as it does for all who truly believe." Throughout, Van Allsburg uses muted yet rich pastel shades to depict fuzzy, indistinct backgrounds with sharply drawn objects in the foreground. *The Polar Express* was only Van Allsburg's second book to use color illustrations, and they have been widely praised.

Van Allsburg has written many more books, almost one each year since his first publication. These tales include *Ben's Dream* (1982), in which young Ben dreams about floating in his house throughout a flooded world, visiting the great monuments; *The Wreck of the Zephyr* (1983), in which a young boy finds an enchanted island where sailing boats can fly; *The Stranger* (1986), in which a mute stranger, whom Farmer Bailey brings home to recuperate after an accident, seems to have some power over the weather; *The Z Was Zapped: A Play in Twenty-Six Acts* (1987), in which the letters of the alphabet are subjected to various abuses; *Two Bad Ants* (1988), in which the dangerous adventures of two ants are depicted from their perspective; *Just a Dream* (1990), in which a young boy dreams about the future devastation of the earth and learns the importance of preserving the environment; and *Swan Lake* (1989), written by Mark Helprin and illustrated by Van Allsburg, a retelling of the classic tale. In his most recent effort, *The Wretched Stone* (1991), the captain and crew of a sailing ship discover an uncharted island, where they find a large, glowing rock that they bring on board ship. The rock seems to have some mysterious power: the sailors are enchanted by it, and, over time, they gradually turn into monkeys.

For many, Van Allburg's success derives from his ability to understand and engage the imagination of the reader. Yet he claims that he doesn't think about his readers when he sits down to write and illustrate his books; instead, he creates stories that interest him. Still, his stories appeal to both adults and children, as his many fan letters and brisk sales demonstrate. As one five-year-old wrote to him, "Dear Mr. Van Allsburg, I love the books you write. I am so glad your books are so weird because I am very weird. I think you are weird but great. I wish a volcano and a flood could be in my room when I am bored. I am happy I am only five because I have lots more years to enjoy magical gardens and crazy games in books by you."

MARRIAGE AND FAMILY

Van Allsburg was married on August 17, 1976, to Lisa Carol Morrison, whom he met when they were both art students at the University of Michigan. They have one daughter, Sophia, born in 1991. Their home is in Providence, where Van Allsburg divides his time among his varied pastimes, sculpting, drawing, teaching at RISD, and writing and illustrating books.

MAJOR INFLUENCES

"If I were to name ten people who have influenced me," Van Allsburg once said, "I would feel that I've neglected the other fifty. Still, there are some, like the German etcher Max Klinger, who left a big impression on me. Also, something about the work of the painter Casper David-Friedrich moves me a lot. I like drawings and images in which the emotional content is not based on the subject matter. That may not be a fair evaluation of the work of Klinger and David-Friedrich, but I think some of their best work has a moody quality which is not dependent on subject matter. The feeling they create is not a consequence of content but of composition. It's easy to get an emotional response by doing a drawing of a little boy and puppy dog. It's much more difficult to create sentiment by drawing a landscape or a still life."

WRITINGS

The Garden of Abdul Gasazi, 1979
Jumanji, 1981
Ben's Dream, 1982
The Wreck of the Zephyr, 1983
The Mysteries of Harris Burdick, 1984
The Polar Express, 1985
The Stranger, 1986
The Z Was Zapped: A Play in Twenty-Six Acts, 1987
Swan Lake, 1989 [written by Mark Helprin; illustrated by Van Allsburg]
Just a Dream, 1990
The Wretched Stone, 1991

HONORS AND AWARDS

New York Times Best Illustrated Children's Books of the Year: 1979, *The Garden of Abdul Gasazi;* 1981, *Jumanji;* 1982, *Ben's Dream;* 1983, *The Wreck of the Zephyr;* 1984, *The Mysteries of Harris Burdick;* 1985, *The Polar Express;* 1986, *The Stranger*
Notable Children's Books (American Library Association): 1979, *The Garden of Abdul Gasazi;* 1981, *Jumanji;* 1983, *The Wreck of the Zephyr;* 1984, *The Mysteries of Harris Burdick;* 1985, *The Polar Express;* 1988, *The Z Was Zapped*
Boston Globe—Horn Book Award: 1980, for *The Garden of Abdul Gasazi;* 1985, for *The Mysteries of Harris Burdick*
Irma Simonton Black Award (Bank Street College of Education): 1980, for *The Garden of Abdul Gasazi;* 1985, for *The Mysteries of Harris Burdick*
Booklist "Editor's Choice": 1981, *Jumanji;* 1983, *The Wreck of the Zephyr;* 1984, *The Mysteries of Harris Burdick;* 1985, *The Polar Express;* 1987, *The Z Was Zapped*
New York Times Outstanding Books of the Year: 1981, *Jumanji;* 1983, *The Wreck of the Zephyr*
Randolph Caldecott Medal (American Library Association): 1982, for *Jumanji;* 1986, for *The Polar Express*

FURTHER READING

BOOKS

Dictionary of Literary Biography, Vol. 61
Something about the Author, Vol. 53
Who's Who in America, 1991-92

PERIODICALS

Horn Book Magazine, Aug. 1982, p. 380; July/Aug. 1986, pp.420, 425
New York Times Magazine, Dec. 24, 1989, p.12; also in *New York Times Biographical Service,* Dec. 1989, p.1238
People, Dec. 11, 1989, p.142
Time, Nov. 13, 1989, p.108

ADDRESS

Houghton Mifflin Company
2 Park St.
Boston, MA 02108

Cynthia Voigt   1942-
American Writer
Author of *Homecoming, Dicey's Song, David and
Jonathan, Orfe,* and Other Young Adult Novels

BIRTH

Cynthia Irving Voigt was born on February 25, 1942, in Boston,
Massachusetts. Her father, Frederick C. Irving, was an executive,
while her mother, Elise (Keeney) Irving, was a homemaker. Cindy,
as she was called, was the second of five children: she had two
sisters until she was thirteen, when twin brothers were born.

YOUTH

There have been few profiles published about Cynthia Voigt, and
little information about her life is available. Even she once said,

"I actually remember very little of my childhood, which makes me think it was quite happy. I suspect it might have been very close to perfect." Yet she does distinctly remember nursery school. "Because my older sister was *thought* to be painfully shy, my parents decided to send us to nursery school together. I was a little young, but they felt I would be able to help her through. When it came time for the nursery school play, however, she was Miss Muffet, and I was the Spider. Later, when we got to dancing school—she was a Sweet Pea, and I was a Head of Cabbage."

EARLY MEMORIES

"My grandmother lived in northern Connecticut, in a house three stories high; its corridors lined with bookcases. I remember reading *Nancy Drew, Cherry Ames, The Black Stallion,* and the Terhune book. One day, I pulled *The Secret Garden* off one of her shelves and read it. This was the first book I found entirely for myself, and I cherished it. There weren't any so-called 'young adult' books when I was growing up. If you were a good reader, once you hit fourth grade, things got a little thin. I started to read adult books, with my mother making sure what I had chosen was not 'too adult.' I read Tolstoy, Shakespeare, Camus, and many classics."

EDUCATION

Because both her mother and father had attended a boarding school, they sent Voigt to Dana Hall, a private girls' school in Wellesley, Massachusetts. Voigt has said that the school gave the students a great deal of intellectual and even physical freedom, rare in a girls' school during that era. "Knowing the school trusted us, I believe, helped us to grow up," she has said. She wrote poems and short stories there and in ninth grade decided to become a writer. She graduated with distinction from Dana Hall, a member of the Cum Laude Society and president of her senior class.

Voigt attended Smith College in Northampton, Massachusetts, a renowned women's college. She took some creative writing courses there, but she was disenchanted with the classes and her teachers were unimpressed with her work. She graduated from Smith College in 1963 with a bachelor's degree. She later took graduate courses at St. Michael's College (now College of Santa Fe), in New Mexico, to earn a teaching certificate.

FIRST JOBS

After her college graduation and a tour of Europe with a friend, Voigt moved to New York City. There she found a tiny apartment in Greenwich Village and a job with the J. Walter Thompson Advertising Agency, doing typing and dictation. As she recalls, "I worked for a wonderful woman in public relations, who at the time was putting together a centennial history. A vaudevillian, her best act was tap dancing while playing the xylophone blindfolded!"

MARRIAGE AND FAMILY

Voigt has been married twice. She and her first husband, whose name she prefers not to reveal, were married in September 1964. They had one daughter, Jessica, who remained with Voigt after her divorce in 1972. On August 30, 1974, she married Walter Voigt; they have one son, Peter, known as Duffle.

CAREER HIGHLIGHTS

After her marriage in 1964, Voigt moved with her new husband to Santa Fe, New Mexico, where he was a student. She looked for secretarial work to help support them while he was in school. Despite her experience in New York, she had trouble finding a job. Discouraged, she went to the Department of Education to find out how to become a teacher. She took courses for six months at St. Michael's College to become certified. Voigt had never planned to become a teacher; in fact, "I vowed I would never teach when I left Smith, and yet, the minute I walked into a classroom, I loved it."

TEACHING CAREER

With her husband, Voigt moved back East, to Maryland, where he finished school. In 1965, she began teaching high school English in Glen Burnie, Maryland. In 1968, she moved to The Key School in Annapolis, where she taught English to second, fifth, and seventh graders. She continued teaching there, eventually part-time, until the late 1980s, through the birth of her first child, her divorce in 1972, her remarriage in 1974 to one of her colleagues on the teaching staff, the birth of her second child, and her appointment to chair of the English department in 1981.

WRITING CAREER

Throughout much of this time Voigt had been writing stories, setting aside time each day to write. It was her experiences as a teacher that ultimately determined the direction of her writing. While selecting books from the library for her fifth graders to use for book reports, she first began to think about writing novels for young adults. As she said, "I would go to the library and starting with the letter 'A' peruse books at the fifth, sixth, and seventh-grade age levels. If a book looked interesting, I checked it out. ...It was then that I realized one could tell stories which had the shape of real books—novels—for kids the age of my students. I began to get ideas for young adult and juvenile books. The first year of teaching, and *reading* really paid off in spades. I felt I had suddenly discovered and was exploring a new country."

Since her first novel appeared in 1981, Voigt has been acclaimed as an insightful and imaginative storyteller whose stories are known for their emotional depth and well-crafted characters. In just over ten years, Voigt has published 21 books, including 18 novels for young adults, one illustrated book for younger readers (*Stories about Rosie,* 1986), one adult novel (*Glass Mountain,* 1991), and a collection of the stories about the Tillerman family. There is a great deal of variety in her young adult books, which consist of some realistic novels, some in other genres, set in the present and in other eras. These include *Tell Me If the Lovers Are Losers* (1982), the story of three college students who forge a bond on their volleyball team; *The Callender Papers* (1983), a gothic mystery set in 1894; *Building Blocks* (1984), a fantasy about a twelve-year-old boy who travels through time to meet his own father as a boy; *Jackaroo* (1985), a mythical tale set in a medieval kingdom, similar to Robin Hood; *Izzy, Willy-Nilly* (1986), a modern story of a girl whose leg is amputated after an auto accident; *Tree by Leaf* (1988), a tale of the family problems faced by Clothilde, age 13, following World War I; *On Fortune's Wheel* (1990), an imaginative fantasy set in the same world as *Jackaroo; The Vandemark Mummy* (1991), which combines a modern story about family problems and a mystery about a missing mummy; *David and Jonathan* (1992), the story of two friends who reassess their values, their friendship, and the legacy of World War II when a self-destructive cousin, a Holocaust survivor, comes to visit; and *Orfe* (1992), a modern reworking of the classic Orpheus myth that tells the story of Enny and her friend Orfe, a musician, and his doomed relationship with Yuri, a former drug addict. Despite praise for these works, it is the stories about the Tillerman family that are considered her best.

THE TILLERMAN STORIES

The inspiration for *Home-coming,* Voigt's first published novel and the first of the Tiller-man stories, came about in a rather mundane way. "I went to the market and saw a car full of kids left to wait alone in the parking lot. As the electric supermarket doors whooshed open, I asked myself 'What would happen if nobody ever came back for those kids?' I made some jottings in my notebook, and let them 'stew' for a year, the way most of my ideas do. When I sat down to write the story that grew from my question (and this is typical of my process) I made a list of character names. Then I tried them on to see if they fit. I knew Dicey was the main character, but was not sure precisely *who* she was. The more I wrote about her, the more real she became to me. I'd planned a book about half the size of *Homecoming*. But a few chapters into the novel, the grandmother became central and I began to see that there was a lot more going on than would fit in one book."

Thus began the Tillerman saga. These novels, seven to date, focus on three generations in a Maryland family. The first novel in the series, *Homecoming* (1981), tells the story of four children abandoned in a shopping center parking lot by their emotionally unstable mother. The book details the experiences of the four Tillerman siblings, led by Dicey, the oldest, as they walk from Cape Cod, Massachusetts, to their grandmother's Maryland home. The next book, *Dicey's Song* (1982), picks up the story at Gram's, recounting how the family, and especially Dicey, adjust to life together. *A Solitary Blue* (1983) focuses on Dicey's friend Jeff, describing his abandonment by his mother and his adjustment to his reserved father. In *The Runner* (1985), Voigt goes back a generation to portray Dicey's uncle Bullet, her mother's brother, as a seventeen-year-old determined and sometimes bigoted runner. In *Come a Stranger* (1986), Voigt tells how Dicey's friend Mina, who is black, learns to deal with being rejected as an outsider. *Sons from Afar* (1987) returns to the experiences of Dicey's family, describing her brothers' search for their father, who had abandoned the family. Finally, in *Seventeen against the Dealer* (1989), which Voigt expects to be the final book in the series, we meet Dicey at age 21, as she tries, but fails, to earn a living building boats.

Voigt's novels in the Tillerman series have been widely praised by readers and critics alike. These works have received a variety of awards, including the 1983 Newbery Medal from the American Library Association for *Dicey's Song*. While many reviewers applaud Voigt's focus on realistic problems in modern family life, they reserve their greatest praise for her characterization. Even the author seems to share this feeling. "[Grandmother] was always very clear to me, and in some ways is a mirror image of her granddaughter, Dicey. I sometimes think that Dicey is the type of kid I would have liked to have been, and grandmother is the kind of old lady I would like to be." These and other characters, according to many, are distinct, strong, and compelling individuals; they draw us into the story and make us care about their lives. It is this ability to depict teenagers and others with honesty, dignity, and compassion that has won Voigt such devoted readers.

THE AUTHOR'S OWN WORDS ON HER LIFE

Voigt once told how two people, a friend and her mother, had said that her life was dull. Voigt then countered with this description. "I'm not about to quarrel with either of them, although I've found my life interesting to live. The facts bear them out: a secure childhood, spent among siblings and friends and books, in a world run by adults who enjoyed taking their responsibilities seriously; that New England women's education, designed to foster independence of mind and recognizing that willfulness and rebellion affirmed rather than undermined its purposes; an employment that, while the world might find it unhonorable and unenviable, is deeply satisfying to the whole person; a failed marriage from which I emerged with a continued friendship and a wonderful child; a more successful marital endeavor with a good friend and good thinker, which has given me another terrific kid. And I get to write books."

ADVICE TO YOUNG WRITERS

From her own experiences, Voigt offers these words of advice to aspiring writers: "Do it, not for awards, but for the pleasure of writing. And remember that publication is often a matter of chance. *Homecoming* was turned down by three of the five editors to whom I submitted the first three chapters."

HOBBIES AND OTHER INTERESTS

In addition to writing and teaching, Voigt enjoys "going out to dinner, shopping with my son or daughter, and in the summer, trips to our island in the Chesapeake Bay where we enjoy the beach, go crabbing, read together, wash dishes. I'd love to have a house in Maine someday. It's so beautiful and quiet, and there are so many stars in the sky. When I see something I like, I always want to try and write it—that makes it *mine*, you see. It's almost as good as buying property—I put something in a book, and I almost own it. I suppose I'll have to write a book about Maine, perhaps that will make the dream come true." And in fact, her dream did come true recently, when Voigt and her family moved to Deer Isle, Maine.

WRITINGS

THE TILLERMAN STORIES

Homecoming, 1981
Dicey's Song, 1982
A Solitary Blue, 1983
The Runner, 1985
Come a Stranger, 1986
Sons from Afar, 1987
Seventeen against the Dealer, 1989

OTHER WRITINGS

Tell Me If the Lovers Are Losers, 1982
The Callender Papers, 1983

Building Blocks, 1984
Jackaroo, 1985
Izzy, Willy-Nilly, 1986
Stories about Rosie, 1986
Tree by Leaf, 1988
On Fortune's Wheel, 1990
Tillerman Saga, 1990 (collection)
Glass Mountain, 1991 (adult)
The Vandemark Mummy, 1991
David and Jonathan, 1992
Orfe, 1992

HONORS AND AWARDS

New York Times Outstanding Books: 1981, for *Homecoming*
Notable Children's Trade Books in the Field of Social Studies (National Council for Social Studies/Children's Book Council): 1981, for *Homecoming*
Best Books for Young Adults (American Library Association): 1982, for *Tell Me If the Lovers Are Losers;* 1983, for *A Solitary Blue;* 1985, for *The Runner;* 1987, for *Sons from Afar;* 1991, for *On Fortune's Wheel*
Newbery Medal (American Library Association): 1983, for *Dicey's Song;* Newbery Honor Book: 1984, for *A Solitary Blue*
Boston Globe/Horn Book Honor Books: 1983, for *Dicey's Song;* 1984, for *A Solitary Blue*
Notable Children's Books (American Library Association): 1982, for *Dicey's Song;* 1983, for *A Solitary Blue*
Parent's Choice Award for Children's Books: 1983, for A Solitary Blue
Edgar Allan Poe Award (Mystery Writers of America): 1984, Best Juvenile Mystery, for *The Callender Papers*
Children's Books of the Year (Child Study Association of America): 1987, for *Come a Stranger*
Best of the Best Books for Young Adults (American Library Association): 1988 (4 awards), for *Homecoming, Izzy, Willy-Nilly, The Runner,* and *A Solitary Blue*
Silver Pencil Award (Holland): 1988, for *The Runner*
Deutscher Jugend Literatur Preis (Germany): 1989, for *The Runner*

FURTHER READING

BOOKS
Contemporary Authors New Revision Series, vols. 18 and 37
Something about the Author, vol. 48

PERIODICALS
Booklist, Apr. 15, 1989, p.1452

Christian Science Monitor, May 13, 1983, p.B2
Horn Book, Aug. 1983, pp.401, 410
Language Arts, Nov./Dec. 1983, p.1025

ADDRESS

Macmillan Publishing Co.
Children's Marketing Dept.
866 Third Ave.
New York, NY 10022

Bill Watterson 1958-
American Cartoonist
Creator of "Calvin and Hobbes"

BIRTH

William B. (Bill) Watterson II was born July 5, 1958, in Washington, D.C., to James and Kathryn Watterson. He has a younger brother, Thomas.

YOUTH

When he was six years old, Watterson moved with his family to Chagrin Falls, Ohio, a suburb of Cleveland. His father was an attorney, and his mother served on the city council. The family remembers Watterson as quietly imaginative, spending hours at a time drawing cartoon characters or making time-lapse movies with his brother. James Watterson told an interviewer a few years ago that his son was "nothing like Calvin. He didn't have an imaginary friend like Hobbes and he wasn't a Dennis the Menace." The outlandish exploits of Calvin, the rude and boisterous little boy of the comic strip, bear no resemblance to Watterson's childhood personality, but the cartoonist admits that there probably is some of his own identity in the more thoughtful and conservative character of the stuffed tiger Hobbes, who turns into a real tiger when there are no adults around.

Information about Bill Watterson's early years is meager. Those who know him well respect his intense wish for privacy, and the little stories and anecdotes that surface about most celebrities have not found their way into the brief profiles of his personal life.

EDUCATION

Watterson earned a degree in political science in 1980 from Kenyon College in Gambier, Ohio. During his student years, he drew cartoons for the school publication, the *Kenyon Collegian,* as he had done earlier for his high school newspaper and yearbook.

FIRST JOBS

The *Cincinnati Post* hired Watterson as a political cartoonist soon after his college graduation, but six months on the job convinced him, and his editor, that he should look elsewhere for a career. He returned to northern Ohio and spent the next few years drawing cartoons for a chain of suburban newspapers and doing layout jobs for a little weekly tabloid.

MAJOR INFLUENCES

Charles Schulz's "Peanuts" was the comic strip that first sparked Bill Watterson's interest in cartooning. He read "Pogo," too, and these early favorites led him to try his own hand at creating characters and story lines. The writing and drawing of Garry Trudeau ("Doonesbury") and Berke Breathed ("Bloom County") have impressed him in more recent years, but it is said that he still reads and enjoys "Peanuts."

CHOOSING A CAREER

There is little doubt that Bill Watterson intended to be anything other than a cartoonist. He started to sketch comic characters as a young boy and has been following his dream in one form or another ever since. In the few interviews he has granted—reluctantly—he comes across as a quiet observer of human nature, which may be an outgrowth of the shyness he demonstrated in childhood. Those traits, combined with his drawing talent and his wry sense of humor, made him a natural for his chosen career.

CAREER HIGHLIGHTS

Watterson turned out strips and submitted them to press syndicates for five discouraging years before success came in late 1985 with "Calvin and Hobbes." One of his many rejected strips had featured two minor characters, an impudent little kid and his faithful toy tiger, and someone suggested that Watterson develop a series around these two. Things clicked. Later, in a rare interview, he said that he didn't regret the years of effort and disappointment. "Some people hit right away, and they have to learn [from their mistakes] on the pages of the nation's newspapers. I could flop and fall on my face without anybody noticing."

The little mischief-maker and his more rational friend appealed to readers immediately with their humorous, and sometimes touching, relationship. The comic strip started with 35 clients and now runs in more than 1,800 newspapers nationwide. When Watterson took a nine-month vacation last year, only a few small papers dropped the wildly popular feature. Others ran strips from the first 14 months of publication without real fear of losing readership. One features editor echoed the majority's sentiments at the time with a comment that "there seems to be such affection for these characters," adding that the reruns "will seem new to kids who were too young to read 'Calvin and Hobbes' when it first came out." Watterson is scheduled to return from his sabbatical in February 1992.

Collections of "Calvin and Hobbes" in book form have sold by the millions, but Watterson has so far refused to license his work for greeting cards, T-shirts, stuffed animals, and other commercial uses. He has felt from the beginning that overexposure would spoil the freshness of the strip. "Money," he insists, "isn't why I got into this...if I got into licensing I might not have the time I want to devote to the strip. And that's all I ever wanted to do."

MARRIAGE AND FAMILY

Watterson and his artist wife, Melissa, lived in the small village of Hudson, Ohio (near Akron) until the late 1980s, but now make their home in New Mexico. There are no children listed in his biographical entries.

HOBBIES AND OTHER INTERESTS

If Bill Watterson has other interests besides producing "Calvin and Hobbes," and occasionally taking time out to paint, few people know what they are. He is said to be friendly enough, but not interested in being a celebrity. He shuns photographers, and is never willing to talk about his private life. Of the fame that has come his way, Watterson says, "There's very little of it that I enjoy." Some years ago, at the beginning of his success, he did reveal something of his whimsical nature, though, by revealing that the naming of his comic strip characters was "an inside joke" for political science students—Calvin, for Protestant reformer John Calvin, and Hobbes for Thomas Hobbes, the political philosopher.

WRITINGS

Calvin and Hobbes, 1987
The Essential Calvin and Hobbes: A Calvin and Hobbes Treasury, 1988
Something Under the Bed Is Drooling: A Calvin and Hobbes Collection, 1988
The Calvin and Hobbes Lazy Sunday Book, 1989
Yukon Ho!, 1989
The Authoritative Calvin and Hobbes: A Calvin and Hobbes Treasury, 1990.
Weirdos From Another Planet: A Calvin and Hobbes Collection, 1990
The Revenge of the Baby-Sat, 1991

HONORS AND AWARDS

National Cartoonists Society Reuben Award: 1987, 1990, for "Outstanding Cartoonist of the Year"

FURTHER READING

PERIODICALS

Detroit Free Press, Apr. 13, 1987, p.B1
Editor & Publisher, Mar. 30, 1991, p.34
Los Angeles Times, Apr. 1, 1987, V, p.1
Plain Dealer (Cleveland, Ohio), Aug. 30, 1987, Sunday magazine, p.7

ADDRESS

Universal Press Syndicate
4900 Main St.
Kansas City, MO 64112

Calvin and Hobbes   by Bill Watterson

Robin Williams 1952-
American Actor and Comedian
Star of *Hook*, *Dead Poets Society*, and
Good Morning, Vietnam

BIRTH

Robin Williams was born on July 21, 1952, in Chicago, Illinois, to Robert and Laurie Williams. According to Robin, his father, a Ford Motor Company vice president, was a "very elegant man with a powerful voice. He looks like a retired English army colonel, except he's not. My mother is the one who has show-business tendencies, but she never exerted them."

YOUTH

The Williams family was wealthy. They relocated frequently when Robin was young, and eventually moved to a 30-room house on a 20-acre estate in Bloomfield Hills, outside Detroit, Michigan. He has two older half-brothers from his parents' previous marriages, but he grew up feeling like an only child. His father was usually working, and his mother was also often away. Always the new kid in school, Williams was basically happy but often lonely, he now says: "My imagination was my friend, my companion." He learned to enjoy solitary activities, reading, watching cartoons on television, and playing with his extensive collection of toy soldiers. Williams once described himself as "a shy, chubby child whose nickname was 'leprechaun.' My world was bounded by thousands of toy soldiers with whom I would play out World War II battles. I had a whole panzer division, 150 tanks, and a board ten feet by three feet that I covered with sand for Guadalcanal." By the age of twelve he began to recognize and develop his talent for comedy, doing imitations and routines for his mother, whom he describes as "always funny."

During Williams's senior year in high school, his father retired and the family moved to Tiburon, outside San Francisco, California, an area heavily influenced by the counterculture movement of the late 1960s. There he enrolled at Redwood High School, a public school with a relaxed atmosphere and curriculum—a far cry from the strict and academically rigorous preparatory school that he had attended in Michigan. "It was very much of a shock," he recalls. "I went from an all-boys private school where we had to wear ties to a school where even socks were optional. Did [California] broaden my horizons? It put them into *hyperspace*." The change seemed to suit him—he lost weight and became interested in athletics, especially wrestling and track. When he graduated in 1969, his classmates voted him "Most Humorous" and "Least Likely to Succeed."

EDUCATION

After high school, Williams enrolled in Claremont Men's College in southern California, planning to study political science. While there, though, he took a course in improvisation and discovered the thrill of making others laugh. Hooked, he transferred to the College of Marin to study classical drama. In 1973, Williams won a full scholarship to the Julliard School, the prestigious performing arts school in New York City. For three years, Williams studied drama and speech under the noted actor John Houseman and others. The program at Julliard was demanding, covering voice, movement, and the development of character through the study of drama, from ancient to modern sources. His teachers discouraged his attempts at humor, which he channeled into weekend performances as a mime on the steps of the Metropolitan Museum of Art, earning up to $150 per day. In 1976, before completing his degree, he left Julliard to follow a girlfriend to San Francisco.

CHOOSING A CAREER

According to Williams, his choice of comedy as a career was inevitable: "Comedy is something I was meant to do, whether it's [some] kind of divine purpose. . .or not. I was meant to do this. I was not meant to sell insurance."

FIRST JOBS

Williams returned to San Francisco, enrolled in a comedy workshop, and began working in an ice cream parlor and as a bartender. One of the waitresses there was Valerie Velardi, a dancer who was working her way through school; she later became his first wife. With Velardi's help he worked on polishing his routines and began appearing in local comedy clubs. By the summer of 1976 they moved to Los Angeles, and Williams began doing stand-up improvisational routines in several comedy clubs. That led to appearances on a few television shows, including a new "Laugh-In," the "Richard Pryor Show," and "America 2-Night" with comedian Martin Mull. His fabled "big break" came in 1977, when Williams auditioned for and won the role of a space alien to appear in an episode of the television series "Happy Days." Viewer response to Williams's performance as Mork from Ork was so overwhelming that a new show was created.

CAREER HIGHLIGHTS

"Mork and Mindy," starring Williams and Pam Dawber, ran for four seasons, from 1978 to 1982. Depicting the surprising habits and startled reactions of a space alien trapped in Boulder, Colorado, the series was an instant hit. Many of the scenes featured Williams's improvisational style, and critics credited his wild and inventive physical and verbal comedy with the show's success.

Williams's comedic style has remained fairly consistent. According to Howard Storm, the director of "Mork and Mindy," "His special quality is his total freedom. It's as if there are no boundaries." This was especially true in his stage performances, which the critic Vincent Canby once described as "so intense that one feels that at any minute the creative process could reverse into a complete personality meltdown." Often frenetic, but also playful and inventive, his routines contain both improvisation and previously crafted material that he hones over time. In his improvisational routines, Williams is known for his lightening-quick reactions and his free-flowing associations. It has been said that he has a genius for voices, but he also has the ability to flesh out those voices

455

into full-fledged, individual creations, and these characters form the basis of his comedy. Although Williams makes his routines look easy, he describes it as hard work: "Inspiration is like drilling for oil. Sometimes I can think for hours and come up with nothing, and then in a few minutes it all comes in waves. Maybe you have to go through those hours of dead time, like a drill bit piercing the shale and old sediment, to get to it, the new stuff."

Yet while Williams was achieving great success in his television series and club appearances, other parts of his life were doing poorly. He appeared in a string of movies that achieved, at best, lukewarm reviews. His two mild successes from this time were *The World According to Garp* (1982) and *Moscow on the Hudson* (1984). In addition to his professional difficulties, his personal life was deteriorating. After the debut of "Mork and Mindy," Williams went through a well-publicized period of personal upheaval that included extramarital affairs and drug and alcohol abuse. He has attributed much of this to the temptations of Hollywood and the pressures of dealing with sudden, unaccustomed fame. In early 1983, Williams quit drinking and using drugs. He later said that he was inspired by several events: the upcoming birth of his first child, his desire to be a good father, and the death of his friend John Belushi by drug overdose only hours after they had snorted some cocaine together. Williams and his wife, Valerie, moved from Los Angeles, first to a 600-acre ranch in northern California and later to San Francisco.

More recently, Williams has had a string of movie successes. In his first, *Good Morning, Vietnam* (1987), Williams portrays Adrian Cronauer, a disk jockey on Armed Forces Radio during the Vietnam War who is credited with originating an early version of shock radio. Williams excelled in the part, according to many critics, because it gave him the chance to show onscreen the sort of unscripted comedy that he does best. His next movie, *Dead Poets Society* (1989), features Williams as John Keating, an original, iconoclastic, and inspiring teacher who returns to teach English at his alma mater, a strict private boys' boarding school. In *Awakenings* (1990), Williams plays the part of Dr. Oliver Sacks, a neurologist who finds a ward of patients who were victims of the sleeping sickness epidemic in the 1920s. They are effectively frozen—not moving, or seeing, or speaking—and Sacks treats them with the drug L-dopa to bring them briefly, but movingly, back to life. *The Fisher King* (1991) followed, in which Williams depicts a former professor of medieval history now homeless and delusional after a personal trauma. In *Hook* (1991), his most recent film, Williams is Peter Banning, a grown-up Peter Pan; the movie was directed by Steven Spielberg and features Dustin Hoffman as Captain Hook and Julia Roberts as Tinkerbell. Peter, now a mergers and acquisitions lawyer, is forced to return to Neverland for a final battle with Captain Hook, who has kidnapped his children. The success of these recent performances, many critics agree, derives from the depth and complexity Williams was able to develop by integrating the comedic skills he has honed for years in live shows and the dramatic skills he gained while studying at Juilliard.

MARRIAGE AND FAMILY

Williams's personal life has had a series of dramatic ups and downs, all well documented in the press. Williams married his first wife, Valerie Velardi, on June 4, 1978, shortly before the debut of "Mork and Mindy"; they have one son, Zachary, born in 1983. Their marital problems, along with Williams's drug and alcohol abuse, received a great deal of press attention. They have since divorced. Williams eventually became involved with Marsha Garces, a painter and sculptor who worked for a time as a nanny for Zachary Williams. Some press accounts have portrayed Garces as a home-wrecker, claiming that she and Williams became involved while she was still working for the family. He vehemently denies it, saying that they became involved a year after he and his first wife separated. Williams and Garces were married on April 30, 1989. They have two children: Zelda, born in 1989, and Cody, born in 1991.

At press time, Williams was scheduled to go to trial this summer in a $6 million lawsuit in which a former lover has charged him with negligent infliction of mental suffering and fraud, claiming that he gave her herpes without warning her about it. Williams has denied the charges and has countersued, accusing her of extortion and intentional infliction of emotional distress.

MAJOR INFLUENCES

Williams has often spoken of comedian Jonathan Winters as his idol. Even as a child, Williams would tape record Winters's performances, studying and imitating his crazy characterizations. Later, Williams was able to perform with Winters on the "Mork and Mindy" show.

TELEVISION PROGRAMS

"Mork and Mindy," 1978-82
"Robin Williams: An Evening at the Met," 1986
"A Carol Burnett Special: Carol, Carl, Whoopi and Robin," 1987
"ABC Presents a Royal Gala," 1988

MOVIES

Popeye, 1980
The World According to Garp, 1982
The Survivors, 1983
Moscow on the Hudson, 1984
The Best of Times, 1986

Club Paradise, 1986
Good Morning, Vietnam, 1987
The Adventures of Baron Munchausen, 1989
Dead Poets Society, 1989
Awakenings, 1990
Cadillac Man, 1990
The Fisher King, 1991
Hook, 1991
Toys, 1992

RECORDINGS

Reality. . .What a Concept, 1979
Throbbing Python of Love, 1979
A Night at the Met, 1987
Good Morning, Vietnam, 1988
Pecos Bill, 1988

HONORS AND AWARDS

Golden Apple Award (Hollywood Women's Press Club): 1978, for Male Discovery of the Year
Golden Globe Award: 1979, for Best Actor in "Mork and Mindy"; 1988, for Best Actor in *Good Morning, Vietnam*; 1991, for Best Actor in *The Fisher King*
Grammy Award: 1979, Best Comedy Recording for *Reality. . .What a Concept''*; 1987, Best Comedy Recording for *A Night at the Met*; 1988, Best Comedy Recording for *Good Morning, Vietnam*; 1988, Best Children's Recording for *Pecos Bill*
People's Choice Award: 1979, for Best Performer in a New Program in "Mork and Mindy"
Academy Award nominations: 1987, for Best Actor in *Good Morning, Vietnam*; 1989, for Best Actor in *Dead Poets Society*; 1991, for Best Actor in *The Fisher King*
Emmy Award: 1987, for Outstanding Individual Performance in "A Carol Burnett Special"; 1988, for Outstanding Individual Performance in "ABC Presents a Royal Gala"
Harvard Hasty Pudding Man of the Year: 1989

FURTHER READING

BOOKS
Who's Who in America, 1990-91

PERIODICALS
Current Biography Yearbook 1979
New York Times Biographical Service, Dec. 1978, p.1285; May 1989, p.495; Nov. 1990, p.1059

People, Sep. 13, 1982, p.92; Feb. 22, 1988, p.79
Reader's Digest, Apr. 1988, p.101
Redbook, Jan. 1991, p.14
Rolling Stone, Aug. 23, 1979, p.40; Sep. 6, 1982, p.19; Feb. 25, 1988, p.28
Time, Dec. 16, 1991, p.70

ADDRESS

P.O. Box 210-520
San Francisco, CA 94121

Oprah Winfrey 1954-
American Talk-Show Host, Actress, Producer

BIRTH

Oprah Gail Winfrey was born January 29, 1954, in Kosciusko, Mississippi, to Vernon Winfrey and Vernita Lee. She was to have been named *Orpah*, for the sister-in-law of Ruth in the Old Testament, but a reversal of letters on the birth record created a new spelling—and the now-famous name, Oprah. Winfrey's young, unmarried parents were unable to take care of her, and she spent the earliest years of her childhood on a rural farm with her paternal grandmother.

YOUTH

Everything about Winfrey's childhood seemed to point in the direction of her eventual career. She talked early and well, and remembers now that, as a young child, she amused herself on the isolated farm, playacting for an "audience" made up of pigs and chickens and a corncob doll. Chatty and bright, she learned to read before she turned three and was confident enough at about that same age to recite short speeches in church. Grandmother Hattie Mae was a loving and deeply religious woman, but also a strict guardian who never hesitated to scold or punish the rambunctious little girl who lived with her; stern discipline was her way of building character. Looking back, Oprah Winfrey credits her grandmother with giving her the strength and "sense of reasoning" that she has today.

After six years in rural Mississippi, Winfrey went to live with her mother in a Milwaukee housing project, but soon was uprooted again. This time she was sent to her father and his wife, Velma, in Nashville. The move gave her a more secure environment for one short and happy year, and she began to make a name for herself with recitations at church and social functions. But her mother, Vernita Lee, wanted her child to come home, and the reluctant father complied. Oprah settled into cramped and less than desirable quarters with her mother's growing family and then, sadly, other forces started to create havoc in her life. The overworked mother had little time to devote to her imaginative, strong-willed daughter. She became the victim of sexual abuse, over a number of years, at the hands of men she trusted. Her frightened silence and growing confusion eventually turned her into a serious discipline problem and led her to acts of defiance that very nearly sent her to a detention center. She lied, she stole from her mother's purse, she was destructive, and she ran away from home. One crisis followed another until, finally, when Oprah was fourteen, her desperate mother sent her back to her father's home in Nashville.

"When my father took me, it changed the course of my life," Winfrey admits, in telling of those rocky years. "He saved me. He simply knew what he wanted and expected. He would take nothing less." Vernon Winfrey, a barber and city councilman, quickly straightened out his wayward daughter with rigid supervision and a structure in her life that she had not experienced for years. He and Velma guided her, encouraged her interest in books, and demanded from her a continuing effort to reach what they felt was her enormous potential. Young Oprah met the challenge. She earned excellent grades in school, became active in drama and speaking circles, was elected president of the student council, and, at sixteen, won an Elks Club oratorical contest that guaranteed her a full college scholarship.

EDUCATION

Winfrey attended two different high schools before leaving Milwaukee. Her district school was Lincoln, a typical big-city, public institution in a poor neighborhood, where there was nothing to motivate a bright and high-spirited girl already ahead of her grade level. Interested teachers, recognizing her unusual abilities, secured a scholarship for her at Nicolet, an exclusive suburban school. Her grades there were superior, but she could not cope with her own poverty in surroundings of such wealth, and these were the unruly times when she was most out of control.

The good years began at East High School in Nashville. Winfrey was chosen one of the Outstanding Teenagers of America, participated in the 1970 White House Conference on Youth, and became involved in a number of school and community projects. After graduation, she enrolled at Tennessee State University, about seven miles from home, and majored in speech and drama. Winfrey was working at a local radio station as well as attending classes. To make her schedule even more hectic, she made public speaking appearances and entered beauty contests, winning both the Miss Black Nashville and the Miss Black Tennessee titles.

FIRST JOBS

A hefty speaking fee, said to be as much as $500, was Winfrey's first real paycheck, and that money convinced her that she would earn her living "being paid to talk." The unusual part of the story is that she was *twelve years old* at the time, visiting her father in Nashville and speaking before a large and spellbound audience.

As a senior in high school, Winfrey had a job reading newscasts for WVOL-Radio in Nashville. Then, in her sophomore year in college, she accepted a spot as co-anchorperson on WTVF-TV, Nashville's CBS affiliate. The offer was a tribute to her widely noted talent and poise, yet she knew that, as the first woman and the first black to appear on Nashville television news, she was a token. Nevertheless she was, by her own admission, "one *happy* token."

CAREER HIGHLIGHTS

Baltimore was the first stop for Winfrey after college graduation. She joined WJZ-TV as feature reporter and co-anchor, but differences soon arose over her emotional style of interviewing and over the producers' efforts to change her looks (and, at one point, even her name). Constantly upset by the ordeal, she turned to food for comfort and began her well-documented and ongoing struggle with her weight.

What seemed like a nightmare, though, turned into a dream when Winfrey was shifted to the station's morning show, "Baltimore Is Talking," as co-host with Richard Sher. She had found her niche. "This is what I was born to do," she said at the time. "This is like breathing."

Seven successful years on the Baltimore talk show led to the acceptance, in 1984, of an offer from WLS-TV in Chicago. There, Winfrey's unique talent for communicating with an audience quickly boosted what had been the poor ratings of "A.M. Chicago." She was in the same time slot as Phil Donahue's long-favored program on a competing station, but she took the ratings lead after only a few months. Donahue eventually moved his show east, but not, insists Winfrey, because of their rivalry in the Chicago television market; he wanted to be in New York with his wife, actress Marlo Thomas. "A.M. Chicago" became "The Oprah Winfrey Show" in 1985 and went into national syndication the following year. The show mirrors the appealing personality of its host, a woman who has been called candid, unspoiled, sassy, spontaneous, and fiercely loyal. To all this, she adds only, "I am truly blessed." She often speaks of how much she has enjoyed the hard work and discipline of building a career. It has been a process that has helped her, she maintains, to find—and be—herself.

In the flurry of all the television activity, Oprah Winfrey was cast as the proud, tough Sophie in the 1985 film, *The Color Purple,* and she received an Academy Award nomination for her moving performance. Winfrey also had a leading role in *Native Son* in 1986. In 1989, she appeared in a prime-time television special, *Just Between Friends,* with Gail King Bumpus, her own best friend from Baltimore days; that same year, she produced and acted in the ABC miniseries, *The Women of Brewster Place.*

Spring 1992 saw still another of Winfrey's many projects come to the television screen. She moved into prime-time with the first of a new series of celebrity interviews called *Oprah: Behind the Scenes.*

MARRIAGE AND FAMILY

Oprah Winfrey is single, but has a close friendship with businessman (and former basketball star) Stedman Graham, who has been her companion for the past few years. She lives in a luxurious condominium above Chicago's Lake Shore Drive, but her weekend and holiday retreat is a farm near Rolling Prairie, in northwestern Indiana.

HOBBIES AND OTHER INTERESTS

Winfrey's keen business sense has made it possible for her to put her considerable wealth to good use. She formed Harpo (Oprah spelled backward) Productions in 1986 to produce videos and films of social importance, and the company has continued to expand and to thrive. Winfrey is deeply involved in community projects, especially those that deal with young people, and generously gives her own time as well as her "forceful advice" in encouraging education and the development of personal goals. An avid reader from her earliest years, she recently was one of several celebrities taking part in the American Library Association's promotional program to encourage reading. Winfrey constantly stresses education as the way to a better life, and has established an important scholarship program at the all-black Morehouse College in Atlanta.

Dark memories of the sexual abuse Winfrey suffered as a child triggered another commitment last year. She and former Illinois Governor James Thompson drafted federal legislation to create a national registry of convicted child abusers and other criminal offenders. She is dedicated to stopping the violation of children and intends next to lobby for mandatory sentencing of child abusers. In a *People* magazine article in late 1991, she is quoted as saying "We have to demonstrate that we value our children enough to say that when you hurt a child, this is what happens to you. It is not negotiable."

Oprah Winfrey has interests other than social or academic issues. She does not deny her passion for jewels and beautiful clothes, or for the antiques which she has started to collect. Her annual income, reported to be $38 million, makes these pleasures easy to indulge.

HONORS AND AWARDS

Miss Black Nashville: 1971
Miss Black Tennessee: 1971
Academy Award nomination: 1986, for *The Color Purple*
Golden Globe Award: 1986, for *The Color Purple*

Woman of Achievement award (National Organization for Women): 1986
One of the Ten Most Admired Women *(Playgirl* magazine): 1986
Emmy Awards: 1987, for Best Daytime Talk Show Host, Best Talk Show
Broadcaster of the Year (International Radio and Television Society): 1988
Image Awards (NAACP): 1990

FURTHER READING

BOOKS

Encyclopedia Britannica Book of the Year, 1988
King, Norman. *Everybody Loves Oprah!,* 1987
Patterson, Lillie, and Cornelia H. Wright. *Oprah Winfrey: Talk Show Host and Actress,* 1990

PERIODICALS

Current Biography Yearbook 1987
Contemporary Newsmakers 86
People, Dec. 2, 1991, p.69

ADDRESS

Harpo Productions
P.O. Box 909715
Chicago, IL 60690

Kristi Yamaguchi 1972-
American Figure Skater
Olympic Gold Medalist

BIRTH

Kristi Tsuya Yamaguchi, the first American woman to win a gold
medal in Olympic figure skating in 16 years, was born July 12,
1972, in Fremont, California. Her mother, Carole, is a medical
secretary and her father, Jim, is a dentist. Kristi has an older sister,
Lori, and a younger brother, Brett.

YOUTH

Kristi's legs were turned in at birth. When she was only two weeks
old, she had to wear casts to correct the problem. The casts were
changed every two weeks until her first birthday. From the ages

of one to four, she wore corrective shoes connected with a bar. She began to skate at six, to continue the process to improve her legs as she grew. At the age of eight, she was competing. By the time she was nine, her mother was driving her to practice at four in the morning, and Kristi skated five hours before going to school.

EARLY MEMORIES

Kristi never seemed to mind the sacrifices demanded by her sport. Of her 4 A.M. to 9 A.M. practice schedule, she said: "It's been an equal trade-off because of what I've gotten back from skating." She used to sleep with a little Dorothy Hamill doll, modelled on the skating star who won the gold medal for the U.S. sixteen years before Kristi.

EDUCATION

Yamaguchi graduated from Mission San Jose High School in 1989 with a grade point average of 3.7. "Her life was skating, skating, skating. I couldn't get over how hard she worked," said Susie Anderson, her high school counselor.

CAREER HIGHLIGHTS

Kristi's remarkable talent and energy motivated her to compete as both a pairs and a singles skater for several years. In 1983, she began to skate in pairs competitions with Rudi Galindo, a young man from San Jose, California. The two formed a very successful skating partnership, winning the 1988 U.S. Junior Championships and the 1989 World Championships. Kristi also won the singles title at the 1989 World Championships, becoming the first woman in 35 years to win both a singles and a pairs title in World competition. In the 1989 National Figure Skating Championships, Yamaguchi placed second after Jill Trenary.

In 1989, Yamaguchi's singles coach, Christy Kjarsgaard Ness, who had been coaching her in California since 1981, married and moved to Edmonton, in Alberta, Canada. In the summer of that year, Kristi moved to Edmonton to live with the Nesses and continue her coaching. Galindo moved with her so that the two could continue to practice as a pairs team.

Yamaguchi's young life has been touched by change and sometimes painful loss. Her pairs coach, Jim Hulick, died of cancer in December 1989. Hulick had been an important part of her life and work with Galindo, and despite the efforts of their new coach, the duo had trouble regaining their former spark.

At the World Championships in 1990, Yamaguchi and Galindo placed fifth, and Kristi placed fourth in the singles competition. It seemed time to make a change. So Yamaguchi decided to concentrate solely on her future as a singles skater. "I knew that to improve in one or the other, I had to drop one, and I figured it would be very tough to break into the top three in pairs. Everyone seemed to think dropping pairs was the best decision to make...except Rudi." Later, Galindo, too, decided to compete in singles competition.

Kristi began a weight-training program, adding muscle and strength to her 5-foot, 90-pound body. Known early in her career for her jumping ability, she now worked with a choreographer to add grace of movement to her routines. In August 1990, she beat Jill Trenary at the Goodwill Games, and in October of that year beat Japanese star Midori Ito at the Skate America competition. Other changes in the rules of the International Skating Union were also in her favor. For years, figure skaters were required to do "school figures," tracing figure eights and other shapes with their skates in the ice. But as of 1988, the school figures were eliminated, and Yamaguchi, who had never scored well on them, was able to concentrate on her strengths in competition: her ability as a free-style skater.

In 1991, with defending U.S. and World Champ Jill Trenary out with an injury, Kristi was favored to win the U.S. Championships. But Tonya Harding of Oregon stunned the skating world by becoming the first American woman to land one of the most difficult jumps in skating: the triple Axel. The 3½-revolution jump is named after Axel Paulsen, a Norwegian skater, and is the only jump a skater tries while moving forward. Kristi is a skilled and capable skater, able to land all the other triple jumps: the lutz, the Salchow, the toe loop, and the flip. But the Axel continued to elude her. On the strength of her program, Harding won the 1991 U.S. Championship, with Yamaguchi finishing second. At the World Championships in March 1991, Kristi skated beautifully and placed first.

But the triple Axel was also the most powerful weapon in the arsenal of Yamaguchi's chief international competition, Midori Ito of Japan. The winner of the 1989 World title and the top free-stylist in the 1990 World Championships, Ito was the first woman skater ever to complete the triple Axel in competition. Ito, 4-foot 7-inches and stocky, is known as one of the "athletes" of women's skating, and with Tonya Harding represents the acrobatic, physical style that threatens to dominate women's skating. Their style is in vivid contrast with that of Yamaguchi and American teammate Nancy Kerrigan, and much debate has centered on how the aggressive, new style of Ito and Harding has changed competition. "The jumps were never supposed to mean so much," said Carol Heiss, former Olympic champion. "You need it all: the lightness and the airiness; the music, the personality. You need the caressing of the ice." The stage was set for the 1992 Olympics in Albertville, France, where Ito was slightly favored to win the gold.

Ito had beaten Yamaguchi in six of their eight competitive meetings; Yamaguchi had won two out of the last three contests. Harding was also considered a top competitor, and Nancy Kerrigan, whose grace on the ice reminded many of the days before triple jumps had become the measure of excellence in the sport, was a threat, too.

Kristi attended the opening ceremonies, which took place 11 days before the skating competition. So that she could focus and avoid the public scrutiny that so often goes with Olympic competition, Yamaguchi spent three days in Megeve, a half hour from Albertville, to complete her preparation, and in the opinion of her coach, she achieved her goal. "She skated beautifully in Megeve," said Ness, "a step above. I sat her down and said, 'That's all. You don't have to try to do anything more than what you just did.'"

Ito looked terrific, too, when she arrived in Albertville. But she appeared to tense up prior to the opening of competition. The short competition took place on February 19, 1992. But if Yamaguchi was feeling under pressure, it certainly didn't show, as she skated to first place with a technically and artistically flawless program. Nancy Kerrigan skated beautifully, too, earning second place. Harding, looking nervous and unprepared, fell trying to land her triple Axel, and ended up sixth. Ito skated uncertainly, falling on a triple Lutz, which earned her a fourth

place position going into the final phase of the competition. She had a great deal of pressure on her, because she felt that she represented the hopes of the Japanese people to bring home the first gold medal in women's skating in 20 years. After her lackluster performance in the short program, she apologized to her people via television.

Yamaguchi received a last-minute visitor before her final performance in Olympic competition: Dorothy Hamill. "She wanted to wish me luck," Yamaguchi said. "Dorothy is part of the reason I'm in the sport, and it was a real inspiration to talk to her. She reminded me how hard I've worked for this and told me to

469

go out and have a good time." That's exactly what she did. Her routine included a group of difficult jumps, but what impressed judges and spectators alike was her grace and poise. Her music was *Malaguena*, and its sweet and rhythmic phrases provided a backdrop for a gold medal-winning performance and Yamaguchi's greatest success on ice. Her routine included a fall on a triple loop, a jump that is normally within her reach. It was a night that found all the major contenders down on the ice. Kerrigan, too, had trouble with three of her triple jumps and ended in third place. Harding also fell several times and ended up in fourth place. Ito made something of a comeback, skating well enough, despite a fall, to earn a silver medal.

Yamaguchi was characteristically low-key in victory. "I'm still a little surprised everything has happened so fast," she said. "I've dreamed about this since I was a little girl and I first put on a pair of skates. To think about how far I've come, it's all still sinking in."

Yamaguchi continued her hold on first-place in the world of women's skating, winning the World Championships in March of 1992. She is the first woman skating for the U.S. to win two world championships in a row since Peggy Fleming in 1966. What lies ahead for her now remains to be seen. There is speculation that she may turn professional, and the International Skating Union is planning to vote on allowing pros to compete in the next Winter Olympics, scheduled to take place in Lillehammer, Norway, in 1994.

Why Yamaguchi has not received the flood of endorsements for products that usually comes with a gold medal is being debated in the press. Some suggest that her lack of endorsements stems from her Japanese heritage in a country where the mood is currently anti-Japanese, due to economic problems between Japan and the U.S. But of her strength and contribution to the sport, the writer E.M. Swift said, "God never gave anyone everything, but Yamaguchi, without the triple Axel, is as close to a complete package as women's skating has ever seen."

MAJOR INFLUENCES

Yamaguchi names her parents as her greatest influence. Their support of her through the years of training and competition has been constant, and they have helped her to keep her down-to-earth approach to skating and to life.

MARRIAGE AND FAMILY

Kristi, who is unmarried, takes pride in her parents and in her Japanese heritage, which includes painful memories for the family. Even though the families of both of her parents had lived in California since the nineteenth century, Carole and Jim grew up in internment camps. The

U.S. government forced more than 120,000 Americans of Japanese descent to move to these camps after the U.S. entered World War II in 1941, during which the U.S. was at war with Germany, Japan, and Italy. The government feared that Japanese-Americans would aid Japan during the war, and so kept them on reservations, restricting their movements until the war ended. Even though his family was interned, Kristi's maternal grandfather, George Doi, served the U.S. bravely in Europe during the war. The families of her mother and father lost their California homes and their livelihoods when they moved, but neither of the Yamaguchis have any bitterness about what happened to them. Kristi was particularly close to her grandfather Doi, who died in 1989. "My grandfather didn't talk much about World War II, but he let me know how proud he was to see me make it as an Asian-American representing the United States," she said.

HONORS AND AWARDS

U.S. Skating Championships: 1991, Second Place
World Figure Skating Championships: 1991, 1992, First Place
Olympic Women's Figure Skating: 1992, Gold Medal

FURTHER READING

PERIODICALS

Business Week, Mar. 9, 1992, p.40
Chicago Tribune, Feb. 8, 1990, p.C4; Feb. 15, 1991, p.C1; Feb. 7, 1992, p.C3
Minneapolis Star and Tribune, Feb. 10, 1991, p.C10
The National, Feb. 14, 1991, p.G10
New York Times, Feb. 20, 1992, p.B7; Feb. 22, 1992, p.33
Newsweek, Feb. 10, 1992, p.46
People, Mar. 20, 1989, p.71
Sports Illustrated, Mar. 2, 1992, p.19
Washington Post, Feb. 8, 1990, p.E11

ADDRESS

IMG
1 St. Claire Ave.
Suite 700
Toronto, Ontario M4T 2V7
Canada

Boris Yeltsin   1931-
Russian Federation President
Leader of the Commonwealth of
Independent States

BIRTH

Boris Nikolayevich Yeltsin was born February 1, 1931, in the Ural
Mountains village of Butka to Nikolai Ignatievich and Klavdia
Vasilieva (Starygin) Yeltsin. The eldest of three children, he has
a brother, Mikhail, and a sister, Valya. Yeltsin's birthplace lies in
a farming area of the Russian Federation's Sverdlovsk Region, 875
miles east of Moscow. The name Sverdlovsk, in use since 1924,
now has been changed back officially to the original name,
Yekaterinburg.

YOUTH

Yeltsin's childhood, he says, was "a fairly joyless time. We had only one aim in life—to survive." At first, the family lived on a collective farm (a group unit), suffering through bad harvests and a frightening environment where gangs of outlaws roamed the countryside. The father later worked on a construction site, and family quarters were part of a large, bleak communal hut that had no conveniences and no privacy. "Winter was worst of all," Yeltsin recalls. "There was nowhere to hide from the cold. . . .We would huddle up to the nanny goat to keep warm. We children survived on her milk."

Young Boris did well in school, although his behavior was often less than praiseworthy. He admits to being "a bit of a hooligan"—a characterization that has followed him into his political life. He tells in his autobiography, *Against the Grain*, of being the mischief-maker who persuaded his entire fifth-grade class to jump out a first-floor window, just to annoy an unpopular teacher. The stunt almost backfired when the teacher punished the class with failing grades. Yeltsin, however, appealed to the headmaster, who allowed the students to be tested and graded on their subject matter and who marked them off only on bad behavior. Another brazen act for which Yeltsin is well remembered is the one when, at his primary school graduation, he dared to publicly expose the cruelty of a teacher who had humiliated her students and abused her authority by making them clean her house and feed her pig. He nearly was denied permission to go on to secondary school, but his appeal for a hearing was granted and he won back his diploma—and caused the teacher to be fired.

Yeltsin paints a picture of teen years filled with foolish adventure. There were neighborhood free-for-alls, with up to one hundred boys pummeling one another with sticks and fists—and there was the dangerous game, too, of leaping across floating logs in the swollen river. In Boris Yeltsin, the love of risk-taking remains today one of his most dominant personality traits.

Sports came into young Yeltsin's life at about the time he was "causing nightmares" for his parents. He tried skiing, wrestling, boxing and, above all, volleyball, which became his passion. He would eventually compete on a national level during his university years. Because he also coached volleyball, only late evening hours were left for studying, but, he says, "I had schooled myself to do without much sleep and I have managed to keep up that regimen ever since, sleeping for no more than three-and-a half hours at night."

EARLY MEMORIES

Of all his youthful escapades, the story of how Yeltsin lost the thumb and index finger of his left hand is the most appalling. The Second World War had begun, and he and his friends, too young to fight, stole some grenades from a local church that was being used as an ammunition dump. They wanted to see what was inside the little hand missiles and carried them to a forest some miles from town. "I volunteered to take the grenades apart," Yeltsin remembers. "I told the other boys to take cover. . .then I put a grenade on a stone, knelt down, and hit it with a hammer. I didn't realize I had to remove the fuse. There was an explosion, and two of my fingers were mangled." Boris's friends took him back to town for treatment, but surgeons later had to amputate when gangrene set in.

Yeltsin learned to compensate so well that he was never hindered by the loss of his fingers during the years he excelled at volleyball.

EDUCATION

Yeltsin attended primary school in his home district and completed his secondary education at the Pushkin School of Sverdlovsk. When he informed his family that he wanted to be a civil engineer, his grandfather insisted that he prove his interest in this type of career by spending the summer before college building a log *banya* (sauna) without help. He completed the chore when he should have been studying for entrance exams. Always a good student, though, he passed his tests successfully and enrolled at the Urals Polytechnic Institute in Sverdlovsk. He graduated in 1955 with a degree in civil engineering.

CHOOSING A CAREER

As a young boy, Yeltsin thought of becoming a ship builder, but the closer he drew to making a career decision the more interested he became in civil engineering. It was a natural choice, since his father worked in the construction business and he, too, had some experience as a building laborer. Politics had never been part of his dreams, although a wise observer might have made such a prediction, given the boy's scrappy style and supreme self-confidence.

Yeltsin worked in the construction industry for several years after becoming an engineer. He learned all the basic trades on the job before moving up to a supervisory level and, eventually, to the post of chief engineer of a large industrial complex in Sverdlovsk.

CAREER HIGHLIGHTS

Boris Yeltsin was thirty years old before he joined the Communist Party—a late move for a man who would rise so dramatically through the ranks. He flourished in public life, forging a reputation as an energetic reformer and becoming, in 1976, first secretary of the Sverdlovsk District Central Committee. He was then, and still is, described as a highly charged leader, direct and rough, but always willing to listen to other opinions.

In 1985, Mikhail Gorbachev, then general secretary of the Politburo (committee of party members in control of government), summoned Yeltsin to Moscow. Gorbachev had already started to introduce sweeping reforms in the Soviet Union and had opened discussions aimed at world peace. Yeltsin became Moscow party leader, but he was fired two years later for criticizing both the Politburo and Gorbachev's style of leadership. A profile of Yeltsin in *Time* tells of how he "nursed himself back to...political health and bided his time."

Always popular with the people, Yeltsin made a stirring comeback in 1989, winning election to the Supreme Soviet (the national parliament). In 1990, he became chairman of the Russian Republic, the largest of the fifteen republics that made up the U.S.S.R., and did the unthinkable—he left the Communist Party. Yeltsin won a landslide victory that same year in an open election, becoming president of the Russian Federation. Gorbachev, by this time, had proposed a treaty that would establish cooperation between the central government and the individual republics. Yeltsin and Gorbachev "buried the hatchet."

A big, gruff, bear of a man—obstinate, combative, and often dismissed as a buffoon—Yeltsin rose to international prominence and new respect in August 1991, when party hard-liners staged what turned out to be a failed coup and placed Gorbachev and his family under house arrest.

Yeltsin defied the coup leaders, the Red Army, and the feared KGB (secret police). He climbed atop a tank in front of the Russian Parliament building and, backed by thousands of demonstrators, persuaded the military force to turn back and recognize the will of the people. He proved then, in those crucial four days of upheaval, his "credit of trust" with the Russian masses. "The man who had been one of Gorbachev's most strident critics," wrote the international editor of Denver's *Rocky Mountain News*, "became his most visible supporter during the coup—and [Gorbachev] will be forever in his debt."

A time of transition and upheaval followed the coup. In late 1991, several republics seceded from the Soviet Union. Then Yeltsin, along with the leaders of the Soviet republics Ukraine and Byelorussia, announced the formation of the Commonwealth of Independent States. As the year came to an end, Gorbachev officially resigned. The Soviet Union, an oppressive regime that terrorized its own people for decades and contributed to world-wide political polarization and massive escalation of military expenditures during the Cold War, had ceased to exist. As *Time* described it, "The event is one of the turning points of world history, proclaiming the end of a totalitarianism that has destroyed so much of the twentieth century."

As the leader of the new commonwealth, Yeltsin has faced a host of political, economic, and social problems. There is an ongoing constitutional crisis, as the various republics decide how to organize their new government. One particular area of concern is the role to be played by Russia, the largest and most powerful of the republics of the former Soviet Union. For many outsiders, the control of the military, and particularly its nuclear capability, has remained a serious issue. The economic system is in disarray, and attempts to shift from a planned, centrally controlled economy to a free-market private enterprise system have, to date, resulted in high prices and lost jobs. Food shortages were anticipated during the winter of 1991-92, although they turned out to be less severe than many feared. Fuel, for transportation, industry, and home use, was also in short supply, as were all basic medical goods.

Many observers have expressed doubt about Yeltsin's ability to fill the role of leader in the new post-Soviet commonwealth of republics. His power base has been shaky, and he faces critics within the government, the military, and opposition groups, many of whom favor a return to authoritarian rule. In addition, charges of excessive drinking have followed him for years, and his rough-edged manners and reckless nature have made many leaders wary of the powers he has amassed. His legion of defenders argue that such concerns are unfounded, citing his resourcefulness, courage, and political daring. Yeltsin may have built his career by being unconventional, but it is he who oversaw the destruction of the Soviet empire and who peacefully brought about the establishment of the Commonwealth of Independent States. All the world is watching as Yeltsin stands at the center of a new chapter in Russian history.

MEMORABLE EXPERIENCES

Yeltsin often speaks about the summer during his university years when he made a journey alone around the Soviet Republic with no money in his pocket. "I traveled and observed during the three summer months," he recalls. "To have a checkbook while traveling is one thing. It is quite another to own only a student card." Yeltsin slept in parks or in sheds with homeless people and traveled on the roofs of railroad cars. He says that, during that trip, he learned things about his country and its people that he will never forget.

MARRIAGE AND FAMILY

Yeltsin has been married since 1955 to Anastasia Girina of Russia's Orenburg province. Naya, as she has been called since girlhood, was Yeltsin's fellow student at Urals Polytechnic. Until they moved to Moscow in 1985, she was chief engineer at Sverdlovsk's Institute of Waterways, where she had worked for twenty-nine years.

The Yeltsins have two daughters. Lena, born in 1957, is married to Valery Okulov, an aircraft navigator, and they are the parents of daughters Katya and Mashenka. Tanya, younger than her sister by two years, is the wife of Lyosha Dyachenko and the mother of another Boris, named for his grandfather. Tanya and her family share a Moscow apartment with the Yeltsins.

HOBBIES AND OTHER INTERESTS

Boris Yeltsin is said to be a workaholic. When asked, though, about what he does with his spare time, he insists that he enjoys vacations with his family and with old university friends. He is known to spend many hours reading and to play weekly games of tennis. He says that he attends the theater often, too—when he must, as an official duty.

WRITINGS

Against the Grain: An Autobiography, 1990 (translated by Michael Glenny)

FURTHER READING

BOOKS

Morrison, John. *Boris Yeltsin: From Bolshevik to Democrat,* 1991

Solovyov, Vladimir, and Elena Klepikova. *Boris Yeltsin: A Political Biography,* 1992 (in English)

Yeltsin, Boris. *Against the Grain: An Autobiography,* 1990 (in English; translated by Michael Glenny)

PERIODICALS

Current Biography Yearbook 1989
Los Angeles Times, Dec. 21, 1991, p.A1
Newsweek, June 11, 1990, p.20; Dec. 30, 1991, p.18; Jan. 6, 1992, p.12
Time, Mar. 25, 1991, p.26; Sept. 2, 1991, pp.18, 24, 33, and 54

ADDRESS

The Kremlin
Moscow
Russian Federation (no ZIP code needed)

Photo and Illustration Credits

Paula Abdul/Photo: Camera Press/Globe Photos.

Andre Agassi/Photos: Dave Chancellor/Alpha/Globe Photos; Erma/ Camera Press/Globe Photos

Kirstie Alley/Photo: AP/Wide World Photos.

Roseanne Arnold/Photos: Edie Baskin/ABC.

Isaac Asimov/Photo: Globe Photos.

Charles Barkley/Photo: AP/Wide World Photos.

Judy Blume/Photo: George Cooper. Cover: Jacket art by Ray Cruz. From DEENIE by Judy Blume. Copyright © 1973 by Judy Blume. Reproduced by permission of Bradbury Press, an Affiliate of Macmillan, Inc.

Berke Breathed/Photo: Copyright © Jody Boyman. Cartoon: From BLOOM COUNTY by Berke Breathed. Copyright © Washington Post Writers Group. Reprinted with permission.

Garth Brooks/Photo: Beverly Parker.

Barbara Bush/Photos: Carol T. Powers/The White House.

George Bush/Photos: David Valdez/The White House

Fidel Castro/Photo: AP/Wide World Photos.

Bill Clinton/Photo: Diane Weiss/*The Detroit News.*

Diana, Princess of Wales/Photos: Patrick DeMarchelier/Camera Press/Globe Photos; Camera Press/Globe Photos.

Shannen Doherty/Photos: Timothy White, Andrew Semel.

David Duke/Photos: AP/Wide World Photos.

Gloria Estefan/Photo: J. Herbert/Camera Press/Globe Photos.

Mikhail Gorbachev/Photos: Tom Stoddart/Globe Photos; U.N. Photo 172529 S.Lwin/Globe Photos.

Steffi Graf/Photos: Erma/Camera Press/Globe Photos; Camera Press/ Globe Photos.

Wayne Gretzky/Photos: Copyright © Photography Ink.

Matt Groening/Photo: Copyright © 1990 Fox Broadcasting Company. Cartoon: The Simpsons TM & Copyright © 1991 Twentieth Century Fox Film Corporation. Used with permission.

Alex Haley/Photo: Dwight Carter for *Essence* magazine. Copyright © 1991.

Hammer/Photo: Lori Stoll/1990. Courtesy of Capitol Records/Globe Photos.

Stephen Hawking/Photo: Stephen Shames.

Hulk Hogan/Photo: Steve Taylor. Copyright © 1990 TitanSports, Inc.

Saddam Hussein/Photo: AP/Wide World Photos.

Mae Jemison/Photo: NASA.

Peter Jennings/Photo: Eddie Adams/ABC.

John Paul II/Photo: AP/Wide World Photos.

Magic Johnson/Photo: AP/Wide World Photos.

Michael Jordan/Photo: Nathaniel Butler. Courtesy of NBA Photos.

Jackie Joyner-Kersee/Photo: AP/Wide World Photos.

Spike Lee/Photo: *Ann Arbor News.*

Mario Lemieux/Photo: Denny Cavanaugh/Pittsburgh Penguins.

Madeleine L'Engle/Photo: Copyright © James Phillips 1989. Cover: Jacket illustration copyright © 1979 by Leo & Diane Dillon from A WRINKLE IN TIME by Madeleine L'Engle, published by Farrar, Straus & Giroux. All rights reserved.

Jay Leno/Photo: NBC Photo.

Yo-Yo Ma/Photo: Bill King.

Nelson Mandela/Photos: Jan Kopec/Camera Press/Globe Photos.

Wynton Marsalis/Photos: Ed Hille. Copyright © 1988.

Thurgood Marshall/Photo: National Geographic Society.

Ann M. Martin/Cover: Copyright © Ann M. Martin. All rights reserved. Reprinted with permission of Scholastic, Inc.

Emily Arnold McCully/Portrait: Emily Arnold McCully. Illustration: Emily Arnold McCully from PICNIC by Emily Arnold McCully. Copyright © 1984 by Emily Arnold McCully. Reprinted with permission of Harper-Collins Publishers.

Sandra Day O'Connor/Photo: Copyright ©, National Geographic Society, courtesy, Supreme Court Historical Society.

Rosa Parks/Photo: AP/Wide World Photos.

Jane Pauley/Photo: NBC Photo.

Luke Perry/Photo: Michael Grecco.

Jason Priestley: Photos: Timothy White; *Vancouver Sun* photo by Mark Van Manen.

Yitzhak Rabin/Photos: A. Galmi/Camera Press/Globe Photos.

Sally Ride/Photos: Wide World Photos/AP.

Pete Rose/Photo: Wide World Photos/AP.

H. Norman Schwarzkopf/Photo: Wide World Photos/AP.

Jerry Seinfeld/Photo: NBC Photo.

Dr. Seuss/Photo: Aaron Rapoport/Onyx 1986. Cover: Copyright © 1986 by San Diego Museum of Art. Published by Random House, Inc.

Clarence Thomas/Photo: Wide World Photos/AP.

Cynthia Voigt/Photo: Walter Voigt. Cover: Courtesy Macmillan Publishing Co.

Bill Watterson/Photo: C.H. Pete Copeland/Plain Dealer. Cartoon: CALVIN AND HOBBES. Copyright © 1988 Universal Press Syndicate. Reprinted with permission. All rights reserved.

Robin Williams/Photo: Reproduced by Special Permission of *Playboy* magazine. Copyright © 1991 by *Playboy*. Photo by Kim Mizuno.

Oprah Winfrey/Photos: Ron Slenzak and Paul Natkin. Copyright © 1991 Harpo/King World. All rights reserved.

Kristi Yamaguchi/Photos: *Detroit Free Press* photo by John Stano. Copyright © 1992; Heinz Kluetmeir/*Sports Illustrated*.

Boris Yeltsin/Photos: Vario Press/Camera Press/Globe Photos; Photograph copyright © V. Kochetov.

Name Index

Listed below are the names of all individuals profiled in *Biography Today*, followed by the date of the annual cumulation, and the individual issue, in which they appear.

General Index

This index includes subjects, occupations, organizations, and ethnic and minority origins that pertain to individuals profiled in *Biography Today*. The name is followed by the date of the annual cumulation, and the individual issue, in which each appears.

Places of Birth Index

The following index lists the places of birth for the individuals profiled in *Biography Today*. Places of birth are entered under U.S. state and city or by country. The name is followed by the date of the annual cumulation, and the individual issue, in which each appears.

Birthday Index

January

2 Asimov, Isaac
8 Hawking, Stephen W.
25 Alley, Kirstie
28 Gretzky, Wayne
29 Winfrey, Oprah
31 Ryan, Nolan

February

1 Yeltsin, Boris
4 Parks, Rosa
7 Brooks, Garth
12 Blume, Judy
15 Groening, Matt
17 Jordan, Michael
20 Barkley, Charles
24 Jobs, Steven
25 Voigt, Cynthia

March

1 Rabin, Yitzhak
2 Gorbachev, Mikhail
Seuss, Dr.
3 Joyner-Kersee, Jackie
18 Queen Latifah
20 Lee, Spike
25 Steinem, Gloria
26 O'Connor, Sandra Day
30 Hammer

April

5 Powell, Colin
12 Doherty, Shannen
14 Rose, Pete
28 Baker, James A.
Hussein, Saddam
Leno, Jay
29 Agassi, Andre
Seinfeld, Jerry

May

18 John Paul II
26 Ride, Sally

June

8 Bush, Barbara
12 Bush, George
14 Graf, Steffi
16 McClintock, Barbara
18 Van Allsburg, Chris
19 Abdul, Paula
21 Breathed, Berke
23 Thomas, Clarence
27 Perot, H. Ross

July

1 Diana, Princess of Wales
Duke, David
McCully, Emily Arnold
2 Marshall, Thurgood
5 Watterson, Bill
12 Cosby, Bill
Yamaguchi, Kristi
18 Mandela, Nelson
21 Williams, Robin
29 Dole, Elizabeth Hanford
Jennings, Peter

August

11 Haley, Alex
Hogan, Hulk
12 Martin, Ann M.
13 Castro, Fidel
14 Johnson, Magic
19 Clinton, Bill
22 Schwarzkopf, H. Norman
23 Novello, Antonia
28 Priestley, Jason

September

1 Estefan, Gloria
25 Pippen, Scottie
27 Handford, Martin

October

5 Lemieux, Mario
7 Ma, Yo-Yo
11 Perry, Luke
15 Iacocca, Lee A.
17 Jemison, Mae
18 Marsalis, Wynton
27 Anderson, Terry
31 Pauley, Jane

November

3 Arnold, Roseanne
29 L'Engle, Madeleine
30 Jackson, Bo

December

7 Bird, Larry

People to Appear in Future Issues

Actors
Trini Alvarado
Richard Dean
  Anderson
Dan Aykroyd
Valerie Bertinelli
Mayim Bialik
Lisa Bonet
Matthew Broderick
Candice Cameron
Kirk Cameron
Chevy Chase
Cher
Glenn Close
Kevin Costner
Tom Cruise
Macaulay Culkin
Jamie Lee Curtis
Ted Danson
Tommy Davidson
Geena Davis
Matt Dillon
Michael Douglas
Richard Dreyfus
Harrison Ford
Jody Foster
Michael J. Fox
Richard Gere
Sara Gilbert
Tracey Gold
Whoopi Goldberg
Melanie Griffith
Jasmine Guy
Tom Hanks
Mark Harmon
Melissa Joan Hart
Michael Keaton
Val Kilmer
Angela Lansbury
Richard Lewis
Christopher Lloyd
Shelley Long
Marlee Matlin
Bette Midler
Alyssa Milano
Demi Moore
Rick Moranis
Eddie Murphy
Bill Murray
Leonard Nimoy

Ashley Olsen
Mary Kate Olsen
Sean Penn
River Phoenix
Phylicia Rashad
Keanu Reeves
Julia Roberts
Winona Ryder
Bob Saget
Susan Sarandon
Fred Savage
Arnold Schwarzenegger
William Shatner
Christian Slater
Will Smith
Sylvester Stallone
Jimmy Smits
John Travolta
Kathleen Turner
Denzel Washington
Damon Wayans
Keenan Ivory Wayans
Bruce Willis
B.D. Wong

Artists
Mitsumasa Anno
Graeme Base
Maya Ying Lin

Astronauts
Neil Armstrong

Authors
Jean M. Auel
Avi
Lynn Banks
John Christopher
Arthur C. Clarke
Beverly Cleary
John Colville
Robert Cormier
Roald Dahl (obit.)
Paula Danziger
Paula Fox
Jamie Gilson
Rosa Guy
Nat Hentoff
James Herriot
S.E. Hinton
Stephen King
Norma Klein

E.L. Konigsburg
Lois Lowry
David Macaulay
Stephen Manes
Norma Fox Mazer
Anne McCaffrey
Gloria D. Miklowitz
Toni Morrison
Walter Dean Myers
Phyllis Reynolds Naylor
Joan Lowery Nixon
Marsha Norman
Robert O'Brien
Francine Pascal
Gary Paulsen
Christopher Pike
Daniel Pinkwater
Anne Rice
Louis Sachar
Carl Sagan
John Saul
J.D. Salinger
Maurice Sendak
Shel Silverstein
R.L. Stine
Amy Tan
Alice Walker
Jane Yolen
Roger Zelazny
Paul Zindel

Business
Minoru Arakawa
Michael Eisner
William Ford, Jr.
William Gates
Anita Roddick
Donald Trump
Ted Turner

Cartoonists
Lynda Barry
Roz Chast
Jim Davis
Greg Evans
Cathy Guisewite
Nicole Hollander
Gary Larson
Charles Schulz
Garry Trudeau

Comedians
Tim Allen
Dan Aykroyd
Steve Martin
Eddie Murphy
Bill Murray

Dancers
Debbie Allen
Mikhail Baryshnikov
Suzanne Farrell
Gregory Hines
Gelsey Kirkland
Darci Anne Kistler
Rudolf Nureyev
Twyla Tharp
Tommy Tune

Directors/Producers
Woody Allen
Steven Bochco
Ken Burns
Francis Ford Coppola
John Hughes
George Lucas
Penny Marshall
Leonard Nimoy
Rob Reiner
Steven Spielberg

**Environmentalists/
Animal Rights**
Marjory Stoneman
  Douglas
Kathryn Fuller
Lois Gibbs
Wangari Maathai
Linda Maraniss
Ingrid Newkirk
Pat Potter

Journalists
Ed Bradley
Tom Brokaw
Dan Rather
Diane Sawyer
Nina Totenberg
Mike Wallace
Bob Woodward

Musicians
Another Bad Creation
Joshua Bell
George Benson

Black Box
Boyz II Men
James Brown
C & C Music Factory
Mariah Carey
Ray Charles
Kurt Cobain
Natalie Cole
Cowboy Junkies
Def Leppard
Gerardo
Guns N' Roses
Whitney Houston
Ice Cube
Ice-T
Janet Jackson
Jermaine Jackson
Michael Jackson
Kitaro
k.d. laing
Andrew Lloyd Webber
Courtney Love
Madonna
Barbara Mandrell
Marky Mark
Branford Marsalis
Paul McCartney
Bette Midler
Midori
New Kids on the Block
N.W.A.
Oakridge Boys
Sinead O'Connor
Teddy Pendergrass
Itzhak Perlman
Prince
Public Enemy
Raffi
Bonnie Raitt
Red Hot Chili Peppers
Lou Reed
R.E.M.
Kenny Rogers
Run-D.M.C.
Carly Simon
Paul Simon
Michelle Shocked
Sister Souljah
Will Smith
Sting
TLC
Randy Travis
2 Live Crew
Vanilla Ice
Stevie Wonder

**Politics/
World Leaders**
Lamar Alexander
Corazon Aquino
Yasir Arafat
Benazir Bhutto
Pat Buchanan
Jimmy Carter
Violeta Barrios de
  Chamorro
Shirley Chisholm
Edith Cresson
Mario Cuomo
F.W. de Klerk
Robert Dole
Louis Farrakhan
Boutros Boutros Ghali
Al Gore
Alan Greenspan
Vaclav Havel
Jesse Jackson
Bob Kerrey
Coretta Scott King
Charles Everett Koop
John Major
Wilma Mankiller
Imelda Marcos
Slobodan Milosevic
Brian Mulroney
Manuel Noriega
Major Owens
Dan Quayle
Marilyn Quayle
Ann Richards
Mary Robinson
Pat Schroeder
Louis Sullivan
Aung San Suu Kyi
Paul Tsongas
Desmond Tutu
Lech Walesa

Royalty
Charles, Prince of
  Wales
Duchess of York
  (Sarah Ferguson)
Queen Noor

Scientists
Sallie Baliunas
Avis Cohen
Donna Cox
Stephen Jay Gould

Mimi Koehl
Deborah Letourneau
Philippa Marrack
Helen Quinn
Barbara Smuts
Flossie Wong-Staal
Aslihan Yener
Adrienne Zihlman

Sports
Jim Abbott
Muhammad Ali
Sparky Anderson
Michael Andretti
Boris Becker
Bobby Bonilla
Jose Canseco
Jennifer Capriati
Michael Chang
Roger Clemens
Randall Cunningham
Eric Davis
Clyde Drexler
John Elway
Chris Evert
Sergei Fedorov
Cecil Fielder
George Foreman
Zina Garrison
Florence Griffith-
  Joyner
Rickey Henderson
Evander Holyfield
Desmond Howard
Brett Hull
Raghib Ismail
Jim Kelly
Petr Klima
Bernie Kozar
Greg LeMond
Carl Lewis
Mickey Mantle
Dan Marino
Willy Mays
Joe Montana
Martina Navratilova
Jack Nicklaus
Greg Norman
Joe Paterno
Kirby Puckett

Jerry Rice
Mark Rippen
David Robinson
John Salley
Barry Sanders
Monica Seles
Daryl Strawberry
Danny Sullivan
Vinnie Testaverde
Isiah Thomas
Mike Tyson
Steve Yzerman

**Television
Personalities**
Downtown Julie Brown
Andre Brown (Dr. Dre)
Phil Donahue
Linda Ellerbee
Arsenio Hall
David Letterman
Joan Lunden
Dennis Miller
Jane Pratt
Martha Quinn
Diane Sawyer

Other
Cindy Crawford
Marian Wright
  Edelman
Jaimie Escalante
Jack Kevorkian
Wendy Kopp
Sister Irene Kraus
Mother Theresa
Eli Weisel
Jeanne White

BUSINESS REPLY MAIL

First Class Mail   Permit No. 174   Detroit, MI

Postage will be paid by addressee

Omnigraphics, Inc.

Attn: Order Dept.
Penobscot Building
Detroit, MI 48226

||.||.||..|...||.||..|.|.||..|.|.||..||...|||..|||..|.|

- -

BUSINESS REPLY MAIL

First Class Mail   Permit No. 174   Detroit, MI

Postage will be paid by addressee

Omnigraphics, Inc.

Attn: *Biography Today,* Editor
Penobscot Building
Detroit, MI 48226

||.||.||..|...||.||..|.|.||..|.|.||..||...|||..|||..|.|

ON-APPROVAL ORDER FORM

Please send the following on 60-day approval:

Copies

___ **BIOGRAPHY TODAY**
ISSN 1058-2347 . . . . $46.00/year (3 issues)

___ _Standing Order_

___ 1992 Hardbound Annual 48.00
___ 1993 Hardbound Annual 48.00
___ 1994 Hardbound Annual 48.00

___ _Standing Order_

___ Annual Subscription
(3 issues and hardbound annual) 92.00

___ _Standing Order_

___ Individual Issues 16.00
___ **BIOGRAPHY TODAY AUTHOR SERIES** 30.00

☐ Payment enclosed, ship postpaid ☐ Bill us, plus shipping

Institution _____

Attention _____

Address _____

City _____

State, Zip _____

Phone (___) _____

4/95

W̲e want to cover the people _you_ want to know about in _Biography Today_. Take a look at the list of people we plan to include in upcoming issues. Then use this card to list other people you want to see in _Biography Today_. If we include someone you suggest, your library wins a free issue, and you get one to keep, with our thanks.

People I'd like to see
in BIOGRAPHY TODAY:

_____

_____

_____

_____

Name _____

Institution _____

Address _____

City _____

State, Zip _____